CONTEMPORARY
CORPUS LINGUISTICS

Also available from Continuum

Contemporary Stylistics
Edited by Marina Lambrou and Peter Stockwell

Contemporary Corpus Linguistics

Edited by
Paul Baker

continuum

Continuum International Publishing Group
The Tower Building   80 Maiden Lane
11 York Road   Suite 704
London SE1 7NX   New York NY 10038

First published 2009
Paperback edition first published 2012

British Library Cataloguing-in-Publication Data
A catalogue record for this book is available from the British Library.

ISBN: HB: 978-0-8264-9610-2
       PB: 978-1-4411-8133-6

Library of Congress Cataloging-in-Publication Data
Contemporary corpus linguistics / [edited by] Paul Baker.
    p. cm. – (Continuum studies in Linguistics)
  Includes bibliographical references and index.
  ISBN 978-1-4411-8133-6 (pbk. : alk. paper) – ISBN 978-0-8264-4034-1 (ebookpdf : alk. paper) – ISBN 978-1-4411-0946-0 (ebookepub : alk. paper)   1. Corpora (Linguistics) 2. Computational linguistics. I. Baker, Paul, 1972–

  P128.C68C63 2012
  410.1'88–dc23   ʼ
                                                      2011046609

Typeset by Newgen Imaging Systems Pvt Ltd, Chennai, India

Contents

Notes on Contributors

Svenja Adolphs is professor of English Language and Linguistics at the University of Nottingham, UK. Her research interests are in corpus linguistics and discourse analysis and she has published widely in these areas. Recent books include *Introducing Electronic Text Analysis* (Routledge, 2006) and *Corpus and Context: Investigating Pragmatic Functions in Spoken Discourse* (Benjamins, 2008).

Laurence Anthony is a professor in the Faculty of Science and Engineering at Waseda University, Japan, where he teaches technical reading, writing, and presentation skills, and is Director of the Center for English Language Education in Science and Engineering.

Paul Baker is a reader in the Department of Linguistics and English Language at Lancaster University. His research interests are corpus linguistics, sociolinguistics and discourse analysis. His books include *Using Corpora in Discourse Analysis* (2006) and *Sociolinguistics and Corpus Linguistics* (2010). He is commissioning editor of the journal *Corpora* (EUP).

Jonathan Culpeper is a professor in the Department of Linguistics and English Language at Lancaster University, UK. His work spans pragmatics, stylistics and the history of English. Corpora and Corpus Linguistics underpins much of his work.

Irina Dahlmann is currently finishing her Ph.D. thesis in the School of English Studies at the University of Nottingham, UK. In her work she integrates psycholinguistic theory with corpus linguistics methods to study aspects of holistic storage and retrieval of multi-word units in learner and native speaker English.

Alice Deignan is a reader in TESOL at the University of Leeds and researches aspects of lexical meaning, especially metaphor and metonymy, using corpus linguistic and discourse analytic techniques. She has also worked as a teacher of English as a foreign/second language and has written materials for language learners.

Patrick Hanks is a lexicographer with a special interest in corpus linguistics. He is a senior research associate at the Institute for Formal and Applied Linguistics at the Charles University in Prague. From 1983 to 1990 he was managing editor (subsequently editorial director) of the Cobuild project at the University of Birmingham. From 1990 to 2000 he was Chief Editor of Current English Dictionaries at Oxford University Press. Since 2000 he has held research and teaching posts at Brandeis University, the Berlin-Brandenburg Academy of Sciences, and Masaryk University, Brno and the Charles University in Prague.

Andrew Hardie is a lecturer in the Department of Linguistics and English Language at Lancaster University. His main current research interests are in corpus annotation, the corpus-based (especially quantitative) study of grammar, and the languages of South Asia.

Brian W. King is employed by the School of Linguistics and Applied Language Studies of Victoria University of Wellington, New Zealand. His research interests include the use of corpus analysis in sociolinguistic investigations of the relationship between language, gender and sexuality.

Robert Lew is employed at the School of English of Adam Mickiewicz University, Poznań, Poland. He has recently published a book comparing the effectiveness of monolingual, bilingual and bilingualized dictionaries for learners of English.

Michaela Mahlberg is Associate Professor in English Language and Applied Linguistics at the University of Nottingham, where she is also the Director of the Centre for Research in Applied Linguistics (CRAL). She is the Editor of the *International Journal of Corpus Linguistics* (John Benjamins), and Co-editor of the series *Corpus and Discourse* (Continuum).

Gerlinde Mautner is professor of English Business Communication at Wirtschaftsuniversität Wien (Vienna University of Economics and Business). She has carried out research at the linguistics departments of the universities of Birmingham (UK), Lancaster, and Cardiff, specializing in the marketization of public discourse as well as methodological issues.

Adam Meyers (New York University) is responsible for the NomBank annotation project. He has chaired/co-chaired numerous annotation workshops, including the recent LAW workshops. In 2007, Prof. Meyers co-founded (with Nancy Ide) the ACL Special Interest Group on Annotation (SIGANN).

Michael P. Oakes is a senior lecturer in Computing at the University of Sunderland, teaching courses in Information Retrieval and Statistics. He also works as a Senior Researcher in the Computational Linguistics Group, Uni Research, Bergen. His research interests include Information Retreival and Corpus Linguistics.

David Oakey is a lecturer in English language in the Centre for Academic and Professional English at the University of Birmingham, UK. His research interests include the use of computers to investigate phraseological aspects of written academic English.

Randi Reppen is professor of Applied Linguistics in the English Department at Northern Arizona University. Her research interests include using corpora to explore language development, inform teacher training, and develop teaching materials.

Yukio Tono is a professor at the Graduate School of Global Studies, Tokyo University of Foreign Studies, Japan. His research interests include learner corpus-based second language acquisition research, corpus applications in English language teaching, and corpus lexicography.

Richard Xiao is senior lecturer and programme leader in Chinese Studies at Edge Hill University. He has published extensively in corpus linguistics with a particular focus on corpus-based contrastive and translation studies of English and Chinese.

Ming Yue is an associate professor at the School of International Studies, Zhejiang University, China. She works in the linguistic Field of Natural Language Processing, in particular examining the automatic understanding of media discourse.

CHAPTER

1

Introduction

Paul Baker

The chapters in this book cover new research by corpus linguists, computational linguists and linguists who use corpora. While all three groups are growing in number, I suspect that the boundaries between them are becoming more blurred than they used to be, and also that it is the last group which is experiencing the most significant increase. As an illustration, in 1995, my university had a large Linguistics and English Language department which encompassed a broad range of fields and research methodologies. There were two corpus linguistics lecturers, but not a great deal of overlap between their work and the other research going on in the department. Now, in the same department, the situation has changed remarkably, with corpora and corpus techniques being used by the majority of the academics to various degrees. Additionally, I regularly receive requests for information and help from researchers in other departments who have heard about corpus-based analysis and think it would be helpful to them. This is in contrast to the response I received ten years ago when I gave a workshop on corpus linguistics to a very resistant group of social scientists. 'Words are beautiful things, like flowers', complained one participant. 'We should not put them inside computers!'

Perhaps the enthusiasm for corpus linguistics at my university is more an example of what is possible, rather than what is typical, yet a look at any online book store reveals numerous examples of published work that is not just about corpus linguistics but the corpus approach as it relates to some other aspect of linguistics (phonetics, language teaching, language acquisition, translation studies, discourse analysis, stylistics, metaphor, functional linguistics, world Englishes etc.).

One aim of this book is to address some of the more recent ways that corpus-based approaches have started to be incorporated in a range of linguistic research. A second aim is to address some of the current trends and themes that are influencing the manner in which corpus research is developing, as well as noting some of the concerns that people working closely with corpora are currently facing. Each chapter in this book follows (to a greater or lesser extent), the format of reviewing key and current work in a particular field of linguistics (e.g. stylistics, language teaching, critical discourse analysis), or aspect of corpus linguistics (e.g. software design, corpus design, annotation schemes) and then providing a recent example or case study of the author's own research in that area. Many of the chapters have multiple foci; for example, David Oakey considers corpus design as well as the analysis of fixed collocational patterns, while Randi Reppen's chapter looks at both the American National Corpus and language teaching. Because of this, it is difficult to divide the chapters in this book into neat subsections such as 'corpus building' 'corpus software' and 'corpus applications', although I have tried to order them in a way where it is possible to note relationships or similarities between those that are closer together. In the remainder of this introduction, I provide a short summary of each chapter, and end with a brief discussion of some of the themes which emerge across the book as a whole.

The book begins with a look at metaphor from a corpus-based perspective. Alice Deignan's chapter reviews how linguists have attempted to identify metaphors in corpora, by applying sampling techniques and concordances, to methods which have used more automatic means – for example deriving lists of strong collocations that are semantically unrelated, which are likely to suggest metaphorical uses of language. She also considers how corpus approaches have helped metaphor theory by providing more detailed and accurate classifications of non-literal language and how corpus-based analysis has helped to challenge existing theories of metaphor. For example, with her analysis of metaphors around the word *speed*, she shows that 'chunking' often occurs, which counters the idea that linguistic metaphors are the product of underlying conceptual metaphorical networks.

A set of related methods are used by Gerlinde Mautner, who shows how corpus approaches can aid critical discourse analysis (CDA), a field which could be criticized for over-reliance on small-scale qualitative analyses, whose results may not be usefully applied to wider contexts. Mautner shows how corpus techniques such as concordancing and collocation can help to reveal semantic prosodies; for example, she finds that in general corpora the expression *the elderly* tends to strongly collocate with negative terms like *infirm* and *frail*. A concordance analysis shows that the exception negating lexical bundle *elderly but* tends to be followed by positive adjectives (*charismatic, sharp-minded*), which indicates how the term *elderly* is regularly constructed negatively in general language use. While Mautner warns that high frequency is not necessarily indicative of popular attitudes, her chapter shows that corpus techniques offer CDA researchers another way of carrying out their analysis, which is likely to make their findings more reliable and valid.

Similarly, in Chapter 4, Michaela Mahlberg reviews approaches in the growing field of corpus stylistics, while providing a case study which focuses on how corpus methods can be used to draw conclusions about language use in fiction. While literary critics may argue that a word or phrase is used to evoke a particular emotion or meaning, Mahlberg shows how concordance analyses of reference corpora and corpora based on an author's complete works can help to provide evidence that a particular use of language has occurred in numerous other, similar contexts. For example, she shows that Charles Dickens uses the cluster *put down his knife and fork* in nine of his novels as a way of contextualizing when a character is shocked by an event. Corpus techniques therefore introduce systematicity to stylistics, allowing meaningful patterns to be identified and quantified.

Jonathan Culpeper's study of metalanguage (in this case language about the language of impoliteness) uses a new piece of corpus analysis software, the web-based Sketch Engine developed by Adam Kilgarriff and David Tugwell. Using the Oxford English Corpus (approximately two billion words in size), Culpeper shows how a large corpus can yield hundreds or even thousands of citations of relatively infrequent words. This data can therefore be used in conjunction with Sketch Engine in order to derive 'word sketches'. A particularly impressive aspect of Sketch Engine is the way that it gives detailed collocational information based on lexico-grammatical relationships. For example, in Culpeper's examination of the terms *impolite* and *rude*, WordSketch is able to distinguish between collocates that are modifiers (*downright, plain*), those which are infinitival complements (*stare, ask*) and those that are adjectival subjects (*doormen, waiter*). Culpeper's study points both to more sophisticated studies of collocational relationships as well as illustrating the analytical potential of the next generation of large corpora.

Staying with research that uses new analytical tools, in Chapter 6, Laurence Anthony describes the software AntConc, an increasingly popular (and free to download via the internet) multi-platform corpus toolkit which supports the Unicode Standard. Being highly functional, AntConc allows users to generate *KWIC* concordance lines and concordance distribution plots. It also has tools to analyse word clusters (lexical bundles), *n-grams*, collocates, word frequencies and keywords. Anthony discusses how tool design is often overlooked by corpus linguists, who instead have tended to focus on corpus-building procedures. However, he argues that it is only with the right tools that corpora can be adequately exploited. Anthony reports how AntConc was designed with input from corpus users, although it has a simple user interface that can be used by novices, for example, in classroom situations.

In Chapter 7, Adam Meyers considers issues surrounding best practice in corpus annotation. With reference to syntactic treebanks, he describes a number of different annotation schemes that are in existence and examines procedures that are used to convert one scheme to the other. Meyers gives a description of GLARF (Grammatical and Logical Argument Representation Framework), a scheme which allows different annotation systems to be merged in various ways. The author argues that the utility and accuracy of annotation will be improved if there is a greater degree of coordination among annotation research groups, and that multiple annotations should be carried out on corpora that are made freely available and shared, in order to facilitate annotation merging systems.

Continuing the theme of annotation, in Chapter 8, Irina Dahlmann and Svenja Adolphs discuss a number of issues in relationship to the annotation and analysis of spoken corpora. Focusing on the concept of the *multi-word expression*, they carry out two separate analyses of the two-word expression *I think*, the first using a corpus based on a mono-modal transcript (where short pauses within speech are not marked), the second where pauses have been fully annotated. While both forms of analysis result in interesting findings with respect to the patterns of *I think* produced by speakers, the authors argue that with the orthographically annotated corpus a fuller and more complex picture emerges, showing that *I think* is virtually never interrupted by pauses and therefore fits the criteria of a multi-word expression. The authors reason that only by using fully annotated multi-modal corpora will analysts be able to develop a more comprehensive understanding of speech.

David Oakey addresses corpus design, with regard to the analysis of *fixed collocation patterns*, a concept similar to the multi-word expressions used by Irina Dahlmann and Svenja Adolphs in the previous chapter. In order to analyse collocations across different genres, Oakey problematizes the fact that individual texts within different genres may be of different sizes (e.g. in the British National Corpus social science texts tend to be longer than texts from the pure sciences). Should comparisons between these genres therefore be *isolexical* (where the sub-corpora all contain the same number of words) or *isotextual* (where the sub-corpora all contain the same number of texts)? Oakey's findings, based on his own analysis of frequent fixed collocations in eight language genres, have implications for corpus builders who want to carry out studies of language variation.

In Chapter 10, Michael Oakes continues the themes that were raised in the previous chapters, also carrying out comparative analyses of a number of different genres of writing, but this time using the well-known Brown family of corpora. He shows how a range of statistical techniques can be gainfully employed in genre analysis (e.g. fiction vs news), synchronic analysis of language varieties (e.g. American vs British English) and diachronic analysis (e.g. 1960s English vs 1990s English). Starting with two-way chi-squared comparisons, Oakes moves on to more sophisticated techniques which involve comparisons of multiple genres. As well as multifactorial analysis, Oakes also considers techniques that produce visual renditions of similarity, such as dendograms and biplots. Additionally, he examines developments in computational stylometry as well as showing how a support vector machine is being used to classify web-based genres. Finally, Oakes critically addresses concerns regarding corpus design, particularly with respect to balance and representativeness.

Moving on, Yukio Tono examines language acquisition from the perspective of learner output, arguing that carefully encoded learner corpora can facilitate the emergence of theories of learner development, based on probabilistic analyses of multiple factors; an approach which echoes Oakes' multifactorial analysis in the previous chapter. Additionally, using statistical models that include Bayesian network theory and Data Oriented Parsing, Tono shows how over-, under- or misuse of linguistic phenomena in essays produced by learners can be explained (or predicted) by interactions between factors such as ability level, first language interference or frequency of a particular linguistic item in textbooks.

Randi Reppen's chapter also focuses on language learning, but from the view of the creation of teaching materials (in this case using the American National Corpus). Drawing on findings from earlier corpus studies on register variation, Reppen shows how corpus analysis can enable teachers to encourage students to focus on linguistic features that are known to be typical and frequent of particular registers, in order to raise awareness about register variation among learners of English. Corpora therefore not only help to provide information about the sorts of salient linguistic features that are worth teaching to students, but they also facilitate an enormous amount of naturalistic data that teachers can draw on in order to create classroom-based exercises.

Similarly, Patrick Hanks reviews the contribution that corpus linguists have made towards dictionary creation in the last twenty years or so. While Hanks demonstrates that corpora afford dictionary creators the potential to add more words and more word meanings as well as accounts of typical and non-typical usage based on frequency data, he warns that a distinction needs to be made between dictionaries intended for language learners, and those for advanced users. Indeed, with the former, frequency information from corpora should be utilized in order to provide cut-off points (what to leave out), rather than offering blanket coverage of every word in a language. Additionally, Hanks discusses how corpus approaches can be of assistance in providing illustrative examples of word uses, raising a note of caution that authentic examples are not necessarily good examples, and that corpus techniques which identify normal usage will be most helpful for dictionary users.

A related area to dictionary creation is translation, which is considered in Chapter 14 by Richard Xiao and Ming Yue. After clearing up the confusion around terms like *parallel, comparable, comparative, multilingual* and *bilingual corpora*, the authors review contributions that corpus linguists have made to the various fields and sub-fields of translation studies. Then, moving away from studies that have compared closely related European languages, the authors focus on a case study which compares a corpus of Chinese fiction with a corpus of Chinese translations of English fiction, in order to examine the extent to which the hypothesized 'translation universals' found so far in similar language pairs, are also present in a language pair that is genetically distinct.

Continuing the focus on corpora of non-Latin writing systems, Chapter 15, by Andrew Hardie, considers developments in the emerging field of South Asian corpus linguistics, where languages spoken in India, Pakistan, Bangladesh, Sri Lanka and Nepal are beginning to be examined by corpus linguists. Hardie discusses the rendering and encoding problems that were originally encountered (and now largely solved due to the Unicode Standard) when building corpora of South Asian languages, as well as describing work on their annotation and mark-up. Finally, he outlines a case study which considers the extent to which Hindi and Urdu are dialects of the same language, by examining vocabulary differences in a range of multilingual corpora. While such work is still in its early stages, it aptly demonstrates the potential that corpus linguistics has for all the world's languages.

While Hardie describes how much of the corpus data of Indic languages he examines was derived from web-based sources, in the following chapter Robert Lew explores the concept of 'web as corpus', discussing the advantages and disadvantages to corpus linguists of considering the whole web as a source of corpus data. While the web clearly offers access to a much larger rate of citations of rare terms and phrases, which is likely to be beneficial in terms of producing collocational analyses, Lew examines the extent to which the web can be considered to be a representative or balanced corpus, as well as looking at the types of interference which are specific to web-based texts: noise, spam and typos. Additionally, he discusses functionality and access mechanisms, concluding that the web may help to resolve language learners' immediate lexical problems, as well as helping linguists in some contexts, but it should not replace traditionally built corpora.

Staying with texts derived from the internet, the final chapter by Brian King examines the feasibility of building, annotating and carrying out a comparative analysis of a corpus of chat-room data. The area of chat-room corpus analysis is still in its infancy, with researchers needing to quickly find solutions to new problems before research can be carried out. For example, King notes how the semi-public nature of chat-rooms raises ethical issues concerned with obtaining consent and retaining anonymity (particularly in this case, where the participants are classed as being from a 'vulnerable' group). Additionally, problems such as defining turn-taking, ensuring that a balanced sample is taken and categorization of linguistic phenomena are addressed.

Although the chapters in this book were chosen in order to represent a wide range of approaches that are currently being adopted within corpus-based research, covering corpus design, annotation and analysis, it is possible to identify a number of themes and trends which have organically emerged, being noted in multiple chapters. As I pointed out at the start of this chapter, it is clear that corpus-based approaches are increasingly being seen as useful to a range of linguistic disciplines, enabling new theories to be developed and older ones to be systematically tested. Fields such as translation studies (Xiao and Yue), metaphor analysis (Deignan), critical discourse analysis (Mautner), stylistics (Mahlberg), conversation analysis (Dahlmann and Adolphs) and metalanguage (Culpeper) are all benefiting from corpus approaches. The widening of corpus methods to a greater range of applications suggests that the field of linguistics (in both its applied and 'pure' senses) would benefit enormously if *all* researchers working with languages were afforded an understanding and appreciation of the ways in which corpus methods can be effectively utilized as an effective means of linguistic enquiry.

Otherwise, as Tono points out, there is a situation where a typical corpus linguist, whose specialisms involve corpus building and annotation along with using corpus software, will attempt to apply such techniques to a field, such as stylistics or critical discourse analysis, perhaps without being fully engaged with existing theory or techniques of analysis. For example, most CDA practitioners are aware of how nominalizations can be used to obscure agency, although this might not be something a corpus linguist, with little experience of CDA might be aware of – thus, nominalizations may either be overlooked or misinterpreted even if the corpus analysis highlights them as salient or frequent.

Conversely, an applied linguist may attempt to use corpus-based methods, but may not have the know-how to build a balanced corpus or carry out a sophisticated analysis, instead relying on an examination of say, the twenty most frequent words in an (unbalanced) corpus, rather than focusing on more complex techniques. As a result, the applied linguist may conclude that the corpus analysis is ineffective and unsuitable for their field. Such early experiences are likely to be damaging in that they will dissuade the applied linguist from engaging with corpus linguistics in the future.

Similarly, Anthony notes that corpus linguists are likely to be the best judges of the sorts of analytical software that could benefit their own research, although most corpus linguists do not possess the computing skills to create such software. On the other hand, computational linguists who do not carry out corpus research, may have the skills to create the software, but not be best equipped to decide how it can be created to give maximum benefit to the user.

The examples above then suggest that corpus linguists need to continue a dialogue with non-corpus linguists – publishing their research in journals and other places where non-corpus linguists are likely to encounter it. If such research is made accessible (containing a minimum of jargon and assumptions about a priori knowledge) and written in a clear style, while demonstrating convincing and interesting results, it is likely to alert a wider range of academics to the benefits of corpus research, meaning that ultimately there will be advances in both corpus linguistics and a range of other types of linguistics (pure, applied, computational).

Another theme that emerges from this collection of chapters is concerned with the number of researchers who are beginning to move away from analysis of traditional corpora (relatively small, balanced samples of previously published writing in English or similar languages). The chapters by Hardie and Xiao and Yue show that corpus research is feasible in languages which do not rely on representation being in an 8-bit encoding system. Two developments in particular: The Unicode Standard and growing global internet participation have made corpus building and analysis in any language a reality. The EMILLE Corus of Indic languages described in Hardie's chapter only became possible when news media started to mount their daily bulletins on the web in languages like Hindi, Punjabi and Bengali.

It is also heartening that corpus toolkits like WordSmith (used by Xiao and Yue), Xaira (used by Hardie) and AntConc (see Anthony's chapter) have incorporated the Unicode Standard into their systems, meaning that Hangul, Devanagari, Arabic, syllabic and logographic writing systems are afforded the same status as the Latin and Cyrillic systems. As well as using non-English corpora, there is an expansion of work in text types other than published writing, with the internet offering a much wider range of language use, as Lew, King and Culpeper illustrate in their chapters. Large *spoken* corpora still remain expensive and time consuming to build, although Dahlmann and Adolphs show that even 368,000 words are adequate for their analysis. However, the internet also allows for new forms of human linguistic interaction to be examined, as King explores in his discussion of chat-room corpora. While such corpora raise new challenges, they also enable corpus linguists to access very large amounts of data, where like speech, users communicate in a synchronous manner.

Clearly, then, the *amount* of available corpus data, as well as its variety looks set to increase: while Lew shows that the whole web could be used in some contexts as a 'corpus', Culpeper's analysis of the Oxford English Corpus indicates that exponential growth in corpus size potential is continuing. In the early 1960s reference corpora of a million words were viewed as large, by the early 1990s the BNC raised the bar to 100 million, and now the OEC looms even larger, with *billions* of words. Additionally, (again using data from the internet) the OEC covers a range of varieties of English (Caribbean, Canadian, Australian, South African, Indian), indicating how the internet allows for examination and comparison of a fuller range of Englishes that enable corpus linguists to go beyond the traditional focus on British and American English.

Finally, it is also clear that statistical and frequency-based methods of corpus analysis are becoming increasingly sophisticated. Consider how Culpeper uses Sketch Engine in order to derive detailed collocational patterns which take grammatical relationships into account. Both Tono and Oakes show how multifactorial analyses can give more detailed explanations for linguistic variation – in Tono's case, by explaining how a range of factors combine in order to help predict learner's language output, and in Oakes' chapter, by showing how multiple language genres can be clustered together in terms of their linguistic similarity. The themes which emerge from this book indicate a growing sense of confidence in corpus linguistics, both in terms of its areas of application, and in terms of the techniques (text extraction, software, statistical tests, analytical methods) that are currently being employed.

Therefore, as I hope this collection of chapters demonstrates, this is a good time to be involved in corpus linguistics. Rather than signifying that the corpus approach is starting to reach the limits of its usefulness, the opposite is clearly the case.

Searching for Metaphorical Patterns in Corpora

Alice Deignan

In the last decade, researchers applying corpus linguistic techniques to the study of metaphor have increasingly challenged the validity of findings not based on naturally occurring language data. There have been two strands of corpus research: analysis of linguistic patterns of metaphor, and research into the use of metaphor in specific genres. Researchers in the first strand (e.g. Deignan 2005a) have sought to test the predictions of metaphor theory for language in use, using large, 'representative' corpora. Their findings challenge aspects of contemporary metaphor theory and suggest the limitations of a theory of thought in explaining language. Researchers in the second strand have analysed metaphor within corpora designed to represent a specific subset of language, such as presidential speeches, religious texts (Charteris-Black 2004), or business discourse (Koller 2004). The second group of researchers have tended to be interested in the specific meanings conveyed by particular groups of metaphors, and by extension, in metaphor and ideology.

*To date, most published corpus research into metaphor has relied on concordancing as the primary research tool. Metaphors have not been identified automatically from the corpus, and researchers have had to make difficult decisions about which lexical items to concordance and analyse. This has generally been done by analysing a sample of the corpus by hand, to identify metaphors which are then searched for in the main corpus, a technique which has obvious drawbacks. Identifying metaphors automatically is a challenge, not least because when a word is used metaphorically it frequently co-occurs with other words from the same literal domain. For instance, the metaphorical use of **attack** is often found collocating with words such as **fierce** and **launch**, which are both from the literal domain of war. This means that trying to identify anomalous collocations is not a reliable means of disambiguating metaphorical meanings of words from literal meanings. Nonetheless, there are several projects which are attempting to develop automatic means of metaphor identification, including works by Berber-Sardinha (2007, 2008) and Semino and Rayson (2006).*

In this chapter, I detail the contributions made to metaphor studies by corpus-based research, comment on the ongoing challenges to developing a rigorous research methodology, and describe current work tackling these.

2.1 Introduction

The study of metaphor has been a topic of considerable interest across a range of academic disciplines, including cognitive linguistics, applied linguistics and philosophy since the 1980s. Despite this breadth of interest, the field was dominated by assumptions, methodology and findings from cognitive linguistics until fairly recently. A major strand in metaphor research has been work by Gibbs (e.g. 1994) and his co-researchers. Their findings have largely been derived from psycholinguistic experimental techniques.

Many applied linguists have watched developments in metaphor research with interest, for their potential for language description and applications for language teaching. Applied linguistic and corpus linguistic techniques have more recently been added to the well-known approaches to metaphor study. Below, I discuss how metaphor theory can contribute towards corpus-based language description, the challenges that investigating metaphor poses for corpus linguistic techniques, and how corpora and corpus-based techniques can contribute to metaphor theory. I begin by outlining the current mainstream view of metaphor.

2.2 Recent Developments in Metaphor Theory

2.2.1 Conceptual Metaphor Theory

Almost all current work in metaphor in applied and corpus linguistics and related disciplines is carried out loosely within the framework of Conceptual Metaphor Theory, also known as Cognitive Metaphor Theory. Conceptual Metaphor Theory developed in reaction to an approach which saw metaphor in language as primarily decorative, and therefore largely of interest to students of literature rather than linguists or cognitive linguists. Lakoff and Johnson (1980), leaders in the development of Conceptual Metaphor Theory, pointed out that conventional metaphors, as opposed to poetic, innovative metaphors, are very frequent in language, and argued that they are therefore worthy of study. For instance, recent headlines from popular news websites have included 'Alcohol related hospital admissions rise' (http://uk.yahoo.com, 15th October 2007) and 'Sainsburys enjoys jump in profits' (http://news.bbc.co.uk, 14th November 2007). Both *rise* and *jump* would be regarded as metaphorical by researchers working in the Conceptual Metaphor Theory tradition, because *rise* is not intended to mean a literal increase in size, and *jump* does not refer to a literal physical movement. Such metaphors are relatively common in everyday written language use.

Proponents of Conceptual Metaphor Theory argue that there are connections at the level of thought between semantic areas or 'domains'. For instance, there is a mental connection between the concrete domain of 'movement upwards or downwards' and the abstract domain 'increase and decrease'. The abstract domain is understood metaphorically in terms of the concrete domain. The domain providing the metaphor, almost always a concrete domain, is known as the source domain, while the domain that is understood metaphorically, almost always an abstract domain, is known as the target domain. The connections between domains are known as 'mappings', or 'conceptual metaphors'. The mapping of literal movement upwards or downwards onto abstract increases and decreases is expressed as the conceptual metaphor MORE IS UP, LESS IS DOWN. This conceptual metaphor generates a number of metaphorical senses of words, including *rise* in 'hospital admissions rise', *jump*, in 'jump in profits', and senses of *fall, soar, plummet* and numerous near synonyms of these words. Accounts of Conceptual Metaphor Theory are given by Lakoff (1993) and Kövecses (2002).

Conceptual metaphor theorists claim that as well as mapping individual entities to produce metaphorical language, conceptual metaphors also map the relationships between entities, processes, actions and attributes. For instance, the opposition between literally rising and falling is mapped onto the domain of abstract increases and decreases. For researchers who are concerned with how the human mind stores and processes ideas, this is important, because it suggests that the way that we perceive relationships within abstract domains is shaped by our understanding of the concrete world.

2.2.2 Primary Metaphors

An important contribution to metaphor theory has been the notion of 'primary metaphors', proposed by Grady (1997). Primary metaphors operate at a much higher level of abstraction than most of the conceptual metaphors discussed in the literature. Among the conceptual metaphors proposed by Lakoff and Johnson (1980) are ARGUMENT IS WAR, LOVE IS MADNESS and THEORIES ARE BUILDINGS, which equate domains at a fairly specific level. Primary metaphors proposed by Grady include ORGANIZATION IS PHYSICAL STRUCTURE, PERSISTING IS REMAINING ERECT and STATES ARE LOCATIONS. Grady claims that primary metaphors can combine to form complex metaphors; these often overlap with metaphors that had been treated as conceptual metaphors in earlier literature. For example, for Grady, THEORIES ARE BUILDINGS is a complex metaphor, which can be decomposed into the two primary metaphors ORGANIZATION IS PHYSICAL STRUCTURE and PERSISTING IS REMAINING ERECT.

Grady's development of Conceptual Metaphor Theory offers a solution to an aspect of the theory that had been potentially problematic – the observation that not all elements of the source domain are mapped onto the target domain. In the case of THEORIES ARE BUILDINGS, aspects of buildings that are mapped onto theories include foundations and structure, but not walls. If THEORIES ARE BUILDINGS is seen instead as a prototypical instance of the interaction between the primary metaphors PERSISTING IS REMAINING ERECT and ORGANIZATION IS PHYSICAL STRUCTURE, the problem disappears. These primary metaphors would generate linguistic expressions referring to structure and the processes of building and remaining stable, but not any non-structural or decorative aspects of buildings. The notion of primary metaphors is less satisfactory for language description, however, as they are too abstract to have much predictive power for the meanings and uses of individual words. Grady's work is widely accepted by conceptual metaphor theorists; nonetheless most researchers continue to use the term 'conceptual metaphor' or 'metaphorical mapping' to describe relatively specific metaphorical connections, rather than analysing them in terms of the abstract mappings pro-posed by Grady.

To date there is little discussion about the degree of specificity with which metaphorical mappings should be described. A related problem is a tendency for researchers to propose conceptual metaphors on the basis of relatively small amounts of linguistic evidence, sometimes at a very specific level. For instance, Kövecses (2002: 61) interprets the Bible story of Joseph's dreams of cows and ears of corn through the proposed conceptual metaphor ACHIEVING A PURPOSE IS EATING. There have been several attempts to draw up lists of conceptual meta-phors; Kövecses gives an index to conceptual metaphors in his 2002 book, and a long list has been compiled by Lakoff's team of researchers.[1] Nonetheless, the lack of consensus about how specific a conceptual metaphor should be, and even what the central conceptual metaphors are, is a serious problem for the application of Conceptual Metaphor Theory as a tool for linguistic analysis.

2.2.3 Metaphor, Metonymy and Embodiment

Since the mid-1990s, conceptual metaphor theorists have become increasingly interested in the notion of metonymy, or mapping within domains rather than across domains, to the extent that metonymy is now seen as very significant, per-haps even more so than metaphor by some researchers. Metonymy occurs when a part is used to refer to the whole. Prototypical examples of metonymy include referring to a car as a *motor*, or a neighbouring house as *next door*.

However, the notion of metonymy can be taken much further than these con-crete examples if we interpret a physical manifestation of an abstract action as being a part of that action. Goossens (1995) argues that expressions such as *close-lipped* are grounded in metonymy; the action of keeping one's lips together is one aspect of being discreet, not giving away secrets. He argues that because there is some mapping from concrete to abstract, the expression is also metaphorical, a combination he terms 'metaphtonymy'. Work within corpus linguistics has devel-oped Goossens' ideas (Deignan 2005*a*, 2005*b*). The implications of this research for descriptions of metaphor and metonymy are described below.

A similar case can be made for treating the physical manifestation of an emotion as being a part of the holistic experience of that emotion, and therefore seeing a metonymical relationship between them. Taking this interpretation, Barcelona (2000) argues that most, if not all conceptual metaphors have their origins in metonymy. For instance, the metaphorical mapping of darkness onto negative emotions and light onto positive feelings can be traced to physical experi-ence. He writes, 'Light is likely to arouse a feeling of confidence, safety, liveliness or happiness [. . .] whereas dark tends to bring about a feeling of insecurity, melancholy, and physical unease, which is negatively valued' (2000: 40). These ideas have been taken further still by cognitive linguists, many of whom now agree with Gibbs (2006: 9) who claims that 'People's subjective, felt experiences of their bodies in action provide part of the fundamental grounding for language and thought'. This view is known as the *embodiment hypothesis*, and it is now widely believed among cognitive linguists that the fundamental metaphorical mappings are expressions of embodied thought.

This section has briefly overviewed some of the central topics in metaphor research within the cognitive tradition. In the next section, the implications of these for corpus linguists are discussed.

2.3 Metaphor Theory and Corpus Linguistics

2.3.1 The Explanatory Potential of Conceptual Metaphor Theory

Lakoff and Johnson's observation that metaphors are highly frequent struck a chord with lexicographers working in the 1980s, when corpora had recently become an essential tool, replacing hand-collected collections of citations, intuition and the study of other dictionaries as the main source of their data. Corpus lexicographers generally observe the phenomenon of metaphor from the perspective of concordance lines rather than the study of continuous text. While the study of continuous, naturally occurring text will almost immediately show that a high proportion of words are used with metaphorical meanings, the study of concordance citations offers a complementary observation: a high proportion of citations of many individual words involve metaphorical meanings. For instance, over half of the citations in a concordance of *rise*, taken from a general reference corpus, are likely to be instances of metaphorical meanings.

This examination of concordances to analyse polysemy, and the first observations of the relative frequencies of metaphorical meaning occurred at almost the same point in time as the development of Conceptual Metaphor Theory, discussed above. Moon (2007) documents this in her discussion of the treatment of the word *impact* in the first edition of the *Collins Cobuild English Language Dictionary*, published in 1987. Prior to this, most dictionaries would give primary focus on the concrete meaning of the term *impact*. In contrast, the *Collins Cobuild Dictionary* puts the abstract sense first, defining it as 'The impact that something has on a situation, process, person, etc is the effect that it has on it', and exemplifying it with 'The new seeds had an immediate impact on food production . . . the impact of computing on routine office work . . . British authors make relatively little impact abroad.' The concrete sense of *impact*, defined as 'the action of one object hitting another, usually with a lot of force', was given second in the entry, a decision 'reflecting frequency of usage and not a historical or logical semantic development' (Moon 2007: 164).

For researchers in language description, including corpus linguists, Conceptual Metaphor Theory was exciting because of the explanation it offered for the frequency of these abstract metaphorical senses – that we think metaphorically about many topics and therefore it is natural that we should also speak metaphorically about them.

Conceptual Metaphor Theory also seemed to offer a model for the systematic classification of non-literal uses of words, with its claim that all non-literal language is the linguistic realization of deeper connections. While conceptual metaphor theorists are especially interested in these connections, language analysts are not usually concerned about their reality or otherwise at the level of thought. Instead, they are interested in their potential as abstractions or generalizations about language. From this perspective, rather than describing a mental connection between domains, a 'conceptual metaphor' would generalize from the observed relationships between words in pairs of semantic fields, and predict the relationships that would hold between other pairs of words from these fields. For instance, MORE IS UP, LESS IS DOWN would predict that the lexical field of words used to talk about concrete direction will be replicated by the lexical field of words used to talk about abstract increases and decreases. It would also predict that the semantic relationships that hold between literal meanings of words will be replicated for their metaphorical meanings. Disappointingly, early corpus research into metaphor (Deignan 1999*a*, 1999*b*) has shown this model to be an oversimplification of semantic relationships in the target domain, as is explained in the next section.

2.3.2 *Problems in Analysing Corpus Data Using Conceptual Metaphor Theory*

The early hope that Conceptual Metaphor Theory would explain and predict metaphorical meanings has only been fulfilled in part. The patterns that Conceptual Metaphor Theory would suggest can often be found in the data, but so would be other semantic patterns which are not explained by the theory. For example, Deignan (2008) analysed concordance data from the Bank of English for lexicalizations of the ARGUMENT IS WAR conceptual metaphor (Lakoff and Johnson 1980). She shows that there are antonymous uses of *attack* and *defend* in the concrete domain of fighting and in the abstract domain of argument, and apparent hyponyms of *attack*, such as *shoot down* and *fire a* [*warning*] *shot* in both domains. These sets of meanings would suggest that there are two domains, argument and war, which have parallel lexical relationships, as famously claimed by Lakoff and Johnson (1980). However, when Deignan analysed the concordance data for *attack* in more detail, she found that it has at least five frequent meanings, which include two literal uses, the 'war' use referred to by Lakoff and Johnson, and a 'personal violence' use. *Attack* is also used to talk about the sudden onset of illness, in expressions such as *heart attack*, a use that could be regarded as metaphorical, depending on how 'metaphor' is defined. There is also a frequent sporting use in citations such as 'we have explosive match winners in our attack', as well as the metaphorical use referred to by Lakoff and Johnson, to describe verbal confrontation, in citations such as '[He] then launched a bitter attack on the Tory press'. Thus even for this central, apparently simple mapping, the semantic relations are entangled.

Relations are even less straightforward for less central lexis. Lakoff and Johnson cite *strategy* as another realization of the conceptual metaphor ARGUMENT IS WAR, but the corpus citations for this word show that it is used in a wide range of contexts, including business, medicine and the environment. There is not a clear case for regarding a 'war' use as the source of these other uses (Deignan 2008).

Ritchie (2003) used intuitively derived data to consider the same mappings and asserts that 'there is a complex field of contentious interactions, ranging from simple discussions through contests to all-out war' (p. 125). He claims that 'argument' could be seen equally well as 'a game of chess' than as 'war'. Examination of concordance data is consistent with his views.

These data suggest a complex picture, in which individual words seem to take on individual sets of metaphorical meanings rather than meanings defined by and contained within a broader semantic transfer. This is typical of findings when corpus data are analysed in detail, and is not explained by Conceptual Metaphor Theory. However, this would not be apparent if the corpus data had been analysed selectively; for instance, it is easy to select corpus citations that apparently illustrate the systematic mapping of argument onto war. This shows the importance of the corpus linguistic principles of accounting for all data and not being led by a pre-determined hypothesis, that is, the analysis being corpus-driven rather than corpus-based (Tognini-Bonelli 2001). Ensuring that analysis is genuinely corpus-driven, or as close to it as possible, is not straightforward when researching a semantic feature such as metaphor. This problem, and attempts to find solutions, are discussed below.

2.4 Challenges for Investigating Metaphor in Corpus Data

For corpus linguists, the investigation of metaphor raises two central problems, first, the identification of metaphor, which is a problem shared by all metaphor researchers concerned with reliability; and second, finding metaphors in a corpus.

2.4.1 Defining Metaphor in Use

Much early research into metaphor was undertaken without using an explicit definition of metaphor, or with a definition that was intuitively sound but too vague to make reliable decisions on borderline cases. More recently, several scholars have tried to establish a definition of metaphor that can be reliably applied to the analysis of text. For instance, Cameron works with the notion that linguistic metaphor entails the presence of a vehicle term 'that is clearly anomalous or incongruous against the surrounding discourse' (2003: 59). She then investigates the nature of the incongruity, as this in itself is not a sufficient condition. She identifies the presence of some kind of semantic transfer as being a further necessary condition. Cameron's procedure was developed for the analysis of single instances of words in continuous stretches of texts. Deignan (2005a) developed a procedure for working with concordance data, where large numbers of citations of the same word form are analysed. Rather than considering the surrounding text, Deignan begins with a comparison of different instances of the word form, and looks for evidence of polysemy, in discontinuity of meaning, following work in lexicography such as in Moon (1987). If polysemy is established, she then, like Cameron, looks for evidence of semantic transfer between two or more of the senses identified.

More recently, the pragglejaz project (Cameron et al. 2007) has developed a procedure for the identification of metaphor in text that involves the identification of the contextual meaning of each word in the text. The analyst then decides whether the word has a more 'basic' sense, and if so, whether there is a metaphorical relationship between the basic sense and the contextual meaning. The procedure is currently being applied to several collections of texts as part of a large research project.[2] While the texts being analysed are very large by the standards of hand-searched discourse analysis, they are inevitably small by modern corpus standards.

Cameron's work, and the work of the pragglejaz group, highlights another aspect of the analysis of meaning in use, currently unreachable by corpus techniques – the stance of the speaker and hearer, and the possibility that the presence of metaphor can only be established in relation to an individual text, through consideration of all aspects of context. Metaphors are marked to different degrees: at one extreme are highly innovative and poetic metaphors, at the other, uses that are so established that most speakers would consider them to be 'dead', while between these extremes are conventionalized metaphorical uses. Speakers have different intuitions about where the boundaries between these different kinds of metaphor should be drawn, and about where each metaphorical use can be placed on this cline, which means that metaphor identification is highly subjective. The best hope for enabling research findings to be comparable is for the central issues to be identified, and for each researcher to then state where he or she stands on them. For instance, some researchers may be uninterested in the metaphorical use of prepositions, or may require that a metaphor is the same part of speech as its literal equivalent, or may only be interested in innovative metaphors. The pragglejaz project has provided a valuable starting point by identifying many of these issues and stating its position on them.

2.4.2 Approaches to Finding Metaphors in a Corpus

The current approach adopted by the pragglejaz project, and that used by Cameron (2003) for her corpus of education discourse, involves examining every word in the corpus manually to decide whether it is used metaphorically. Clearly, this is impractical in all but very small corpora. Assuming they wish to use a corpus which is too large to analyse manually, metaphor researchers are faced with the challenge of deciding which word forms to focus on. The traditional approach to analysing word meaning in a corpus is to examine concordances of words or multiword expressions. However, this approach is potentially flawed in that the researcher will only find out information about metaphors they have already decided to look for – there could be many important patterns of metaphor use in the corpus which would remain undiscovered. A more refined version of this approach is one based on sampling, and has been carried out by several researchers, including Charteris-Black (2004). Here, analysts manually examine manageable samples of their corpora to identify words or multi-word units which are used in metaphorical constructions, which they then use as the basis for further concordance searches over the whole corpus. Because every word in the sample is examined, the researcher avoids the problems associated with selecting word forms to study. However, this technique will never capture all the metaphorical uses in the whole corpus and is likely to give more reliable results for a relatively homogeneous corpus than for one containing very disparate texts.

Stefanowitsch (2006) outlines the problems of finding metaphors in a corpus and lists some other strategies for doing so, including manual analysis. Several of the strategies that he lists involve deciding in advance which words to concordance. The analyst decides to investigate a particular conceptual metaphor, and concordances lexis from the source domain, for example, lexis from the domain of journeys to investigate the conceptual metaphor LIFE IS A JOURNEY. In a related strategy, the analyst concordances lexis from the target domain, 'life' in the case of LIFE IS A JOURNEY, and searches the text surrounding the node word for metaphors. Alternatively, he/she may search for sentences containing lexis from both domains.

The strategy of searching for source domain vocabulary has led to some valuable research. For instance, Boers (1999) studied metaphors in *The Economist* by concordancing lexis with literal meanings associated with health, that is, source domain lexis. He found that these words were more frequently used with metaphorical meanings in articles written during the colder months of the year. He points out that this is a time when writers might be expected to be more preoccupied with their literal health, a finding that adds support to the embodiment hypothesis (see above). However, deciding to search for realizations of a particular conceptual metaphor, which is assumed to exist in advance of hard linguistic evidence, is a long way from the corpus-driven approach described by Tognini-Bonelli (2001), in which the analyst makes no a priori assumptions about the content of the corpus.

Stefanowitsch also suggests searching for 'markers' of metaphor, following Goatly (1997), who proposes that metaphors are often signalled by expressions such as *kind of* and *so to speak*. However, such markers are not used for all metaphors; further, they seem to be used to signal anything that may be unexpected by the hearer – sometimes a metaphor, but also on occasion the unexpected literal use of a term that is usually metaphorical, or simply a switch to a more formal or less formal register. Stefanowitsch's other strategies involve using a pre-annotated corpus: first, one annotated for semantic fields or domains; second, one annotated for conceptual mappings. This creates a new problem; many corpora are too large to annotate by hand, so a system of automatic annotation would be desirable. In the following section I describe recent work towards the automatic identification of metaphor in corpora.

2.4.3 The Automatic Identification of Metaphors in a Corpus

The automatic identification of metaphors in a corpus is a daunting objective, but a small number of researchers are making progress in this area. Two approaches have been taken: the most popular technique is for researchers to tag words according to their semantic fields, while a second approach attempts to identify formal properties of metaphorically used language that might distinguish it from literal language.

Mason's (2004) software, CorMet, takes the first approach, identifying words typical of certain semantic fields, and then looking for their occurrences in text types where they would not be expected. For instance, a word might be identified as belonging to the semantic field of chemistry, which means that it would not be expected to occur in a text from the genre of economics. Like most programs of this type, it uses a thesaurus or similar lexicon organized by semantic fields, in this case the electronic dictionary WordNet[3] (Fellbaum 1998). An underlying assumption is that the literal and metaphorical meanings of a word have different sets of collocates, which can be used to identify the meaning automatically. For example, *pour* collocates with *liquid* in the domain of the chemistry laboratory when it is used with its literal meaning, while *pour* collocates with *assets* in the domain of finance when it is used with its metaphorical meaning. However, the current success of CorMet in finding instances of metaphorical language is limited, and it 'is not designed to be a tool for reliably detecting all instances of a particular metaphor' (Mason 2004: 24).

Berber-Sardinha (2008) has also used semantic grouping as a way of detecting metaphoricity. His initial research in this area is based on dissertations in Portuguese, written by Brazilian University students. Like Mason, he uses collocation to find potential metaphors, and assumes that metaphorical and literal uses of the same word will have markedly different collocational patterns. His software searches for collocational relationships within his corpus, and then isolates words that have collocates that fall into distinct semantic groups, identified using WordNet (see above). He computes the semantic distance between the semantic fields of these collocates, using a program that supplements the database in WordNet. Where the semantic distance between two or more semantic sets of collocates of a word is sufficiently great, he considers the meanings of the words as potentially metaphorical. He then examines concordances for these words in order to confirm or refute this hypothesis. For instance, *waste, save* and *spend* all collocate with words associated with time and also with words associated with money. The semantic distance between 'time' and 'money' is judged to be reasonably great, meaning that *waste, save* and *spend* should be examined to see whether they are used metaphorically in these texts. The technique produces an overwhelming number of collocates to be evaluated for semantic distance, and to reduce the task, only those above a certain frequency, relative to a reference corpus, are studied.

Semino and Rayson (2006) are extending work on semantic annotation to develop a tool for identifying potential metaphors in text, named Wmatrix. They use a semantic annotation program based on the *Longman Lexicon of Contemporary English* (McArthur 1981), which classifies the lexicon into semantic fields. The program automatically assigns each word in a text to a semantic field, with an accuracy of around 92 per cent, and then compiles a list of the most frequent semantic fields in a text or corpus. The results for a particular text or corpus can be compared with those for a reference corpus, which will highlight semantic fields that are especially frequent in a single text or specialized corpus. These highly frequent semantic fields can suggest possible metaphors, especially where a particular semantic field seems incongruous with the nature of the text. Semino and Rayson used the program with a text about economics, finding that lexes from the fields of health and disease were relatively very frequent. Manual analysis of concordances for these lexes showed a number of metaphorical uses. As for Mason's and Berber-Sardinha's programs, Semino and Rayson's software does not identify metaphors, but because it semantically tags every word or multi-word unit with a high degree of accuracy, it gives the researcher a very complete set of data as a starting point. Assuming the researcher checks this thoroughly, significant metaphors in the text are unlikely to be missed.

Berber-Sardinha (2007) is attempting an alternative approach to the identification of metaphor in a corpus. As for the other research described in this section, the goal, at least at this stage, is limited to automatically identifying metaphor 'candidates', which are then examined manually. Berber-Sardinha follows the work of Sinclair (e.g. 1991), and Hunston and Francis (2000), in which it is argued that form coincides with meaning. When applied to metaphor, the implication is that metaphorical meanings of words are found in different lexicogrammatical patterns to their literal counterparts. The program uses a training corpus, in which metaphors have been identified manually by the analyst. Lexicogrammatical structures in the training corpus are given a probability rating indicating the likelihood of their containing metaphorical senses. The trained tool can then be used to analyse a new corpus, to assign a probability for each word as being metaphorically used or not, depending on its lexicogrammatical structure in context. Berber-Sardinha writes that there is currently insufficient training data for the first stage of the procedure, and it is clearly time consuming for the analyst to produce these. Ultimately, the success of the tool depends on whether the starting assumption, that metaphors are found in distinctive structures, is correct; current thinking among corpus linguists would strongly support the assumption.

2.5 Contributions of Corpus Linguistics to the Study of Metaphor

The previous section briefly described some procedures for identifying metaphors in text, and developments towards automatically finding them in large corpora. This section considers some of the contributions that corpus linguistic research has made to our understanding of metaphor, through a discussion of a sample of recent studies and ongoing research.

I have shown that for conceptual metaphor theorists, the role of metaphor in thought is central; its linguistic form is not the goal of study. Conceptual metaphor theorists generally research thought processes using experimental techniques established within the psycholinguistic school, often supplemented with intuitively derived linguistic data. Corpus linguists have contested the use of this kind of linguistic data (e.g. Deignan 2005a) on the grounds that intuition is a poor guide to language in use (Sinclair 1991). The studies discussed in this section analyse naturally occurring language, at a level of detail that would not be possible without computerized corpora and automatic search tools. Each of the studies described faces the challenge discussed in the previous section, of finding a way into the corpus. Each tackles some aspect of metaphorical form using corpus data, and has produced findings that are a contribution to language description, and in some cases also feed back to metaphor theory. The discussion is organized around three aspects of metaphorical language and thought: the function and ideological use of metaphor, the complex interaction between metaphor and metonymy, and the relationship between metaphor and collocation.

2.5.1 Ideology and the Function of Metaphor

Lakoff and his co-researchers state as a fundamental tenet of Conceptual Metaphor Theory that metaphor is ideological (e.g. Lakoff and Johnson 1980). Lakoff (2003) examined the linguistic metaphors found in short texts (such as presidential speeches) and claimed that metaphor has consistently been used to present a biased view of world events and governments' responses to them, most notably the United States' and allies' roles in the Gulf Wars of 1991 and 2003.

A number of corpus researchers have investigated the ideological use of metaphor, including Koller (2002, 2004) who built a corpus from business newspapers and magazines, of around 165,000 words. She studied concordances of 48 lemmas from the domains of war and marriage, identified from 'anecdotal evidence from M&A [merger and acquisition] discourse' (2002: 188). From the linguistic metaphors that she found in these concordance data, she proposed the conceptual metaphors HOSTILE TAKEOVERS ARE RAPES and MERGERS ARE MARRIAGES, and argued that overall, violence metaphors such as war and rape are more frequent in the corpus than romance and marriage metaphors. Koller points out that for many language users, these conceptual metaphors may not play any active role in text construction. Nonetheless, she concludes that her research

> throws a critical light on the metaphors employed in a particular discourse, showing that selective metaphor usage and usage of metaphorical expressions in specific contexts can indeed construct both a discourse and the sociocultural practice it originates in as a male domain excluding women. (2002: 197)

Corpus linguistic techniques are well adapted to the study of register-specific language use, and a number of corpus researchers have analysed the types of metaphors frequently found in different registers, with particular regard to their ideology and function. One of the most wide-ranging studies to date is that of Charteris-Black (2004), which consists of a series of comparative analyses of corpora from different registers, including British Conservative Party and Labour Party manifestoes, US inaugural speeches, and newspaper reporting of sport and finance. He finds some interesting and suggestive differences; for instance, that for political texts, 'journey' metaphors are more common in the United States while 'building' metaphors are more common in Britain, while of the natural world metaphors, the US texts favour 'landscape' metaphors such as *valley, horizon, jungle* and *desert*, while the British texts favour 'gardening' metaphors. These choices are attributed to the relative ideologies, histories and interests of the two countries. Charteris-Black holds that all metaphor is evaluative, and uses his corpus data to argue that social and ideological factors contribute to metaphor choice.

These and other corpus studies of metaphor have confirmed the assertion by conceptual metaphor theorists that metaphor is ideological, and have added a weight of detailed evidence that would have been unobtainable using data from single texts or intuition.

2.5.2 Metaphor and Metonymy

Metonymy and its current importance within Conceptual Metaphor Theory were discussed above, as was Goossen's (1995) observation that many linguistic expressions have their origins in both metaphor and metonymy. Corpus research has supported this observation, and added important detail. Deignan and Potter (2004) used corpora of English and Italian to study concordances of four body part terms in English and Italian (*mouth, nose, eye* and *heart* and their Italian equivalents). Their initial interest was cross-linguistic and cultural, and they found some differences in the uses of each word which could be ascribed to cultural factors. Interestingly, they also found that many of the expressions they studied had their roots in both metaphor and metonymy, as had been argued by Goossens (1995) in his study of dictionary data. Deignan (2005*a*, 2005*b*), studied further words in detail, and her findings were consistent with this. She also found a number of linguistic expressions, such as *keep an eye on* and *get hot under the collar*, which seemed prototypically to be cases of metaphor from metonymy but that became more difficult to classify when concordance data were examined in detail. The problem arises because in some citations the expressions appear to be metaphorical – that is, having no element of literal meaning – while in others they were metonymical or even almost entirely literal. In other cases, the meaning was ambiguous. Charteris-Black (2003) and Moon (1998) had made the same observation from their corpus studies; Moon writes: '*Put one's feet up* has both literal and metaphorical meanings. The metaphorical meaning 'relax' may involve the raising of one's feet, but does not necessarily have to' (1998: 184), and Charteris-Black notes, about the expression *lick one's lips*, 'It is often ambiguous whether the action actually occurs . . . In those cases where the physical action does not occur, we are perhaps already beginning to shift a boundary from metonymy in the direction of metaphor' (2003: 296–7).

Deignan (2005*a*, 2005*b*) claims that there is a further category of expressions, closer to metaphor than metonymy, in which the origin of the word or phrase is metonymic but the expression is currently a metaphor – there is no ambiguity. She terms this 'metonymy-based metaphor'. Many of the expressions which map temperature onto the emotions come into this category. Conceptual metaphor theorists such as Kövecses (2002) argue that they are grounded in physical experience, for instance the experience of increased body temperature which coincides with anger, leading us to describe anger as *heated.* Deignan (2005a) argues that rather than thinking in terms of discrete categories, we should see a cline from metaphor to metonymy, with labels such as 'metaphor from metonymy', and 'metonymy-based metaphor' providing useful points of description along the cline. The fact that individual expressions can be placed at different points on this cline does not invalidate it as a way of describing metaphorical use.

Goossens' (1995) dictionary-based study helped enormously in the analysis and classification of corpus data. However, dictionary data have limitations; the standard dictionary format forces lexicographers to draw discrete boundaries between senses, to ostensibly 'tidy up' the language. Further, almost all current corpus-based dictionaries were designed with language learners as the target reader, which means that the classifications, definitions and examples need to be easily accessible. This demand is sometimes in conflict with the desire to represent language use in detail and with accuracy, and for these reasons, a dictionary is no substitute for the study of raw corpus data.

2.5.3 Metaphor and Collocation

The final contribution of corpus research to understandings of metaphor to be discussed in this section concerns linguistic description, but, like the contributions discussed above, has implications for cognitive theory.

From the early days of corpus research, the importance of collocation in the formation of text has been recognized (e.g. Sinclair 1991). In a review of the research into formulaic sequences, Conklin and Schmitt (2008: 74) write 'the basic conclusion that formulaic sequences make up a large part of any discourse seems inescapable'. As in the above discussion of the frequency of metaphor, collocations can be counted as a proportion of continuous texts, the perspective that Conklin and Schmitt take, or as a proportion of the uses of each word, established by examining concordances.

Taking the latter view, in the semantic analysis of concordance data, it has been observed that metaphorical meanings have a tendency to occur in relatively fixed expressions. Deignan's (1999a) analysis of the lemma SHOULDER shows that the literal meaning occurs in a wide range of linguistic contexts, and only occurs in a small number of chunks, such as *shoulder injury*. However, when SHOULDER is used metaphorically, most citations are in two, three or four word chunks such as *rub shoulders, head and shoulders above, shoulder a burden* and *cold shoulder.* Analysis of the lemma HEEL (Deignan 2007) also shows a very large number of semi-fixed non-literal expressions, including *down at heel, snap at someone's heels, be hard on the heels of [someone]* and *drag one's heels*, which together account for all but 3 of the 476 non-literal citations of HEEL in the corpus. These observations suggest that the metaphorical meanings of words may be more likely to occur in semi-fixed expressions than the literal meanings of the same words: that is, metaphorically used words may have a stronger tendency than literally used words to bind with their linguistic surroundings and become part of larger expressions.

However, this is not always the case. The relationship between fixedness and metaphor was investigated in the concordance of a number of lemmas including SPEED. These lemmas were chosen because they appeared in a text covering a central and current news story, an attempt at an unbiased selection of reasonably frequent and contemporary words. The corpus searched was the section of the Bank of English that is available online. This consists of 59 million words of written and spoken contemporary texts, from a range of sources including informal speech, radio broadcasts, newspapers, magazines, fiction and non-fiction books, and ephemera such as letters and advertisements. Around 70 per cent of the corpus is British English, 20 per cent US English and the remainder Australian English.

For *speed*, fixedness occurs with both literal and non-literal meanings, but is a great deal more pronounced for the verbal use than the nominal. There are 3,606 citations of *speed* that were tagged as noun, from which a random sample of 1,000 was taken. The pragglejaz method was used to decide which uses were metaphorical; the basic meaning was defined as one that denotes movement from one physical location to another. This may refer to a part of a body or entity rather than the whole entity; for example, where *speed* referred to the physical movement of parts of a machine this was considered literal, even where the machine itself is stationary. Of the 1,000 citations, 18 referred to drugs (amphetamines), 16 were verbs that had been mistagged, and 23 were proper names. These were discounted. Of the remaining 943 citations, 130 were metaphorical and 813 were literal. The metaphorical meanings described abstract processes, often at an institutional level, such as changes in government procedures, and sometimes natural processes. Other frequent metaphorical uses described computer processing, actions such as performing non-physical work, and thinking.

It is clear that defining a fixed expression is not straightforward. For consistency, I counted as fixed expressions all citations where another word form appeared in the same slot relative to the node *speed* (e.g. immediately to the left, two words to the left, etc.) three or more times. I only considered slots up to three words to the left and right of the node. This is a frequency-based approach to fixedness, and will leave out some instances that might seem intuitively to be fixed. For instance, the metaphorical use of *two-speed*, in citations such as '. . . a two-speed approach to Europe', seems likely to be a fixed expression, but as it only occurred once in the 1,000 citation sample, it is not classified as such here.

Speed is used with its literal meaning in a large number of fixed expressions, many of which border on compound nouns; these include *speed limit, shutter speed* and *speed camera*. Other frequent fixed collocations of the literal use included *top speed* and *high speed*. In total, 409 of the 813 citations of the literal sense occurred in fixed expressions. *Speed* is used with its metaphorical meaning in far fewer lexical collocations; *breakneck speed*, which is mainly metaphorical in meaning, is the most frequent. However, the metaphorical meaning is very frequent in two collocations with grammatical words; the expressions [*the*] *speed at which* and [*the*] *speed with which* were largely used metaphorically. If these grammatical collocations are included as fixed expressions, *speed* is used in a fixed expression in 59 citations of the 130 identified as metaphorical. This is shown in Table 2.1.

Numbers and examples of citations found in each fixed expression are given in Table 2.2.

The concordance of *speed* used as a verb was also examined, and here it was found that a much higher proportion of metaphorical uses were in fixed expressions. The concordance showed 371 citations, of which 24 had been mistagged, and 6 were proper names. Of the remaining 341 citations, 73 were literal and 268 metaphorical. Of the literal citations, 21 occurred in fixed expressions, while of the metaphorical citations, 205 occurred in fixed expressions. This is shown in Table 2.3.

Numbers and examples of citations found in each fixed expression are given in Table 2.4.

The hypothesis that metaphorical meanings of words are more likely to occur as components of larger chunks requires further investigation using large corpora. It seems that this is a general tendency, but the examination of nominal *speed* showed that it is not the case for all words. There is no obvious reason why this should be so. It may be that words from particular source domains, such as the human body, are more likely to be used within fixed expressions, because they are more likely to form components of metonymical rather than metaphorical mappings.

If confirmed as a general tendency, the relationship between metaphor and collocation would have implications for conceptual metaphor theorists' view that linguistic metaphors are purely the product of mappings at the mental level, because this view offers no explanation for formal differences between literal and figurative language. It has been claimed that chunks are probably stored, produced and processed as single units by individual speakers (Sinclair 1991; Wray 2002). Further, it is possible they are acquired holistically, only later, if at all, being

Table 2.1 Analysis of 1,000 citations of nominal *speed* by metaphoricity and fixedness.

Meaning	*Number found in fixed expression (%)*	*Number not found in fixed expression (%)*	*Total*
Metaphorical	59 (45)	71 (55)	130
Literal	409 (50)	404 (50)	813
Discounted (mistagged etc.)			57

Table 2.2 Literal and metaphorical meanings of nominal *speed* found in fixed expressions.

Fixed expression	Number of literal citations	Example	Number of metaphorical citations	Example(s)
High-speed (compound)	73	. . . a high-speed national rail network.	11	. . . a high-speed connection to the Net. . . . high speed development of plants and animals.
Speed limit	51	Most of us have exceeded the speed limit at some time or other.		
High speed	43	They turned at once and made for home at high speed.	1	Haig's early life is an insignificant road upon which they must unfortunately travel in order to arrive at the real point of interest. But, whilst they race through this period at high speed . . . .
Top speed	35	It had reached a top speed of 106 mph.	1	He mentally rifled through the possibilities, his mind working at top speed.
Average speed	30	The average speed for all London roads during the morning peak has fallen from just over 17 mph to 15 mph.		
Five-speed	24	. . . if you choose a manual five-speed transmission.		
At speed	16	If you are driving at speed, it is as dangerous as black ice.	1	. . . responding to events at speed sometimes resulted in grammatical errors.

(Continued)

Table 2.2—Cont'd

Fixed expression	Number of literal citations	Example	Number of metaphorical citations	Example(s)
Full speed	13	There was nothing we could do and they rammed our bows. They hit us at full speed.	3	. . . with the presidential campaign going full speed into its last four weeks.
Shutter speed	13	The slowest shutter speed enables you to take night shots.		
Speed of light	12	. . . Einstein's claim that the speed of light is fixed.	1	. . . folk heritage played at the speed of light.
Low speed	10	. . . using a fan at low speed.		
Wind speed	9	. . . the weather forecast, including wind speed and direction.		
. . . speed automatic	9	. . . a three-speed automatic gearbox.		
Maximum speed	8	. . . battery powered cars with a maximum speed of 6 mph.		
A speed of	8	. . . the fastest rider of the night at a speed of 116.62 mph.		
Great/greater speed	6	He was soon back in action, covering ground at great speed and firing shots at goal.	4	. . . the great speed at which the royal family hurtles from one drama to another.
Speed and power	6	It was obvious from the start he was never going to be able to cope with Hamed's speed and power.		
Pick up speed	5	The traffic outside was picking up speed.	2	The economic recovery is picking up speed.
Land speed	5	. . . attempts on the world land speed record.		
Speed camera	5	. . . the long overdue introduction of speed cameras.		

Term	n	Example	n	Example
Speed of sound	5	. . . flying at more than four times the speed of sound.		
At the same speed	4	We'll be travelling at the same speed as the original convoys.		
Film speed	4	. . . buttons on the camera back. The first selects [. . .] a variety of features from film speed, auto-exposure . . .		
Speed ramp(s)	3	They've put those speed ramps up [. . .] they've slowed traffic down.		
Variable speed	3	. . . three variable speed zoom and long play playback.		
Lightning speed	2	Suddenly, he pulled a knife and struck with lightning speed.	2	Companies that want to succeed in today's cut-throat commercial-insurance market need to be able to produce competitive quotations at lightning speed.
Speed and accuracy	2	. . . the speed and accuracy of its movements.	2	Kids begin with key location, then move on to lessons that build speed and accuracy.
Breakneck speed	2	. . . the tale of a rogue asteroid hurtling towards Earth at breakneck speed.	5	He forced the country to industrialize at breakneck speed and at great cost.
Up to speed			3	If you want to keep up to speed, friendly society Liverpool Victoria is offering a free guide and information service.
Speed and efficiency			3	In fact he wrote to commend them on the speed and efficiency of the claims process after having his car stolen.

(Continued)

Table 2.2—Cont'd

Fixed expression	Number of literal citations	Example	Number of metaphorical citations	Example(s)
Speed of processing			3	. . . speed-of-processing differences may be built in at birth.
Speed at which	2	The Science Centre's radar gun is set up for visitors to test their strength and measure the speed at which they can throw a tennis ball.	12	Liquidity is the speed at which an asset can be turned into cash for meeting bills and short-term debts.
Speed with which	1	The amount of the shift is a measure of the speed with which the star is approaching or receding from the earth.	16	[He] issued a statement deploring her arrest and the speed with which details of it had been made public.
	Total 409		**Total 59***	

* The total number of citations in which a metaphorical use of speed appears in fixed expressions is 59. However, 11 citations of speed appear in more than one fixed expression; as in the expression 'the great speed at which'. This means that there are 70 instances of metaphorical fixed expressions in the 59 citations.

Table 2.3 Analysis of 371 citations of verbal *speed* by metaphoricity and fixedness.

Meaning	Number found in fixed expression (%)	Number not found in fixed expression (%)	Total
Metaphorical	205 (72)	79 (28)	284
Literal	21 (36)	36 (64)	57
Discounted (mistagged etc.)			30

Table 2.4 Linguistic fixedness of literal and metaphorical meanings of verbal *speed*.

Fixed expression	Number of literal citations	Example	Number of metaphorical citations	Example(s)
Speed up	15	Drivers will be radioed to slow down or speed up to avoid bunching.	171	Its creators claim it will speed up the design process.
Speed (one word) up			28	Fat loss must be done over a long period because physiologically, we cannot speed it up.
Speed away	3	She could speed away to 100 mph in less than nine seconds.		
Speed through	3	Amtrak soon found itself sidetracked repeatedly to let express freight trains speed through.		
Speed healing			3	Bed rest can help relieve back pain, but may not speed healing.
Speed towards			3	. . . the underlying message was one of encouragement for the Germans as they speed towards unity.
	Total **21**		**Total** **205**	

analysed into their component words (Wray 2002). It follows that when speakers use chunks that consist of some metaphorically used words, they may have selected them ready-made, and, at an earlier stage, acquired them as such. This would call into question the nature of internal metaphorical links for individual speakers. For instance, Lakoff and Johnson cite the chunk *run out of steam* (1980: 27) as a realization of a metaphorical mapping between the 'domains' of THE MIND and A MACHINE. This may be so from the researcher's perspective, but if the chunk has been acquired holistically, individual speakers may never, or very rarely, analyse it. There may not be a direct link in their minds from the linguistic expression to a mapping of machinery onto the mind, especially as a corpus search suggests that it is not usually used with a literal meaning.

The discussion also has implications for the study of chunking. It is argued that formulaic language offers a processing advantage for both speakers and hearers (Wray 2000; Conklin and Schmitt 2008), and that it has social functions (Wray 2000; Wray and Perkins 2000). If, as seems likely from these preliminary studies, metaphorical uses of some words are more likely to occur in fixed expressions than literal uses of the same words, there are implications for the function of formulaic language.

In this section, I have argued that corpus linguistic research can contribute to metaphor theory and description in several important ways: first, I have shown that corpus data confirm the assertion of conceptual metaphor theorists that metaphor is ideological, and can offer detailed insights into its ideological use and function more generally. Second, I have argued that study of corpus linguistic data can contribute to more detailed and accurate classifications of non-literal language and thought in the area of the metaphor-metonymy overlap. Finally, I have argued that the possible significance of chunking for metaphor challenges the notion that linguistic metaphors are purely the product of underlying conceptual metaphorical networks, and I have discussed some concordance analyses that explored this possibility.

2.6 Conclusion

Interest in metaphor and developments in corpus linguistics have grown alongside each other over the last thirty years. In this chapter, I have described some of the interaction that has taken place between the two fields. To date, this interaction has been relatively limited, because the fields have different research agendas, and have radically different, often opposing notions as to what constitutes evidence. I have argued that the study of metaphor has the potential to inform language description in several ways. Corpus linguistics can likewise inform theoretical understandings of metaphor. There are formidable technical difficulties in harnessing the full power of corpus linguistics to analyse metaphors, but as this chapter has hopefully demonstrated, pioneering work is taking place to tackle these.

Notes

1 See http://cogsci.berkeley.edu/lakoff/.
2 http://www.let.vu.nl/english/research/projectSites/pragglejaz/start.htm.
3 http://wordnet.princeton.edu/.

3

Corpora and Critical Discourse Analysis

Gerlinde Mautner

In recent years, awareness has been growing that corpus linguistic techniques can be harnessed profitably in order to uncover relationships between language and the social – one of the central concerns of discourse analysis generally and its 'critical' variety in particular. Clearly, the value of accessing large computer-held corpora lies in boosting the empirical credence of analyses. This serves to counteract the charge, frequently levelled at critical discourse analysis (CDA), that individual texts are cherry-picked to suit the researcher's own political agenda (Koller and Mautner 2004: 225; Partington 2004b: 13; Orpin 2005: 38).

This chapter reviews key works in this area (e.g. Hardt-Mautner 1995; Krishnamurthy 1996; Fairclough 2000; Baker and McEnery 2005; and Mautner 2008) and adds original data analyses to illustrate how CDA can benefit from the application of corpus linguistic techniques to both smaller custom-built corpora and large reference corpora. This is followed by a critique pointing out the limitations of such an approach. A case is made for the use of mutually supportive methodologies originating in CDA and corpus linguistics respectively.

3.1 Introduction

Corpus linguistics and critical discourse analysis (CDA) are both relatively young approaches to linguistic enquiry, and for significant parts of their short but vibrant history they have led largely separate lives. Yet, as this chapter aims to demonstrate, they can cooperate fruitfully and with mutual gain, building on a shared interest in how language 'works' in social rather than merely structural terms.

CDA is a branch of linguistics concerned with links between language and the social, and generally pursuing an emancipatory agenda in doing so, particularly where power asymmetries are involved (cf. Fairclough 1992; Fairclough 1995; Fairclough and Wodak 1997). In this context, it is worth remembering that the scholar widely acknowledged to be one of the founding fathers of corpus linguistics, J. R. Firth, framed his approach very much as a socially oriented endeavour. In his writings dating from the mid-1930s to the 1950s, one finds tell-tale and, in hindsight, prophetic, references to semantic phenomena being referred to as 'sociologically symptomatic', and to the potential involved in using 'a contextual and sociological technique' (Firth 1935 [1957]: 13). Foreshadowing what came to be called keyword analysis a good 40 years later (Williams 1976; Stubbs 1996: 157–95), Firth also called for research into 'the detailed contextual distribution of sociologically important words, what one might call *focal* or *pivotal* words' (Firth 1935 [1957]: 10; original italics). Another quote likely to resonate strongly with researchers located within a CDA framework is Firth's reference to the 'language of social control in the whole of education' (Firth 1957: 179).

While it is true, quite generally, that '[C]orpus linguistics sees language as a social phenomenon' (Teubert and Čermáková 2004: 37), it is arguably its specific applications in CDA that foreground this concern particularly well, bringing to fruition the 'contextual and sociological technique' whose foundations were laid by Firth. This rediscovery, boosted by computer technology, has resulted in a variety of studies applying corpus linguistic techniques to research questions that respond, broadly speaking, to discursive reflections of social issues rather than originating from concerns with linguistic structure *per se*.

3.2 CDA and Corpus Data

Before we look at possible points of contact between corpus linguistics and CDA, and ask why they are occasionally seen as uneasy bedfellows, let us briefly call to mind what CDA is about. Fairclough and Wodak begin their 1997 programmatic paper by stating that CDA 'analyses real and often extended instances of social interaction which take a linguistic form, or a partially linguistic form' (Fairclough and Wodak 1997: 258). They continue by naming eight principles governing CDA:

1. CDA addresses social problems.
2. Power relations are discursive.
3. Discourse constitutes society and culture.
4. Discourse does ideological work.
5. Discourse is historical.
6. The link between text and society is mediated.
7. Discourse analysis is interpretative and explanatory.
8. Discourse is a form of social action.

None of these is inherently inimical to a corpus-linguistic approach. Quite on the contrary, there is shared understanding about the importance of data authenticity and language in use – witness Fairclough and Wodak's (1997: 258) introductory comment on 'real and often extended instances of social interaction'. That alone might tempt one to conclude that corpus linguistics and CDA are a natural match, and in the next section I will review key work that proves this point. Nevertheless, it cannot be denied that there are areas of concern – not prohibitive by any means, but serious enough to explain why the two communities of researchers have so far, to labour the romantic analogy once again, clearly preferred occasional dating (exciting, but essentially non-committal) to a formal exchanging of vows.

What, then, are the impediments? First, CDA considers it essential to relate linguistic evidence to in-depth analysis of extra-linguistic context. The individual text is 'deconstructed and embedded in its social conditions, is linked to ideologies and power relationships' (Fairclough and Wodak 1997: 279). If you work with corpora consisting of hundreds or thousands of texts and running to millions of words, as corpus linguists are wont to do, then such in-depth exploration of context is simply not feasible. In most cases, it is not just a shortage of person hours that makes this impossible, but that most of the large corpora currently available were compiled with only very rudimentary contextual information left intact and accessible. Usually this information stretches only as far as identifying the mode (spoken vs written), medium (newspapers, radio, fiction) and regional provenance (British, US, Canadian, etc.). Admittedly, some corpora are more versatile than others. The British National Corpus (BNC),[1] for example, has been demographically sampled and allows comparative studies that are sensitive to speaker age, socioeconomic class and gender (see, e.g. McEnery and Xiao 2004 for a study of swearing in British English). In the CANCODE[2] part of the Cambridge International Corpus, there are even codes indicating the relationship between speakers, thus allowing investigations into the impact of different levels of formality. However, none of this is likely to impress discourse analysts, who generally want to peg their interpretation on microscopic scrutiny of when, how and why a text was produced, and by whom. That Wordbanks, for example, gives access to nearly 60 million words from *The Times* (not to mention the further 450 million or so from other sources) may not be as appealing as one might think if what the analyst is really interested in is the unfolding of a particular news story over a few days, and its differential treatment in various journalistic genres (e.g. reports vs editorials). Understandably, if you want one thing, then getting lots of another, no matter how generously provided, can offer only paltry comfort. You cannot argue away that, in essence, large corpora contain decontextualized language (Flowerdew 2005: 324; Baker 2006: 25). In addition, they are semiotically impoverished, reduced to text-only format without any information on accompanying visuals, layout, typography, gesture, facial expression and intonation, all of which can of course contribute crucially to the creation of meaning. These limitations do not make corpora useless for CDA applications, but they might go some way towards explaining why critical discourse analysts have not been quite as enthusiastic about reaching out to corpus linguistics as they might be.

On the other hand, the aggregation involved in corpus building, and the decontextualization that goes with it, can also be seen as a help and not merely a hindrance. Generalization undoubtedly rests on a firmer footing if you work with more data, and not having to grapple with all the contextual baggage can, at least for certain stages in the analysis, be helpful in focusing the research (which novices to the trade, bewildered by the multi-layeredness of discourse, may want to read as a euphemism for saying that corpus methods make it is easier to know where to start). Thus, as I hope to show in the following sections, working with large corpora can contribute to counteracting one of the most fundamental and persisting criticisms levelled against CDA, namely that it supposedly cherry-picks small and unrepresentative data samples in order to suit researchers' preconceived notions about hidden ideological meanings; in short, that the analysis is allowed to be shaped by the desired result, which, in turn, is often said to be shaped by the researcher's own political agenda (e.g. Widdowson 2004: 102).

Like other linguists using corpus methods, the critical discourse analyst too basically has a choice between building their own corpus (called 'tailor-made' or 'DIY'/'do-it-yourself') and using those that are ready-made and publicly (usually commercially) available ('off the peg' corpora, McEnery, Xiao and Tono 2006: 59, 71). At the time of writing, the best-known and most widely used publicly available corpora are the BNC and Wordbanks Online.[3] Very often the biggest potential lies in combining the use of both types of corpora, tailor-made and off-the-peg, so that in a sense the potential drawbacks of one can be offset by key advantages of the other. CDA, of course, has a strong interest in socially and historically situated text, and is concerned never to lose sight of precisely the type of wider context that large off-the-peg corpora routinely obscure from vision. This makes it very likely for CDA projects to start out from purpose-built corpora which are stored on and processed by computer, but whose files remain cross-referenced with their hard copy counterparts, which constitute semiotically rich, multimodal and 'tangible' text in its most traditional form. This ensures that, whenever necessary, a full-blown discourse analysis would not be unduly starved of its typically multimodal fare.

If a purpose-built corpus is used as the starting point of an inquiry, the path of methodological choice again bifurcates. One option is to begin with a close reading of selected texts in the corpus, identify salient items and patterns, and then search both the whole corpus and any reference corpora we may be using, to see how the item or pattern 'behaves' collocationally throughout one's corpus or indeed in larger universes of discourse. Large reference corpora are crucial in safeguarding against both 'over- and underinterpretation' (O'Halloran and Coffin 2004): against the risk, that is, of either reading too much into certain usages, or of failing to identify socially significant patterns.

Instead of first doing a qualitative discourse analysis of individual texts in the corpus, there is the option of turning to concordance software straightaway and beginning by what may, inelegantly though perhaps rather aptly, be called 'playing around' with the data. This usually involves compiling and studying a frequency list, and looking at the concordances of particularly frequent lexical items. Finally, a case can be made for critical discourse analysts to occasionally work only with data aggregates, temporarily forsaking their preoccupation with textual integrity (see Case Study 2). The discovery of usage patterns in large reference corpora can be seen as a worthwhile pursuit in its own right, making as it does a legitimate contribution to the critical study of language and society.

3.3 Review of Existing Work

There is now a substantial and growing body of research that responds to the challenges mentioned in the previous section – so substantial, in fact, that in the space available my review has to be brief and selective. Among the earliest examples of this kind of research are Stubbs and Gerbig (1993), Hardt-Mautner (1995) and Krishnamurthy (1996). Stubbs' *Text and Corpus Analysis* (1996), subtitled *Computer-Assisted Studies of Language and Culture*, was instrumental in putting this approach on the map. Not on everyone's map simultaneously, one might add. As is to be expected, researchers with a background in corpus linguistics were the first to pursue this lead and still remain key drivers in producing insightful case studies of ideologically loaded lexis, while also developing the analytical concepts needed for extracting socially significant information from corpora. Two of these concepts, semantic preference and semantic prosody (Louw 1993; Partington 2004*a*; Xiao and McEnery 2006), will be examined later on in this chapter. In the same vein, John Sinclair's (2003) volume, *Reading Concordances*, devotes a chapter to 'Words as Liabilities' (his example being the negative semantic load carried by *regime*) and one to 'Hidden Meanings' – both reflecting concerns quite clearly up the CDA street.

In discourse analysis, an early reference to corpus linguistics was made by de Beaugrande in a two-volume edited collection of state-of-the art discourse studies. He declares, '[l]arge corpuses offer valuable support for the project of discourse analysis to return to authentic data' (de Beaugrande 1997: 42) and proceeds to illustrate how what he refers to as 'large-corpus linguistics' can be harnessed to extracting information from data that would not be accessible to intuition alone. However, none of the 21 other contributors to the volume felt inclined to pursue this lead.

All in all, it has been with some time lag that critical discourse analysts have begun to appreciate the potential lying in this methodology, and there is still no consistency. Even in fairly recent, quasi-canonical works – consolidating CDA, showcasing seminal research and presenting essential toolboxes – corpus linguistic methodology does not feature prominently. For example, Wodak and Meyer's first (2001) edition of *Methods of Critical Discourse Analysis* was silent on corpus linguistic methods. However, its second edition – perhaps tellingly so, given the growing awareness of the field – does include a chapter on applying corpus linguistics in CDA (Mautner 2009). While corpus linguistic techniques are thus only just taking root in CDA's methodological canon, there have, since around 2000, been a fair number of individual publications going down this road. Fairclough's (2000) study of New Labour's discourse ought to be mentioned; Piper's (2000*a*, 2000*b*) work on the discourse of lifelong learning, and Orpin's (2005) analysis of the lexis of corruption (revolving around words like *sleaze* and *bribery*). There have been corpus-based contributions to the discourse of ageing (Mautner 2007), courtroom discourse (Cotterill 2001), political discourse (Baker and McEnery 2005) and risk communication (Hamilton, Adolphs and Nerlich 2007), as well as inquiries into business English (Nelson 2005; Alexander 2007), newspaper discourse (Mautner 2008) and several corpus-informed approaches to metaphor analysis (Koller 2004; O'Halloran 2007*a*; Deignan, this volume). Awareness is also increasing that the World Wide Web represents a treasure trove for building corpora that reflect current social developments much better than static corpora ever can (Mautner 2005; Sharoff 2006; Lew, this volume). As might be expected, there is probably an increasing number of researchers who are in fact unable and quite possibly unwilling to be pigeonholed as either 'corpus linguists' or 'critical discourse analysts'. This can be taken, first, as a healthy sign that intradisciplinary boundaries are beginning to crumble, and second, as a reflection of the rather compelling argument that corpus linguistics 'should be viewed as a methodology rather than an independent branch of linguistics' (McEnery et al. 2006: 11); as such, it should be compatible with many other approaches without concerns about disciplinary traditions and boundaries getting in the way.

Summing up, at the interface of corpus linguistics and discourse analysis, a fair amount of ground has been covered, and important theoretical and methodological foundations laid. Nevertheless, substantial areas are still left to be explored, and will indeed keep emerging as new issues of social, political and cultural concern arise. How such explorations may proceed will be illustrated below.

3.4 Case Studies

The case studies that follow are limited in two ways. There is, inevitably, the usual waiver referring to constraints of space. More importantly, what such brief snapshots cannot adequately demonstrate, but will be high on the CDA agenda, is the question of integrating whatever insights corpus linguistic techniques provide into the wider interpretative framework that underpins the analysis. Thus, the examples below are given on the understanding that, if they were elaborated and developed into larger-scale investigations, then this contextual integration would clearly have to be achieved.

The key analytical tools and concepts that I will draw upon in what follows are frequency, collocation, semantic preference and semantic prosody. Semantic preference is understood as an item's co-occurrence with 'a class of words which share some semantic feature' (Stubbs 2001*b*: 88). Semantic prosody, on the other hand, equates roughly with evaluative meaning, the 'semantic aura' around a word (Louw 1993; Partington 2004), or, more simply, 'the indication that something is good or bad' (Hunston 2004: 157).

3.4.1 Case study 1: Civil Liberties Versus Anti-Terrorism Legislation

My first case study is one that involves a very small tailor-made corpus – quite deliberately, because while it is true that corpus linguistic techniques are shown off to their best advantage when dealing with large amounts of data, there are also clear benefits from applying them to small corpora. The group of texts I am using here constitute an e-mail exchange from 2006 between the then Prime Minister of the United Kingdom, Tony Blair, and the columnist Henry Porter, published in the British Sunday paper *The Observer*.[4] The debate between the two men deals with so-called 'anti-terror laws': what Porter sees as an attack against civil liberties and what Blair regards as a legitimate part of the fight against terrorism. The written dialogue consists of just over 4,000 words: three messages from Blair, totalling about 2,200 words, with the remaining 1,800 taken up by three messages from Porter. For the concordance analysis, their contributions were split and reassembled in a 'Blair' and a 'Porter' corpus respectively.

What a discourse analyst would be interested in is to find out how the opposing views held by the two authors translate into argumentative strategies and lexical choices. Although 4,000 words would generally be considered a corpus size that can still be handled reasonably comfortably without computer support, the use of concordancing software (in this case, Wordsmith Tools[5]), shows up interesting leads and of course does so at a fraction of the time that a manual search would take – if, indeed, the purely manual approach would yield these leads at all. As always, the word frequency list is a good entry point to the corpus, highlighting collocational patterns that will probably be worth following up with a qualitative analysis of concordance lines. Table 3.1 lists the absolute and relative frequencies for 30 items from the top of the word frequency list of the Blair and Porter corpora. The cut-off point is largely arbitrary, dictated by the need to keep the list at a manageable length for the purposes of the present demonstration (though in a 'real' project, too, any initial round of analysis would have to be restricted in some way).

Predictably, the figures for the high-frequency grammatical items (*the, of, to, and, is* etc.) are very similar in the two corpora. Such words are not, after all, generally amenable to stylistic choice on the part of the writer or speaker, and hence of little interest to critical discourse analysts. But there are several disparities in the word lists that would be worth investigating, such as the much higher incidence of *we* in the Blair corpus and of *you* in the Porter corpus. Pronoun usage, with its relevance for the discursive construction of identities and relationships, crops up routinely in CDA studies, and could also make a worthwhile contribution to our example. Without being able to go into too much detail here, what the frequencies for *you* indicate is that the two contributors have a different interactive style, one addressing the other personally more often than is the case vice-versa (and as the concordances confirm, all but one of the instances of *you* are of the personal-address type rather than examples of its generic usage). Blair's more frequent use of *we*, on the other hand, is at least partly accounted for by the fact that his position allows him to use *we* to refer to the government (in quotes such as *If we hadn't legislated*). This, in turn, might help explain why the word *government* itself is not part of his list of high-frequency items, but is of Porter's (item 25). Another difference in the two wordlists, and a particularly conspicuous one considering that a legal topic is being debated, is that between the frequencies for *law*, and this is one which I would like to discuss in more detail. *Law* occurs six times (or 0.27 times per 100 words) in the Blair corpus, and fourteen times (or 0.74 times per 100) in the Porter corpus. If you add the plural form *laws* (three occurrences in Blair, and eight in Porter), the gap opens up even more. From the concordances, it becomes apparent that the difference is not only quantitative but also manifestly qualitative. In the two writers' texts, *law* attracts different collocates as shown in Figures 3.1 and 3.2.

For example, Porter has five occurrences of *Rule of Law*, and Blair none. Four of Porter's uses of *Rule of Law* position it as an object of actions directly or indirectly attributed to the British government: cf. *eroding, has . . . attacked,*

Table 3.1 The top 30 items from the word frequency lists for the contributions by Tony Blair and Henry Porter.

	Blair				*Porter*		
	Word	*Frequ.*	*%*		*Word*	*Frequ.*	*%*
1	THE	127	5.6646	1	THE	121	6.4327
2	OF	76	3.3898	2	OF	64	3.4024
3	TO	58	2.587	3	TO	62	3.2961
4	AND	56	2.4978	4	AND	41	2.1797
5	IS	48	2.1409	5	IS	40	2.1265
6	IN	45	2.0071	6	**YOU**	39	2.0734
7	A	36	1.6057	7	A	37	1.967
8	ARE	31	1.3827	8	IN	37	1.967
9	**WE**	31	1.3827	9	THAT	35	1.8607
10	IT	28	1.2489	10	I	25	1.3291
11	FOR	26	1.1597	11	HAVE	24	1.2759
12	I	25	1.1151	12	BY	20	1.0633
13	THAT	22	0.9813	13	THIS	19	1.0101
14	BUT	19	0.8475	14	FOR	18	0.9569
15	THEY	19	0.8475	15	ARE	16	0.8506
16	THIS	18	0.8029	16	BE	16	0.8506
17	**YOU**	18	0.8029	17	IT	16	0.8506
18	**PEOPLE**	17	0.7583	18	HAS	14	0.7443
19	WITH	17	0.7583	19	**LAW**	14	0.7443
20	HAVE	15	0.669	20	NOT	14	0.7443
21	WOULD	15	0.669	21	YOUR	14	0.7443
22	AS	13	0.5798	22	AS	13	0.6911
23	ON	13	0.5798	23	ON	13	0.6911
24	BY	12	0.5352	24	BUT	12	0.638
25	WHO	12	0.5352	25	**GOVERNMENT**	12	0.638
26	OR	11	0.4906	26	WHICH	12	0.638
27	OUR	11	0.4906	27	BEEN	11	0.5848
28	NOT	10	0.446	28	**WE**	9	0.4785
29	THEM	10	0.446	29	LAWS	8	0.4253
30	AN	9	0.4014	30	PARLIAMENT	8	0.4253

Note: Figures are based on output from Wordsmith Tools (Frequ. = absolute frequency; % = what percentage of the total word count does the item in question represent). Items referred to in the discussion below are in bold.

tamper with, this wholesale assault on. The fifth admonishes Blair *to adhere to the Rule of Law.* That Blair, in turn, completely omits the expression from his responses[6] indicates that this is one of Porter's lines of argumentation that Blair does not engage with at all – presumably, if one were to hazard a guess, because for Blair's

```
1    esses were the answer to these crime and law and order problems that are an age
2    clarify (in the light of subsequent case law) the circumstances under which infe
3    except the usual process of the criminal law, which was hopelessly inadequate. R
4    civil liberties, what about theirs, the  law-abiding people; the ones who treat
5    t where these powers are being used, the law-abiding no longer live in fear of t
6    e victim. If the practical effect of the law is that people live in fear because
```

Figure 3.1 Concordance of *law* from the Blair corpus.

```
1    he job of the law lords is to uphold the law and see that justice is available t
2    not classed as an offence under British  law. The broader point is that in these
3    of your measures have been subject to a law of unintended consequences. That is
4    ished until a court has decided that the law has been broken, the right to demon
5    of innocence. To tamper with the Rule of Law is not the right way for a healthy
6    iminals, merely to adhere to the Rule of Law. If there is no respect for its tra
7    rights and freedoms, eroding the Rule of Law and profoundly altering the relatio
8    or this wholesale assault on the Rule of Law. One of the results of your moderni
9    nt has cumulatively attacked the Rule of Law by reducing liberties in many diffe
10   en justified - but you have produced bad  law which allows gossip and rumour to b
11   you suggest. Either way, the job of the law lords is to uphold the law and see
12   ory Reform Bill proposed an extension of law by ministerial decree. There has be
13   d drug dealers do you mention a court of law. I am not asking you to be weak on
14   it likes. The point about anti-terrorist law is that we do have control orders a
```

Figure 3.2 Concordance of *law* from the Porter corpus.

position this is in fact the thinnest part of the ice. To gauge the full significance of *not* mentioning the *Rule of Law* even though one's counterpart in the argument does so repeatedly, one would have to follow CDA traditions and reach outside the text, into the legal, political and historical spheres that have come to shape the concept and underpin its factual and highly symbolic significance as 'a pillar of constitutional thought' (Alder 2005: 124) and 'a central feature of western liberal democratic governments' (Pollard et al. 2001: 35). Given this symbolism, it does not seem too far-fetched to interpret Blair's not using the term as an avoidance strategy (and, at least from a politician's pragmatic point of view, a rather sensible one at that).

What also stands out from the concordance for *law* is the fact that the compound *law-abiding* appears twice among Blair's six occurrences, but not at all among Porter's thirteen. The evaluative load of *law-abiding*, and the significance of using or not using it, is not entirely clear. On the surface, the word seems unequivocally positive: it is a good thing to be law-abiding, surely; if you are not, you are a criminal. How, then, are we to assess the complete absence of the expression in Porter's letters? It is in cases like this that it is useful to match up evidence from a large reference corpus with what we found in our small corpora. A search in the Wordbanks *Times* corpus, featuring nearly 60 million words from this British upmarket newspaper, shows that *law-abiding* occurs 111 times, or 92 times if we remove all the direct quotes and only include editorial uses in a narrower sense (i.e. where the paper's own voice is heard, rather than someone else's). This equals 1.2 occurrences per one million words. In the 45-million-word corpus of articles from the popular tabloid *The Sun*, by contrast, *law-abiding* occurs 145 times, or 127 if we exclude the quotes. This equals 2.8 instances per one million words, more than double the frequency in *The Times*. Both papers would generally be regarded as (small-c) conservative, but differ significantly in terms of their editorial style and core readership, with *The Sun* being at the populist end of the spectrum and appealing largely to a working-class audience; 62 per cent of its readers belong to the C2, D and E social grades. *The Times*, on the other hand, is a paper with 89 per cent of its readership in the ABC1 socio-economic stratum.[7] Also, from the Wordbanks concordance output, *law-abiding* emerges as a richly connoted expression which conveys so much more than simply describing someone who 'abides by the law'. Those that are law-abiding are also, to quote just a few of the surrounding adjectival collocates from both newspapers, *honest, garden-tending, upright, decent, peaceful, quiet, God-fearing, hard-working, sensible, mild-mannered, responsible, respectable, middle-class* and *abstemious*. We can see from these collocates how *law-abiding* is bound up in a moralizing discourse that goes far beyond mere compliance with the law. That it is, in addition, also part of an exclusionary and potentially polarizing discourse is borne out by the collocates *ordinary* and *normal*. The 'law-abiding' person thus emerges as a discursively constructed conglomerate of mainstream values and, if we go back to the different frequencies in the *Sun* and *Times* corpora, it is a construction evoked more commonly in populist discourse. In everyday parlance we could say that this explains the 'ring' that Blair's use of *law-abiding* has to it. In more technical terms, what we have uncovered is how the word is 'primed' (Hoey 2004), that is, what patterns of co-occurrence we typically expect because we have encountered them frequently in the past. Either way, the discursive profile that we have extracted from the large reference corpus provides a clue as to why Porter does not use the expression at all.

These observations on *law-abiding* tie in with another difference between the Blair and Porter texts, namely the frequency with which they use the word *people*. As the word list shows (see Table 3.1), *people* is actually the most common content word in Blair's letters, occurring 17 times, or 0.76 times per 100 words. In the Porter corpus, by contrast, it occurs only 5 times (or 0.27 times per 100 words). As far as its dictionary definition is concerned, one can hardly imagine a more semantically bland word than *people*, but examining the concordances reveals that the semantics predominant in this discourse is both rather richer and more specific than its purely descriptive meaning suggests. The most common use of *people* in the Blair corpus (12 out of 17) refers to a group of 'ordinary folk' that his legislation claims to protect: people who *mourn the loss of respect*, people who *live in fear* and *whose lives have been turned into a daily hell* (by anti-social behaviour, that is), to quote from just a few lines. In this rhetoric, *people* clearly plays a role in constructing a group that the politician aligns himself with.

It is probably too bold a claim to say that none of the above could have been tackled with only CDA's traditional discovery procedures, but I would argue that, with corpus linguistic support, the account is less speculative and includes insights on patterns most likely to have otherwise gone unnoticed.

3.4.2 Case study 2: A Contribution to the Discourse of Ageing

Unlike the first example, my second case study, dealing with the word *elderly* (published previously in Mautner 2007), does not start out from an individual text or texts but instead goes straight to the very large corpus that in the previous example was only used for comparative purposes. All the same, the investigation was at least initially prompted by observations of fully contextualized language: of entries in learners' dictionaries not agreeing on the evaluative meaning of the word (is *elderly* more polite than *old*, or less so?), of quotes culled from the Web in which the synonymity of *elderly* and *old* was being challenged ('I am elderly, but not old!'), and of *elderly* being rejected as ageist by pressure groups. All of these pointed to *elderly* being a contested expression, and the aim of the corpus-based inquiry was to throw more light on how and why this might be so.

The study begins by looking at the collocation lists for *elderly* and picking out the lexical collocates with the highest joint frequency and high *t*-scores (of 5 and above).[8] In addition to the predictable [+human] nouns such as *people, woman* and *man*, the list of top-10 collocates also includes *care, disabled* and *sick*. Ordered by MI score, which measures the strength of the collocation, more items from this semantic domain appear, and they are also predominantly negative: *infirm, frail, handicapped, mentally* and *blind*. This pattern of semantic preference and prosody (Partington 2004a) turns out to be particularly prominent when the search is limited to the collective expression *the elderly*.

Having established that adjectives with a negative semantic load have a higher than random probability of occurring in the vicinity of *elderly*, the investigation then moved on to a qualitative analysis of concordance lines. This is probably the juncture at which corpus linguistic work begins to look most familiar to critical discourse analysts. The stretch of coherent language that is available for closer inspection may be unusually short by CDA standards (typically, between 80 and 120 characters, and 512 maximum in Wordbanks) but it does allow meaningful insights. For example, in trying to establish the attributes that make up the semantics of *elderly*, there is quite a lot of mileage in examining occurrences of *elderly* that refer to humans and are followed by the exception-marking co-ordinating conjunction *but* and another adjective (with up to one word in between to allow for adverbial modification). This allows a process of indirect definition by contradiction because, by implication, the adjectives following *but* tell us what kind of qualities are not associated with being elderly (*charismatic, powerful, vigorous, imposing* etc.). The concordances raise to the textual surface a whole range of meaning elements that would arguably be impossible to catalogue without corpus evidence (see Figure 3.3).

```
the expression `your number's up". Elderly  but boyish locals Jackie O'Shea (

2002 </dt> <p> ISTANBUL Final scores Elderly-but-charismatic world academics 2,

be crazy." <p> Ghassan Atiyyah, the elderly but diamond-sharp editor of the

screen appearance since 1981 as the elderly but feisty Aunt Ginny. Even with

country skiing, once the preserve of elderly but fit Europeans, has become a

2002 </dt> <p> ISTANBUL Final scores Elderly-but-charismatic world academics 2,

Act: New York studio - 26 feet - An elderly but gay broker is seated at his

        on the outskirts of Munich. An elderly but imposing figure gets out and

and by her teachers, especially the elderly but imposing headmistress,

    the Party unlike some of the other elderly but less famous leaders of the

        of sexual intercourse with an elderly but libidinous man who may or may

sort of dying--the person is quite elderly but loved. Deliver what the

        Stokes - Adams attacks are often elderly but physically youthful with a

and its leader, Haji Saifullah, an elderly but powerful local tribesman, are

Comment 2<h1> Treat Radio 4 like an elderly, but rather wise, old friend (786)

rang. It was Ambrose Pendleton, the elderly but razor-sharp solicitor who

    injects droll comic relief as the elderly but razor-sharp nurse. Those who

        Stephane is befriended by the elderly but robust Izidor (Isidor Serban,

    an unlikely friendship with the elderly but still foxy Mae, when he was

Mr Simes, as personal adviser to the elderly, but still sharp-minded, Richard

    second act role of Marie, the now elderly but still sprightly daughter of

legacy was still in the hands of an elderly but still vigorous aunt; she no

    lifeguards were backed up by an elderly but vigilant clientele drying out
```

Figure 3.3 Concordance of *elderly* followed by *but* and another adjective.

Finally, concordances can be harnessed to systemic functional analysis (Halliday 2004), another staple in the CDA diet. Examining verbal collocates of a search word sheds light on the kind of verbal processes that a particular person or group is commonly engaged in. In our *elderly* example, it turns out that a mere 9 per cent of verbs linked with *the elderly* are of the 'material' process type. On the whole, that is, the elderly do not get to fill the semantic role of 'Actor'. Put more simply and bluntly, the elderly are not shown to be doing very much at all, let alone emerging as masters of their own destiny. When *elderly* is used attributively, on the other hand, that is, modifying a noun, that figure stands at 26 per cent. From the standpoint of an anti-ageist agenda, this is still a far cry from a satisfying result, but it does confirm our earlier quantitative evidence that *elderly* as a pre-modifier is not as negatively loaded and discriminatory as the collective use *the elderly*.

Without a doubt, the type of analysis presented here is no substitute for the detailed, context-sensitive unravelling procedures that critical discourse analysts normally engage in. Nor does it wish to be: the evidence that large-corpus work allows one to access is altogether of a different nature and fulfils a different purpose. Still, there are numerous points of contact, with the most compelling one probably being the qualitative analysis of naturally occurring data.

3.5 Concluding Caveats

As in so many areas of application, in CDA contexts, too, corpus linguistics helps the analyst tackle research questions in ways that other methods cannot, or indeed to deal with new kinds of questions that manual analysis alone would not have thrown up in the first place. Nevertheless, the account would be incomplete if it did not mention some limitations and reservations that the methodology has from a CDA perspective. Two of these were dealt with earlier in the chapter, such as the decontextualization of language data, and the semiotic impoverishment of text once it has been edited for processing by corpus linguistic software. But there are other concerns. One is the preoccupation with frequency of occurrence, a tried-and-tested principle of corpus-driven work, nowhere enshrined more clearly and memorably than in Sinclair's advice (2003: xvi), 'Decide on the strongest pattern and start there'. Certainly, highly frequent items make good starting points, and very often chart a sensible path through the data. On the other hand, it should not be forgotten that rare occurrences of a word can sometimes be more significant than multiple ones. High frequency should be a guide, not an obsession. The lexicographer or syntactician may be comfortable ignoring outliers, but the discourse analyst might do so at their peril, especially when they are working with relatively small 'DIY' corpora.

Furthermore, much as I have been extolling the virtues of large reference corpora, their static nature clearly limits their usefulness for CDA. Whenever you wish to work at the sharp end of language, charting the linguistic reflexes of real-time social dynamics, these multi-million word corpora, treasure chests though they are, often turn out to be empty. A random example should illustrate my point.

In recent newspaper reports, the social class label *chav* has been widely commented on (e.g. Blacker 2007). It refers to a particular type of working-class lifestyle, behaviour and dress code. There are websites dedicated exclusively to the issue,[9] and even books (e.g. Bok 2004; Wallace and Spanner 2004). The expression has all the hallmarks of being a CDA gem: rich in socially divisive connotations, used in a derogatory fashion by ruling elites, and multimodally complex as it encompasses discursive and life-style practices. Yet there is no trace of it in Wordbanks' 500+ million words: it is simply too new.

What, then, should follow from our awareness of these limitations? For current CDA practice, not a great deal, except the sobering realization that no methodological tool can do it all. This chapter has tried to make a case for appreciating the potential of corpus linguistics for CDA, but the method should be taken on board without unduly and unfairly burdening it with overly ambitious expectations. It would be as unrealistic as it would be misguided to assume that corpus linguistic methods could altogether replace the classic discourse analytical repertoire of methods, and least of all at points in the analysis where linguistic evidence needs to be related back to the social environment in which it occurs. It remains firmly the job of the human analyst, rather than that of any software, to interpret the evidence that corpus linguistic techniques lay before them, dovetail the findings with insights gained through other means, and reactivate whatever contextual information the work with large data volumes may have pushed into the background. Essentially, the merit of enriching CDA with a corpus-driven approach lies in allowing researchers to look at data from a different perspective, triangulating other forms of analysis, and in the process making results more reliable.

Acknowledgements

Material from the Bank of English® reproduced with the kind permission of HarperCollins Publishers Ltd.

Notes

1 http://www.natcorp.ox.ac.uk/.
2 CANCODE stands for the Cambridge and Nottingham Corpus of Discourse in English. See http://www.cambridge.org/elt/corpus/cancode.htm.
3 http://www.collins.co.uk/books.aspx?group=154.
4 See http://www.guardian.co.uk/commentisfree/2006/apr/23/humanrights. constitution.
5 For information on how to obtain Wordsmith Tools, see the website of Oxford University Press at http://www.oup.com/elt/catalogue/guidance_articles/ws_ form?cc=global, accessed 3 August 2007.
6 In this particular instance, we need not be concerned about having missed synonyms (a constant worry in corpus-based studies of lexis) because *Rule of Law* is a distinctive

technical term which comes with a sizeable baggage of historical, constitutional and legal theory, all of which are attached to this particular term, and none other.

7 According to figures from the National Readership Survey, available at http://www. nrs.co.uk, accessed 9 August 2007.

8 As Hunston (2002: 72) reports, *t*-scores above 2 are generally considered to be statistically significant.

9 For example, http://www.chavtowns.co.uk/ accessed 5 August 2007.

CHAPTER

4

Corpus Stylistics and the Pickwickian *watering-pot*

Michaela Mahlberg

In large general corpora individual features that characterize a specific literary text tend not to receive much attention. Linguistic studies aim to find generalizations about language that are visible in a range of texts and that can be described as grammatical categories and structures. However, recent developments in corpus linguistics place greater emphasis on the language of particular discourses and the role of the text as a linguistic unit. Moreover, Carter (2004: 69) points out that 'literariness' is not an absolute quality, but should be viewed on a continuum and can be found in 'common' language, too. Similarly, Sinclair (2004: 51) stresses that literature is language in use and thus has to be describable in terms of categories that are part of a general systematic apparatus. Literary stylistics has tradition- ally been the field that tries to bring the study of language and literature closer together. More recently, corpus approaches to literature have been suggested, and with the new technology come new questions. Corpus methodology can help to base stylistic studies on exhaustive quantitative and statistical information and add to the amount of detail that a stylistic analysis can achieve. But stylistic questions approached from a corpus linguistic point of view can also point to the need to refine and develop corpus linguistic categories of description. This chapter reviews different approaches in the growing field of corpus stylistics, discussing theoretical questions and providing examples from texts by Charles Dickens.

4.1 Introduction

Corpus stylistics is seen as a new discipline with plenty of potential still to be explored (Wynne 2006; O'Halloran 2007*b*: 228). In the introduction to their book on 'Corpus Stylistics', Semino and Short (2004: 17) point out that one of the aims of the approach they suggest is to make stylisticians and corpus linguists more aware of each other's work. Such a cross-disciplinary approach opens up new routes in stylistics where previously some reservations had been voiced with regards to the usefulness of computer methodologies. It also opens up new routes for corpus linguistics. A key strand in corpus linguistics research has focused on build- ing increasingly large corpora in order to investigate phenomena that can be described on the basis of quantifiable parameters and generalizations that hold across a number of texts. The corpus revolution has allowed linguists access to empirical evidence; a vast improvement on our poor intuitions about language. However, large corpora may not be equally useful for the stylistic analysis of literary texts. Creative features of a literary text that could be of great interest to a stylistician may not figure in a description of general patterns. As Sinclair (2007: 3) points out, 'a distinctive literary text is just not worth including in a general corpus because it will disappear below the waves'. So we may want to see corpus stylistics as a discipline where literary texts receive more attention from corpus linguists and stylisticians find valuable tools in corpus approaches. Talking about a new discipline of corpus stylistics does not imply that computer methods have not been employed on literary texts before. Computers have been used to assist the study of literature for almost as long as computers have been used for the study of language (Hockey 2000: 67ff.). Crucial to corpus stylistics is not only the application of quantitative methods to literary texts but also the reflection on the types of questions we can ask and attempt to answer. In Section 4.2, I give a brief overview of corpus stylistic examples taking different types of approaches. Then I want to explore how corpus stylistics can add to the analysis of a short text extract. Section 4.3 looks at an extract from *The Pickwick Papers* and the functions of the word *watering-pot* in this example. In Section 4.4, functions associated with *watering-pot* are compared across a corpus of texts by Charles Dickens. Section 4.5 then relates the findings of the previous sections to a wider textual perspective that draws on clusters as pointers to local textual functions and building blocks of textual worlds. This approach is further supported by an analysis of the functions of the cluster *down his knife and fork* in Section 4.6.

4.2 Systematicity and Qualitative Analysis

According to Leech and Short (1981: 13) the aim of literary stylistics is 'to relate the critic's concern of aesthetic appreciation with the linguist's concern of linguistic description'. With reference to Spitzer's philological circle, the authors describe literary insight and linguistic observation as being in cyclical motion (Leech and Short 1981: 13). However, the relationship between interpretation and linguistic description can also be seen in a less favourable light. Approaches to literary stylistics may be criticized for their arbitrariness and circularity – an argument that is sometimes referred to as the Fish Fork (Stubbs 2005) or Fish Hook (O'Halloran 2007*b*, following Toolan 1996) in reference to the critical position adopted by Stanley Fish (cf. Fish 1996). The advantage of corpus stylistics is then seen as a way to add systematicity to stylistic analysis: 'observational data can provide more systematic evidence for unavoidable subjective interpretation' (Stubbs 2005: 22; see also O'Halloran 2007*b*: 228). One of the links between literary stylistics and corpus linguistics that yields operationalizable concepts draws on the description of linguistic norms and deviations from these norms (cf. also Mahlberg 2007*a*: 21). Norms for stylistic analysis can be derived on the basis of corpora so that deviations from these norms can be described in corpus stylistic terms as the result of comparisons, that is, accounting for frequencies of words or specific linguistic phenomena across different sets of texts or with regard to reference corpora. Corpus stylistics not only adds systematicity to but reduces subjectivity from stylistic analysis by drawing on computer methods. Corpus stylistics also raises our awareness about the need for interpretation in corpus work. Only then can the relationship between the two disciplines be mutual and both corpus linguists and stylisticians profit from it. I will briefly look at some examples of how literary texts have been approached with computer methods, starting both from corpus linguistic and stylistic contexts. Due to space limitations, I will not refer to computational or statistical approaches, as they are used, for instance, in authorship attribution (for further overview information see also Archer 2007).

Without explicitly referring to what is now seen as a corpus stylistic approach, corpus linguists have used literary texts for illustration purposes or in the context of language teaching. In his introductory textbook, Barnbrook (1996) uses, for instance, Mary Shelley's *Frankenstein* to illustrate basic corpus methodologies such as frequency lists. Tribble and Jones (1997) present a variety of concordancing tasks for the language classroom, where they also include a chapter on literature. They show how concordancing can help literary analysis, for example, when focusing on a specific character in a short story. Kettemann and Marko (2004) outline their ideas for a course on corpus-based stylistics. They argue for a better integration of language and literary studies at university level. They see the study of literature as a valuable cultural skill where the use of corpus methods can add to awareness raising along the dimensions of language, discourse, methodology and metatheory.

Corpus linguistic case studies demonstrating how corpus approaches can add to literary analysis or to the exploration of literary creativity may be grouped according to the methods they use. While Stubbs (2005) illustrates a range of quantitative methods, there are other case studies that concentrate on a specific aspect of repeated patterns such as collocations (e.g. Hori 2004), clusters (e.g. Starcke 2006), key words (Culpeper 2002; Scott and Tribble 2006; O'Halloran 2007*b*) and key semantic domains (Archer et al. 2006). To characterize subtle meanings the concept of the semantic prosody has been employed (Louw 1993; Adolphs and Carter 2002), literary creativity has been interpreted in terms of lexical priming (Hoey 2007) and the analysis of collocation and phraseology has been linked to schema theory bringing cognitive stylistics and corpus stylistics together (O'Halloran 2007*c*). This list is not intended to be exhaustive, but is to illustrate how methods and concepts that belong to the range of corpus linguistics can be employed to extend approaches in literary stylistics.

To highlight questions that arise in the realm of literary stylistics I focus on the approach by Semino and Short (2004). Semino and Short constructed and annotated a corpus to test and develop the Leech and Short (1981: chapter 10) model of speech and thought presentation. The model was originally developed to account for literary prose fiction. Semino and Short's (2004) study was designed to test whether the model could be systematically applied and used to compare twentieth-century fictional, journalistic and autobiographical/biographical narratives. To achieve those goals, a corpus containing 258,348 words with 120 text samples of approximately 2,000 words each was compiled and manually annotated. The annotation of the corpus is different from more standard practice in corpus linguistics. It is to some extent similar to what McEnery et al. (2006: 43) call 'problem-oriented' annotation in that an annotation scheme had to be specifically developed for the research question. The main attributes in the tags are the categories of the discourse representation scales, for example, the value FDS indicates that the annotated text is free direct speech. This process of annotation can also be seen as a detailed textual analysis. To successfully account for the data, the Leech and Short (1981) model was extended and modified: Semino and Short (2004) introduce a new writing presentation scale and add new categories and subcategories.

The main achievements of the Semino and Short (2004) approach are at least twofold. They arrived at a more comprehensive model of speech, writing and thought presentation carrying out a quantitative analysis of the categories of the model across different genres. At the same time, their approach highlights key issues that corpus stylistics has to address. First, the theoretical context for the development of descriptive categories has to be linked to a systematic approach to the data. While stylistic categories of the type that Semino and Short apply require a time-consuming process of manual annotation, the process itself contributes to the development of the underlying theory: 'the re-examination of the corpus data in the light of the completed annotation [. . .] can lead to further changes in theorization' (Semino and Short 2004: 40). By aiming to account not only for fictional but also for non-fictional prose, the authors also extend the usefulness of their categories and contribute to bringing linguistic and literary studies closer together. Second, the focus on textual phenomena requires interpretation of contextual features. The systematicity that comes with corpus linguistics and that is referred to as a means to reduce subjectivity in stylistic analysis, depends on a close relationship between meaning and form: linguistic features can be accounted for because they are tied to identifiable patterns. Semino and Short (2004: 224) stress that '[t]he aim of consistency and replicability in annotation is best achieved by privileging, as much as is practically possible, the formal over the contextual and pragmatic'. However, they also make it clear that contextual and pragmatic criteria are indispensable. In this way, Semino and Short's (2004) approach links in with recent developments in corpus linguistics that give emphasis to textual and functional features that go beyond lexico-grammatical patterns (cf. e.g. Biber et al. 2007; Flowerdew 2008).

To sum up, corpus stylistics can draw on the systematicity that goes with corpus methodology and it can add categories developed in the field of corpus linguistics (e.g. semantic prosodies) to the inventory of stylistic description. But corpus stylistics is not only the application of corpus approaches to literary texts. Equally important are the types of questions a study sets out to answer, and the qualitative analysis that literary texts require, which in turn links up with literary criticism. In practical terms, qualitative analysis can also mean the focus on a very small language sample where the task of corpus linguistics is to find a way of relating it to other relevant reference points.

4.3 Mr Tupman Proposes to the Spinster Aunt

In the following example of stylistic analysis I take an extract from *The Pickwick Papers* by Charles Dickens. The comedy of this scene is linked to the function of the word *watering-pot* that receives prominence in the extract. The question I want to address is how a corpus stylistic approach can deal with the analysis of a concrete text example. The novel *The Pickwick Papers* (abbreviated as PP) is about four members of the Pickwick Club who set out to travel around England and to report on their encounters with various people and places. Dickens' first novel is well known for its entertaining comedy of the Pickwickian adventures. In the extract below from chapter 8, Mr Tupman, one of the Pickwickians, proposes to Miss Wardle. The comedy of the proposal is to some extent due to the passiveness of Rachael Wardle – the spinster aunt. The spinster aunt stands out from the other young ladies, as we learn at the beginning of the chapter, because of her 'touch-me-not-ishness'. The extract begins when Mr Tupman accompanies the spinster aunt to go and water her flowers:

(1)   The spinster aunt took up a large *watering-pot* which lay in one corner, and was about to leave the arbour. Mr. Tupman detained her, and drew her to a seat beside him.

'Miss Wardle!' said he.

The spinster aunt trembled, till some pebbles which had accidentally found their way into the large *watering-pot* shook like an infant's rattle.

'Miss Wardle,' said Mr. Tupman, 'you are an angel.'

'Mr. Tupman!' exclaimed Rachael, blushing as red as the *watering-pot* itself.

'Nay,' said the eloquent Pickwickian — 'I know it but too well.'

'All women are angels, they say,' murmured the lady playfully.

'Then what can you be; or to what, without presumption, can I compare you?' replied Mr. Tupman. 'Where was the woman ever seen who resembled you? Where else could I hope to find so rare a combination of excellence and beauty? Where else could I seek to – Oh!' Here Mr. Tupman paused, and pressed the hand which clasped the handle of the happy *watering-pot.*

[. . .] Mr. Tupman had sunk upon his knees at her feet.

'Mr. Tupman, rise,' said Rachael.

'Never!' was the valorous reply. 'Oh, Rachael!' He seized her passive hand, and the *watering-pot* fell to the ground as he pressed it to his lips.—'Oh, Rachael! say you love me.'

(*The Pickwick Papers*)

In this extract, Rachael's emotions appear to be transferred to the watering-pot. When she trembles, the pebbles in the watering-pot rattle. When she blushes, the colour of her face is compared to that of the watering-pot. When Tupman presses her hand, it is not Rachael who seems happy, but the watering-pot. And after

Tupman has declared his love for her and gets down on his knees, her hand is still passive and the only action it causes is the watering-pot falling to the ground. The watering-pot can be seen as 'the only real object' in this subverted proposal (cf. Kincaid 1971: 30). The word *watering-pot* is repeated five times over a very short stretch of text that takes up about a page in the book and the comical function of this object is additionally foregrounded in various ways, for example, through the collocation with *happy*, or through the comparison hinted at by Tupman's question: '[. . .] to what [. . .] can I compare you?'

This example raises questions about what corpus stylistics can do for 'practical' stylistics to analyse a specific extract. Louw (1993), for instance, illustrates how poems and short text extracts can profit from a corpus approach by comparing the functions of specific occurrences of lexical items with the patterns of those items in a reference corpus. Such comparisons can reveal subtle meanings that characterize the semantic prosodies of lexical items. In the above extract from PP, however, part of the comedy is due to the fact that Dickens draws attention to contrasts and in fact highlights unusual descriptions. So it seems a search for subtle clues may be less promising. Additionally, for patterns of *watering-pot*, corpus evidence seems more difficult to find. In the British National Corpus (BNC), for instance, *watering-pot* does not occur (although a similar term *watering can* occurs 25 times). Perhaps this is due to diachronic change – the BNC contains texts from the late twentieth century, whereas Dickens wrote in the nineteenth century. However, in a corpus of 29 novels by nineteenth-century authors other than Dickens that I have used for comparisons with Dickens before (Mahlberg 2007*b*), there are no matches for *watering-pot* either – although we find people watering their flowers.

As Lew (this volume) has argued, the web can be used as an effective source of corpus data, particularly in cases of rare usage. Concordance 4.1 has been retrieved with WebCorp. A search for *watering-pot* yields 41 hits, five of these are the five instances from PP, which I have deleted from the concordance.[1] Four of the examples refer to a type of shell (lines 10, 16, 21, 22). The great majority, that is, 19 examples, come from web pages on gardening, and pages with gardening tools or children's toys (e.g. beach toys); these pages can also contain photographs. Additionally, lines 17 to 19 are from youtube (a site which hosts user-generated videos) and line 33 is from ebay (an online marketplace and auction site). Finally, there are five examples from literary prose. Lines 25 and 29 are from a short story by Maupassant ('Old Mongilet') and lines 1, 26 and 27 are from Charlotte Brontë's novel *Villette*. In the fictional texts the watering-pot is used by the characters as a gardening tool.

It seems that Concordance 4.1 is of limited use to the analysis of the extract from PP. Repeated patterns in the concordance either distinguish the 'shell' meaning, or point to the same webpage: the collocation with *Elephant* in lines 8 and 9 refers to a toy, as do the collocations with *Huge*, the repetition of *Julia* leads to the youtube video, and the repetition of *your* in lines 34 to 36 point to a webpage with gardening tools. This page, however, seems to be of questionable content because of the poor English used on the page. Altogether seven of the gardening tool

```
 1              with a spade or a,watering-pot, soothed his nerves; it was
 2            eye of the gardener. A,watering-pot, with a pierced rose, and
 3            of going round with a,watering-pot, and giving a driblet to
 4   336" title="watering-pot" alt=,watering-pot, ">Lyudmila Rudyuk</a
 5   EMBLY KW's: poly flex assembly,watering-pot, pipe meet watering funny Use
 6   different species. The common,watering-pot, is a tinned iron or
 7  and tube surmount Ideal despite,watering-pot, systems, spigot aerators, and
 8   te toy, Zousan Zyoro, Elephant,watering-pot, turns into finger size and
 9    te toy, Zousan Zyoro, Elephant,watering-pot, turns into finger size and
10   variety of extant endobenthic,watering-pot, shells. It has been argued
11   features CAMPBELL FT6-100 For,watering-pot, or watering systems 1-1/2
12             1-1/2" - 60 GPM For,watering-pot, or watering systems. 1-1/2
13     Includes:- Push Truck/ Huge,watering-pot, / Mini Bucket/ Mini Rake/ Mini
14     Mini Rake/ Mini Spade/ Huge,watering-pot, / Sand Mould- Castle A Model
15    stration Vector Isolated items, watering-pot, © Lyudmila Rudyuk #5041336 Size
16  entitious tube of the Japanese,watering-pot, shell Stirpulina ramosa (Bivalvi
17       December 19, 2006 Julia, watering-pot, ( less ) Added:
18        About This Video Julia, watering-pot, ( more ) Added:
19            Julia ( 1 yr 8 mo, watering-pot, Hello, you either have JavaScript
20  surmount. Ideal on account of, watering-pot, systems, spigot aerators, and bar
21    extends into the complex of, watering-pot, tubules and forms the pedal
22  a Class Bivalvia Waterspout or,watering-pot, Shell Brechites penis Family Clav
23        rose; and, 3d, the shelf, watering-pot, , which is a small cartouche-shap
24      of the rightful owner the, watering-pot, is generally entrusted with a
25  e; enough--now this one.' "The,watering-pot, leaked and my feet got
26  ing the returning paletôt; the,watering-pot, was deposited beside the well
27  y round Villette. To-night the,watering-pot, might rest in its niche
28  required, and it cushions the, watering-pot, head up to secure in
29          ten minutes to fill the, watering-pot, , and I was in a
30  fotolia.com/id/5041336" title=,watering-pot, " alt="watering-pot">Lyudmila Ru
31            Up PVC pipe to Toro, watering-pot, heads. Funny Pipe gives flexiblen
32  ance toy watering watering-can,watering-pot, Country Ukraine Url Copy / Paste
33     stonia: boy as sailor with, watering-pot, . Unfortunately city and year is
34  -Off (Nelson) Shut turned your,watering-pot, according to comfort! This foot-
35  ut-Off (Nelson) Shut sour your,watering-pot, by the agency of comfort
36           flux of water to your, watering-pot, . The hose down coupler is
```

Concordance 4.1 Thirty-six occurrences of *watering-pot* retrieved with WebCorp.

examples come from this webpage and another three from a similarly question-able page. Thus it could be argued that this concordance shows that data from the web does not provide an adequate reference corpus for the analysis of nineteenth-century novels. However, the concordance does illustrate a point that is relevant to the functional interpretation of the word *watering-pot* in PP but is almost too obvi-ous to make: Dickens uses a concrete object that has an apparently unambiguous function when it is used as a gardening tool. A watering-pot will be easy to visualize for the reader.

4.4 The Pickwickian *watering-pot*

For a more detailed analysis of the functions of *watering-pot* in PP a comparison with other occurrences in Dickens proves useful. Concordance 4.2 is from a 4.5 million corpus containing 23 texts by Charles Dickens that I refer to as the Dickens Corpus.[2] The singular form *watering-pot* occurs 18 times.

Patterns in Concordance 4.2 show collocations of *watering-pot* with the adjectives *little* and *large*. There are references to the colour of the *watering-pot* (*red* line 2, *green* line 15). There is a group of words that hint at the function of the gardening tool: *out of every hole, replenish, sprinkling, content, inverting, filled and emptied* and *inverting*. And there are some more general verbs that indicate actions of carrying and moving: *put, took up, lugs*. The collocation with *little* seems notable as it occurs in 6 of the 18 lines (lines 5–9 and 15) and the adjective can be used to express attitudinal meaning. This overview can only provide an initial picture. An important point is the distribution of *watering-pot* across the texts in the Dickens Corpus. In fact, five of the six collocations with *little* come from the novel *Dombey and Son* (DS). Table 4.1 shows the distribution of *watering-pot* across texts and provides information on the number of different chapters in the respective text that contain the word.

As with PP, the occurrences in DS are all from the same chapter, and a closer analysis of context reveals similarities with the scene in PP. In chapter 29 of DS, Mrs Chick visits her friend Miss Tox to tell her that Mr Dombey, who is Mrs Chick's brother, is getting married again. Miss Tox herself has romantic feelings for

```
 1  !' He seized her passive hand, and the watering-pot fell to the ground as he p
 2  laimed Rachael, blushing as red as the watering-pot itself. 'Nay,' said the
 3  ay; at the plants, at the bird, at the watering-pot, at almost everything withi
 4  and affection, out of every hole in the watering-pot; when I think of him never
 5  a can of water to replenish her little watering-pot, and sufficiently divined t
 6  the very last sprinklings of the little watering-pot, as if he were a delicate
 7   to receive the content' of the little watering-pot in his shoe; both of which
 8  owing upon her, that she put the little watering-pot on the table for the prese
 9  o verbal answer, but took up the little watering-pot with a trembling hand, and
10   s. The spinster aunt took up a large watering-pot which lay in one corner, a
11   On a summer's evening, when the large watering-pot has been filled and emptied
12  dentally found their way into the large watering-pot shook like an infant's rat
13  the Master. Miss Peecher inverting her watering-pot, and very carefully shakin
14  d which clasped the handle of the happy watering-pot. The lady turned aside h
15      too. Miss Tox filled a little green watering-pot from a jug, and happening
16  erseverance with which he lugs a great watering-pot about is perfectly astonish
17  and putting down, the sprinkling from a watering-pot and hydraulic pressure, Mr
18   poor little Mrs. Tibbs; crying like a watering-pot. 'Hush! hush! pray--Mrs.
```

Concordance 4.2 Eighteen occurrences of *watering-pot* from the 4.5 million Dickens Corpus.[3]

Table 4.1 Eighteen occurrences of *watering-pot* in the Dickens Corpus.

Text	Frequency	Chapters
Dombey and Son (DS)	6	1
Pickwick Papers (PP)	5	1
Sketches by Boz (SB)	3	2
Our Mutual Friend (OMF)	2	1
Little Dorrit (LD)	1	1
David Copperfield (DC)	1	1
Total	**18**	**7**

Mr Dombey and the way in which Mrs Chick breaks the news is awkward and depicted in a comical manner. During the conversation Miss Tox is arranging and watering the plants. Her occupation with the plants is described so as to reflect her emotional involvement and the watering-pot becomes part of the scene: it is taken up, put down and looked at in support of the development of the conversation. The watering-pot has already been mentioned four times, when the climax of the conversation is reached: Miss Tox faints and happens to fall into the arms of the expatriated Native who incidentally enters the room. As Miss Tox loses control over herself, she spills the contents of the watering-pot on the expatriated Native:

(2) [. . .] the expatriated Native, amazed supporter of Miss Tox's swooning form, who, coming straight upstairs, with a polite inquiry touching Miss Tox's health (in exact pursuance of the Major's malicious instructions), had accidentally arrived in the very nick of time to catch the delicate burden in his arms, and to receive the content' of the little *watering-pot* in his shoe; both of which circumstances, coupled with his consciousness of being closely watched by the wrathful Major, who had threatened the usual penalty in regard of every bone in his skin in case of any failure, combined to render him a moving spectacle of mental and bodily distress.

For some moments, this afflicted foreigner remained clasping Miss Tox to his heart, with an energy of action in remarkable opposition to his disconcerted face, while that poor lady trickled slowly down upon him the very last sprinklings of the little *watering-pot*, as if he were a delicate exotic (which indeed he was), and might be almost expected to blow while the gentle rain descended.

(*Dombey and Son*)

What the extracts from PP and DS have in common is that the watering-pot assumes a role in the situation. And in both cases, the situation involves the feelings of a woman for a man that are not expressed because the woman is too passive or it would be inappropriate in the given situation. Further evidence for the functional link between the watering-pot and the description of emotions is found in OMF. Miss Peecher, who is in love with Bradley Headstone, is watering the flowers in her garden, when Headstone passes by. They greet each other and exchange a few words that appear very brief in comparison to the careful attention Miss Peecher gives to her flowers:

> (3) Miss Peecher inverting her *watering-pot,* and very carefully shaking out the few last drops over a flower, as if there were some special virtue in them which would make it a Jack's beanstalk before morning, called for replenishment to her pupil, who had been speaking to the boy.
>
> (*Our Mutual Friend*)

In PP and DS the functions of *watering-pot* relate to its repetition within a short context. Although less strikingly, example (3) is also preceded by another occurrence of the word, listed here as example (4).

> (4) Miss Peecher's favourite pupil, who assisted her in her little household, was in attendance with a can of water to replenish her little *watering-pot,* [. . .]
>
> (*Our Mutual Friend*)

The above examples illustrate watering flowers as an activity of women who at the same time are unable to express their feelings openly. The remaining five occurrences of *watering-pot* appear in slightly different contexts, where all, however, are to do with emotions or relationships. In SB, we find Mrs Tibbs *crying like a watering-pot,* in LD, Mrs Clennam's interest in Little Dorrit is described as fluctuating between *the sprinkling from a watering-pot and hydraulic pressure,* in DC, David describes how Mr Dick wants to be Annie's friend and carries *huge watering-pots* after her and showers *sympathy, trustfulness, and affection, out of every hole in the watering-pot,* and SB contains a description of an elderly couple who enjoy their garden and their life together. In the evening the man typically *lugs a great watering-pot about* and this recreational activity illustrates the couple's happiness:

> (5) On a summer's evening, when the large *watering-pot* has been filled and emptied some fourteen times, and the old couple have quite exhausted themselves by trotting about, you will see them sitting happily together in the little summerhouse, [. . .]
>
> (*Sketches by Boz*)

All 18 occurrences of *watering-pot* show how Dickens employs a concrete object that is part of the environment of the characters to describe emotions or relationships. The analysis has revealed what can be described as 'local textual functions' of *watering-pot,* that is functions that characterize a specific item in a specific set of texts (see also Mahlberg 2007*b*, 2007*c*). To what extent similarities can be found with other literary texts is a question that cannot be investigated further in this chapter, although the initial comparison with the corpus of nineteenth-century novels suggests that the local textual functions are specific to Dickens. What I want to do in the following, is relate the findings to other functional features in Dickens.

4.5 Clusters as a Way into the Dickensian World

In the above analysis the concordance helped a close reading of the immediate contexts of *watering-pot*. This step can be complemented with a wider textual perspective. Corpus stylistics can help to identify components of the world of a novel or the worlds that are described in several texts by one author. An approach that I have used to find a way into the worlds of Dickens' texts is the investigation of clusters, that is repeated sequences of words. Based on the assumption that repetition is linked to functional relevance, I have identified five functional groups of 5-word clusters (Mahlberg 2007*b*) and I have shown for two novels that these groups not only cover most of the 5-word clusters that occur, but also link to topics in the novel (Mahlberg 2007*a*, 2007*c*). The five groups are (1) labels, (2) speech clusters, (3) time and place clusters, (4) As If clusters and (5) body part clusters. Labels are clusters such as *Mr Winkle and Mr Snodgrass, said Mr Pickwick with a* or *the man with the camp-stool* that contain a name of a person (or place) or are used as a name; speech clusters contain a first or second person personal pronoun or possessive, or other signals of interaction, such as imperatives or terms of address, examples are *very much obliged to you* or *will you allow me to*. Examples of time and place clusters are *at the bottom of the* or *a few seconds and then*. As If clusters contain *as if*, for example *as if he had been*, and body part clusters contain a noun referring to a part of the human body, as in *his head out of the*. The clusters in each of these groups share formal and functional similarities. I have argued that such clusters can be seen as pointers to local textual functions. They can be interpreted as building blocks of textual worlds in the sense that the clusters point to aspects of the world[4] of Dickens that is built through the labelling of characters and themes, characters' speech, references to time and place, comparisons with *as if*, as well as body language and the description of characters with regard to their appearance.

The description of textual building blocks is only meaningful when it is based on patterns associated with each functional area. An important aspect of local textual functions is that the emphasis is on functional similarity to group different formal patterns together. The fact that the functions in the Dickens Corpus have been identified initially on the basis of clusters is not to imply that the functions can only be fulfilled by clusters. What clusters do is provide an initial set of examples that is sufficiently manageable to be submitted to a more detailed analysis, and can thus serve as a systematic starting-point.[5] The more detail we can accumulate on the initial components of textual worlds, the better we can assess individual examples, such as *watering-pot*, as part of a larger picture. The approach I have taken in previous corpus stylistic analyses progresses from a corpus of Dickens texts for the identification of cluster categories, to the analysis of all clusters in a specific text with regard to the initially identified categories, to the interpretation of clusters as pointers to a more detailed analysis of specific themes or extracts of a text. In the following, I want to start from the other end and explore to what extent foregrounded features of a text extract can be related to the more general textual features that cluster groups present.

The *watering-pot* examples relate to local textual functions of clusters in a number of ways. Specifically the functions associated with body part clusters and labels are relevant to the analysis presented in Sections 4.3 and 4.4. A body part cluster contains a noun referring to a part of the human body, for example, *his hand upon his shoulder* or *his hands in his pockets*. Body part clusters illustrate functions such as in (6) and (7) where the cluster has a contextualizing function and accompanies other activities which are more central to the story (cf. also Mahlberg 2007*b*: 21f.):

(6) 'No!' exclaimed Perker, putting *his hands in his pockets*, and reclining against the sideboard.

                                                                                (The Pickwick Papers)

(7) Orlick, with *his hands in his pockets*, slouched heavily at my side.

                                                                                (Great Expectations)

In contrast, body part clusters can also have a highlighting function. In example (8) the comparison with *as if* helps to draw attention to Mr Chuckster's conscious attempt to appear inconspicuous[6]:

(8) [...] Mr Chuckster put *his hands in his pockets*, and tried to look as if he were not minding the pony, but happened to be lounging there by accident.

                                                                                (The Old Curiosity Shop)

The *watering-pot* examples are to some extent similar to functions associated with body part nouns. Example (9) from DS shows how the *watering-pot* contributes to a contextualizing function. When the conversation becomes more complex and emotionally intense Miss Tox pauses to focus her attention on what Mrs Chick is telling her, so she puts the *watering-pot* down:

(9) Miss Tox filled a little green *watering-pot* from a jug, and happening to look up when she had done so, was so surprised by the amount of expression Mrs Chick had conveyed into her face, and was bestowing upon her, that she put the little *watering-pot* on the table for the present, and sat down near it.

                                                                                (Dombey and Son)

The way in which the watering-pot forms part of a highlighting function is illustrated by the extract from the PP (example 1) and the climatic scene in DS that we saw above (example 2). In both cases, the repetition of *watering-pot* contributes to the progression from contextualizing to highlighting.

Another aspect of the relationship between the noun *watering-pot* and functions of body part nouns is connected to a watering-pot being a household item that is part of the environment of the characters. The fact that women water plants and 'take up' watering-pots to do so, does not strike the reader as unusual until the watering-pot takes on a more central role or even hits the ground. Similarly, the body language associated with clusters fulfils a contextualizing function until specific attention is drawn to it. What patterns with household items and body part nouns have in common is that they can reveal mental states of characters, as they can be related to activities that the characters do not do deliberately or are not aware of. In this function, an item like a watering-pot can almost be seen as an extension of the body. Links to functions of body part nouns are also reflected in the textual context. In PP, the word *hand* occurs twice in the context of *watering-pot* and underlines the connection between the spinster aunt and the watering-pot:

(10) Here Mr. Tupman paused, and pressed the *hand* which clasped the handle of the happy *watering-pot.*

(11) He seized her passive *hand,* and the *watering-pot* fell to the ground as he pressed it to his lips.

(The Pickwick Papers)

Similarly in DS, the noun *hand* highlights how the watering-pot is linked to Miss Tox. In example (12) Dickens makes it clear that the watering-pot is a substitute for verbal expression of feelings:

(12) Miss Tox *made no verbal answer, but* took up the little *watering-pot* with a trembling *hand [. . .]*

(Dombey and Son)

4.6 Body Language and Household Items: The Example of
down his knife and fork

The link between body language and household items such as the watering-pot can be illustrated further with the cluster *down his knife and fork.* On the surface the cluster does not relate to the five groups of clusters described in Section 4.5. A closer, analysis, however, reveals some functional similarities with body part clusters. The cluster *down his knife and fork* occurs 20 times in the Dickens Corpus and across nine different texts (shown in Table 4.2).

Concordance 4.3 shows that all occurrences collocate with LAY.[7] Similar to body part clusters, examples of *lay/laid/laying down his knife and fork* illustrate the contextualizing function, in that they occur together with other activities. The concordance shows that in lines 1, 2, 6, 9, 10, 12 and 19 the cluster accompanies speech.

Table 4.2 Twenty occurrences of *down his knife and fork* in the Dickens Corpus.

Text	Frequency	Chapters
Pickwick Papers (PP)	4	4
Nicholas Nickleby (NN)	3	3
Martin Chuzzlewit (MC)	3	3
Dombey and Son (DS)	3	3
Barnaby Rudge (BR)	2	1
Little Dorrit (LD)	2	2
David Copperfield (DC)	1	1
The Mystery of Edwin Drood (ED)	1	1
The Chimes (Chi)	1	1
Total	**20**	**19**

```
1       ye hear thot?' cried John, laying down his knife and fork. 'A godfeyther! Ha!
2   eak that,' said Squeers, as he laid down his knife and fork, after plying it, in
3   ery two or three mouthfuls, he laid down his knife and fork, and stared at his so
4   ing his dinner out of a basin, laid down his knife and fork, and put on his wife'
5    uite forgotten his own dinner, laid down his knife and fork, and drew his chair t
6     , eh? ha, ha!' Mr Lillyvick laid down his knife and fork, and looked round the
7   of his friends, that gentleman laid down his knife and fork, and with a mournful
8    ure Mr. Tupman was observed to lay down his knife and fork, and to turn very pa
9     ,'said John. 'Why--no--I--'laying down his knife and fork, and taking a long b
10   'Bob,' said Mr. Ben Allen, laying down his knife and fork, and fixing his eyes
11   elled, exceedingly: and even laid down his knife and fork  for a moment, to rub
12    ha!' observed the doctor, laying down his knife and fork  for one instant, and
13   begin eating when he suddenly laid down his knife and fork, leaned forward in hi
14   han he had yet maintained, he laid down his knife and fork  on either side his
15    obliged every now and then to lay down his knife and fork, rub his hands, and
16    loved him. If he so much as laid down his knife and fork, somebody put out a
17   sed the gentle Minor Canon, laying down his knife and fork  to rub his ear in a v
18   said the pensioner, slowly laying down his knife and fork  to consider. 'How o
19    much of 'em. By the by'; he laid down his knife and fork, which he had been us
20    ttle and little he began; laying down his knife and fork  with a noise, taking
```

Concordance 4.3 Twenty occurrences of *down his knife and fork* from the Dickens Corpus.

Although not immediately visible in the concordance, it turns out that most of the occurrences of the cluster appear together with speech, sometimes in longer stretches leading up to speech, as in the following example:

(13) [. . .] and Mr Toodle, who had just come home from Birmingham, and was eating his dinner out of a basin, *laid down his knife and fork*, and put on his

wife's bonnet and shawl for her, which were hanging up behind the door; then tapped her on the back; and said, with more fatherly feeling than eloquence, 'Polly! cut away!'

(*Dombey and Son*)

The fact that *down his knife and fork* occurs together with other activities is also visible in the occurrence of *and*, at the right of the cluster, and the fact that in most cases the cluster is part of a unit that is followed by a comma. Examples of the contextualizing function can also serve to give support to other activities (cf. Mahlberg 2007*a*: 22). In example (14) Mr Tupman puts down his knife and fork because he is shocked by the news he hears:

(14)   The man gasped for breath, and faintly ejaculated–
'They ha' gone, mas'r!–gone right clean off, Sir!' (At this juncture Mr. Tupman was observed to *lay down his knife and fork*, and to turn very pale.)
'Who's gone?' said Mr. Wardle fiercely.

(*The Pickwick Papers*)

Example (14) already moves towards the highlighting function by giving greater emphasis to the mental state of the character. More striking, however, is example (15) that shows Tom Pinch at the centre of a happy celebration:

(15)   If he so much as laid *down his knife and fork*, somebody put out a hand to shake with him.

(*Martin Chuzzlewit*)

The cluster *down his knife and fork* can be interpreted as a pointer to body language expressed through practical actions. In this sense it shares functional features with *watering-pot*. However, the examples of the cluster tend to be associated more with the contextualizing than the highlighting function. This tendency seems to relate to the patterns and distribution of the cluster. The cluster is part of a larger unit LAY *down his knife and fork* that tends to accompany speech. Additionally, the occurrences of the cluster are spread across more different chapters. Table 4.2 shows that there is only one chapter with two examples of *down his knife and fork*. The two examples from BR occur in one chapter, and more specifically in one paragraph. The paragraph describes in a detailed way how Mr Willet, who is having supper in the company of his son and a few other people, is trying to understand what happened to his son who lost an arm. Mr Willet is described as being very slow and the slowness of his thought processes is underlined by his behaviour and actions. The cluster adds to highlighting how he pauses to think and then finally understands the situation.

To argue how body language can occur on a continuum where the Pickwickian watering-pot is at one end and examples of the contextualizing function of *down his knife and fork* are at the other, an examination of labels will be useful.

Label clusters contain names or function in a similar way to names. In some cases it can be argued that what looks like a body part cluster is – depending on the context – better classed as label. In *Bleak House* we find, for instance, the cluster *his head against the wall* that always refers to Mr Jellyby. Although the cluster contains a body part noun, it actually labels a character who is characterized through some aspect of body language (cf. Mahlberg 2007*c*: 231). An example of a label that specifically relates to the Pickwickian watering-pot is the cluster *the leg of the table*. All five occurrences of the cluster appear in chapter 4 of *Great Expectations* (GE). The cluster highlights Pip's anxiety through the way in which he holds on to *the leg of the table*. The cluster is classified as a label as it only occurs in one text. Its function in GE resembles the function of the watering-pot in PP and in DS: in each case the emotional state of a character is highlighted through repeated references to an object that takes on a role in a specific scene.

The various strands of the analysis of the example of the Pickwickian watering-pot can be summed up in the following way. With the help of functional groups of 5-word clusters broad areas of repeated features in the texts by Dickens can be identified. Body part clusters indicate aspects of body language on a continuum of contextualizing and highlighting functions. The extreme end of the highlighting function is reached when a body part cluster turns into a label for a specific character or situation. However, body language is not restricted to clusters that contain body part nouns, as the cluster *down his knife and fork* (and similarly *the leg of the table*) shows. One aspect of body language is that it involves practical actions and objects in the characters' environment that are used to perform these actions. With regard to these objects there is again a continuum. Some objects are used more often than others and their distribution and patterns can hint at a tendency for a contextualizing function. Other objects are more restricted to a specific situation or character and fulfil a stronger highlighting function. Although it is not a 5-word cluster, the functions of *watering-pot* fit into the picture that the clusters provide.

4.7 Conclusion

This chapter has argued that the main potential of corpus stylistics lies in the combination of different approaches. Quantitative methods can add systematicity but detailed textual analysis is also indispensable for the analysis of literary texts. From a corpus linguistic point of view, corpus stylistics also stresses that meaningful patterns in individual texts are difficult to pin down to exact formal criteria that allow for detailed quantification. The discussion of the *watering-pot* example in relation to functions identified on the basis of clusters shows that the systematicity of a corpus approach can contribute to finding starting-points for a framework of analysis. It is clear that these starting-points have to draw on a selection of examples and cannot provide a full picture. The focus on clusters is a methodological decision to find patterns, but does not imply that the cluster is seen as a unit of meaning. Meaningful patterns are often very flexible and varied. The formal variety associated with functions identified in the Dickens Corpus is illustrated by the examples of *watering-pot, knife and fork* and *leg of the table* that all refer to household items and show functional similarities but different formal patterns. The cluster approach was used to provide a reference point for the comparison of functions and to relate the *watering-pot* example to features that are repeatedly found in Dickens. For the above analysis of examples from the Dickens Corpus it may now be asked how the findings relate to well-known truths in Dickens criticism? The use of body language is not a new discovery. In fact, Dickens is famous for his notorious identification of characters by idiosyncratic body language (cf. e.g. Korte 1997: 135) and for the blurring of boundaries between human beings and objects (cf. e.g. Brook 1970: 35f.). The fact that a corpus stylistic study arrives at results that relate to findings in criticism can be seen as encouraging about the usefulness of the approach (cf. also Stubbs 2005: 6). Additionally though, the advantage of corpus stylistics is that it can take a fresh view on the reference points for the interpretation of linguistic phenomena. Categories that are useful for the analysis of Dickens's texts can be built up starting from the linguistic evidence, whereas in literary criticism linguistic examples often tend to be provided as exemplification in such a way that parallels across a range of features are difficult to ascertain. What I have attempted with the *watering-pot* example is a description along dimensions of a functional continuum that takes into account reoccurring linguistic features and similarities between patterns.

Notes

1 WebCorp. 1999–2008. Available at: http://www.webcorp.org.uk/ (last accessed: February 2008). A WebCorp search for *watering pot* without hyphen gave over 300 hits and also illustrated patterns referring to a concrete object.

2 The text are taken from Project Gutenberg, 2003–2006, http://www.gutenberg.org/ (last accessed: July 2006).

3 Concordances for the Dickens Corpus were retrieved with WordSmith Tools (Scott 2008).

4 In the present context, textual worlds are not to be understood in the sense of text world theory (cf. Gavins 2007), but in a more basic way where textual functions associated with repeated patterns contribute to the creation of textual worlds. A discussion of links to text world theory remains to be taken up in future work.

5 With observations on *as if*, for instance, I have started to investigate more flexible patterns (Mahlberg 2007a).

6 Examples (6) to (8) show that functions of clusters can also be described with a greater level of detail than 'contextualizing' and 'highlighting': *reclining, slouched* and *lounging* in the context of *his hands in his pockets* point to what could be called a semantic prosody of laziness, indolence or feeling relaxed. Such aspects of meaning play a role for the interpretation of clusters as signals of habitual behaviour and features of characters, but this aspect is beyond the scope of the present paper.

7 LAY here collects the forms *lay, laid, laying*. It is not meant to refer to the full lemma.

5

The Metalanguage of IMPOLITENESS: Using Sketch Engine to Explore the *Oxford English Corpus*[1]

Jonathan Culpeper

Corpus-based studies on metalanguage have examined the use of terms like 'political correctness' (Johnson et al. 2003) and gendered use of language (Ensslin and Johnson 2006). This chapter contributes and expands on corpus analysis of metalanguage. Scholars have not done much to investigate lay people's metalanguage for politeness and even less for impoliteness; certainly, the full armoury of corpus-based techniques that characterize most present-day dictionaries has not been deployed. This study attempts to fill this gap by focussing on the metalanguage of impoliteness. The study specifically addresses the following questions: What linguistic expressions do people use to refer to impoliteness? What do those expressions mean, how are they used and in what contexts? I first generate a comprehensive range of terms using thesauri, including terms such as: impolite, rude, opprobrious, scurrilous, aggressive, threatening, abusive, offensive, insulting, discourteous, ill-mannered. Then, taking a corpus-based approach, I consider a subset of these in more detail (particularly the words rude(ness) and impolite(ness)), examining their frequencies and co-textual characteristics (e.g. genre distribution, collocations) and thereby working towards an understanding of their meanings. The corpus I will explore in particular is the 2 billion word + Oxford English Corpus (OEC). Metalinguistic impoliteness expressions are generally rare. It is only with the advent of huge corpora that their study has become a possibility. The corpus is used in conjunction with Sketch Engine, which allows a more detailed examination of collocates based on grammatical uses of a word, allowing a fuller understanding of the metalanguage of impoliteness and the difference between lay and academic definitions.

5.1 Introduction

Corpus-based studies of metalanguage are not entirely new. For example, Johnson et al. (2003) examine metalinguistic expressions relating to 'political correctness', and Ensslin and Johnson (2006) examine expressions relating to 'Englishness'. Both these studies deploy keyword analyses (and also analyses of collocations) in corpora comprised of specific newspapers, and relate results to underlying ideologies. Methodologically, this chapter is very different. It includes explorations of metalinguistic expressions not in corpora of a few million words but in a corpus of two billion, along with other data sets. It neither deploys keyword analysis nor simple collocational analyses, but includes 'word sketch' analyses, which are based on collocational analyses within relevant grammatical relations, along with other techniques. However, this chapter is similar in that it contributes to and expands on the corpus-based analyses of metalanguage, specifically by examining expressions referring to IMPOLITENESS (small capitals are used in this chapter to indicate a mental concept). Some work in the field of politeness studies, of which we can view impoliteness as a sub-part, emphasizes the importance of metalinguistic expressions (used by the ordinary lay person, as opposed to the academic) in identifying what might count as IMPOLITENESS. However, no serious investigation of those expressions has been carried out, and certainly not a corpus-based investigation. These expressions are inadequately treated in dictionaries (if at all), because even dictionaries that used corpora did not have access to large enough corpora. Herein lies a particular problem with corpus-based research on impoliteness in general. Consider this quotation:

> Any natural corpus will be skewed. Some sentences won't occur because they are obvious, others because they are false, still are those because they are *impolite*. The corpus, if natural, will be so wildly skewed that the description would be no more than a mere list. (Chomsky 1962: 159, a conference paper delivered in 1958, my emphasis)

Of course, Chomsky's solution of using constructed data is hardly likely to be less skewed than a corpus of naturally occurring data. My main point is that Chomsky made this statement in a period when corpora *were* small and biased towards scholarly or literary texts, but that is not the case now. Of course, Chomsky is talking about language or behaviour that can be labelled impolite and not the labels – the metalanguistic expressions – themselves. But the two things are obviously linked, as behaviours that can be labelled impolite drive the labelling (although a metalinguistic comment following an impolite behaviour can be delayed). Certainly, it is the case that impoliteness metalinguistic expressions are also rare. A pilot study of such expressions in the 100-million word *British National Corpus* revealed that it was too small for robust conclusions to be drawn. One needs huge corpora to pursue the study of either impoliteness devices or impoliteness metalinguistic expressions, and this fact partly explains the dearth of previous studies deploying this methodology. The corpus I will explore is the *Oxford English Corpus* (hereafter OEC), which contains in excess of two billion words. This corpus is used in conjunction with *Sketch Engine*, which allows a detailed examination of collocates within the grammatical relations in which a word engages. So, in addition to furthering research on impoliteness, this chapter will incorporate a brief description and demonstration of the OEC and *Sketch Engine*, and an evaluation of some of their features.

5.2 The Metalanguage of IMPOLITENESS

I use the term 'metalanguage' in the broad sense of language which focuses on language itself (see Jakobson's 1960 definition of the metalingual function). Although I am primarily interested in the metalanguage of IMPOLITENESS, the study of metalanguage is of general importance in sociolinguistics. The reason for this is neatly put by Jaworski et al. (2004*b*: 3):

> How people represent language and communication processes is, at one level, important data for understanding how social groups value and orient to language and communication (varieties, processes, effects). This approach includes the study of folk beliefs about language, language attitudes and language awareness, and these overlapping perspectives have established histories within sociolinguistics. Metalinguistic representations may enter public consciousness and come to constitute structured understandings, perhaps even 'common sense' understandings – of how language works, what it is usually like, what certain ways of speaking connote and imply, what they *ought* to be like.

It is those 'structured understandings', those social evaluations that may be represented in language and have a role in influencing the usage of linguistic forms (Lucy 1993: 18). They can be linked to the notion of ideology (see Jaworski et al. 2004*a*: especially 105–62). A corpus-based analysis offers a way of revealing the metalanguage relating to a particular linguistic or communicative area, and through this we have a way of tapping into those 'structured understandings'. Of course, any particular instance of metalanguage could have local strategic purposes and meanings (e.g. telling somebody that they were 'polite' could be a strategy to facilitate ingratiation), which could be disputed. But here I am interested in the metalanguage that people generally share in their particular speech communities.

Some recent work on politeness has bewailed the fact that scholars, including the authors of the much cited [1978] 1987 study of politeness by Brown and Levinson, have constructed pseudo-scientific politeness theories that seem remote from or pay little attention to the lay person's usage of politeness terms (e.g. *polite, tactful, courteous*) and what they might describe (e.g. Eelen 2001; Watts 2003). Politeness, they argue, is a notion that is constructed and contested in discourse, and looking at those constructions and contexts will provide a firmer ontological basis for politeness studies than has been the case hitherto. Even if one does not accept (or not fully accept) that the way forward for politeness studies is the investigation of the lay person's usage, all politeness or impoliteness studies need to adopt a metalanguage to describe the linguistic phenomena that relate to POLITENESS (or IMPOLITENESS). So, the issue here is not whether to adopt or consider a metalanguage, but which metalanguage to adopt or consider – the academic's or the lay person's. Rather oddly however, scholars, of whatever persuasion, have not done much to investigate the lay person's metalanguage.

My specific research interest is impoliteness. Linguistic impoliteness plays a central role in many contexts (e.g. military recruit training, exploitative TV shows) and is often of great interpersonal significance (e.g. family breakdowns, suicides as a result of bullying). Yet there is no systematic or comprehensive treatment of impolite language use. A comprehensive model of impoliteness should accommodate impoliteness metalanguage at some level. I view an individual's impoliteness metalanguage as driven by evaluative beliefs about what counts as IMPOLITENESS. They may express their evaluations as opinions or impoliteness-metapragmatic comments. And these comments may involve words and phrases conventionally understood within a speech community to refer to an assessment of behaviour in context as IMPOLITE – the impoliteness-metalanguage. Cameron (2004: 313) points out that morality is an important theme in studies of metalanguage: '[m]etalinguistic resources seem very often to be deployed to connect various aspects of linguistic behaviour to a larger moral order'. This is particularly pertinent to impoliteness, as instances of impoliteness-metalanguage are generally occasioned by perceived breaches of that moral order.

Whether one should use the metalinguistic terms *rude/rudeness* as opposed to *impolite/impoliteness* has been emerging as a controversial issue in (im)politeness studies. Culpeper (2008) and Terkourafi (2008) defined them in contrary ways, both appealing to metalinguistic evidence; mine drawn from the British National Corpus, Terkourafi's drawn from etymological and cross-linguistic observations. Neither of us are conclusive.

5.3 The Oxford English Corpus and Sketch Engine

5.3.1 The Oxford English Corpus

In an earlier study of linguistic items related to the notion of 'over-politeness' (see Culpeper 2008), in order to ensure sufficient quantities of data, I used the web as a corpus, accessing it through *Webcorp* (see http://www.webcorp.org.uk). The major problems with this 'corpus' are that it is (a) unstable (web pages are constantly being changed) and (b) unstructured. The first problem means that one's findings can never be precisely replicated, and the second one means that certain research agendas, notably those relating to the observation of distributional patterns, cannot be pursued.[2] Regarding the latter, one cannot, for example, examine of an expression's stylistic characteristics via distribution across text-types, its dialectal characteristics via distribution across Englishes and varieties of English, or its historical characteristics via its distribution across time (see also Robert Lew's chapter, this volume for detailed discussion of using the web as a corpus). As an alternative large source of corpus data, the *OEC* claims to have over 2 billion words of twenty-first-century English. With the benefits of both size and structure, this makes it an ideal resource to use.[3] To be precise, the version of the OEC used in this study has 1,889,417,697 words (the figure is given by *Sketch Engine*). In the remainder of this section, I will describe how the OEC was constructed and its structure. Information in this subsection and all quotations unless specified otherwise are sourced from http://www.askoxford.com/oec.

The OEC is comprised of material largely collected from the web, with some supplements drawn from printed texts for certain subject areas (e.g. academic journals). Material was retrieved by a specially designed web crawler. The web crawler was designed to be selective (not to take all or any material within a website). Pages considered related according to topic, author and so on were retrieved. Although this method meant that the collection of each document required 'a new entry to be added to the configuration file in order to specify the crawler's route and behaviour', there were two benefits: (1) 'it means that meta-data (domain, year, author, etc.) can be accurately defined in advance', and (2) 'it facilitates removal of "boilerplate" text'. Material was then 'stripped of tags, links, and other coding, and normalized to plain-text ASCII'. The text was then processed, that is, '[e]ach token is annotated with its lemma and its part-of-speech tag (drawn from the Penn Treebank tag set)', and '[s]entences are then shallow-parsed to bracket token sequences into noun and verb groups'. No information is given on the OEC website about how the lemmatizing and parsing was done, what program was used to do it (this is not part of the program *Sketch Engine* described below), or what the error-rates might be. Finally, the text was converted to XML, and the following metadata were added to each document:

- title
- author (if known; many websites make this difficult to determine reliably)
- author gender (if known)
- language type (e.g. British English, American English)
- source website
- year (+ date, if known)
- date of collection
- domain + subdomain
- document statistics (number of tokens, sentences, etc.)

Furthermore, each document page metadata represents the URL of the source webpage (this allows users to access the original text).

The OEC is structured according to subject domain, text type, variety of (world) English and date. There are 20 subject domains or areas, each divided into more specific categories. These are displayed in Figure 5.1.

Text type (or register) 'refers to the different levels of language that may be used in different contexts', for example, 'writing about soccer may range from the formal (official regulations) to the very informal (fans' weblogs or chatroom discussions)'. Note that weblogs, chatrooms, newsgroups and so on contain largely unedited data (i.e. it is less standardized), and thus more promising for the exploration of impoliteness phenomena (see also Brian King's chapter, this volume, on building corpora of computer mediated communication). In addition to its domain and register variation, the OEC is made up of various world Englishes.

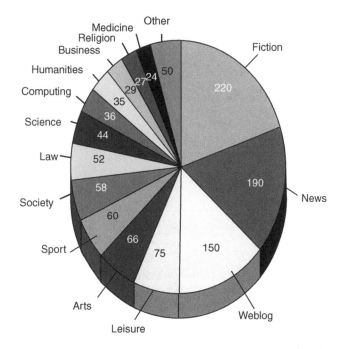

Figure 5.1 The 20 subject domains of the OEC (raw frequencies in millions of words). Figure sourced from http://www.askoxford.com/oec/mainpage/oec01/?view=uk.

It includes material from regions where English is the first language (including British, American, Australian, South African, Canadian and Caribbean), as well as material from where it is a second language (including India, Singapore and Hong Kong). The distribution of material is weighted towards British and US English, which together account for 80 per cent. Regarding period, the OEC spans 2000 to 2006. Although this is quite a narrow timeframe, it does enable some scrutiny of diachronic shifts.

5.3.2 Sketch Engine

The OEC is accessed and manipulated via *Sketch Engine*, software developed by Lexical Computing Ltd. (see www.sketchengine.co.uk). Useful, introductory demonstrations, with screenshots, can be found at http://www.askoxford.com/oec/oecdemos. More detailed information can be found via the documentation link available within *Sketch Engine* itself. Furthermore, the key published paper describing it is Kilgarriff et al. (2004), but further description and application can be found in Kilgarriff and Tugwell (2001), Kilgarriff and Rundell (2002) and Krek and Kilgarriff (2006).[4] *Sketch Engine* is a tool that can produce 'word sketches' for particular words, 'sketch differences' for two (usually semantically related) words, a corpus-based thesaurus, as well as more familiar corpus query functions

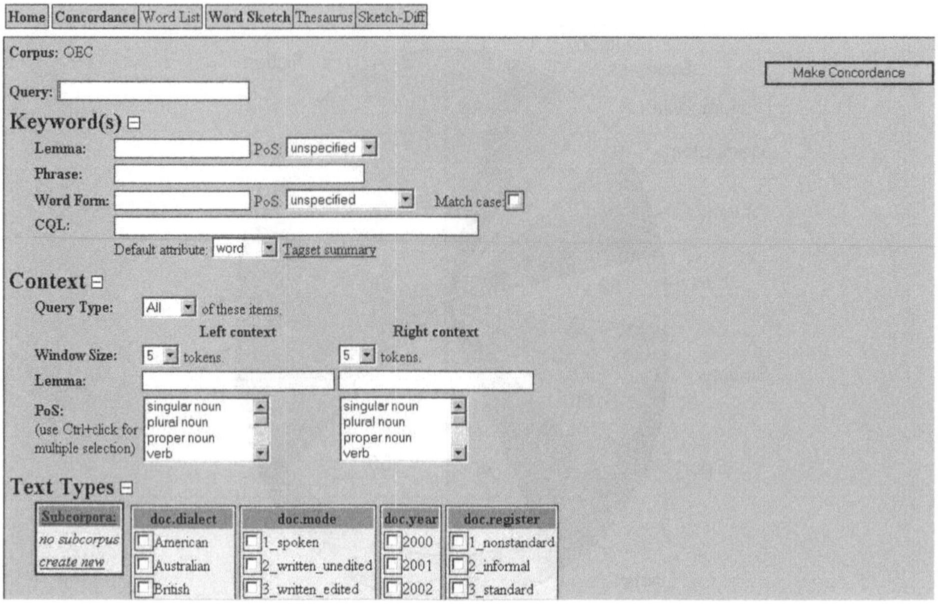

Figure 5.2 Basic concordancing options.

(e.g. a key word in context (KWIC) concordance). However, the corpus will need appropriate markup (ideally lemmatization information, and certainly part-of-speech (POS) tagging) and be in an appropriate format (as specified for Stuttgart Corpus Tools). The interface for basic concordancing options is displayed in Figure 5.2. (Note that Text Types refers to subsections of the corpus, which can conveniently be selected by checking boxes, and that these extend far below what is visible in the screenshot.)

A *Word Sketch* is defined as a one-page, automatic, corpus-based summary of a word's grammatical and collocational behaviour. The key feature is that rather than searching some possibly arbitrary window of text surrounding a particular word for collocates, each grammatical relation a word participates in is searched for collocates, and then those collocates are then presented in separate lists according to statistical salience. According to Kilgarriff and Rundell (2002: 814), that statistic is 'the product of MI [mutual information] and the logarithm of the raw frequency of the collocate', but after September 2006 the statistic was changed to logDice, based on the Dice coefficient (see 'Statistics used in the Sketch Engine', a document available via *Sketch Engine*). For example, if our target word were a verb, its collocates are considered and presented according to the grammatical relations of which it is a part, including, in this case, the subject, the objects, conjoined verbs, modifying adverbs, prepositions and prepositional objects. For English, *Sketch Engine* has been used for a repertoire of 27 grammatical relations, which are either automatically identified from the POS-tagging or can be user-defined.

Sketch Differences is useful for exploring near-synonyms by considering the behaviours that they share or that set them apart. *Sketch Differences* considers whether a word shares a statistical relation with another word in the same grammatical relationship (e.g. *beer* and *wine* share a statistical relationship with *drink*). The *Thesaurus* function has the opposite aim to *Sketch Differences*. It applies statistical operations, following Lin (1998), to the items that enter into the same grammatical relation. Thus, *beer* might be grammatically related to *drink* as an object, as might *wine*, and so both *beer* and *wine* can be allotted to the same thesaurus category.

A concern lingering from my overview of the OEC is that we know little about its lemmatization and POS-tagging. Currently, the OEC uses a POS-tagger developed in-house at Oxford University Press by James MacCracken, though they are currently evaluating alternatives (Kilgarriff, pers. comm.). Interestingly, Kilgarriff et al. (2004: 111) comment:

> Our use of word sketches to date suggests that POS-tagging errors are more frequently the source of anomalous output than weaknesses in the grammar. The use of sorting based on salient statistics means that occasional mis-analyses rarely result in the wrong words appearing in collocate lists.

Given that a considerable amount of the OEC is comprised of the 'non-standard' language of weblogs, one might wonder whether there will be more 'anomalous output' than usual; perhaps even requiring a re-examination of whether it is the output that is anomalous or the grammar. Finally, it should be noted that *Sketch Engine* is best suited to the analysis of relatively frequently occurring words in relatively large corpora. For example, in Kilgarriff et al. (2004) it is reported that word sketches were generated for all words that occurred more than 1,000 times in a 120-million-word corpus of Czech. Kilgarriff (pers. comm.) suggests that '[i]n general, you want at least (say) 500 occurrences for a decent word sketch (this of course needs all sorts of qualifications . . .)'.

5.4 The Metalanguage of IMPOLITENESS in the Linguistics Academic Community

The point of this section is to provide a contrast between what is happening in academia and what the 'lay person' is doing in relation to the metalanguage of IMPOLITENESS. Below I give a list of labels used in the politeness or impoliteness literature for IMPOLITENESS-related phenomena (see, e.g. Culpeper et al. 2003, for a reasonably comprehensive bibliography). In order to make sure that these labels were fulfilling a metalinguistic function, I only included labels that were used in indexes, figures, titles and subtitles, and abstracts.

- *Impolite(ness)*
- *Rude(ness)*

- *Aggravation, aggravated/aggravating language/facework* (also *aggravated impoliteness*)
- *Aggressive facework*
- *Face attack*
- *Verbal aggression*

I have not attempted a precise quantification of how frequently these labels are used, my main aim being to discover the range of labels that were used. However, by any estimation, the labels *impolite(ness)* and *rude(ness)*, either in their nominal or adjectival forms, emerge as vastly more frequent than the other labels. Interestingly, some authors use both of these labels interchangeably (Spencer-Oatey 2000, e.g., is explicit about them being nearly synonymous). And we should note the absence of other possible labels in other disciplines (e.g. psychology, sociology), particularly the label *verbal abuse*, which I will include in later analyses.

My next step was to cast the net wider, and consider the usage of the above set of labels in various academic fields. To do this, I used the Social Sciences Citation Index combined with the Arts and Humanities Citation Index, performing a search on each item and recording both its frequency and the field of study in which it appeared.[5] The results are displayed in Table 5.1, for nominal expressions, and Table 5.2, for adjectival expressions. My search expressions also include 'verbally aggressive' and 'verbally abusive', which are clearly closely related and relevant, though they did not emerge in my research to produce the list in the previous paragraph. However, my search expressions did not include 'aggravating language' or 'aggravating behaviour', because only three instances arose in the OEC in total. It should be remembered that these search terms do not constitute an entirely

Table 5.1 Frequency and distribution of hits for IMPOLITENESS-related nominal expressions in the Social Sciences Citation Index and the Arts and Humanities Citation Index. (searched 1/2/08)[7]

Search item	Verbal aggression	Verbal abuse	Rudeness	Impoliteness
Top 5 subject categories	Psychology, multidisciplinary (155)	Psychiatry (158)	History (8)	Language and Linguistics (12)
	Psychiatry (151)	Psychology, clinical (116)	Humanities, multidisciplinary (5)	Linguistics (10)
	Psychology, clinical (129)	Family studies (115)	Sociology (4)	Acoustics (1)
	Psychology, developmental (107)	Psychology, multidisciplinary (59)	Psychology, social (3)	Asian Studies (1)
	Family studies (98)	Psychology, social (55)	Architecture (2)	Communication (1)
Overall total	874	705	37	17

Table 5.2 Frequency and distribution of hits for IMPOLITENESS-related adjectival expressions in the Social Sciences Citation Index and the Arts and Humanities Citation Index. (searched 1/2/08)[8]

Search item	Rude	Verbally aggressive	Impolite	Verbally abusive
Top 5 subject categories	History (113) Humanities, multidiscipli- nary (39) Political science (24) Sociology (18) Literature (16)	Psychiatry (27) Gerontology (21) Geriatrics and Gerontology (18) Psychology, clinical (17) Psychology, multidisciplinary (14)	History (10) Linguistics (8) Language and Linguistics (7) Communication (5) Psychology, social (5)	Family studies (3) Psychology, clinical (3) Psychology, developmental (3) Communication (2) Law (2)
Overall total	384	101	48	23

level playing field with respect to the focus on the verbal behaviour: *rude(ness)* and *impolite(ness)* can apply to any kind of behaviour, not just verbal, but this is not true of the other expressions.[6]

Comparing the two tables, it is clear that adjectival forms of the pairs *rude/rudeness* and *impolite/impoliteness* tend to occur more frequently than the nominal forms, but that the opposite is true for *verbal aggression/verbally aggressive* and *verbal abuse/verbally abusive*. In all cases it is the more complex form that is used less. There are differences in the frequency ranking of the items in the tables, most notably in the positioning of *rude* relative to the much less frequent *rudeness*. This is possibly evidence that *rudeness* is not so often theorized and researched as a concept in itself. Turning to the distribution of subject categories in the tables, nominal and adjectival variants of particular pairs distribute across subject categories in broadly similar ways. The top five subject categories for *verbal aggression* reveal a heavy emphasis on psychology and psychiatry. In these disciplines, aggression is considered a feature of personality, a cognitive disposition, and is often related to personality disorders and mental illnesses. This is particularly transparent in the subject areas for *verbally aggressive*, where we see gerontology and geriatrics, that is, subject areas that cover mental illnesses associated with ageing processes. *Verbal abuse* bears some similarities to *verbal aggression*, but there is a difference of emphasis: *verbal abuse* is used in disciplines where there is a greater concern with the social context, with the effects of the abuse, hence family studies appears higher in the list and we also see social psychology. This is also reflected in *verbally abusive*. *Rude* is distinctly different, having a strong humanities profile, with a particular emphasis on history, as does *rudeness*. Generally, these terms refer to the social, cultural or historical aspects of offensive behaviour. *Impoliteness* is strongly related to linguistics and communication, and this pattern can also be seen in *impolite*. The reason for this may be due to the monumental success of Brown and Levinson's (1987) book labelled *politeness*. Subsequent publications in the area of pragmatics may have selected *impoliteness* partly as a way of positioning themselves in relation to this major work, as well as the many other works that use the label politeness (there is also now a journal that uses this label). Regarding overall frequency in these tables, it is clear that just two terms, *verbal aggression* and *verbal abuse*, account for the bulk of the metalanguage in academia. *Impolite/impoliteness* occur much less frequently than *rude/rudeness*. In particular, *impoliteness* emerges as a highly specialized term used in a particular academic niche – linguistics and communication.

5.5 IMPOLITENESS-Related Terms in the OEC

5.5.1 A Glance at the Word Sketch Thesaurus

If we move beyond the domain of academia, there are of course numerous terms that relate to IMPOLITENESS. There is not space in this chapter to explore each of these, but we can get a sense of the range of items by using the *Word Sketch* thesaurus function. Table 5.3 displays such associated items for *rude*, and also for *impolite*.

Not surprisingly, for both *rude* and *impolite*, the thesaurus companions are all adjectives and all attribute negative qualities (with the possible exception of *funny*). All of the items of both *rude* and *impolite* can describe language; that is, they could fit the frame 'that was a(n) X thing to say'. However, the meanings generated in this frame tend to vary according to whether the judgement focuses more on the language and the speaker, as opposed to the language and effects on the hearer (these of course are not mutually exclusive; an item focusing more on

Table 5.3 *Rude* and *impolite*. Words sharing the same corpus-based thesaurus category (top 30 in order of statistical significance). (accessed 6/2/08)

Rude	Impolite
arrogant, selfish, obnoxious, cruel, sarcastic, stupid, ignorant, nasty, insensitive, disrespectful, abusive, cynical, ugly, vulgar, foolish, lazy, silly, unpleasant, angry, harsh, violent, funny, pathetic, offensive, irresponsible, ridiculous, stubborn, dumb, boring, inappropriate	discourteous, presumptuous, hurtful, demeaning, insulting, flippant, bossy, unprofessional, unappreciative, overbearing, impertinent, insolent, disrespectful, distasteful, pushy, disloyal, nosy, ill-mannered, unbecoming, inconsiderate, unladylike, tactless, ungenerous, unsportsmanlike, blasphemous, thoughtless, boorish, derogatory, flirtatious, uncalled [for]

the speaker can also have implications for the hearer, and vice versa). For *rude*, the following items could happily describe the social and personality characteristics of an individual without reference to either communicative or relational behaviour: *stupid, ignorant, vulgar, foolish, lazy, silly, angry, pathetic* and *dumb*. For *impolite*, it is difficult to find the same kind of items; a possibility is *boorish*, or the more questionable *unprofessional, unladylike* and *unsportsmanlike*. The key point is that these thesaurus words help reveal those 'structured understandings' of the social world. The tendency is that *rude* belongs to a set of items that links speakers and their talk (i.e. rude speakers doing rude talk); *impolite* belongs to a set of items that links hearers, someone else's talk and contexts (i.e. hearers perceiving impolite talk). This supports Gorji's (2007) (unsubstantiated) observation that although the dominant sense of the word '"rude" describes behaviour or language which causes offence', additionally it is used as a 'term of social description' (p. 3) for the uneducated, the uncultured, the unintelligent – those of low social class. Finally, we shall briefly note that a difference between the items for *rude* and those for *impolite* is in length: items associated with *impolite* tend to be longer. This hints that *impolite* has a more formal, a more highbrow flavour.

5.5.2 *Raw Frequencies of* IMPOLITENESS-*Related Terms*

This section aims to get a sense of the wider, more general currency of the metalinguistic items for IMPOLITENESS used in academia. I have added one further item to those mentioned in Section 5.4. The word *impolite* has evolved through *polite* plus a negative prefix. My concern is that that is not the only way in which *polite* can be negated and thereby refer to impoliteness. Consequently, I have added *not polite.*[9] To retrieve instances, I used the following search query:

"not" [tag != 'VB.*']{0,1}"polite"

The query yielded 473 instances. A screenshot of a randomized sample concordance of *not polite* is given in Figure 5.3. Table 5.4 displays the raw frequency counts in the OEC for the metalinguistic items in focus.

   Rude is clearly the impoliteness-metalinguistic expression of general currency. In contrast, in academia *rude*, though the most frequent adjectival expression, ranks well behind *verbal aggression* and *verbal abuse* (see Tables 5.1 and 5.2). *Rudeness* is in second position in Table 5.4, but *rudeness* in academia is relatively much lower. Close behind *rudeness*, *verbal abuse* emerges near the top of the OEC frequency list, as it did with that for academia. This is despite the fact that *abuse* is constrained by the modifier *verbal*, unlike some other items in the list. For the sociologically and humanities-oriented disciplines, then, there seems to be a reasonable match between their metalanguage and that of the lay person, at least as far as currency relative to the other metalinguistic items considered is concerned. *Verbal aggression*, the most frequent nominal term in academia, emerges near the bottom of the OEC frequency list, with a mere 164 instances.[10] It is in mainstream

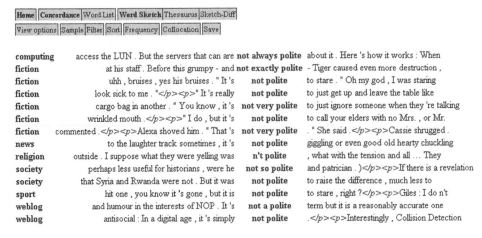

Figure 5.3 A randomized sample concordance of *not polite*.

Table 5.4 Frequency of IMPOLITENESS-related expressions in the OEC. (accessed 5/2/08)

Search item	Rude	Rudeness	Verbal abuse	Impolite	Not polite	Verbally abusive	Verbal aggression	Verbally aggressive	Impoliteness
Total	18,387	1,546	1,522	871	473	201	164	64	30

psychology and psychiatry that there seems to be a dramatic mismatch between the academic metalanguage and that of the lay person. *Impolite* appears roughly in the middle of the OEC frequency list, and interestingly somewhat higher than *not polite*. *Impoliteness*, the term of linguistics and communication, appears at the bottom of the OEC frequency list, being similarly infrequent in academia. Thirty instances out of almost 2 billion is of course an exceedingly small number: *impoliteness* has almost no general currency – it is very much an academic metalinguistic term.

5.5.3 OEC Distribution of rude and impolite in English: Year, Dialect, Gender, Domain

Here, as in Section 5.5.1, I will focus on *rude* and *impolite*, because their usage is disputed in academia (see Section 5.2); they are on a level playing field for comparison (both are adjectives and both are unmodified by *verbally*); *rude* is the most frequently occurring item in the OEC; and *impolite* has a particular association with linguistics, the broad area within which this study is positioned. All frequencies in

Table 5.5 The distribution of *rude* and *impolite* over the years 2000 to 2006.[11]

	Rude			Impolite	
Year	Freq.	Rel. freq.	Year	Freq.	Rel. freq.
2000	718	53.5	2000	30	49.2
2001	1207	65.6	2001	47	56.3
2002	2341	82.9	2003	129	98.6
2003	3905	104.7	2004	221	108.8
2004	5347	102.4	2002	167	100.6
2005	4894	128.7	2005	258	127.9
2006	600	237.6	2006	-	-

Table 5.6 The distribution of *rude* and *impolite* over dialect.

	Rude			Impolite	
Dialect	Freq.	Rel. freq.	Dialect	Freq.	Rel. freq.
Caribbean	390	327.3	Unknown	36	199.3
Canadian	855	116.2	East Asian	41	151.7
American	10,604	113.6	Canadian	45	124.6
New Zealand	309	99.0	American	501	109.4
British	4,713	96.3	Australian	53	109.3
Australian	947	95.8	British	152	63.3
South African	178	67.7	-	-	-
Indian	268	63.6	-	-	-
East Asian	332	60.3	-	-	-
Unknown	150	40.8	-	-	-
Irish	266	25.8	-	-	-

all tables in this section have a cut-off point of a minimum of 25 instances, and were generated on 5th February 2006.

Tables 5.5 to 5.8 display distributions of *rude* and *impolite* according to year, dialect (which here means World English), gender and (major subject) domain. In Table 5.5, although the distribution is not completely even, one can see a general increase in the use of both words from 2000 to 2005. This might reflect increasing anxiety and awareness of impoliteness. Interestingly enough, as far as the United Kingdom is concerned, it was 2005 that saw the arrival of Lynne Truss's book *Talk to the Hand: The Utter Bloody Rudeness of Everyday Life*, which became a best-seller; and in January 2006 the British Prime Minister Tony Blair launched his 'Respect'

Table 5.7 The distribution of *rude* and *impolite* over gender.

	Rude			Impolite	
Gender	Freq.	Rel. freq.	Gender	Freq.	Rel. freq.
Female	6,118	279.9	Female	249	247.8
Unknown	2,300	252.2	Unknown	91	217.1
Male	3,445	151.2	Male	171	163.3
Mixed	7,149	52.4	Mixed	363	57.9

Table 5.8 The distribution of *rude* and *impolite* over domain (up to the most frequent 10 domains).

	Rude			Impolite	
Domain	Freq.	Rel. freq.	Domain	Freq.	Rel. freq.
Fiction	7,814	268.9	Fiction	340	198.7
Weblog	3,650	211.5	Humanities	50	168.4
Life and leisure	1,791	130.6	Weblog	149	146.7
Transport	92	85.3	Life and leisure	65	80.5
Arts	964	78.2	Society	41	57.1
Paranormal	42	69.7	Arts	36	49.6
Humanities	293	58.1	News	102	39.9
Religion	250	55.7	-	-	-
News	2,250	51.8	-	-	-
Computing	263	50.7	-	-	-

Action Plan. In Table 5.6, Canadian English, for some reason, ranks highly in both lists. Usage is roughly similar in British and American English, though rather more so for *rude*. *Rude* is strikingly more frequent in Caribbean English than any other. We will return briefly to this observation in the following section. In Table 5.7, for both the terms, the most frequent users are female. This would fit claims by socio-linguists (e.g. Labov 1990, 2001) that women favour overtly prescribed forms. *Rude* and *impolite* label behaviours that are typically proscribed and have low social value, behaviours of which perhaps women are more acutely aware. In Table 5.8, the distribution over major public subject domains is similar. The fact that fiction is the highest listed for both *rude* and *impolite* is perhaps surprising. Maybe it is because IMPOLITENESS-related behaviours are entertaining and make for high drama (see Culpeper 2005), and their presence gets talked about. In contrast, the appearance of weblogs fairly high in each list can easily be explained by the fact that it is in

Table 5.9 The distribution of *rude* over dialect and gender.

	Rude in Caribbean English		Rude in British English		Rude in Australian English		Rude in American English		Rude in Canadian English	
	Freq.	Rel. freq.	Freq.	Rel. freq.	Freq.	Rel. freq.	Freq.	Rel. freq.	Freq.	Rel. freq.
Male	277	592.8	1,330	235.5	263	231.8	1,302	102.5	71	69.3
Female	27	60.2	733	135.3	270	248.0	4,601	377.4	248	252.3
Un-known	25	133.7	204	90.2	53	116.7	1,918	377.1	91	221.9
Mixed	61	21.8	2,446	72.4	361	53.1	2,783	36.6	445	72.6

weblogs that many people discuss salient events, most notably IMPOLITENESS events.

It is difficult to be more precise about what lies behind these distributions without much closer investigation. It is possible within the *Sketch Engine* software to restrict searches to certain categories of the OEC. This means that it is possible to combine categories, thereby helping to shed more light on what is really going on. As an illustration, Table 5.9 displays the distribution of *rude* across five Englishes and gender. Clearly, it is not always the case that the most frequent users of *rude* are female. In Caribbean English, *rude* is used almost ten times more frequently by men than women, and in British English it is used almost two times more frequently. Of the remaining Englishes, usage is weighted in favour of women. For Australian English the difference is fairly marginal, but in both American and Canadian Englishes women use *rude* more than three times as often as men. Minimally, what this shows us is that caution is required when making claims in a diverse corpus.

5.6 *Sketch Engine:* rude **and** impolite **Compared**

The fact that *rude* and *impolite* are single items means that they are amenable to *Word Sketch* analysis. I shall undertake a comparison of these expressions as adjectives (including their comparative and superlative forms), using Sketch Differences (performing a statistical comparison of two Word Sketches). A slight limitation of this comparison is that the number of instances of *impolite*, 871 instances compared with 18,387 for *rude*, is somewhat low for achieving rich Word Sketches. For this reason, I adopted a relatively low cut-off point of five for any collocate of *impolite/rude* to be taken into consideration. This, of course, increases the danger of idiosyncratic results creeping in, for which reason, I scrutinized concordances of all resulting collocates.

Word Sketches and Sketch Differences results are displayed with a colour scheme that helps the user observe tendencies, but for practical reasons of space this is not rendered in Tables 5.10, 5.11 and 5.12. However, in order to give the flavour of the output, Figure 5.4 is a screenshot of the top of the *impolite/rude* Sketch Differences comparison. It captures in one block grammatical relations and collocates which are common to both expressions (scrolling down would reveal other blocks capturing differences). The information in this figure is also represented in Table 5.10. In Tables 5.10 to 5.12, collocates are ordered in terms of the density with which they occur within a particular grammatical relation. Where two frequencies are given in round brackets, the first refers to the grammatical relation with *rude* and the second the same relation with *impolite*. All results in this section were produced on 6th February 2008.[12] Results that are errors, usually tagging errors, are enclosed within square brackets. (Remember that *Sketch Engine* operates on lemmatized forms; for example, *awakening*, listed in Table 5.12 below, also includes instances of the plural form *awakenings*.)

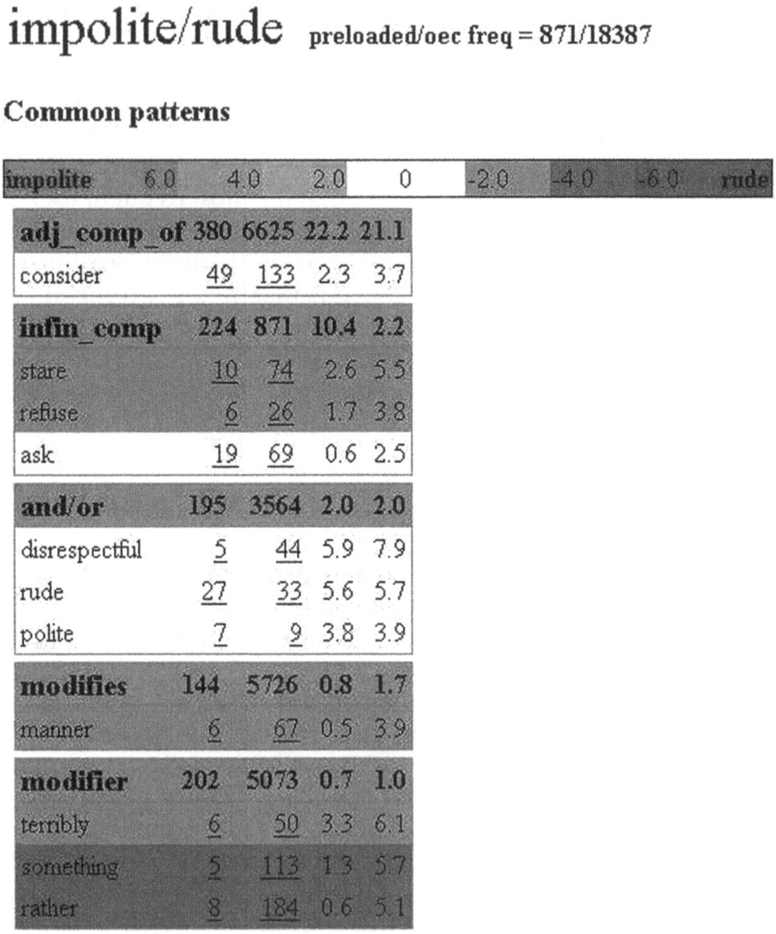

impolite/rude preloaded/oec freq = 871/18387

Common patterns

impolite	6.0	4.0	2.0	0	-2.0	-4.0	-6.0	rude
adj_comp_of 380 6625 22.2 21.1								
consider		49	133	2.3	3.7			
infin_comp 224 871 10.4 2.2								
stare		10	74	2.6	5.5			
refuse		6	26	1.7	3.8			
ask		19	69	0.6	2.5			
and/or 195 3564 2.0 2.0								
disrespectful	5		44	5.9	7.9			
rude	27		33	5.6	5.7			
polite	7		9	3.8	3.9			
modifies 144 5726 0.8 1.7								
manner	6		67	0.5	3.9			
modifier 202 5073 0.7 1.0								
terribly	6		50	3.3	6.1			
something	5		113	1.3	5.7			
rather	8		184	0.6	5.1			

Figure 5.4 Sketch Differences: Similarities between *impolite/rude*.

Table 5.10 *Rude* and *impolite*. Lexico-grammatical patterns in common.

Grammatical pattern (frequency impolite/ frequency rude)	Collocates of impolite and rude in that grammatical relation, and their frequencies
Adjectival complement (6625/380) It is *considered impolite* to visit someone's home unannounced . . .avoid pointing as well as it is *considered rude*.	consider (133/49)
Infinitival complement (871/224) It's *impolite* to *stare*. It's *rude* to *stare*.	stare (74/10), refuse (26/6), ask (69/19)
And/or (3564/195) I believe that you were *impolite* and *disrespectful* to your host Such conduct is *rude* and *disrespectful*.	disrespectful (44/5), rude (33/27), polite (9/[7])
Modifies (5726/144) The manager, in a very *impolite manner*, told them to leave the bar. . . .the fellow brushed past me in a *rude manner*	manner (67/6)
Modifier (5073/202) It would be *terribly impolite* to impinge upon another chap like that Not only was it *terribly rude* to discuss such matters generally	terribly (50/6), [something (113/5)], rather (184/8)

Table 5.11 Lexico-grammatical patterns peculiar to *impolite*.

Grammatical pattern, its frequency and an example with impolite	Collocates of impolite in that grammatical relation, and their frequencies
Infinitival complement (224) Some worry that it is somehow undiplomatic or *impolite* to *speak* the language of right and wrong.	[speak (14)], discuss (6), eat (6)
And/or (195) [see above]	undiplomatic (8)

In the *Sketch Engine* documentation on grammatical relations, the authors acknowledge that the pattern-matching approach:

will always be less than perfect – there will be cases where they fail to capture the relation between two words, and cases where the grammar incorrectly supposes a relation exists. Such 'noise' in the system is in most cases of little importance

Table 5.12 Lexico-grammatical patterns peculiar to *rude*.

Grammatical pattern, its frequency and an example with rude	*Collocates of* rude *in that grammatical relation, and their frequencies*
Adjectival complement (6625) I knew it *sounded rude,* but I was curious.	sound (187), [damn (25)], seem (168), be (3030), [bite (16)], realize (23), appear (46), [care (6)], act (15), [mention (13)], is (2626), feel (32)
NP adjectival complement (445) Some cultures *consider* it *rude* for students to question a teacher.	consider (22), [sound (6)], think (28), find (40)
Adjectival subject (1114) *Doormen* are so *rude* to some customers	doorman (8), bouncer (7), staring (10), bartender (5), [tad (5)], waitress (6), waiter (5), [bit (138)], yorker (5), staff (78), french (5), [stop (7)]
Infinitival complement (871) Julius knew that it was *rude* to *eavesdrop* on conversations	eavesdrop (6), interrupt (25), [staff (8)], point (17), print (5), ignore (15), decline (5), invite (7), smoke (5), listen (6), refer (6), laugh (6)
'to' PP (429) A person who is nice to you, but *rude* to the *waiter,* is not a nice person	waiter (8), stranger (12), guest (16), customer (17), host (6), reporter (5), journalist ([5])
And/or (3564) I don't much care for kids; they're loud, *rude,* and usually *obnoxious.*	obnoxious (93), arrogant (151), inconsiderate (38), impolite (27), crude (93), [awakening (17)], discourteous (16), sarcastic (42), unhelpful (22), dismissive (24), lewd (18), pushy (15)
Modifies (5726) She experiences a series of extremely *rude awakenings.*	awakening (672), bwoy (132), yute (21), gesture (171), remark (140), boyz (13), mechanical (16), bwoys (10, interruption (23), shock (156), comment (266), jolt (10)
Modifier (5073) Beyond ignoring the widely posted 'no cell phone' signs, this just seemed *downright rude.*	downright (117), plain (69), fucking (28), awfully (34), incredibly (106), unspeakably (12), [sound (25)], unnecessarily (17), unbelievably (12), outright (11), horribly (17), little (96)
PP of-i (36) Tretiak delivered the *rudest* of *awakenings* to the North American hockey	awakening (5)

as the word sketches only display relations which occur much more often than expected.

'Errors' in the above analyses included: (1) tagging errors (e.g. *a little bit rude* or *a tad rude,* where *bit* and *tad* are treated as independent nouns), (2) erroneous repetition of the same example and its source (e.g. four of the seven instances of *polite* as a collocate of *impolite* in a coordinated relationship are all from exactly the same source), and (3) natural repetition of the same example (e.g. 'speak' as an infinitival complement). This final case is shown in Table 5.11. Seven of the fourteen instances of this particular example emanate from a single instance in President Bush's West Point speech in June 2002: 'it is somehow undiplomatic and and impolite to speak the language of right and wrong'. This speech was quoted by various news agencies, and thus 'speak' as an infinitival complement emerges as a pattern. Still, overall there are not a large number of errors.

I do not have space to comment in detail on the tables, but will make the following observations:

- The prototypical linguistic context shared by both *impolite* and *rude* is : 'It/that is [considered] [terribly/rather] *impolite/rude* [and disrespectful] to stare/ refuse/ask'. The two adjectives are used to evaluate certain behaviours, both verbal and non-verbal.
- Considering that the contents of Table 5.11 are so scant as to be discounted, we can say that *impolite* has no real identity separate from *rude*; its usages overlap with a subset of the usages of *rude.*
- *Rude* differs from *impolite* in its wider array of usages.
- *Rude* differs from *impolite* in that it has potentially positive uses, notably, 'rude boyz', 'rude yute', 'rude bwoys', reflecting a usage of *rude* that originated about 50 years ago in Jamaica, but is now also current in the United Kingdom, and has the sense of being loud, sexy and fashionable (this also relates to its popularity in the language use of Carribean men c.f. Table 5.9).
- *Rude* differs from *impolite* in that it is used to describe sex and nudity taboos. Note that it coordinates with the item 'lewd'.
- *Rude* differs from *impolite* with regard to the frequent collocational pattern 'rude awakening(s)'. This is similar to 'rude shock' and 'rude jolt'. All of them relate to unexpected and unpleasant change.
- Unlike *impolite, rude* also has social description usages. Note 'rude mechanicals', a usage that originated in Shakespeare's Midsummer Night's Dream, meaning rough and unsophisticated.
- Subjects regularly described as *rude* include: 'doorman', 'bouncer', 'bartender', 'waitress', 'waiter', 'yorker', 'staff' and 'french'. 'Doorman', 'bouncer', 'staring', 'bartender', 'waitress', 'waiter' and 'staff' nearly all relate to public service contexts, where people have expectations of 'service' entitlements, which are not always met or are disputed. In addition, we find 'yorker' (as in 'New Yorker') and 'french', suggesting that people evaluate some national or place stereotypes as IMPOLITE (remember that the bulk of the OEC emanates from North America).
- Actions regularly described as *rude* include: 'eavesdropping', 'interrupting', 'pointing', 'printing', 'ignoring', 'declining', 'inviting', 'smoking', 'listening' and 'laughing'. These actions give particular insight into the social underpinnings of behaviours regularly evaluated as IMPOLITE. Note, in brief, that 'eavesdropping', 'pointing' and 'listening' relate to unwarranted intrusions; 'interrupting' and 'declining' relate to unwarranted impositions; 'ignoring' relates to unwarranted exclusion; 'laughing' relates to devaluing somebody; and 'printing' and 'smoking' relate to what is allowed in a particular context (i.e. they break a prescriptive norm).

- Similar to subjects regularly described as rude, *rude* is often applied to people inhabiting particular social roles: 'waiter', 'guest', 'customer', 'reporter' and 'journalist'. 'Waiter' and 'customer' again relate to contexts where people have expectations of 'service' entitlements, which are not always met or are disputed. Similarly, a 'guest' might be thought to have a claim to special treatment, a claim which might not be met or could be disputed. Those scenarios could lead to the use of *rude*. 'Reporters' and 'journalists' presumably attract use of *rude* because they are regularly involved in conflictual situations. We should also note the collocate 'stranger'. Interestingly, Brown and Levinson's (1987) politeness framework predicts that strangers attract more politeness work. As with 'waiter', 'customer' and 'guest', it is perhaps situations of assumed special entitlement that, if a rupture occurs, attract evaluation as IMPOLITE.
- The items that are regularly coordinated with *rude* include: 'obnoxious', 'arrogant', 'inconsiderate', 'impolite', 'crude', 'discourteous', 'sarcastic', 'unhelpful', 'dismissive', 'lewd' and 'pushy'. It is no surprise to see the item 'impolite', given that I have claimed that the usages of *impolite* are subsumed within *rude*.
- Both *rude* and *impolite* vary in intensity (see 'terribly' / 'rather'). However, for *rude*, even allowing for the mis-tagged items 'a little bit rude' or 'a tad rude', the bulk of modifiers indicate a generally high degree of IMPOLITENESS.

5.7 Conclusions

As far as impoliteness-metalanguage is concerned, this chapter found that:

- Academic metalanguage is not in tune with the lay person's metalanguage for IMPOLITENESS, notably with respect to the items *verbal aggression* and *(im)politeness*. *Rude* is by far the more frequent metalinguistic expression, followed by *verbal abuse*.
- *Impolite* and *rude* distribute similarly across varieties, both have increased in frequency since 2000 (perhaps reflecting growing anxieties about impoliteness), both are used more frequently by men in British English (but this is not the case for all Englishes), and both are most frequent in fiction and weblogs.
- *Impolite* is not synonymous with *rude* but more precisely matches a subset of its meanings. *Rude* differs from *impolite* in the following ways: it is somewhat more 'low-style', it can be used explicitly as a term of social/personal description, it can be used for sex or nudity taboos, it has positive usages as well as negative, and it is distinctively frequent in Caribbean English.
- An analysis of the grammatical relations and collocates of *rude* revealed some of the 'social understandings' underpinning its usage. It is a scalar notion, varying in intensity (this is also true of *impolite*), though weighted towards the more intense end. It is mainly applied in contexts (particularly public) where perceived entitlements to certain treatment are thwarted by individuals performing the social roles associated with those contexts. It is applied to both verbal and non-verbal behaviours which are unwarranted intrusions, impositions and exclusions,

as well as behaviours which devalue somebody or simply break a prescriptive norm.

These findings were made possible by a huge structured corpus, the OEC, and the sophisticated search software, *Sketch Engine*. The high-value of both has been demonstrated by what this paper has achieved. One particular limitation of the OEC is that it only includes written data. Spoken data is of course much more difficult to prepare for an electronic corpus. It would also have been useful to have had more information about the reliability of the grammatical tagging applied to the OEC. *Sketch Engine* was, as far as one can tell, not prone to error and those errors made no difference to the overall picture. A current limitation of Word Sketch is that it can only handle single words, though there are plans afoot to allow multi-word Word sketches (Kilgarriff, pers. comm.). I would have liked to have examined *verbal abuse*. This is the most frequent expression in the social sciences and also in public sign prohibitions. Do its meanings and usages lie outside what might be described as *impolite* or *rude*, or are they a subset within it?

Notes

1 The project of which this publication is a part is funded by the United Kingdom's Economic and Social Research Council (ESRC) (RES-063-27-0015).
2 Not all corpus linguists would necessarily see these as problems. Sinclair (e.g. 2004: 188–90) would argue that it is size that matters, and used huge unstructured (unprincipled) corpora, notably, the Bank of English, in his own research. If it is size that is all important, then the web is clearly an important resource.
3 The Oxford University Press (henceforth OUP) has what it describes as a 'positive attitude' towards licensing the use of its dictionaries and research sources, and this extends to the use of the OEC, at least for specific research projects. An application must be made to the OUP outlining the research project for which findings from the OEC are needed. If this is approved, you will be given permission to use the OEC via *Sketch Engine*. To use *Sketch Engine*, the subscription fee will have to be paid (currently, £42.97 including VAT, for one year). Initial contact and other user queries for the OEC can be directed to: oec.uk@oup.com.
4 All papers listed in this sentence can be downloaded from Adam Kilgarriff's web page http://www.kilgarriff.co.uk.
5 The Social Sciences Citation Index claims to index fully 'more than 1,725 journals across 50 social sciences disciplines', and the Arts and Humanities Citation Index claims to index fully '1,144 of the world's leading arts and humanities journals'.
6 'Verbally rude' occurs once and 'verbally impolite' occurs twice.
7 The totals refer to total number of documents indexed for the search term in the top row, not just the total of the top-five subject categories.
8 The totals refer to total number of documents indexed for the search term in the top row, not just the total of the top-five subject categories.
9 Of course, there are yet further ways in which *polite* can be negated, but they are less central to my concerns here. For example, 'he was never polite' is not an assessment

of an immediate or particular interaction, and 'he was scarcely polite' still implies a degree of politeness.

10 *Aggro* has 382 instances in the OEC. However, many if not most of these cases are not metalinguistic. Many refer to unnecessary effort or hassle endured by an individual. Some refer to a type of music and fashion ('aggro punk').

11 The frequency of 'impolite' for 2006 is 22, i.e. below the minimum frequency cut-off point.

12 I undertook the same analyses in June 2007. Disconcertingly, while the overall picture was broadly the same, some grammatical relations and/or collocates appeared, while others disappeared, and there were some changes to rankings. This may be partly due to the continual expansion of the OEC, but that is unlikely to account for all the changes.

6

Issues in the Design and Development of Software Tools for Corpus Studies: The Case for Collaboration

Laurence Anthony

Corpus linguistics is a field that is inextricably linked with developments in computer science and engineering. Without corpus tools in the form of concordancers, word frequency counters, and collocate profilers, many of the actions that we usually complete in seconds would take years of work. Despite this, there have been few discussions on the role of software in the field, and the limitations of our most popular tools are rarely addressed in the literature. Even though corpus linguistics is now nearly 50 years old, we are still relying mostly on methods of observation that were developed at its conception. If we hope to advance contemporary corpus linguistics in new and exciting directions, there is a clear need for new tools of the trade. In this chapter, I discuss some of the important issues that we need to consider if we hope to create the next generation of software tools. First, I discuss the relationship between corpora and corpus tools, and show that by clarifying their different roles, some of the common debates in the literature can be easily resolved. Next, I present some of the arguments for and against corpus linguists developing purpose-built tools through programming. Following this, I propose that collaborative software development offers us an alternative route to new and useful tools. To illustrate the advantages of this approach, I describe the case of AntConc, a freeware, multi-platform corpus toolkit that has been developed with the advice of some of the leading corpus linguists in the world, as well as the feedback and suggestions of researchers, teachers and learners.

6.1 Introduction

It is often said that corpora have revolutionized the study of language over the last 50 years (e.g. Chapelle 2001: 21; Hunston 2002). We know, however, that corpora have been used in language studies for much longer. Biber et al. (1998: 21–2) report that Johnson used a corpus of texts to create authentic examples of use for his dictionary in 1755, and that a corpus was also used in the late 1800s in the construction of the first edition of the Oxford English Dictionary. McEnery and Wilson (2001: 3) describe studies on child language in the late nineteenth and early twentieth century that also used primitive corpora as a source of data.

The so-called revolution that began in the 1960s can perhaps be attributed to two main factors. First, the 'early' corpora mentioned above, while being constructed from naturally occurring language, were not designed to be representative of the language in any way. The early 'modern' corpora (e.g. the Brown Corpus (Francis 1965)), on the other hand were created according to an explicit design with the aim of being representative of a particular language variety. Subsequently, patterns observed in the corpus could in theory be extended to the language in general. Although there are still disagreements on the definition of a modern corpus, most agree that it is a collection of *naturally* occurring texts, gathered according to an *explicit* design so that it is *representative* of the target language and can be used for linguistic analysis (Tognini-Bonelli 2001: 54; McEnery and Wilson 2001: 29; McEnery et al. 2006: 5).

The second reason for the corpus revolution, which is the focus of this chapter, relates to the way corpora are stored and analysed. Early corpora were paper-based. Sinclair (2006), for example, describes how Jesperson used to scribble on sheets of paper and post them in little drawers and pigeonholes in his desk when carrying out his studies on grammar. The modern corpus, in contrast, is almost by definition electronic. The huge advances in computer technology over the last 50 years have allowed us to store far more data than could have been conceived in the 1900s. It could be conjectured that the 500-million word Bank of English (Jarvinen 1994; Baker et al. 2006: 18) probably contains more electronic texts than all the electronic texts in the world in the 1960s. More importantly, perhaps, computers allow us to easily search, retrieve, sort and carry out calculations on corpora via specialized text analysis tools like concordancers. As corpora get larger, the importance of software becomes even greater. In a similar relationship to search engines with the Web, if our corpus tools cannot locate and display what we are searching for, the corpus itself is essentially worthless. McEnery and Wilson (2001) remind us of the importance of software when they say,

> After using a concordancer program it is all too easy to become blasé about the ability to manipulate corpora of millions of words. In reality, we should temper that cavalier attitude with the realization that, without the computer, corpus linguistics would be terrifically difficult and would hover grail-like beyond reasonable reach. (p. 18)

Corpus linguistics is inextricably linked to computer technology in a more fundamental way than any other applied linguistics field, with the exception of perhaps CALL (Computer Assisted Language Learning). Developments in computer technology will have an immediate washback effect on the size and kinds of corpora we can store and analyse. Unfortunately, corpus linguists can contribute little to the development of faster computers and larger memories. In this respect, we are at the mercy of scientists and engineers. Already, limitations in hardware are becoming apparent as we attempt to analyse huge corpora such as the British National Corpus (BNC) (Aston and Burnard 1998; Baker et al. 2006: 24). All we can do is wait for the next generation of computers and hard disk technology.

On the other hand, corpus linguists can and should play a major role in the creation of software tools to analyse corpora. Computer software engineers are notoriously poor at creating software for a purpose they do not fully understand, and for an audience they are unfamiliar with. In contrast, corpus linguists have a clear understanding of what they want to analyse, why they want to analyse it and who will be using the software. In the rare case when a corpus linguist under-stands software development, the result is a tool that quickly becomes a standard in the field, as shown for example by WordSmith (Scott 1999) and the BNCWeb interface (Hoffmann and Evert 2006). The importance of these tools in the field cannot be overstated. Without WordSmith, for example, it is doubtful that many of the post millennium research studies would have been carried out, or that corpora would have become such a useful resource in the classroom.

Strangely, however, it seems that most corpus linguists have been largely reactive when it comes to tools development. The number of people involved in the devel-opment of corpus tools is still incredibly small, and as a result, there exist a rather limited set of tools that mostly offer identical features. On David Lee's Devoted to Corpora site (http://devoted.to/corpora/), which is probably the most extensive corpus site on the Web, 32 concordance tools are listed. However, none of these can smoothly handle annotated data in a wide range of corpora on the three main operating systems: Windows, Macintosh and Linux. Teachers often complain about the lack of tools that can be used easily in the classroom, and researchers are beginning to find that many of the tools cope poorly with huge amounts of data, unless they have been purposively built for a particular corpus. Even basic features, such as the ability to sort or rank concordance results based on part-of-speech tags or vocabulary difficulty level, are surprisingly lacking in our most popular tools.

In this chapter, I want to focus on the tools of the trade; the software that we use when we need to consult a corpus. First, I will discuss one of the common misconceptions we have in the field, that is the relationship between the corpus itself and the tools we use to probe it. In accordance with Sinclair (2004), I will argue that a corpus can be defined in terms of how texts are observed, putting the tools we use at the centre of all corpus research. Next, I will discuss some of the limitations of existing tools that limit the range of corpora applications, and also undermine many of the proposals that have emerged from corpus studies. Biber et al. (1998) have argued that some of these limitations can be overcome if corpus linguists program their own tools. I will discuss the advantages and disadvantages of the so-called Do-It-Yourself (DIY) corpus tools, and propose an alternative model for tools development based on collaboration between corpus linguists and computer engineers. To illustrate this point, in the final part of the paper I will discuss the results of a collaborative approach to software design and development using *AntConc* as an example. *AntConc* is a freeware, standalone, multiplatform corpus toolkit developed by the author in collaboration with some of the leading corpus linguists in the world. Unlike many of the standard tools, *AntConc* is under constant development, with new features and options added regularly in response to feedback and suggestions from some of the 70,000 or more users of the software. I will argue that adopting a similar model in the creation of other corpus tools would enable us to analyse texts in new and exciting ways, pushing the field of corpus linguistics in directions we cannot yet conceive.

Although this chapter does not aim to give readers a step-by-step guide to using *AntConc* and other tools (which can be easily found on the developers' websites),

I hope that it will lead to a better understanding of the position of software tools in corpus work, and provide new insights into the concerns of software developers, the advantages and disadvantages of direct programming of tools, and approaches for dealing with the limitations of standard software when conducting a corpus study.

6.2 The Relationship Between Corpora and Corpus Tools

Over the years, there have been several debates about what corpus linguistics represents. Some researchers, for example, say that it is a methodology (e.g. Kennedy 1998; Meyer 2002; Scott and Tribble 2006), while others argue that it is closer to a new branch of applied linguistics (e.g. Tognini-Bonelli 2001). Researchers have described at length the differences between corpus-based and corpus-driven studies (e.g. Tognini-Bonelli 2001), while others have shown that the two approaches are more similar than they first appear (e.g. McEnery et al. 2006). At the centre of all these discussions has been the corpus itself. In any standard reference book on corpus linguistics, there will undoubtedly be a major section or even chapter dedicated to defining corpora and explaining how they should be created in terms of size, balance, sampling and representativeness. There will also usually be a discussion on the different types of corpora, such as specialized, comparable, parallel, learner, diachronic, monitor and even pedagogic corpora. There is also inevitably a discussion on the advantages and disadvantages of part-of-speech tags and other corpus annotation.

Of course, these discussions are necessary if we are to improve our understanding of corpus studies; a poorly constructed corpus will inevitably lead to poor results. However, the heavy focus on corpus design issues leads us to forget that it is not the only essential component of a corpus study. For a successful study, two further components are necessary; (1) human intuition (to interpret the data derived from corpora, and more importantly perhaps, (2) software tools to extract the data in the first place.

One reason why the importance of software is often forgotten is that corpora themselves are often referred to as the 'tools' of the corpus linguist (Tognini-Bonelli 2001: 185; Bernardini 2002a: 20; Sinclair 2004: 2). When corpora are discussed in such a way, it is easy to think that they are *directly* providing us with the important information we need, in a similar way to dictionaries and reference books. In reality, a corpus does not provide us with any information directly. In fact, as (Hunston 2002: 3) acknowledges, 'a corpus by itself can do nothing at all, being nothing more than a store of used language'. A corpus is certainly a useful resource in the same way that libraries and the Web can be considered resources. However, it only becomes valuable when we start observing it *indirectly*. For example, a library provides us with little information when we look at it directly; all we see are the doors, walls, windows and roof that could be part of any building. Even entering a library and randomly flicking through the pages of its many volumes will unlikely lead to us acquiring the knowledge we seek. Libraries become useful when we start using reference *systems* that place books on related topics in the same areas of the building. More importantly, we can gain the information we require when we use *tools* in the form of computer search engines to identify where the books are located. The same argument can be made about corpora. In the words of Sinclair (2004),

> The essence of the corpus as against the text is that you do not observe it directly; instead you use tools of indirect observation, like query languages, concordancers, collocators, parsers, and aligners . . . the whole point of making something a corpus rather than a collection of texts is in order to observe things which cannot be directly observed because they are too far apart, they are too frequent or infrequent, or they are only observable after some kind of numerical or statistical process. (p. 189)

A number of interesting points can be inferred from Sinclair's statement. First, even a single text can be considered a corpus if we observe it using the same procedures and *tools* that we would use to observe more traditional large-scale bodies of texts. Second, and more importantly for the discussion here, it puts software tools at the centre of all our studies. Regardless of how big or well designed corpora are, if the tools are unable to reveal the features we search for, we are back in the world of McEnery and Wilson's (2001) 'grail-like' searches.

Hunston (2002: 20) suggests that many people compare the development of corpora with that of telescopes in astronomy, referring to Stubbs (1996: 231) as an example. If this is true, then it is another example of seeing the corpus itself as a tool that reveals to us the mysteries of the universe of language. On careful reading, however, it seems that Stubbs understands the role of corpora in corpus studies better than most when he says,

> The combination of computers, software, and large corpora has already allowed linguists to see phenomena and discover patterns which were not previously suspected. (pp. 231–2)

Following Stubbs's analogy, we can see that corpora are more like *regions of space*, such as stars, planets and nebulae that we observe with telescopes. Seeing corpora in this way allows us to resolve some of the common issues in the field. For example, there has been a great debate about the value of small corpora with some people seeing them as simply an unfortunate limitation (Sinclair 2004), and others seeing their great potential (McEnery and Wilson 2001). If we see corpora as regions of space, the value of both large and small corpora is immediately apparent. Investigating large corpora can be compared with investigations of galaxies, from which we can learn about the building blocks of the universe and create models about how it all 'works'. A study of a small corpus can be compared with looking at a small group of stars, from which we can gain more detailed information about their unique properties. The value of analysing even a single text, as illustrated by Scott and Tribble (2006: 179), can be understood if it is compared with the study of a single star. However limited the 'corpus' is in terms of size and representativeness, nobody can doubt the value of astronomical observations of the nearest star to us, the Sun. The usefulness of a corpus is dependent not on its size but on what kind of information we hope to extract from it with our tools.

There has also been a long and sometimes passionate debate about the value of 'enriching' corpora with part-of-speech data and other annotation (Tognini-Bonelli 2001). Again, by comparing corpora with regions of space, the value of annotation becomes immediately apparent. In astronomy, there has been an ongoing debate about what should be defined as a 'planet' (http://www.iau.org/iau0601.424.0.html). However, irrespective of whether we label eight, nine, or eleven bodies orbiting the sun as planets, the model itself provides us with essential information for understanding the movement of objects in the night sky, and ultimately our model of the solar system. Likewise, annotated data provide us with essential information for understanding how linguistic objects operate within texts, and ultimately help us to refine our models of language itself.

If we accept that corpora are more similar to areas of space in Stubbs's analogy, then clearly corpus tools, in the form of concordancers, collocators, word frequency generators, and so on, are the real *telescopes* of corpus linguistics. This leads us to one of the main conjectures in this chapter. In astronomy, a great many scientists and engineers have strived to create more reliable, accurate and powerful telescopes to investigate the heavens. For example, to observe a greater range of features of stars they have complimented traditional optical telescopes with radio telescopes. To reduce the impact of noise and light scattering from the atmosphere, they have created sophisticated noise filtering software or simply designed telescopes that work in space. In corpus linguistics, on the other hand, there is still a general lack of concern about the essential tools we use for observation. As mentioned in the introduction, corpus linguists are far more reactive than proactive when it concerns software development. When faced with tools with poor interfaces or limited features, rather than working to improve them, many researchers in the field of corpus linguistics simply turn their existing telescopes to a different part of the sky and begin making a new set of recordings. This attitude is revealed in the fact that although corpus linguistics is now almost 50 years old, we are still effectively using the same tools that we developed at its conception. What we need is a more proactive approach to tools development. If we can develop new tools in corpus linguistics, like radio telescopes or the Hubble space telescope in astronomy, we can gain new perspectives of the universe of language. How to achieve this is the concern of the sections that follow.

6.3 Advantages and Disadvantages of DIY Corpus Tool Development

There is no doubt that the tools we use today have improved tremendously since the days of black screen command line applications and even those that ran under early Windows and pre-Macintosh OS X environments. As mentioned earlier, modern tools such as WordSmith (Scott 1999), BNCWeb (Hoffmann and Evert 2006), MonoConc (http://www.athel.com/mono.html), and Concordance (http://www.concordancesoftware.co.uk/) have hugely improved our experience of working with corpora, and have enabled many more people to carry out corpus research that would have been impossible without them. Nonetheless, anyone who uses corpus tools will have experienced occasions when the software is either not sophisticated enough to perform an action, or is too complex for the user to figure out how the action should be performed (Sinclair 2004: 296). Even simple operations can sometimes be surprisingly difficult to achieve. For example, none of the major corpus tools can display key word in context (KWIC) concordance lines aligned by the search word in a 'sentence' mode. There are also no tools that filter KWIC concordance lines to show only those with high frequency words, or allow sorting of lines by tag and word position independently. In this respect, it is questionable whether the tools we use in corpus linguistics are really improving, or are able to carry out even the majority of operations we desire.

To deal with the problems of standard tools, Biber et al. (1998: 255) strongly encourage researchers to develop their own tools through computer programming. They give four reasons to support their argument:

1. You can conduct analysis not possible with standard tools.
2. You can carry out analyses more quickly and accurately.
3. You can tailor the results to fit your research needs.
4. There is no limit to the size of the corpus you can use.

There is no doubt that if the researcher has good programming skills, all these claims can be justified. Biber et al. (1998) demonstrate the power of such DIY corpus tools in their own studies on the analysis of complex grammatical constructions, word endings, and the so-called 'valency' patterns of two target verbs. In the early years of modern corpus linguistics work, Sinclair's group not only created specialized tools for their pioneering studies on lexical phrases, but also developed a new programming language geared towards text analysis (Krishnamurthy 2004).

The reality for most corpus researchers, however, is that computer programming is in a completely different world. Biber et al. (1998) rightly state that programs can be written without a special aptitude in computer science or mathematics. On the other hand, without extensive training in programming it is certainly doubtful if corpus linguists can develop tools that demonstrate any of the four advantages given above. On the contrary, it is likely that these tools would be more restrictive, slower, less accurate and only work with small corpora.

To illustrate this point, we can consider the case of developing a simple word frequency generator. In her noble attempt to introduce programming to corpus linguists (Danielsson 2002) describes two simple programs written in the Perl programming language. Combined, these programs effectively count all strings of characters in a text that are formed from the letters 'a' to 'z'. At first sight, this may seem sufficient for the majority of tasks. However, extending the programs to serve as an accurate word frequency counter is quite daunting. One problem is the issue of what counts as a word. Scott and Tribble (2006: 11–32) describe many cases where the simple 'a' to 'z' model of a word does not work. For example, how should the tool deal with words containing hyphens or apostrophes? Barlow (2002: 207) describes the many problems that are introduced when the corpus data are annotated in some way or other. There is also the issue of whether the raw form of the word should be counted or if word forms should be conflated into a single lemma before counting. The problem of counting words increases in complexity when we introduce texts containing both upper and lower case letters (as is normally the case), and there are decisions to make when we need to sort the results in some way. Another layer of complexity is introduced when we want to count non-English words. For example, Japanese words are written using a set of over two thousand Chinese characters and two additional, mutually exclusive alphabets, each composed of 48 phonetic symbols. How should we adapt our word frequency generator for this language?

All the above complications in counting words have to be dealt with in some way when designing a word frequency counter. The advantage of DIY tool development is that the designer can make a decision that suits his or her particular needs. The danger is that through inexperience the above issues will simply be overlooked leading to spurious results. It should also be remembered that word counting programs are some of the simplest programs that exist in corpus linguistics. The complexities increase dramatically when we consider even a rudimentary KWIC concordancer or collocation program.

In addition, we should not forget that as well as researchers, there are many teachers and learners who can find great value in using corpora and corpus tools for materials development and in-class data-driven learning or discovery learning (Johns 2002). The tools needed for these users are likely to be at a different level of sophistication to the research tools described by Biber et al. (1998) or Danielsson (2002). Classroom-oriented tools need to be intuitive to use, stable and even sometimes attractive. They have to conform to the user's expectations of how software operates (Lonfils and VanParys 2001) and perhaps even work on multiple platforms and within the technical constraints of language laboratories. DIY tools run via the black screen command line of Windows, for example, will in most classroom contexts be clearly inappropriate. Not surprisingly, even among the standard tools available for corpus linguistics studies, few adapt well for use in the classroom.

In summary, there is a clear benefit for corpus linguists to write their own programs if they have the expertise. However, for the majority of people in the field the only option is to use standard tools. Even so, as illustrated above, Biber et al. (1998) are correct when say that there are many tasks that the standard tools cannot accomplish. In these cases, should the corpus linguist just sit back and wait for software developers to create the tools they need, as they have to do with hardware related problems? In the following section, I will propose an alternative solution that addresses the problems associated with DIY programming and also the limitations of standard tools. In our astronomy analogy, it is unreasonable to expect regular astronomers to start building new and advanced telescopes to carry out their observations. Although there are some exceptional astronomers that will use their engineering skills to develop new tools, the field has been advanced by astronomers working in *collaboration* with engineers to develop the next generation of tools. I will argue that such a model can also be successfully adopted in corpus linguistics, using the experience of developing *AntConc* as an example.

6.4 Collaboration in the Design and Development of Corpus Tools: The Case of *AntConc*

AntConc is a freeware, multiplatform corpus toolkit originally developed for classroom use, but now commonly used by researchers, teachers and students around the world. *AntConc* includes a tag aware concordancer and plot distribution tool, word and keyword generators, and tools for cluster, N-gram and collocate analysis. The software is completely Unicode compliant, meaning that it can work smoothly with almost all languages of the world, including Asian languages such as Japanese, Chinese and Korean. It also incorporates a full regular expression engine (Baker et al. 2006: 138) that enables users to extend traditional wildcard searches with a powerful set of search functions. For easy use in the classroom, all colours, font sizes, font styles and tool settings can be imported or exported, and the next major upgrade of the program should work smoothly with massive, annotated corpora saved in a variety of formats, including Microsoft Word and PDF. A summary of the features in the latest version of *AntConc* (3.2.1) are listed in Table 6.1. A screenshot of the concordance tool in the program is shown in Figure 6.1.

Although *AntConc* boasts an unusually wide range of features for a freeware program, what is perhaps unique about the program is that it has been developed almost completely as a result of comments, suggestions and feedback from many of the leading corpus linguists, as well as some of the 70,000 users of the software around the world. A detailed account of all the features in the program can be found in Anthony (2005 and 2006). Here, I will illustrate how collaboration in three key areas of its design has led to it becoming a useful tool that has found favourable reviews (Diniz 2005; Wiechmann and Fuhs 2006).

6.4.1 Windows, Macintosh, or Linux?

Figure 6.2 shows the first version of *AntConc* that was released in 2002. *AntConc* 1.0 was a extremely simple Windows program offering just a basic KWIC concordance. It did not have any sorting features, could not search for differences in case, and had no Unicode support. The program was originally created as an exercise in programming a modern software application in the Perl programming language (Wall 2000) as part of an unrelated project (Anthony and Lashkia 2003). At the time, there was no intention for the program to ever leave the laboratory.

At the same time that *AntConc* was being written, colleagues at Osaka University in the west of Japan were beginning to organize a new technical writing course for their 700 graduate school engineering students. A feature of the course was

Table 6.1 Summary of tools and features in *AntConc* 3.2.1.

- Freeware license
- Small memory requirement (~3.5 MB of disk space)
- Multiplatform
  - Windows 95/98, 2000, NT, XP, Vista
  - Linux
  - Macintosh OS X 10.0 or later
- Extensive set of tools
  - KWIX Concordance
  - KWIC Concordance Plot
  - File View
  - Word Cluster/N-gram
  - Collocates
  - Word List/Keyword List
- Powerful search features
  - Regular expressions (REGEX)
  - Extensive wildcards
- Multiple level sorting
- HTML/XML tag handling
- Fully Unicode compliant
- Easy-to-use, intuitive graphical user interface (GUI)

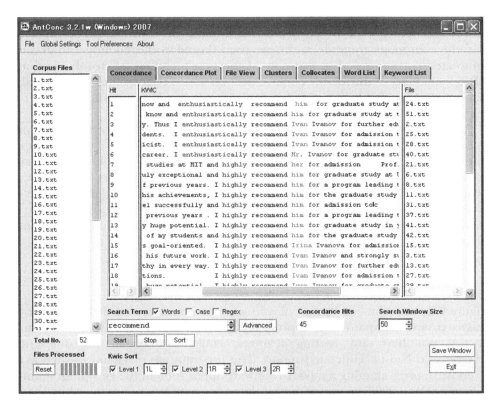

Figure 6.1 *AntConc* 3.2.1 Concordance Tool showing results of a search for 'recommend' in a corpus of 52 graduate recommendation letters. The KWIC lines have been sorted on the 1st word to the left, and then the 1st and 2nd words to the right.

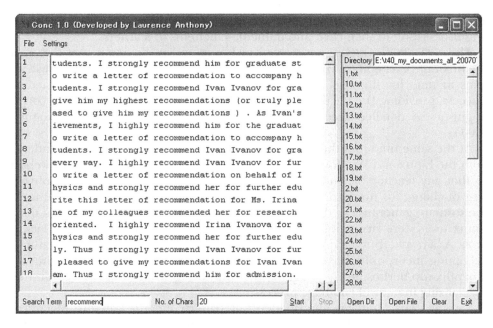

Figure 6.2 *AntConc* 1.0, released in 2002. The window shows the same results as those in Fig. 6.1, when searching for 'recommend' in a corpus of 52 graduate recommendation letters.

that students would create mini-corpora of target texts for their varied specialized fields, and use these to identify and make hypotheses on language following the data-driven approach to learning mentioned earlier (Johns 2002). Unfortunately, the organizers had two problems. First, they had little funding to purchase commercial software for the many terminals to be used by the learners. The second and more serious problem was that the language laboratory where the classes were to be held was a Linux environment. Although several Linux tools existed, none were suitable for the novice corpus linguists who were to take the course.

Through our work on various other projects, one of the Osaka course organizers, Judy Noguchi, soon became aware of *AntConc* and on learning that the Perl programming language allowed for easy porting of programs to different operating systems asked if I would port the program to Linux for use in her course. The benefits to all parties were clear. For the Osaka students, they would obtain a simple, freeware KWIC concordancer that could be used to analyse specialized texts on the Linux machines. For the course organizers, they would have a direct route to the software developer who would be able to deal with any problems or serious limitations that were found with the software. For me, the teachers and students on the course would provide valuable feedback for future developments of the program, and also at a more theoretical level, provide insights on the value of data-driven learning in a classroom setting. It should also be added that seeing so many students using the software to solve real-world writing problems provided a great deal of motivation to improve the program. Few research projects in applied linguistics result in such clear and immediate benefits to learners.

Through 2002, *AntConc* was ported to Linux and in September of that year, the first Linux version of *AntConc* (version 2.2.1) was uploaded onto the Osaka systems in time for the start of the new course. The software was an immediate success, providing the ideal tool for teaching non-specialists basic skills in corpus linguistics. A detailed account of the Osaka course can be found in Noguchi (2004).

At the same time that the software was released for use by the Osaka students, both the Linux and Windows versions of *AntConc* were uploaded onto my website so that any teacher or student around the world could download the software free of charge for non-profit use. What was surprising, however, was the interest the software generated in the Linux community as a whole. It seemed that many Linux users were struggling to carry out corpus work simply due to the lack of tools. As a result, *AntConc* quickly spread through the Linux community eventually becoming incorporated as the standard corpus tool in Morphix NLP (http://morphix-nlp.berlios.de/), a Linux distribution geared towards researchers specializing in natural language processing.

Several years later, an almost identical pattern emerged in the Macintosh community. Through feedback from students at Osaka University and other users around the world, it became clear that the corpus tools available on the Macintosh were also extremely limited. Some researchers were even running their modern Macintosh OS X systems in a virtual 'classic' mode (a much older version of the operating system), simply to access the useful but clearly outdated Conc program (http://www.sil.org/computing/conc/). Therefore, in 2006, *AntConc* was ported to Macintosh OS X, and has since quickly established a strong user base on that platform. Figure 6.3 shows the three different versions of *AntConc* running on Windows, Linux and Macintosh. What is important to note is that the three programs look the same, and offer identical features. This allows users to easily move from one version, for example in their Linux language laboratory, to another version at home.

The experience of developing *AntConc* for multiple platforms has revealed a number of important points. First, even though a great deal of research has demonstrated the value of using corpus techniques in the classroom (e.g. Sinclair 2004), many teachers and learners have struggled to implement these ideas simply due to a lack of tools on their chosen operating system. In the case of the Osaka program, for example, it was only after the release of *AntConc* for Linux that data-driven learning in the classroom became a possibility. Second, the need for multiplatform tools only became apparent through discussions and direct feedback from researchers, teachers and learners using software tools in their everyday studies. The need for multiplatform tools has been almost completely ignored in the literature. Third, it is clear that many users will not switch to a different operating system simply to carry out a corpus study with a more advanced tool. Rather, they will opt to carry out a simpler study with the available tools on their own system, or not carry out the study at all. This is particularly true of students, who may learn how to do corpus analyses in their university classes on a

Windows (XP)   Macintosh (OSX)

Linux (Vine 3.2)

Figure 6.3 *AntConc* 3.2 running on Windows, Macintosh OSX and Linux operating systems.

Linux system, but then struggle to apply those skills at home on their preferred Macintosh or Windows computers. What this implies is that the availability of limited tools on different operating systems may be more important than having advanced tools on a single system. If this is the case, there are clear advantages to having a fully functional corpus tool that works in an identical fashion on all major operating systems, as is the case with *AntConc.*

6.4.2 English, Japanese or Arabic?

As described above, *AntConc* was originally designed for learners of English. As *AntConc* increased in popularity in Japan, however, more and more teachers of *Japanese* began requesting a similar tool that would work with their Japanese corpora. This was not just a local problem. Requests began to arrive for tools that would work with other languages, such as Chinese and Korean and then European languages. Clearly, there were many people around the world who wanted to carry out corpus studies in non-English environments but were struggling to find tools that would process their corpora. Working in collaboration with a number of users in Japan and Germany, a major decision was taken to convert *AntConc* from an English only corpus tool to one of the first fully international tools for corpus linguists.

Earlier in the chapter, it was mentioned that Japanese is a complicated language based on three separate 'alphabets' and composed of thousands of characters. When we want to view Japanese texts on a computer screen, the situation becomes even more complex. Traditionally, computers displayed texts using a small set of 256 characters called ASCII (Baker et al. 2006: 12). Unfortunately, the huge number of characters in the Japanese language cannot be mapped directly to the ASCII character set and so various ways to encode Japanese, such as using two character codes to represent a single Japanese character, were proposed. Many of these so-called legacy encodings are still in use, including 'Shiftjis', 'EUCJP', and 'iso-2022-jp'. It is important to note that the problem of displaying characters on a computer screen is not restricted to Japanese but all languages. English, for example, becomes a problem if we want to display special characters such as 'curly' quotation marks. As a result, there are literally hundreds of legacy encodings in use around the world. The Japanese version of Microsoft Word 2003, for example, supports over 50 legacy encodings as standard, including seven legacy encodings for Japanese.

In recent years, the complex relationship between languages and character sets has been simplified with the introduction of Unicode, a internationally recognized character set which provides mappings to every letter, punctuation mark, digit and other marks used in virtually all languages in the world (The Unicode Consortium, 2006; Baker et al. 2006: 163). In practice, there are various ways in which computers can store the Unicode character set, although an approach called UTF8 encoding has largely become the standard due to a clever design that allows the characters to be stored in a small amount of memory, and also allows ASCII characters to be processed without change.

In response to requests from international users, *AntConc* was modified to process all texts internally with the UTF8 'flavour' of the Unicode character set. More importantly, *AntConc* was revised to include two features not found in any other corpus tool that are essential for the smooth processing of international texts. First, a menu of options was added to seamlessly convert data in one of the legacy encodings, such as 'Shiftjis', into the UTF8 version of the Unicode character set. Users would then be able to use existing texts without external conversion tools. Users still need to know what legacy encoding their data is in. However, once this is established, processing English, Japanese, German, French or even Arabic, is effectively the same. Figure 6.4a shows *AntConc* processing a four-million word corpus of Japanese texts in an identical fashion to an English corpus.

A second and equally important feature was the introduction of a Unicode aware token definition menu (See Fig. 6.4b). As discussed earlier, defining what a word means in the context of a corpus study is an essential step which affects all other results (Scott and Tribble 2006). The word definition also affects how wildcards will work in a concordancer. Unfortunately, most of the standard tools

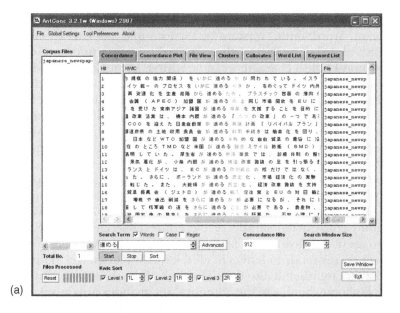

(a)

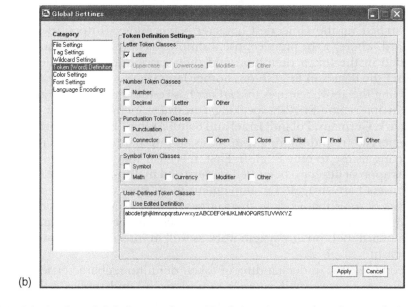

(b)

Figure 6.4 (a) *AntConc* 3.2.1 Concordance Tool showing results of a search for the Japanese translation of "recommend" in a Japanese corpus of newspaper articles. (b) The Unicode compliant token definition menu.

have remained fixed in an English paradigm when it comes to defining what a word means. WordSmith (version 4), for example, appears to include letters of the English alphabet as part of the standard token definition. However, it is not clear how non-English characters can be added. MonoConc Pro adopts a different approach. Here, the characters that are NOT to be included in the token definition, that is, word delimiters, need to be typed in directly. Again, for English and most European languages this is not a problem as there is significant overlap. However, adding non-token characters for every language of the world is impossible, especially considering that even Japanese has numerous punctuation marks, numerals and so on, that have no similarity to English.

In *AntConc*, characters that form the token definition can be specified directly. However, to deal with all the languages of the world, standard Unicode character sets can also be explicitly included in the token definition. Unicode character sets are carefully constructed subsets of the entire Unicode character set that corresponds to useful subdivisions of language we use in everyday life. For example, the 'Letter' set corresponds to letters in all the world's languages. This would include 'Aa' to 'Zz' in English, but also the characters of the three different writing systems found in Japanese. Similarly, the 'Number' set includes not only 0 to 9 for English, but also the representations for all the numbers in Japanese and other languages. These subsets are huge and so it is impossible to simply view them as we would normally view the alphabet in English. However, the sets are well documented and can be searched via the Unicode Character Name Index (http://www.unicode.org/standard/where/). In practice, users simply select different character sets to be included in the token definition and then carry out their studies regardless of whether the data is in English or another language.

Adding the above features to *AntConc* has resulted in the program being widely used in many non-English speaking countries, including Japan, China, Korea, Denmark, Germany, Poland, Israel and Saudi Arabia. Three important points have also emerged from designing *AntConc* as an international corpus tool rather than restricting its use to only English. First, it is clear that although the advantages of corpus approaches have been well understood in non-English speaking countries, many users have struggled to implement ideas from corpus research simply due to a lack of tools that work in their target language (McEnery and Wilson 2001). Moving to a different operating system has also not been an option since none of the standard tools on any system work as well in international contexts as they do in English.

Second, a clear understanding of token definition, character set and language encoding are necessary if we want to understand and replicate the results from corpus studies. However, the concepts are poorly understood by many researchers, teachers and students in the field. Our standard tools do not help either, sometimes using confusing terminology when referring to the concepts, and other times hiding the exact implementation of the concepts below the user interface. Even Microsoft Word adds to the problem when it refers to saving files in 'Unicode' format without making it explicit which 'flavour' of Unicode is being used. Without this knowledge, successfully loading files created in Microsoft Word into other software tools becomes an exercise in trial and error.

Finally, feedback from users suggests that successfully loading a file into a corpus tool is perhaps the most difficult step for them. All our software tools can hugely improve the experience by providing clearer guidance on token definition settings, character sets, language encodings and even font settings. The current interfaces and documentation of all the standard tools, including *AntConc*, are clearly insufficient.

6.4.3 Research, Teachers, or Learners?

AntConc has always been designed primarily for learners in a classroom environment. As a result, it is not surprising that many features and tools that have been added to the program since version 1.0 have been the direct result of feedback from teachers and learners. These include the addition of the distribution plot tool, the n-gram generator, search options in the word and keyword generator tools, and even more obscure features, such as the ability to sort KWIC concordance lines by character position from the start and end of a search word, in addition to the normal word position sort. (This feature was added at the request of a teacher who hoped to use the software in the teaching of spelling to German students.)

Other teachers have wanted to generate worksheets based on the results of corpus searches, and so have asked for editing features of KWIC concordance lines. In response, concordance lines in *AntConc* can now be easily extracted or deleted, and search terms can be hidden to allow the simple production of exercises where learners are supposed to guess the target word or phrase from the surrounding context. Another important feature of the program that was added at the request of an English teacher was the ability to adjust colours, font sizes and font styles so that learners would always be able to easily see the results of searches on a central projector in the classroom, regardless of the quality of the projector or their distance from the screen. It is surprising how few other tools offer such a useful feature for classroom use, demonstrating the importance of collaboration in tool design. Implementing a colour and font settings menu is trivial but it is highly unlikely that the feature would have been included in *AntConc* without the direct input from a classroom teacher.

As more and more researchers who need multiplatform, Unicode aware tools have started using *AntConc*, they have also begun requesting additional features. A commonly requested feature that was added to version 3.00 was the ability to handle annotated data, and produce lemma lists. There have also been requests to include more advanced statistical measures for the collocation tool, and options to save all the user modified settings. These requests have been met but with the understanding that the tool is still primarily designed for learners. As a result, some novel solutions have been devised. For example, annotated corpora can now be imported into the software and processed either with all tags visible, all tags hidden, or more usefully for learners, in a mixed mode where tag-based searches can be carried out with the software stripping the tags automatically from the hits to provide a clean and easy to understand set of results.

What is noticeable about the suggestions from expert researchers is that they are generally happy with the specialist tools they use to carry out highly complex corpus studies. Unlike other corpus users, they have no problem switching from one operating system to another to access a particular tool. They will also persevere with the idiosyncrasies, poor support, weak documentation and even bugs associated with their tools if the job can be eventually completed. The problem arises when they want to introduce new corpus techniques to novices, for example, in their graduate school corpus studies classes. It is here that the tools can become a heavy burden on students, slowing the pace of the class, and even restricting the amount and type of homework that can be issued due to licensing issues and platform restrictions. In these situations, a tool like *AntConc* can be valuable as it is designed for learners, but also includes a robust set of features for serious corpus work.

6.5 Discussion

In this chapter, I have argued that corpus tools are an essential but largely ignored component of corpus studies. In previous research, issues such as corpus size, sampling, balance and representativeness have received great attention, as have discussions on whether or not corpora should include part-of-speech and other annotation. Corpora have long been referred to as the 'tools' corpus linguists use to observe language in action, in a similar way to dictionaries and reference books. These discussions have drawn our attention away from the real tools of corpus studies, that is, the software applications that provide an interface between us and the huge sets of data stored on our computer hard disks.

The standard tools we use today certainly have many limitations and problems. If we hope to advance the field of contemporary corpus linguistics and develop new theories and models of language, we need to give software far more attention that it currently receives. We need to strive to improve our existing tools, and actively push for the creation of new ones. Biber et al. (1998) and Danielsson (2002) suggest one way to achieve this is for corpus linguists to develop their own programming skills. No doubt, having a grounding in programming is useful for anyone entering the field of corpus linguistics. However, in this chapter I have proposed that a more realistic and productive approach is for corpus linguists to work in collaboration with software developers to create new tools.

Of course, the software I have used to demonstrate the advantages of collaborative software development, *AntConc*, is certainly not a finished product. In fact, each week I receive numerous problem reports, requests and suggestions for improvements. What is important is that corpus linguists are able to participate in its development. If more corpus linguists become interested in software tools, and become proactive when it comes to improving existing tools and creating new ones, the future of all our tools and the field itself will be a very bright one. Using Stubbs's astronomy analogy one final time, by corpus linguists becoming proactive rather than reactive to software, our telescopes will be able to show us more stars and galaxies, let us see further into the depths of space, and perhaps even reveal to us the fundamental building blocks of the universe.

Compatibility Between Corpus Annotation Efforts and its Effect on Computational Linguistics

Adam Meyers

Many automatic analysers in Computational Linguistics follow the following pattern: (1) the system acquires statistics-based rules from manual annotation of a particular corpus; (2) on the basis of these data, the system can apply a similar analysis to new corpora. Participants in shared tasks typically produce these sorts of systems. For example, the Conference on Computational Natural Language Learning (CONNL), Automatic Content Extraction (ACE) and others provide participants with annotated corpora to train their systems and, then later (for a short time only), they provide participants with new data to test their systems. The availability of annotation determines the scope of phenomena covered by annotation-trained systems, the analyses assumed and the types of corpora represented. This chapter discusses evolving views of best practice, relating to: (1) the compatibility of the theoretical frameworks for annotation of the same or related phenomena; (2) the merge-ability of annotation of different phenomena into unified representations; and (3) choice of corpora. The chapter will also focus on how these issues relate to the linguistic content rather than the form of annotation.

7.1 Introduction

In the Computational Linguistics community, a division of labour exists between manual annotation of corpora and automatic statistics-based analysis. The annotators of corpora provide knowledge bases realized as particular analyses of particular phenomena for particular data. System developers train automatic systems on these data using machine learning. The resulting systems can analyse new data, modelled on the analyses found in the original annotation. Shared tasks are typically defined in terms of the annotation guidelines and annotation prepared according to those guidelines. For example, the Conference on Computational Natural Language Learning (CONNL)[1] X and XI tasks (2006 and 2007) involve modelling dependency analyses based on dependency-annotated data. The availability of annotation determines the scope of phenomena covered by annotation-trained systems, the analyses assumed and the types of corpora represented. The unavailability of corpora annotated with scope[2] information makes it difficult to create corpus-trained programs that analyse corpora with respect to the scope of quantifiers, negative adverbs and other lexical items. For example, parsers trained on the Wall Street Journal Section of the Penn Treebank (PTB) are notoriously better for parsing financial text than for parsing non-financial text (Ratnaparkhi 1999). Although annotation teams determine the phenomena being recorded, decisions such as the way the information is recorded, which corpora are used and so on will have major effects on the systems trained on their annotation.

This chapter discusses evolving views of best practice, relating to the linguistic content (not the physical form) of corpus annotation.[3] These issues include: (1) the compatibility of the theoretical frameworks for annotation of the same or related phenomena; (2) merge-ability of annotation of different phenomena into unified representations; and (3) choice of corpora.

7.2 The Desirability of Compatible Theories of Corpus Annotation

Different theoretical frameworks/theories underlie different corpus annotation schemata. These theories are indispensable sets of ideas which make the specifications and other annotation standards clear and consistent. An annotation schema for describing a particular phenomenon is only suitable for annotating a text if it can describe the full range of instantiations of that phenomenon in that text. Given this constraint, attempts at annotating the same phenomena in the same type of data often yield theories that can 'mostly' translate from one to the other. In other words, there is a constraint of descriptive adequacy on the set of possible theories, relative to samples of actual language.[4] This means that some theories may not be annotation-friendly (Minimalism, Optimality Theory, etc.) if descriptive adequacy is sacrificed at the expense of other properties (e.g. features of explanatory adequacy). Although some researchers claim that their annotation projects are 'theory neutral', what they seem to really mean is that they are adopting one of the descriptively adequate theories. It is also sometimes claimed that particular analyses are generally accepted by the community (i.e. they have become *de facto* standards) and that theory-neutral approaches favour such analyses. However, such claims are difficult to substantiate for two reasons: (1) consensus is difficult to quantify; and (2) the descriptive-adequacy constraint provides important reasons to reject particular 'standard' analyses when they are inadequate for describing particular data.

Sometimes different annotation schemata represent the same phenomenon for different languages or for different genres of text. These differences raise issues of portability for developers of systems who want to use this information from a number of different types of data.

System developers may also decide to train their systems on annotation from different sources so that their systems can benefit from different types of annotated information. Even putting aside differences in the format of encoding, annotation schemata that have different underlying theories may not be easy to integrate together.

In Meyers et al. (2006), compatibility issues were explored by 22 participants from around the world. That paper discusses compatibility issues between alternative specifications of parts of speech, syntax, coreference, gap filling, predicate argument relations, temporal relations and other factors. In the next section, we will focus on one such issue: the difference between dependency and phrase structure approaches and how it relates to the same-phenomenon/different schemata problem. Then, in Section 7.4, we will discuss the problem of merging different information sources, in the context of the encoding of predicate argument structure.

7.3 Phrase Structure and Dependency Approaches to Treebanking

Syntactic treebanks, representations of the syntactic analysis of natural language corpora, currently adopt some version of either a phrase structure or dependency grammar approach. Under the phrase structure approach, sentences are describable as trees constructed by recursive applications of phrase structure rules, rules of the form:

$$\textbf{XP} \rightarrow \textbf{AB} \ldots \textbf{C}$$

where XP, representing the left hand side of the rule, is a nonterminal symbol and symbols on the right hand side can either be terminal symbols (leaves of the tree) or nonterminal symbols (internal nodes of the tree). For example, a phrase structure analysis of the NP *John read a nice book* might be the tree in Fig. 7.1, derived by applications of the following rules:[5]

$$S \rightarrow NP \ VP$$
$$VP \rightarrow V \ NP$$
$$NP \rightarrow (D) \ (A) \ N$$

In contrast, a dependency analysis of this same sentence is provided as Fig. 7.2. In a dependency analysis, binary directional relations between the words in the

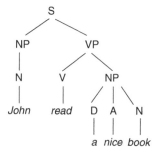

Figure 7.1 Phrase Structure: *John read a nice book.*

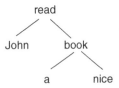

Figure 7.2 Dependency Structure: *John read a nice book.*

sentence are assumed. These relations, when realized as directed edges, are typically assumed to form a rooted, directed graph, usually a tree (the edges in dependency graphs are often labelled with grammatical relations, e.g. SBJ, OBJ, etc.)

Theories that assume a phrase structure analysis usually assume that most phrases have a special constituent called the *head* which determines the phrasal category and other properties of that phrase that are important for semantic selection, morphological agreement and the like For several reasons (as we will discuss), few phrase-structure-based annotation schemata explicitly mark the heads of phrases. Nevertheless, we will begin our discussion of conversion between phrase structure and dependency analyses with the following idealizations: (i) every phrase has a head (not just most phrases); and (ii) it is possible to uniquely identify the head of a phrase. With these assumptions Fig. 7.1 can be replaced with Fig. 7.3, where the head arcs are explicitly marked. Based on this, we propose the initial rule in Fig. 7.4 for converting back and forth from a phrasal to a dependency representation.

Note that the rule in Fig. 7.4 does not adequately handle the VP in Fig. 7.3. In Dependency frameworks, it is typically assumed that all dependency relations are between words and, furthermore, arguments depend on heads – the edges in Fig. 7.2 connect each head word to each of its argument words.[6] In contrast, phrase structure theories assume that heads can be either words or phrases. For example, VP is marked as the head of the S in Fig. 7.3. Since phrases do not exist in most Dependency frameworks,[7] true compatibility would require us to flatten phrase structure analyses so that only leaves can be heads, as in Fig. 7.5, or assume that

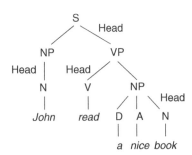

Figure 7.3 Headed Phrase Structure: *John read a nice book.*

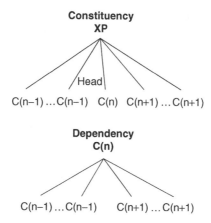

Figure 7.4 Dependency ↔ Constituency.

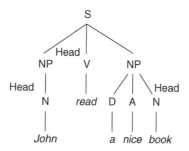

Figure 7.5 Flat Headed Phrase Structure: *John read a nice book.*

something is lost in conversion from phrase structure to dependency structure, for example, assuming that the edge labelled *Head* in Fig. 7.4 can be a path of edges, each edge labelled *Head.*

In summary, the differences between phrase structure and dependency that make information-preserving conversion difficult are as follows:

1. Dependency analyses assume that a set of head-argument relations between words can be created that completely cover a sentence.
2. Although phrase structure does not include a representation of the head of a phrase, many phrase structure-based theories define *heads* for at least a subset of phrases. However, the phrase structure version of *head* is assumed to be either a word or a phrase, rather than just a word. The phrase-as-head idea has no clear correlate in dependency analyses.

Therefore dependency analyses have one additional type of information (head-identification) and phrase structure analyses can have one additional piece of information (phrasal heads). Conversion routines must either use heuristics to deduce these pieces of information or lose this information during conversion.

7.3.1 Assumptions about Heads

While it is extremely useful to identify the head in most cases, there are well-known problems with assuming that every phrase has a head or that all dependency relations are between heads and arguments.

First of all, there are several cases for which the identity of the head is confusing due to the occurrence of closed class items with little semantic content. While some theories assume the closed class items are the head, others assume that content words near the closed class items are the heads. For example, consider the bracketed subordinate clause *John said [that Mary can leave]*. Penn Treebank's theory (Marcus et al. 1994) assumes the following structure: (*SBAR that* (*S Mary can leave*)).[8] Penn's framework is compatible with both an interpretation in which *that* is the head of the SBAR and an interpretation in which the *S* is the head. Furthermore, in finding the head of the *S*, theories vary as to whether the modal *can* or the verb *leave* are to be considered as the head. Closed class items that cause this confusion in English include: complementizers, modals, auxiliary verbs, the infinitival *to*, prepositions, subordinate conjunctions, and adverbial modifiers of prepositions. These sorts of cases make it difficult to convert between dependency and phrase structure analyses. Suppose that you are converting back and forth between a particular phrase structure analysis (e.g. the analysis assumed in the PTB) and a particular dependency analysis (e.g. the analysis assumed in the Kyoto Corpus[9]). Before writing any conversion procedures, you must first: (1) select a set of head choosing heuristics that are compatible with the phrase structure analysis; and (2) determine which of these analyses is compatible with the assumptions of the dependency analysis.

There are also many constructions that do not seem to have heads at all.[10] For example, it would seem to be inappropriate to choose a head in coordinate structures, such as (*NP* (*NP the book*) *and* (*NP the pencil*)). Nevertheless, dependency grammars usually do choose a head, typically either the conjunction (*and*) or the head of the first conjunct (*book*).

Finding the head of a proper noun phrase (a name) is complicated by the fact that there does not seem to be any standard definition of a name. Even ignoring this problem, treatment of names is difficult to standardize. One approach is to assume that a name is a word that contains spaces, in which case the whole name is its own head, that is, *John Smith* is treated as a single word. However, this does not seem to be standard practice. For example, many named entity guidelines, for example Chinchor and Robinson (1998), stipulate that the extent of *Dr. John Smith III* does not include the title *Dr.*, but does include the first, middle and last name, as well as any post honorifics or similar modifiers (*Jr., Ph.D.* or *III*). Furthermore, without clear guidelines, it is unclear how to treat names that take the form of noun phrases. In other words, is the phrase *The Association of Computational Linguistics* to be treated as a 'word with spaces' or should we assume that *Association* is the head? The answer really depends on specifications. The conversion procedure would need to account for the specifications for both the phrase structure and dependency analyses assumed for all these kinds of cases.

Numerous other types of phrases requiring special considerations for determining the head include: comparatives (*John ate more than Fred*), range expressions (*from five to ten*), verb particle constructions (*call up*), idiomatic expressions (*pull strings, at all*), complex prepositions (*with respect to*), number expressions (*one hundred twenty*), dates (*January 3, 1905*) and times (*5 o'clock AM*). In all these cases, it is necessary to understand the underlying assumptions of both the dependency analyses and the phrase structure analyses in order to convert accurately between them. Furthermore, in cases where this sort of detail is missing from the phrase structure analysis, one must be able to identify the head that the dependency analysis would choose by means of a set of rules, perhaps heuristic ones.

7.3.2 Why are there Nested Heads in Phrase Structure?

When a phrase consists of a head word and some other set of constituents, this can be represented in a dependency structure as dependencies between the head word and each of the heads of the sister phrases (by the method of conversion described above). However, when the head of a phrase is itself assumed to be a phrase, it is unclear how to represent this embedding in a dependency framework. For example, the bracketing (*NP the* (*NBAR big* (*NBAR green cat*))), arguably suggests that the green cat in question is big rather than merely describing a cat that is both big and green. Similarly, the following bracketing arguably represents that the relative clause in (*NP* (*NP the red book*) (*SBAR that was destroyed*)) modifies the NP *the red book*, rather than the head word *book*. These sorts of distinctions do not arise in every phrase structure analysis. Furthermore, dependency theories such as that of the Prague Dependency Treebank[11] can represent this sort of distinction by ordering dependencies, for example, representing that the dependency between *green* and *cat* takes precedence over the one between *big* and *cat* in the example above. Accurate conversion requires that these assumptions be made explicit.

Most phrase structure analyses assume (for some languages) that a verb phrase is (essentially) the head of the sentence. The VP analysis has a long theoretical history. One argument is that a VP constituent is required in order to fill certain gaps, for example, *John did* (*VP eat a sandwich*)$_i$, *but Mary didn't* (*VP e$_i$*). Another common argument is that different VPs with the same verb impose different selection restrictions on their subject, e.g., both *the robotic arm* and *Fred* can be the subject of the VP *threw the ball*, but only *Fred* can felicitously be the subject of the VP *threw the party* (Marantz 1984). This is not intended as an endorsement or rejection of a VP analysis. However, the existence of these views are relevant to this discussion because a VP analysis is not representable in most dependency frameworks.

7.3.3 Existing Conversion Programs and Proposed Constraints

The problems discussed above can most efficiently be solved by means of careful specification. Special attention should be placed on defining what the head of a phrase is and what to do when a phrase should be classified as not having a head. One should always convert a particular theory of phrase structure to a particular theory of dependency structure, where the definition of *head* is made clear in both theories.

Xia and Palmer (2001) describe a procedure for converting phrase structure to dependency structure by means of a set of heuristic rules. While consistent, these rules have a number of counter-intuitive consequences: the final constituent is the head of a date or name, for example, *29* is the head of the NP *Nov. 29* and *Smith* is the head of *John Smith*. It would seem that similar unexpected results should occur for other examples of headless phrases because the set of heuristics do not specifically account for the types of phrases that are actually headless. In contrast, Hockenmaier and Steedman (2007) give a detailed account of the conversion of the PTB into a Combinatory Categorial Grammar (CCG) treebank, representable in terms of both phrase structure and dependencies. That approach relied on various Categorial Grammar-based lexical resources and Categorial Grammar-based definitions of syntactic dependency. The theory of Categorial Grammar provides a basis for making determinations of dependencies that are intuitive as well as consistent. Hockenmaier (2006) provides an account of a similar conversion of the German Tiger dependency corpus into a similar Categorial Grammar-based representation. Although this paper describes a Categorial Grammar-based phrase structure account, it would seem that the techniques described in Hockenmaier and Steedman (2007) could be applied and a dependency analysis could be generated as well. The existence of a consistent theory (like CCG) as a guide is an extremely important factor in making it possible to do a number of such conversions.

7.4 A la Carte Approaches and the Merging of Annotation

We will now lay out two approaches to annotation: the *single-theory* approach and the *a la carte* approach. *Single-theory* approaches are taken by corpus annotation research groups who annotate a corpus with a complex of information organized according to a single theoretical framework, for example, The Tübingen Treebank of Written German,[12] the Czech Dependency Treebank and the Kyoto Corpus Treebank. New information that is added to these corpora are incorporated into the old data structures to produce new, more complete versions of the annotation (and perhaps an updated version of the theories that includes the new phenomenon). In contrast, under the *a la carte* approach, new linguistic phenomena are annotated separately, by research groups who do not necessarily share the same theoretical views. Under the single-theory approach, it is easy for users of the annotated corpus to see how the different types of information fit together because the annotation of all the information is specifically designed to be interconnecting.

Under the *a la carte* approach, annotation researchers can focus on describing a single phenomenon well, without worrying how their description of the new phenomenon can be worked into an existing theory. However, it is up to the users of the annotation to determine how (or if) the different types of annotation inter-relate. While both annotation strategies have been fruitful, one can characterize the single-theory approaches as providing large comprehensive resources and the *a la carte* approaches as producing smaller, more diverse resources, covering a wider variety of linguistic phenomena.

This section discusses some research undertaken at New York University (NYU) to merge several a la carte style linguistic resources in order to produce a simulated single-theory analysis using the Grammatical and Logical Argument Representation Framework, aka GLARF (Meyers et al. 2001*a*, 2001*b*; Meyers et al. 2002). GLARF has been used as part of several information extraction efforts (Zhao et al. 2004; Shinyama and Sekine 2006) at NYU. GLARF has also provided predicate argument information for NYU's Automatic Content Extraction (ACE)[13] system for the past few years.

7.4.1 The Unified Linguistic Annotation Project

Researchers at New York University, the University of Pennsylvania, the University of Colorado, the University of Pittsburgh and Brandeis University are collaborating to produce unified linguistic annotations, consisting of merged representations of annotation produced for the following schemata (and possibly others): PTB, PropBank, NomBank, Penn Discourse Treebank, TimeML and Pittsburgh Opinion Annotation (Wilson and Wiebe 2005). Cooperation between these groups includes: (1) the annotation of a common corpus, a part of which is distributable without licensing restrictions (cf. Section 7.5); and (2) research on merging the annotation (Pustejovsky et al. 2005; Verhagen et al. 2007).

Developers of many current applications (Question Answering, Information Extraction, etc.) typically tune their systems to very few sources of annotated data. Some systems only tune to the data modelling the task itself. The use of additional sources of annotation, for example, part of speech, phrase structure, and the like, each involve incorporating a different source of information and a different format of annotation input data. Systems that model these phenomena can be trained on different training sets (depending on what has been tagged already) and systems that have been trained by other people can also be used (e.g. the Charniak 2001 parser). Each automatic processor will need to be run on test data. In order to incorporate these data sources into the final analysis, the system developer will need to have a way to process the format and should understand the content of the output provided by each processor. A minimal step towards solving these problems would be to find a common format for representing all the annotations, for example, LAF (Linguistic Annotation Format – an ISO standard; Ide and Romary 2007) or UIMA (Unstructured Information Management Architecture; Verhagen et al. 2007).[14] Let us call these 'weak' merging approaches. In contrast, the GLARF approach that will be described in the next section can be viewed as 'aggressive' because the input sets of annotation are forced to be compatible with each other, that is, annotation is changed at the discretion of the merging procedures. Essentially, aggressive merging derives single-theory representation from *a la carte* annotation input.

Under both approaches, system developers should find it easier to incorporate multiple sources of hand-coded information into their machine learning applications. Since all schemata are in the same basic format, incorporating new types of annotated information should take less effort than before. Aggressive merging approaches go one step further than weak merging approaches because they force all annotated information to fit into a general theoretical framework. This may mean that some annotation (automatic or hand-coded) will be changed in the process. Thus developers of the aggressive merging system instil their own theoretical biases into the resulting merged representation. It also means that the resulting data will be more internally consistent and, therefore, the chances of finding conflicting predictions from the annotation should be reduced. This is especially important for the creation of systems with a large number of components. For example, developers creating systems for participation in the US Government's ACE and Global Autonomous Language Exploitation programs[15] have had a difficult time trying to integrate components assuming different tokenizations, constituency structures, heads of phrases, and so on. Integration of components is much easier when these theoretical decisions are forced into uniformity.

7.4.2 Merging Annotation in GLARF

Consider the following (simplified) annotations based on four different schemes for the sentence: *Meanwhile, they made three bids*:

- Penn Discourse Treebank
  o *Meanwhile: ARG1 = Previous S, ARG2 = current S*
- PropBank
  o *made: ARG0 = they, ARG1 = three bids*
- NomBank
  o *bids: ARG0 = they, Support = made*
- Penn Treebank
  o *(S (ADVP (RB Meanwhile)) (, ,)*
    (NP (PRP they))
    (VP (VBN made)
    (NP (CD three)
    (NNS bids))) (. .))*

PropBank (Palmer et al. 2005), NomBank (Meyers et al. 2004) and the Penn Discourse Treebank (Miltsakaki et al. 2004) are three projects for annotating the predicate argument structure, respectively, of verbs, nouns and discourse connectives. PropBank and NomBank use a lexicon to define numbered arguments ARG0, ARG1, . . ., ARGN. In addition, certain other items are annotated as ARGMs (mostly modifiers such as temporal adverbials). The Penn Discourse Treebank uses a similar annotation (just ARG1 and ARG2) for discourse connectives, lexical items that join together two clauses (subordinate/coordinate conjunctions, conjunctive adverbials, etc.). All three of these presuppose much (but not all) of the constituency structure as marked in the PTB. The GLARF-based system merges all these annotations into (a more complicated version of) the following typed feature structure,[16] which represents a phrase structure analysis:

```
(S (ADV (ADVP (HEAD (ADVX (HEAD (RB Meanwhile))
        (P-ARG1 (S (EC-TYPE PB) (INDEX 0+0)))
        (P-ARG2 (S (EC-TYPE PB) (INDEX 0)))))
            (INDEX 1)))
(PUNCTUATION (, ,))
(SBJ (NP (HEAD (PRP they)) (INDEX 2)))
(PRD (VP (HEAD (VX (HEAD (VBN made))
        (P-ARG0 (NP (EC-TYPE PB) (INDEX 2)))
        (P-ARG1 (NP (EC-TYPE PB) (INDEX 4)))
        (P-ARGM-TMP (ADVP (EC-TYPE PB) (INDEX 1)))
        (INDEX 3)))
    (OBJ (NP (T-POS (CD three))
        (HEAD (NX (HEAD (NNS bids))
            (P-ARG0-SUPP (NP (EC-TYPE PB) (INDEX 2)))
            (SUPPORT (VX (EC-TYPE PB) (INDEX 3)))))
        (INDEX 4)))))
(PUNCTUATION (. .)) (SENT-NUM 1) (INDEX 0))
```

The structure of the GLARF representation assumes a typed feature structure according to the following rules:

$$\text{TFS} \rightarrow \text{ATOM}$$
$$\text{TFS} \rightarrow \text{PART-OF-SPEECH WORD}$$
$$\text{TFS} \rightarrow \text{TYPE FV}_1 \text{ FV}_2 \ldots \text{FV}_N$$
$$\text{FV} \rightarrow \text{FEATURE TFS}$$

In the above typed feature structure, types are phrasal categories like *S, ADVP* and *VP*.
Features can be:

- Grammatical roles (*SBJ, OBJ,* etc.)
- P-Features: PropBank/NomBank/PDTB features (*P-ARG0, P-ARG1,* etc.)
- Other attributes such as SENT-NUM and INDEX

Grammatical roles and P-Features are used to represent the linguistic relations between phrases and/or words. SENT-NUM is a feature used to indicate the sentence number (sentences in a file are numbered sequentially starting with zero). INDEX is a feature used to indicate binding between empty categories and phrases. For example, the NP *they*, bearing an index of 2, is the ARG0 of *made* and *bids*, as indicated by the empty categories that are sisters to these words in the feature structure. The whole sentence has an index of 0 and is therefore the ARG2 of *meanwhile*. Note that the index *0+0* indicates that the ARG1 of *meanwhile* is the first sentence in this file. The *0* before the plus sign points to sentence number 0 (the first sentence), the *0* after the plus sign indicates the index of that sentence (indices of other phrases in that sentence would be *0+1*, *0+2*, etc.). By convention, whole sentences are always assigned the index *0*. As the current sentence is sentence number 1 (see the feature SENT-NUM in the TFS), sentence 0 is the previous sentence, as one might expect when finding arguments of an adverb like *meanwhile*.

The GLARF program can also convert the above feature structure into a dependency-style analysis, represented as tuples. For expository purposes the 23-tuples currently used have been simplified to 9-tuples as follows:

ADV | ADV | TMP | made | 139 | VBN | Meanwhile | 123 | RB TMP
PUNCTUATION | PUNCTUATION | NIL | made | 139 | VBN |, | 132 |,
SBJ | SBJ | ARG0 | made | 139 | VBN | they | 134 | PRP
PUNCTUATION | PUNCTUATION | NIL | made | 139 | VBN |.| 154 |.
OBJ | OBJ | ARG1 | made | 139 | VBN | bids | 149 | NNS
T-POS | T-POS | NIL | bids | 149 | NNS | three | 143 | CD
NIL | NIL | ARG1 | Meanwhile | 123 | RB TMP | took | 57 | VBN
NIL | NIL | ARG2 | Meanwhile | 123 | RB TMP | made | 139 | VBN
NIL | NIL | ARG0 | bids | 149 | NNS | they | 134 | VBN
NIL | NIL | SUPPORT | bids | 149 | NNS | made | 139 | VBN

The first three fields on each line indicate the relations between the words in the fourth and seventh fields. The other fields provide details about these words. For example, there are three relations listed in the tuples as occurring between the words *made* and *they*: a logical and surface SBJ relation, as well as a PropBank ARG0 relation (logical and surface SBJ relations are different for all regularizations and gap filling constructions, e.g., passive, relative clauses, etc.). The last four lines indicate relations that are specific to PropBank and PDTB, for example, the ARG2 of *meanwhile* is taken to be the matrix verb of the sentence and the ARG1 is taken to be the matrix verb of the previous sentence. As we will discuss, recording annotation in this dependency notation avoids many of the compatibility issues discussed below.

The GLARF program adds GLARF regularizations (Meyers et al. 2001*a*, 2001*b*) to the PTB II and merges in the following other annotations: (1) PropBank 1.0; (2) NomBank 0.91; (3) The overt relations of the Penn Discourse Treebank (PDTB);[17] and (4) Named Entity annotation of this corpus created at BBN Technologies and distributed through the Linguistic Data Consortium at the University of Pennsylvania.[18]

7.4.3 Merging Compatibility Issues

The merging procedure is simplest if each component assumes the same break-down of the sentence into constituents and tokens. However, some differences in breakdowns are easier to resolve than others. In comparing pairs of annotation schemata, one annotation sometimes breaks down the constituents of the other into subconstituents or subtokens. In such cases, we usually choose the schemata that assumes more constituents, assuming that this analysis is a more fine-grained version of the other. In each of the following cases, one annotation scheme adds subconstituents to the PTB, such that the merged GLARF analysis contains these subconstituents. The round brackets represent PTB constituents and the square brackets represent constituents added due to another annotation scheme.[19] Both NomBank and Named Entity Annotation provide evidence for adding pronominal constituents, constituents that are known to be underspecified in PTB specifica-tions. In the case of the Penn Discourse Treebank (PDTB) there is a general rule that can derive many of the added constituents. In the PTB a subordinate conjunc-tion clause is typically a sister to the subject and predicate of the sentence. The PDTB often marks the rest of the sentence (NP + VP) as a single argument of the discourse connective. The merging procedure merely adds an S that covers these subconstituents. In the resulting phrase structure, the sentence is an S con-sisting of the SBAR subordinate conjunction phrase and a lower S. The resulting adjunction structure is standard in many theories.

- Nombank
  - *(NP [NP cotton and acetate] fibers)*
  - *(NP [NP lung cancer] deaths)*
- BBN NE annotation
  - *(NP [NP Republican] [NP Rudolph Giuliani]'s)*
  - *(NP its (UCP Canadian and [NP United Kingdom]) headquarters)*
- Penn Discourse Treebank
  - *(S (SBAR although (S preliminary findings suggest one thing))*
    [S (NP the latest results) (VP suggest something else)])

Similarly, in the following example, BBN NE annotation marks U.S. and Japan as distinct NEs in the phrase *U.S.-Japan relations.* The NE annotation thus assumes that this 'word' constituent is further broken down into 'subwords', as follows:

(NP (NP [NNP U.S.] [HYPH -] [NNP Japan]) (NNS relations)).

In some cases, the constituent/token boundaries assumed by one annotation crosses the boundaries assumed in another. In these cases, an aggressive merging program must choose between conflicting constituents. In principle, this can be done on a case by case basis with a human adjudicator choosing between alternatives and changing one or the other annotations accordingly. Of course, the human adjudicator would have to follow strict guidelines in order to maintain consistency. Rather than engaging in this laborious endeavour, automatic rules were implemented in the GLARF system, based on knowledge of the input annotation schemata. By default, the PTB analysis of phrase structure is favoured. However, there were exceptions. For tokenization, the PTB annotation on the Wall Street Journal (WSJ) corpus did not include the breaking up of hyphenated words. In some subsequent annotation, PTB does break words at hyphens. Thus when named entity annotation assumes constituents that violate the WSJ corpus's tokenization on this basis, the GLARF-based unified representation assumes the analysis from the NE annotation as shown:

- PTB Phrase Structure: *(ADJP (JJ New) (JJ York-based))*
- Altered based on BBN NE Annotation:
    (ADJP (NP (NNP NEW) (NNP York)) (HYPH -) (VBN based))

It is not clear that all types of annotation can be merged together in this way. For example, syntactic phrases and intonation phrases cross under most current accounts. The same holds for syntactic phrases and theme-rheme structure. This chapter does not claim that all annotation need be compatible, but merely that there is a benefit to making annotation compatible when one can do so in a principled way. Thus, whenever possible, incompatibilities between the units assumed should be settled by rules. In this vein, Hockenmaier and Steedman (2007) note changes from the PTB's analysis of small clauses to Categorial Grammar's analysis. During the 1970s and 1980s, there were extensive arguments about whether the bracketed NP in sentences like *I consider [John] to be my friend* is part of the matrix clause (Rosenbaum 1967; Postal 1974; Postal and Pullum 1988) like CCGBank or part of the subordinate clause (Chomsky 1980, 1981) like the PTB. Given that these sentences involve very specific structures (often licensed by particular verbs),[20] conversion from one analysis to another is straightforward. Thus adopting a different analysis than input annotation for these instances would not be too difficult (as well as being reversible). It is in this spirit that the GLARF program attempts to solve incompatibilities between the constituents assumed by PropBank, NomBank and the PDTB on the one hand and the PTB on the other.

It is very common for a phrase *X* to modify a phrase *Y*, where *Y* contains *X*. We will refer to this as the *self-phrase* issue. For example, the parenthetical phrase *John imagined* is assumed to modify the sentence containing it in *The cow, John imagined, could jump over the moon.* In PropBank annotation, the sentence minus the parenthetical phrase would be marked as the ARG1 of *imagined*, that is, the concatenation of the NP *The cow* and the VP *could jump over the moon*, two phrases which do not form a constituent in the PTB. In PTB, an empty category bound to the matrix sentence would be a sister to the verb *imagined*, that is, the empty category is bound to a phrase that contains itself. A similar analysis is assumed in the GLARF-ULA, that is, the matrix clause including the modifier should be the ARG1 of *imagined*. However, the following stipulation is assumed:

- Given an argument phrase *A* of a predicate *P* such that *P* is a descendant of *A*,
  - *Find P+, the immediate child of A that contains P.*
  - *Assume that P+ is excluded from A.*

This child *P+* is the *self phrase*, the phrase that is subtracted from the argument to obtain an interpretation that is not self-referential. This analysis allows for a simple representation of argument structure for PropBank, NomBank and PDTB and is derivable by a simple, generally applicable procedure. Examples from Prop-Bank, NomBank and PDTB follow, where the predicate is indicated in bold and the broken up arguments are indicated as discontinuous arguments in the form: *ARG1a, ARG1b,* . . . The original analysis is indicated assigning some set of con-stituents to ARG1 or ARG2. Under self-phrase analyses, however, the entire sen-tences would fill these argument roles.

- PTB + PropBank
  - *(S-1 (NP (DT The) (NN cow))/ARG1a*
    (PRN
    (,,)
    (S (NP (NNP *John*)) /ARG0

    (VP (VBD **imagined**)
    (SBAR (-NONE- 0)

    (S (-NONE- *T*-1)))))
    (,,))
    (VP (VBD *jumped*)
    (PP (IN *over*) (NP (DT *the*) (NN *moon*))))/ARG1b
    (..))
  - *ARG1 of imagined = The cow + jumped right over the moon*
- PTB + NomBank
  - *(S (NP (DT The) (NN legislation))/ARG1a*

    (VP (VBD *was*)/ARG1b
    (VP (VBN *introduced*)/ARG1c
    (PP (IN *at*) (NP (PRP$ *their*)/ARG0 (NN *request*))))))
  - *ARG1 of request = The legislation + was + introduced*
- PTB + PDTB:
  - *(S (NP (DT The) (NN company))/ARG2a*

    (ADVP (RB *also*))
    (VP (VBD *disclosed*)
    (SBAR (WHNP-1 (WP *what*))
    (S (NP (PRP *it*))

(VP (VBD *did*)
    (VP (-NONE- *T*-1))))))/ARG2a
)
o *ARG2 of also = The company + disclosed what it did*

7.4.4 How can Annotation Researchers Facilitate Merging?

The ease with which *a la carte* annotation schemata can be merged with each other seems to be governed by several factors. Annotation is easier to merge if annotation researchers borrow specifications from other annotation schemata or focus their annotation to exclude specifications that are not relevant to the phenomenon they are annotating.

Also, more focused annotation might help. For example, in the dependency representation of the GLARF-ULA, there are no conflicting phrase structure boundaries, although there may be some tokenization conflicts. Thus dependency representations of NomBank, PropBank and PDTB might be preferable to phrase-based ones, as they focus entirely on predicate-argument relations, leaving constituency issues to other annotation efforts. This view would suggest a division of labour among the *a la carte* annotation schemata in which PropBank, NomBank and PDTB were deferring completely to PTB, NE annotation, and perhaps others, for phrase structure.

It may not be possible to build in compatibility along the lines proposed in this section for every type of annotation. Theories being assumed may be incompatible with previous approaches. In addition, accurate descriptions of some sets of phenomena may necessarily entail conflicting analyses. As mentioned above, the well-known differences between syntactic constituency, intonation phrases and theme-rheme structure are probably just facts of life. However, in all these cases, it would be helpful if the annotation specifications included a discussion of these factors to aid both those researchers who would like to merge annotation and those system developers who would like to use annotation from multiple sources in their applications.

7.5 Choosing Corpora for Multiple Annotations

It has become increasingly clear that there is added value in annotating the same corpus with different annotation schemata. The preceding sections of this paper have suggested at least two reasons for this: (1) if two research groups annotate the same corpus with similar information, the multiply annotated corpus can become a testing ground for the comparison of the two underlying frameworks, that is, to figure out how one schema translates into the other; and (2) if several research groups annotate the same corpus with different information, the multiply annotated corpus can become a testing ground for procedures for merging the annotation schemata into a single representation. Meyers et al. (2007) describe an effort which attempts to organize annotation researchers around a shared corpus, beginning with a 40,000 word piece of the ULA corpus (cf. Section 7.4.1).

An ideal corpus to share would have the following properties:

1. It would be diverse, including many different genres (fiction, news, advertisements, correspondence) and modalities (written, spoken). It would include a wide range of linguistic phenomena and lexical items.
2. There would be parallel or comparable corpora available in other languages.
3. The corpus would be available in a standard format (standard mark-up, headers, character encoding, etc.).
4. The corpus would be in the public domain or its usage would be governed by a very permissive licence.

Unfortunately, there are no corpora that we are aware of which fit all of the above criteria. Meyers et al. (2007) discuss the progress of our working group in preparing such a corpus. At the meeting where that report was presented, it was agreed that a 40K subcorpus of the American National Corpus (Ide and Macleod 2001; Ide and Suderman 2004, 2006; Reppen this volume) which is being adopted by the ULA project would be a starting point for developing a larger shared corpus. In addition, there was some discussion of translating this corpus into other languages. The 40K ULA corpus consists of:[21]

- Spoken Language
  - *Charlotte: 5K words*
  - *Switchboard: 5K words*
- Letters: 10K words
- Slate (Journal): 5K words
- Travel guides: 5K words
- 911report: 5K words
- OUP books (Kaufman): 5K words

The ULA corpus is therefore fairly diverse and is freely distributable under the Open American National Corpus (OANC) licence. This licence should be distinguished from the GNU[22] document licence or various Creative Commons Share-Alike licences in that the OANC licence is not viral, that is, the OANC licence does not require that derivative works be placed under the same licence. It should be noted that until the legal implications of GNU and Creative Commons licences are better understood, corpora released under such licences will not be considered ideal for annotation (e.g. WikipediaXML,[23] a corpus of Wikipedia data).[24] There are also plans for the 40K corpus to be translated into other languages.

7.6 The Future of Corpus Annotation

The summer of 2007 marked the birth of SIGANN, A Special Interest Group (SIG) of the Association for Computational Linguistics (ACL). The creation of SIGANN was the culmination of several different annual annotation workshops over the years. The final merged workshop was held at ACL 2007 and was called the Linguistic Annotation Workshop ('The LAW'). Previous workshops included: Natural Language Processing and XML; Frontiers in Linguistically Annotated Corpora; Frontiers in Corpus Annotation; and Linguistically Interpreted Corpora. Over the years, members of the corpus annotation community met regularly at these workshops to discuss issues of best practice including the sort of issues raised above. We hope that SIGANN will help usher in an era of greater coordination among annotation efforts.

The SIGANN website http://www.cs.vassar.edu/sigann/ was launched during the Fall of 2007, approximately at the time of this writing. The official version of the 40K ULA corpus (and other shared corpora) will be made available on that website. In addition, we will maintain a repository for hand-annotation and machine-annotation of this corpus, annotation guidelines, and other information that will aid in cooperation between annotation research groups.

7.7 Concluding Remarks

This chapter supports the view that a greater degree of coordination among annotation research groups would vastly improve the utility and accuracy of annotation. Specifically, the content of different annotations can be made more compatible with each other if the factors discussed above are taken into account. Furthermore, it has been suggested that the annotation of the same shared, freely distributable documents will facilitate cooperation and comparison of annotation.

Acknowledgements

Much of the research discussed in this chapter was supported by the National Science Foundation, award CNS-0551615, entitled *Towards a Comprehensive Linguistic Annotation of Language.*

Notes

1 http://www.ifarm.nl/signll/conll/.
2 The scope of quantifiers, negation, verbs of *belief* etc. refers to how features of these items interact when there are more than one of them. For example, the following sentence could be ambiguous: *Every dog loves some cat.* If *every* has wider scope than *some*, than for each dog d, there is a cat c, such that d loves c. Under the interpretation where *some* has wider scope, there is a single cat, e.g., *Fred the cat*, such that all dogs love that cat (*Fred*). In the hypothetical annotation, the scope for each such item would be marked for the text. For example *some* presumably takes wide scope given the pair of sentences: *Every dog loves some cat. That cat is sitting right here.*

3 We are specifically ignoring issues about the physical encoding of annotation. For example, there will be no discussion of whether to annotate text by editing the input document to include the annotation (inline annotation) or to annotate using external documents that point to parts of the text being annotated (offset annotation), whether to use XML (eXtensible Markup Language) and if so, which standard of XML. For more information on that area of research, see for example, Ide and Romary (2007) and the sources cited there.

4 In principle, a theory underlying annotation used for a sublanguage (medical language, legal language, etc.) may have different properties than that used for annotating newspaper text, even if both annotation schemata are for representing the same phenomenon.

5 Parentheses mean that symbols are optional. Thus the third rule is equivalent to the set of four rules derived by explicitly representing the presence and absence of each symbol in parentheses.

6 In some Dependency Grammar traditions the edges are drawn in the reverse direction: from argument word to head word.

7 The framework described in Shaumyan (1977) is unusual in that it assumes both phrases and dependencies.

8 SBARs in the PTB (and early Chomskian theories) consist of two items: (a) a subordinate conjunction, complementizer or relative pronoun; and (b) a sentence.

9 Kurohashi and Nagao (1997).

10 Some linguistic frameworks, notably Head Driven Phrase Structure Grammar, explicitly distinguish headed phrases from non-headed phrases.

11 http://ufal.mff.cuni.cz/pdt/.

12 http://www.sfs.uni-tuebingen.de/en_tuebadz.shtml.

13 http://www.nist.gov/speech/tests/ace/.

14 For more information on UIMA, cf. www.research.ibm.com/UIMA/.

15 http://www.nist.gov/speech/tests/ace/index.htm and http://projects.ldc.upenn. edu/gale/.

16 Features structures are used in many contemporary linguistic theories. The ones employed by GLARF are perhaps most similar to those of Head Driven Phrase Structure Grammar (Pollard and Sag 1994).

17 In the PDTB, overt relations are relations anchored by lexical items (coordinate and subordinate conjunctions, conjunctive adverbs, etc.). Covert links between sentences will be merged into the representation in future work.

18 There are future plans to merge in TimeML, Opinion annotation, as well as PDTB's covert relations between sentences.

19 There are some exceptions. For example, person names like *Dr. John Smith III* are often broken up as follows according to many NE (Named Entity) guidelines:

(NP [NP (NNP Dr.) (NNP John) (NNP Smith)] (NNP III))

As the GLARF program is an aggressive merging procedure, it overrides this specification of the NE guidelines. Those guidelines conflict with assumptions of the GLARF framework, under which both the title and the posthonorific are viewed as modifiers and the first and last name together act like the head of the phrase.

20 For example, several classes of these verbs (NP-TOBE, NP-TO-INF, NP-NP-PRD, etc.) are marked in the COMLEX Syntax lexicon, available from the Linguistic Data Consortium. See Macleod et al. (1998) and http://nlp.cs.nyu.edu/comlex/index.html for more details.

21 These refer to sections of the American National Corpus, as they appear on the disks distributed by the Linguistic Data Consortium (www.ldc.upenn.edu).

22 The recursive acronym GNU stands for 'GNU's Not Unix' and is the (trademark-like) name applied to software, documents, licensing agreements, etc. produced by the Free Software Foundation.

23 Denoyer and Gallinari (2005) describe WikipediaXML, a corpus which embodies many of the ideal properties discussed. In particular, it is a large, consistently formatted, multilingual corpus. It is subject to the GNU document licence, which is problematic for the reasons discussed in this section.

24 It is unclear whether an application (machine translation, information extraction, etc.) trained on annotation of a copyleft corpus is automatically subject to a copyleft licence. Most annotation researchers want their work used by private companies as well as by other researchers and therefore do not want to risk annotating copyleft material. Clarifying these legal issues would be a major benefit to the community. Under a common sense interpretation, it would seem that systems derived from the annotation should not be subject to the copyleft licence. However, this author is not a copyright lawyer.

8

Spoken Corpus Analysis: Multimodal Approaches to Language Description

Irina Dahlmann and Svenja Adolphs

Methodologies in corpus linguistics have revolutionized the way in which we study and describe language, allowing us to make accurate and objective observations and analyses using a range of written and spoken data from naturally occurring contexts. Yet, current corpora, whether spoken or written, are only concerned with textual representations and do not take account of other aspects that generate meaning in conjunction with text, especially when we are dealing with spoken corpora. Gesture, prosody and kinesics all add meaning to utterances and discourse as a whole and recent research in the area of spoken corpus analysis has started to explore the potential impact of drawing on multimodal corpus resources on our descriptions of spoken language (see, e.g. Knight et al. 2006). In addition to offering a more comprehensive resource for describing discourse, multimodal corpora also allow us to reflect on and evaluate some of the methods for analysing textual renderings of spoken discourse established so far. In this chapter, we contrast a purely text-based analysis of spoken corpora with an analysis which uses the additional parameter of pauses measured and integrated into a multimodal corpus resource.

The unit of analysis we will focus on is that of multi-word expressions (MWEs). The description and extraction of MWEs has been a key topic in a variety of areas within applied linguistics and natural language processing for some time. However, there seem to be a number of problems associated with a purely textual and frequency-based approach, especially in terms of understanding the boundaries of such expressions. One of the main problems with computational extraction methods is that we cannot be sure whether corpus-derived MWEs are psycholinguistically valid. In this study, we argue that an analysis of the placement of pauses represented within a multimodal corpus resource can contribute to our understanding of MWE candidates extracted automatically from a spoken corpus consisting of transcripts only. We argue that the analysis of different modalities in spoken corpora allows us to address some of the issues that have caused methodological and conceptual difficulties in the past.

8.1 The Case of Multi-Word Expressions

Erman and Warren (2000) argue that more than 50 per cent of every-day speech and writing consists of 'prefabs', that is, prefabricated, formulaic language. The term *multi-word expression* (MWE) is used in this context as an umbrella term for a phenomenon which has gained wide recognition over the last few years, especially in the areas of computational linguistics, natural language processing (NLP) (e.g. Sag et al. 2002) and areas of applied linguistics such as lexicography (e.g. Moon 1998), language acquisition and teaching (e.g. Nattinger and DeCarrico 1992; Weinert 1995; Wray 1999, 2000, 2002) and psycholinguistics (e.g. Schmitt 2004; Jiang and Nekrasova 2007; Conklin and Schmitt 2008). We use the term *MWE* to mean a 'holistic unit of two or more words' (Moon 1998: 2). This is, admittedly, a very broad description; however, it captures the basic idea that two or more words form a single unit (e.g. *as soon as possible, I don't know, Ladies and Gentlemen, kick the bucket, not only x, but also y*) without pre-defining in advance the nature of the 'glue' which holds such a unit together.

The definition and identification of MWEs are still among the major challenges in the field (e.g. Sag et al. 2002; Wray 2002), and are mainly determined by the angle or field from which they are approached. Wray (2002: 9) suggests the following working definition for a formulaic sequence: 'a sequence, continuous or discontinuous, of words or other elements, which is or appears to be prefabricated: that is, stored and retrieved whole from memory at the time of use, rather than being subject to generation or analysis by the language grammar.'

Research in computational linguistics relies predominantly on statistical approaches to, and observable phenomena of, MWEs, such as frequency and semantic or structural properties of MWEs. Sag et al.'s definition is widely used in NLP related research, evident in its occurrence in the majority of papers presented in recent MWE related workshops at the *Association of Computational Linguistics* (ACL and the European Chapter EACL). Sag et al. (2002: 2) define MWEs as 'idiosyncratic interpretations that cross word boundaries (or spaces)'. They specify further that MWEs can be classified broadly into two categories according to their syntactic and semantic flexibility, that is, lexical phrases and institutionalized phrases.

The main difference between the two definitions is the inclusion of holistic storage in the mental lexicon of MWEs by Wray, whereas Sag et al.'s definition focuses mainly on syntactic and semantic properties of MWEs.

One of the reasons why the criterion of holistic storage may not have found its way into NLP research might be due to the fact that it is almost impossible to measure holistic storage directly. However, it has been proposed that prosodic cues and pauses might be considered to be indirect indicators of prefabricated language and holistic storage, and that MWEs in speech apparently exhibit more phonological coherence (e.g. Van Lancker and Canter 1981; Peters 1983; Hickey 1993; Weinert 1995) than creative language.

Our case study explores a multi-method approach to the identification of MWEs by integrating statistically-based MWE extraction methods with the psycholinguistic notion of holistic storage. The development of a multimodal corpus resource is a key requirement for this approach as it forms the basis of the process of MWE definition and identification.

Our discussion focuses on the sequence *I think*. We explore whether a multimodal analysis of *I think* will allow us to assess whether this highly frequent MWE candidate might be stored and retrieved from memory as a holistic unit, thus satisfying the psycholinguistic criterion for MWEs. The placement of pauses will be used as a guide to assessing holistic storage in this context.

While current research of spoken corpora mainly focuses on orthographic transcriptions, our aim is to illustrate the gains achieved by pause annotation for the description of the MWE candidate *I think* as captured in a corpus of spoken English. This is achieved by comparing a purely textual corpus analysis of *I think* with an analysis that draws on additional information retrieved from audio files, inserted into the corpus transcript, that is mainly pauses, but also improved overlap marking as well as improved speaker and turn indication.

8.2 Textual Analysis of *I think*

This section is concerned with the textual analysis of *I think* in the orthographic version of ENSIC. We draw mainly on frequency information and concordance analysis to extract patterns in the usage of *I think*.

8.2.1 Descriptive Statistical Information

For the purpose of this study we use the English Native Speaker Interview Corpus (ENSIC) which contains transcriptions and recordings of 35 interviews. The interviews are dyadic and carried out with native speakers of British English. This data was collected as part of a previous research project on speaker attitudes to public services, family life and sports. The corpus comprises a total of 368,698 words totalling almost 30 hours of recordings.

The number of words per interviewee ranges from 2,507 words to 18,489 words. *I think* occurs 1,256 times in the interviewee speech (which totals 272,298 words). All 35 interviewees used *I think* (on average 4.67 times per 1,000 words), but the speakers differ in their frequency of use (between 1.12 and 10.60 times per 1,000 words). This might be due to idiosyncratic preferences, but can also depend on different characteristics and functions of the phrase *I think*, such as the possible use of *I think* as filler in order to gain planning time, or as a fluency device (MacKenzie 2000: 174). This function can also be realized in other ways (e.g. pausing, using other fillers such as *I suppose, I mean*), thus individuals may or may not choose to use *I think* as a matter of course.

8.2.2 Prominent Patterns in ENSIC

A concordance search of *I think* resulted in 1,256 instances which were sorted at N–1 and N+1 in order to generate the most prominent patterns. The results are summarized in Tables 8.1 and 8.2. In the following and as a first stage of our investigation, patterns emerging from the concordance output, occurring 15 times or more at N–1 and N+1, are listed here as well as being described and analysed in more detail.

8.2.2.1 Patterns at N–1

The following patterns figure frequently in the ENSIC (Table 8.1).

A noticeable pattern occurring to the left of *I think* is that the MWE starts a new thought or clause. Almost 10 per cent of the instances occur at the beginning of a speaker turn, more than 11 per cent after a full stop indicating the end of a previous sentence, or after the coordinating conjunctions *and* and *but*.[1] The subordinating conjunctions *because* and *so* – usually introducing a new clause as well – also occur relatively frequently before *I think*.

Table 8.1 Patterns to the left of *I think* (sorted to the *left* of I THINK (minimum occurrence 15 instances). (<S2> is the tag used for Speaker 2))

Main patterns	Before	I THINK	After	Instances: absolute (%)
and I think	and	**I THINK**		163 (**12.98**)
	and	**I THINK**	it/it's	6 (0.84)
	and	**I THINK**	that/that's	61 (4.85)
<S2> I think	<S2>	**I THINK**		115 (**9.20**)
	<S2>	**I THINK**	it/it's	24 (1.91)
because I think	because	**I THINK**		20 (**1.59**)
but I think	but	**I THINK**		80 (**6.37**)
em/er I think	er/em	**I THINK**		48 (**3.82**)
I I think	I	**I THINK**		48 (**3.82**)
know I think	know	**I THINK**		21 (**1.67**)
	you know	**I THINK**		16 (1.28)
	I don't know	**I THINK**		5 (0.4)
I mean I think	I mean	**I THINK**		21 (**1.67**)
no (.) I think	no (.)	**I THINK**		19 (**1.51**)
so I think	so	**I THINK**		47 (**3.74**)
I think I think	I think	**I THINK**		31 (**2.47**)
well I think	well	**I THINK**		39 (**3.01**)
what/when/where which/ whilst I think	wh=	**I THINK**		26 (**2.07**)
yeah I think	yeah	**I THINK**		38 (**3.03**)
. I think	.	**I THINK**		145 (**11.54**)

A second pattern seems to include a kind of hesitation before *I think*, that is *em/er, yeah,* and repetitions (*I I think, I think I think*). Furthermore, *you know, I don't know, I mean* and *well* before *I think* may function as fillers, which are sometimes also classified as hesitations. This accounts for 12.4 per cent (155 instances) and may indicate that *I think* is being used while on-line planning of speech is in process.

In summary, the overall patterns to the left of *I think* indicate that this sequence occurs frequently at beginnings of clauses or turns (see Aijmer 1997 and Kärkkäinen 2003 for similar results), or is used in connection with hesitation markers which may indicate the use of *I think* as a time buyer in on-line speech planning.

8.2.2.2 Patterns at N+1

The most prominent pattern on the right of *I think* (43 per cent of the cases) is *I think* followed by a personal pronoun, in particular *it* (more than 15 per cent, see Table 8.2). The vast majority of these instances introduce a new clause, where the personal pronoun is the subject followed by a verb. In the very few cases where this does not apply a false start is involved.

In almost 10 percent of the cases, there is some evidence that *I think* terminates a thought/clause or sentence. This is indicated by subsequent full stops (see also below for punctuation in ENSIC), the beginning of a new speaker turn by speaker 1, or the subsequent beginning of an unfinished sentence, repeat or false start.

Both these patterns seem to confirm the observations outlined in the previous section, namely that *I think* does not tend to be syntactically or semantically closely related to its immediate co-text. In this respect *I think* seems to be a very independent unit. This independence, however, does not refer to its pragmatic value and discourse functions, which have been shown to be important in previous studies (see e.g. Aijmer 1997; Kärkkäinen 2003).

A further prominent pattern is *I think that ('s)*. However, this actually comprises two patterns as *that* represents different functions. It can be used as a subject in a new clause following *I think* or at the beginning of a dependant that-clause.

> **Example 8.1**
> . . . things like that. Em and *I think* **that that's** about as close as we're going to get
>
> **Example 8.2**
> . . . and *I think* **that** was it.
>
> **Example 8.3**
> . . . And *I think* **that** says a lot about the type of people that work in it. . . .
>
> **Example 8.4**
> . . . So *I think* **that** they should leave the process to the people who are managing . . .

Table 8.2 Patterns to the right of *I think* (sorted to the *right* of I THINK (minimum occurrence 15 instances). (<S1> is the tag used for Speaker 1))

Main patterns	Before	I THINK	After	Instances: absolute (%)
I think.[1]		I THINK	.	39 (3.01)
I think <S1>[1]		I THINK	<S1>	26 (2.07)
I think <$=> (marker for following unfinished sentence, repeat or false start)		I THINK	<$=>	58 (4.64)
I think I think		I THINK	I think	30 (2.40)
I think er/erm		I THINK	em/erm	41 (3.28)
I think [personal pronoun]		I THINK	[personal pronoun]	542 (43.36)
		I THINK	I	121 (9.68)
		I THINK	I 've/I have	10 (0.80)
		I THINK	you	51 (4.08)
		I THINK	you know	14 (1.12)
		I THINK	she	15 (1.20)
		I THINK	he	30 (2.40)
		I THINK	they	64 (5.12)
		I THINK	we	62 (4.96)
		I THINK	it	195 (15.6)
		I THINK	it was	31 (2.48)
		I THINK	it's/is	103 (8.24)
I think if		I THINK	if	32 (2.56)
I think that('s)		I THINK	that('s)	140 (11.20)
and I think that('s)	and	I THINK	that('s)	61 (4.88)
I think the		I THINK	the	52 (4.16)
I think there		I THINK	there	40 (3.20)
		I THINK	there (+ some form of verb to BE)	39 (3.12)
I think more/most/ mostly		I THINK	more/most/ mostly	18 (1.44)
I think so (.)		I THINK	so	17 (1.36)

Example 8.5
. . . I mean joking apart *I think* **that** he was very impressed with
what we were doing . . .

I think that as used in the last two examples (8.4 and 8.5) seems to be one of the few
patterns where *that* is closely related to *I think*. Whereas in most cases, *I think* could
be omitted from the context without violating grammaticality, this is not true for
these last two examples. The dependence between *I think* and *that* is unidirectional. *I think* can occur on its own while *that* cannot occur in isolation in this
context. This structure is one of the strongest links between *I think* and another
item. However, it is purely grammatical and not semantically founded. Nattinger
and DeCarrico describe structures such as *I think (that) X* as being 'sentence builders'. 'Sentence builders are lexical phrases that provide the framework for whole
sentences. They contain slots for parameters or arguments of expressions of an
entire idea [. . . and] allow considerable variation of phrasal (NP, VP) and clausal
(S) elements' (Nattinger and DeCarrico 1992: 42–3).

The structure *I think that* has been discussed in previous research. Taking *that*-
clauses as a starting point, Biber et al. (1999: 660) state that '*that*-clauses are commonly used to report the speech, thoughts, attitudes, or emotions of humans'.
They are controlled by verbs which 'fall into just three major semantic domains:
mental verbs, mainly of cognition (e.g. *think, know*), (. . .) speech act verbs (e.g. *say,
tell*); and other communication verbs that do not necessarily involve speech (e.g.
show, prove, suggest)' (p. 661). This mirrors the reporting function of *that*-clauses.
Think and *say* are the most common verbs used with *that*-clauses and Biber et al.
(1999: 666) conclude that 'the most common use of *that* complement clauses is
clearly to report people's mental states and processes' particularly in the genre of
conversation. Thus, the high frequency of *think* in connection with *that*-clauses in
conversation is largely a reflection of the use of the clause *I think* to report one's
own personal thoughts.

The only other strong link between *I think* and another word in our data lies
in the phrase *I think so(.)*, which occurs 17 times. In 16 cases, a new or unrelated
lexico-grammatical unit follows. This is indicated by: full stop (11 times), conjunctions (2 times), the response token *yeah* (2 times), and a new clause (1 time). In
one occurrence (Example 8.6) *so* is linked to the subsequent expression and not
to *I think*:

Example 8.6
. . . Cos it doesn't matter in an odd sort of way. *I think* **so** long
as you're getting people to talk to each other and . . ..

Thus, aside from very few exceptions (*I think so* and *I think that* [introducing a
noun clause/direct object]) the evidence from the corpus suggests that *I think* is
used as a disconnected unit in speech.

8.2.2.3 *I think* according to 'sentence' position

WordSmith Tools was used to sort the data by 'sentence'. This is defined within the program as 'punctuation followed by a space followed by a capital letter' to mark a 'sentence' boundary (Scott 2004). Although the concept of a 'sentence' is problematic in speech, the term will be used here in its technical sense relating to punctuation. The accuracy of the results depends on the consistency of the punctuation applied to the corpus. A high level of consistency is difficult to achieve when it comes to naturally occurring speech. Consequently, results in this section are tentative. However, the punctuation which has been put in, nevertheless gives an indication as to any pattern emerging from sentence position. This analysis can be used as a starting point for further validation, for instance, in a multimodal representation which includes pause annotation.

Two main patterns emerge from the data:

1. . *I think* at the beginning of a 'sentence'/clause
2. *I think.* at the end of a 'sentence'/clause

The cases where *I think* occurs in mid-utterance are too varied and their analysis would be beyond the scope of this study.

8.2.2.3.1 . I think *at the* beginning *of a sentence*

There are 281 instances (more than one-fifth (22.4 per cent)) where *I think* or *I I think* is preceded by punctuation, that is, occurs in sentence initial position.

In addition, there are a large number of instances where semantically empty items occur in-between the punctuation and *I think*, that is, repetitions (*I think I think*), hesitations (*er/em I think*), the response token *yeah* before *I think*, the conjunctions *and*, *but*, and *because* before *I think*, and certain discourse markers (*well, I mean*). If these cases are included, then almost half of the instances (612; 49 per cent) of *I think* do occur at the beginning of a sentence (see Table 8.3).

8.2.2.3.2 I think. *at the* end *of a sentence*

There are 39 instances where *I think* occurs at the end of a sentence. Compared to the use of *I think* in sentence initial position this number is very low, amounting to a mere 3.12 per cent. Eighteen of these instances are preceding a speaker change. Further analysis of the audio files show that in many cases the interviewee's speech flow is not interrupted, although the linear representation in the transcript would make it appear that way.

8.2.3 Mono-Modal Transcript Analysis: A Summary

Overall, the findings from the purely text-based analysis of the corpus show the following: Structural patterns occur in our data set of spontaneous speech

Table 8.3 *I think* in relation to punctuation.

I think *at the beginning of a sentence*	Occurrences
. I (I) think	281
. I think I think	12
. Er/Em I think	55
. Yeah I think	9
. And I think	76
. But I think	44
. So (so) I think	23
. Because/Cos I think	24
. Well I think	8
. I mean I think	16
. [cluster consisting of a combination of two of the following: and, but, so, well, yeah, er/erm] I think	64
	Σ **612**

of British English around *I think*, such as *and I think, I think its/that's, I think [personal pronoun]*. It can be used as what Nattinger and DeCarrico call sentence builders, for example, *I think that*. More semantically meaningful embedding is rare in our data. This seems to suggest that *I think* is mostly a self-contained unit which is not strongly integrated syntactically. However, there is strong indication that the preferred place for *I think* is at the beginning of a sentence.

Although a large number of instances of *I think* can be subsumed under the patterns identified above, there is still a substantial proportion which remains unaccounted for in terms of describable patterns. This is partly due to the lack of prosodic information which would allow additional patterns to be derived both in terms of sentence placement and lexical integration.

8.3 *I think* and Pauses

Moving on from a purely textual analysis of *I think* the next section illustrates the benefits of adding pause annotation to an orthographically transcribed corpus (ENSIC) in terms of our understanding of MWEs, such as *I think*.

As outlined above, there are a number of problems associated with the identification of MWEs. A purely textual and frequency-based approach, as we have attempted in the previous section, seems inadequate to capture the physical reflexes of holistic storage, as well as the boundaries of such expressions. It has been claimed that 'phonological coherence' may be an additional criterion to account for holistic storage in the identification process of MWEs in spoken language (e.g. Van Lancker et al. 1981; Hickey 1993; Wray 2002). As readily available chunks, MWEs are believed to be retrieved automatically and as one single unit from

long-term memory, which makes 'pauses within lexical phrases (. . .) less acceptable than pauses within free expressions, and after a hesitation the speaker is
more likely to restart from the beginning of the expression' (Pawley 1986: 107).
These characteristics of storage and retrieval from memory of MWEs will be
explored by the examining pause placement around the MWE candidate *I think*.

   The main focus of our analysis is on pause distribution, and the following
patterns have been identified as relevant to our study (see also Dahlmann et al.
2007*a*):

(a) M W < > E (pause within the MWE)
(b) < > MWE < >
(c) < > MWE _____< >
(d) < > _____ MWE < >
(e) < > _____ MWE _____ < >

('_____' indicates text of any length, < > indicates pause)

As outlined above, the high frequency of *I think* marks it as a MWE candidate.
Thus, we would expect that *I think* is stored holistically and not interrupted by a
pause. Furthermore, and referring to pause patterns (b)–(e), MWE boundaries
are investigated in terms of pause placement, that is, whether there are any regular
pause patterns which indicate boundaries.

8.3.1 Data and Procedure

A pause annotation scheme based on fluency research, psycholinguistic approaches
and existing pause coding has been developed specifically for the purpose of
studying MWEs and holistic storage (Dahlmann et al. 2007*b*). One of the requirements of this annotation scheme is a high level of accuracy in terms of pause and
hesitation descriptions, as well as in the measurement of pauses. Pauses and hesitations which have been identified as meaningful for fluency and the processing
of speech are

- filled pauses (non-lexical fillers, e.g. *erm*; and syllable stretches),
- silent pauses (at least 0.2 seconds),
- repairs, false starts/restarts,
- start of an utterance, and
- laughter/sigh.

Furthermore, the newly aligned transcriptions reflect a better representation of
the speaker organization and overlap marking. The accompanying audio files
enable us to clearly identify the main speaker. Pure back channelling, for example,
can be integrated into speech flow of the main speaker, instead of claiming a new
turn (see the changes in the example transcript in Figure 8.1).

Transcript *without* pause annotation

> <S2>   I don't know they just they sighs they seem to appreciate I mean th= they seem
>   to know that y= appreciate the fact that you know where they're coming from
>   you know
>
> <S1>   Yeah.
>
> <S2>   you appreciate some of the pressures. Although they'll say em But I mean in
>   actual fact they say Oh you don't want to go back to it I mean they you know
>   And then some of them say Oh don't you get fed up with doing this with us all
>   whinging and moaning all the time and I just say No no I don't. But I think
>   they they know you've got the same background to them and you've been
>   through it so I think it does help. I mean I don't know whether FX finds it any
>   different coming from a radiography
>
> <S1>   Yeah.
>
> <S2>   background. Em
>
> <S1>   Yeah it'd be interesting wouldn't it to

The transcript *with* pause annotation and improved speaker organization

> <S2>   I don't know <r> they just </r> <1.3> they <sighs 0.5> <r> they seem to
>   appreciate </r> I mean <r> th= they seem to know that y= </r> <0.3>
>   appreciate the fact that you know where they're coming from you know **<S1>**
>   **Yeah. </S1>** you appreciate some of the pressures. <r> Although they'll say
>   <r/> <0.7> <em 0.5> <1.1> But I mean in actual fact they say Oh you don't
>   want to go back to it I mean you know <0.22> And then some of them say Oh
>   don't you get fed up with doing this with us all whinging and moaning all the
>   time and I just say No no I don't. <0.5> But **<mwu> I think </mwu>** <r> they
>   </r> <0.5> they know you've got the same background to them and you've
>   been through it so **<mwu> I think </mwu>** it does help. <0.8> I mean I don't
>   know whether FX finds it any different coming from a radiography **<S1>**
>   **Yeah. </S1>** background. <0.5> <em 0.7>
>
> <S1>   Yeah it'd be interesting wouldn't it <r> to </r>
>
> <0.4>

Figure 8.1 Transcript example with added pause annotation and improved speaker organization.

The pause annotation has been inserted manually by using audio-visual clues, that is, the combination of audio recording and wave forms, both analysed using Adobe Audition.

The first ten instances of *I think* of ten different speakers were taken as a sample. The 100 sample instances were annotated manually to reflect pause placement and duration. The actual annotation follows XML and TEI standards, which can be transferred back into readable format (as in the above example).

8.3.2 Results: Pause Placement Around I think

Patterns in the placement of pauses are of foremost interest (see Table 8.4).

The five identified different patterns of pause placement will be discussed in more detail below.

8.3.2.1 M W < > E (pause within the MWE candidate)

This pattern runs counter to the notion of holistic storage and our results confirm that this is not a prominent pattern for the MWE *I think*. However, pauses may occur in this context depending on the speech situations and circumstances, and there is one instance in 100 examples where the speaker pauses within *I think*:

> **Example 8.7** (talking about how he spends Christmas day)
> Well as far as as far as it goes I mean I would s= **<mwu> I <0.26> think </mwu>** I would sooner stop at home <0.21> but <0.7> <er 0.27> when your family <0.5> ask you to do these things then it's only fair that one should <0.6> kind of cooperate.

Overall, this interviewee is a slow speaker and the pause is relatively short (0.26 seconds). Considering the content of his utterance, the pause may be used for emphasis.

8.3.2.2 < > MWE < >

Nine instances of *I think* (9 per cent; used by seven different speakers) follow this pattern, where *I think* is immediately surrounded by pause phenomena. Two instances are preceded by a false start, and in six cases *I think* is preceded by a substantial silent pause (length between 0.4–2.0 seconds), in three cases as part of a pause cluster. The context suggests that these instances of *I think* involve a fair amount of planning, and the use of *I think* may be a part of the thinking process. In one of the nine instance *I think* is used as an evaluative and stance marking afterthought.

Table 8.4 Pause placement pattern for 100 instances of *I think*.

Pause placement patterns	For 100 instances of I think
a. M W < > E (pause within the MWE candidate)	1
b. < > MWE < >	11
c. < > MWE _____ < >	22
d. < > _____ MWE < >	18
e. < > _____ MWE _____ < >	48
	100

8.3.2.3 < > MWE ____< >

Twenty-two per cent of the 100 instances follow this pattern, which is used by seven of the ten speakers (1–6 instances per speaker).

Two-thirds of the preceding pauses are silent pauses, and the majority of these are of substantial lengths (0.3–2.2 seconds). Two of the three filled pauses are part of a pause cluster and all these instances display comparatively lengthy pause phenomena before *I think*. The remaining five pause instances are unmeasured phenomena, such as repetitions and false starts, the beginning of a new utterance by the speaker (preceded by a silence between the speakers) and occasions of overlap.

Overall, and as seen in the previous '< > MWE < >' case, when *I think* is preceded by pause phenomena, it seems to be a substantial pause and not a transient one (i.e. just above threshold of 0.2 seconds).

8.3.2.4 < > _____ MWE < >

Seventeen instances follow this pattern. At first sight, and taken out of context, this pattern suggests syntactic regularities, such as a syntactic boundary. However this is only the case in three instances. In terms of pause types following *I think* more than half of the pauses are silent pauses of mixed lengths, four of them are very short (from <.> [perceptible but below 0.2] to 0.25), the other six are at least 0.4 seconds long. In three instances, the speaker finishes his turn with *I think*, and four times *I think* is followed by repetitions (*I think it is it is that balance*).

8.3.2.5 < > _____ MWE _____ < >

This pattern is the most common (48 per cent) but it arguably offers the least reliable information about possible MWE boundaries as there is no adjacent pause on either side of *I think*. However, patterns which emerged from the text-based analysis are prominent in this set. There are 22 instances of the following pattern in this category:

<pause> /and, but, because, so well, yeah/ *I think.*

The kinds of pauses are almost exclusively silent pauses or filled non-lexical pauses, and some pause clusters. Combined with the observations in the text-based analysis, this strengthens the case for flexible boundaries. It can be assumed that *I think* is a core unit and variations can be longer, such as *and I think.*

8.3.3 Further Observations

A few other observations are interesting against the background of our previous text-based results. For example, none of the 9 cases of *I think that* or of the 18 cases of *I think it/it's* is interrupted by a pause. We have highlighted these instances on the basis of their overall frequency. Combined with the analysis of pause patterns we may assume that these two-word clusters may also be separate MWEs.

However, we acknowledge that our data set is relatively small and more evidence is required to establish more robust patterns of this kind.

8.3.4 Is I think A Psycholinguistically Valid MWE?

Our aim has been to explore an approach which draws on multimodal information to develop a frequency-based and psycholinguistically motivated description of MWEs. As expected, in our data, *I think* is virtually never interrupted by pauses. This is one possible indicator for holistic storage.

In half of the cases, pauses seem not particularly meaningful in terms of boundary alignments, simply because they do not occur (48 < > ___ MWE ___ < > cases). However, it should be noted that language is commonly organized in bigger chunks. Pawley and Syder (2000) suggest that 'the average number of words per fluent unit is about six' (p. 195) for fluent native speakers. And we know from research in psychology that 'the memory span is a fixed number of chunks' (Miller 1956: 93), that is, seven plus/minus two. However, each chunk can be built up with more information. Thus it is not unlikely that *I think* is embedded in a larger chunk of language as the memory is able to handle more than one chunk. The absence of a pause then does not exclude the possibility that there might in fact be a boundary.

The occurrence of pauses at one or either side of *I think* that we find in the remaining examples might offer valuable evidence of possible boundaries. It is interesting that pauses occur evenly at both sides of the unit (33 times before and 27 times after *I think*). This supports the results from the textual analysis that *I think* is a largely independent chunk in language use.

8.5 Conclusion

Multimodal corpus research into pauses and MWEs is still in its infancy and there are few spoken corpora that are annotated in a way that allows a detailed analysis of different types of pauses. As such resources are currently being developed, additional prosodic markers such as intonation and stress patterns can be studied.

In terms of the description of *I think* and the aspect of 'phonological coherence' of MWEs, the approach we have taken would not have been possible with a purely text-based resource. We have illustrated the results of the text-based corpus analysis; however, these remained tentative as important information was missing. By adding pause annotation, the re-organization of speaker alignment and alignment of audio files to the transcripts, we were able to arrive at a more accurate representation of the actual speech event, which in turn allowed for a new layer to be added to the description of the MWE *I think*.

Using a multimodal corpus as a basis for analysis opens up possibilities for a considerable range of studies particularly in the area of (spoken) language description. There has long been a discussion of the limitations of using text-only corpora as the basis for analysing spoken discourse (see, e.g. Cook 1995). While textual corpora have contributed substantially to the description of spoken language, the new generation of multimodal corpora promises a much more comprehensive representation of speech situations. This development should, in the long term, lead to better descriptions of spoken discourse, and to improved applications based on those descriptions.

Note

1 Note that the percentages cannot be used cumulatively as the full stop cases have been compiled manually and may overlap with the other instances (the speaker identification *<S2>*, and the conjunctions *and,* and *but*).

Fixed Collocational Patterns in Isolexical and Isotextual Versions of a Corpus

David Oakey

Comparative studies of the discourse functions of fixed collocational patterns require a comparable amount of corpus data. One approach is to subdivide existing normative (Sinclair 2005) corpora to allow comparisons to be made between different registers or between different genres. The amount of data in each resulting subcorpus is often unequal, however, and results might be biased in favour of the subcorpus with the greatest number of texts or tokens. Another approach is to balance the number of tokens in each subcorpus by using text samples, although this can mean that individual subcorpora do not completely represent all areas of the discourse. Some patterns which perform discourse functions relating to these areas may be missed as a result. This chapter reports on a comparative study of fixed collocational patterns in two versions of a corpus of research articles from eight academic disciplines. It first presents results from a comparison of an equal number of tokens in each discipline, i.e. an isolexical comparison, and then presents results from a comparison of an equal number of texts in each discipline, i.e. an isotextual comparison. The results indicate that the same fixed collocational patterns are frequent in both versions of the corpus. This suggests that further comparative studies of fixed collocational patterns should be isotextual, so that their functions can be investigated across similar numbers of communicative acts rather than across similar amounts of language.

9.1 Introduction

This chapter begins with an overview of previous work on collocation in English, and shows how the increasing use of corpora over the last few decades has influenced shifts in theoretical positions towards the phenomenon. The principal development has been that longer, multi-word stretches of language have come to be regarded as collocations with roles in the discourse of particular areas of English use rather than in the language as a whole. There are two possible methodological approaches to corpus-informed comparisons of the role of such collocations: data in existing representative 'off-the-shelf' corpora can be grouped into categories reflecting different areas of language use, or original corpora of data chosen from different categories can be constructed. Depending on the goals of the study, various overlapping labels can used for these different categories: comparing different 'registers' (Biber et al. 1998: 135) reveals linguistic features typical of different situations of use, such as purpose, topic and setting; making comparisons between texts belonging to different 'genres' (Lee 2001) can show how language varies according to socio-culturally determined factors.

However, both register and genre-based work on collocations using data from existing 'off-the-shelf' corpora is limited by two considerations. First, while such corpora can be subdivided to allow the study of collocation across different registers or genres, the amount of data from each subcorpus is often unequal, and so studies of collocation using these subcorpora may be inaccurate. Second, some corpus compilers achieve a balanced number of tokens by using text samples, with the result that discourse features from the parts of the texts which are not included in the sample are not represented in the corpus. This chapter attempts to address these considerations by introducing a distinction between 'isolexical' and 'isotextual' versions of a corpus when comparing extended collocations in research articles in eight academic disciplines. One version allows results to be compared across a similar number of tokens, while the other allows results to be compared across a similar number of texts. The chapter concludes with some initial findings of a comparison of isolexical and isotextual frequencies of 3-word strings in different disciplines.

9.2 Firthian Collocation

Collocation has been an area of study in British linguistics since the work of Otto Jespersen at the beginning of the twentieth century and H. E. Palmer in the 1920s (Cowie 1998: 211). Collocation is also studied in the Eastern European phraseological tradition (Howarth 1996), but this chapter will focus on the notion of collocation which became prominent in J. R. Firth's work on the theory of meaning in the 1930s. Starting from the anthropologist Bronislaw Malinoswski's notion of meaning as 'context of situation' (Malinowski 1923), Firth argued that words derived their meanings from their use in texts in particular situations: 'the *placing* of a *text* as a constituent in a context of situation contributes to a statement of meaning since situations are set up to recognise *use*' (Firth 1957: 11; original emphasis). Firthian collocation was an abstract, linear, syntagmatic relationship between individual words which contributed to their meaning. Later work by Firth's student Michael Halliday, and in turn Halliday's student John Sinclair, prepared the ground for empirical studies of collocation using corpora.

Halliday proposed a definition of collocation which specified both linear and statistical elements:

> the syntagmatic association of lexical items, quantifiable, textually, as the probability that there will occur, at n removes (a distance of n lexical items) from an item x, the items a, b, c . . .. Any given item thus enters into a range of collocation, the items with which it is collocated being ranged from more or less probable. (Halliday 1961: 276)

Halliday (1966: 159) reasoned that it was 'not known how far collocational patterns are dependent on the structural relations into which the items enter' which formed the basis for his argument that the analysis of lexis should be performed in tandem with the analysis of grammar. This was a somewhat radical position as it implied a suspension of the basic distinction in linguistics between grammar and lexis. Halliday also pointed out that the empirical investigation of collocational relations between items 'would require the study of very large samples of text' (ibid.).

The development of electronic language corpora during the 1960s meant that such a study could now take place in order to determine the frequency with which words occur and the frequency with which they occur with other words. One consequence of this application of computer power to the study of collocation was the emergence of divergent stances on its syntagmatic dimension. Researchers adopted different views on how far apart collocational relations between words, i.e. between a node and a collocate, operate. One position is that, when words combine with each other to create textual coherence, there is no practical limit to the distance (measured in words) between the node and the collocate. *All* words in a text, i.e. 'any group of sentences/utterances that functions as a unity, whether spoken or written' (Hoey 1991: 270) are in a collocational relationship with each other simply because they are all in the same text. Words repeatedly combine in text so that 'connections between sentences across long distances of text are subconsciously recognised by the reader' (ibid.: 219). Scott (1999) terms words in this type of collocational relationship with another word as 'coherence collocates', similar to the collocational meaning ascribed by Sinclair to words like *edition, bookshop, paper* and *print* occurring with *tome* and *paperback* (Sinclair 1966: 411). For words which actually co-occur very close to the word *letter* – (*my, this, a,* etc.), Scott uses the term 'neighbourhood collocates'. This approach to collocation has been taken furthest by Hoey (2005), who uses corpus evidence as a way of explaining how language is acquired. When a language user is repeatedly exposed to the various frequent contexts of a word, namely its collocational environments, the user's knowledge of and ability to use that word is developed, or 'primed'.

Sinclair's work on collocation, by contrast, is more concerned with relationships between words over shorter distances. Sinclair proposed that any point in a text can be considered to be either part of a collocational relationship, or not. Sometimes, at points between words in a text, the choice of the next word is largely open. The lexicon, once it has satisfied local constraints, can provide virtually any word. At other times the language user's choice is restricted to 'a large number of semi-preconstructed phrases that constitute single choices, even though they might appear to be analysable into segments' (Sinclair 1991: 110). Text is interpreted according to either of these 'open choice' and 'idiom' principles, but not at the same time. The idiom principle is 'as least as important as grammar in the explanation of how meaning arises in text' (ibid.: 112). An attempt to quantify the relative quantities of these choices confirmed that 'the production of a text involves frequent alternation between prefab and non-prefabricated strings' (Erman and Warren 2000: 51), and that in a text of around 100 words on average only 45 single-word choices were made.

This closer proximity of a word with its collocate along the syntagmatic plane, Halliday's 'n removes', is referred to as the 'span' by Sinclair, who estimates it as being approximately five words to the left or right of the word. This criterion was applied to the *COBUILD Collocations Dictionary* (COBUILD 1995) when the definition of a collocate used was a lexical item 'occurring within five words either way of the headword with a greater frequency than the law of averages would lead you to suspect' (Krishnamurthy 1987: 70). Later research has questioned whether a span should be symmetrical, i.e. the same number of words to the left or right of the node. It has instead been argued that different nodes have different spans, since 'each word form has an individual influence on the variability of its environment' (Mason 1997: 361). This influence Mason calls 'lexical gravity', and results in a unique span for any word, based on the restriction the word imposes on the variability of its context.

More recent work on collocation in the Sinclairian tradition has seen the word as less of a unit of meaning in its own right and more as a constituent of longer meaningful collocations, such as Stubbs' construct of the 'extended lexical unit' (Stubbs 2001: 87). Hunston and Francis proposed the construct of 'pattern', such as *N n* or *link verb V that* (Hunston 2002: 139). They argue that 'words have no meaning in isolation, or at least are very ambiguous, but have meaning when they occur in a particular phraseology' (Hunston and Francis 2000: 270). Multi-sense words tend to associate each sense most frequently with a different set of patterns, and words with the same pattern tend to share aspects of meaning. Meaning thus belongs 'to the whole phrase rather than to individual words in it' (Hunston 2002: 140). A pattern is a useful compromise between an instance of specific behaviour of a lexical item and a generalization for which the specific examples are evidence (Hunston and Francis 2000: 81).

This approach to meaning was incorporated into empirically produced reference materials for English language learners. *The COBUILD Advanced Learner's Dictionary* (Sinclair 2006) has a column containing the pattern of a word used for a particular sense, and the two books on grammar patterns (COBUILD) 1996*a, b*) contain a list of patterns and the most common verbs, nouns or adjectives used in them. These resources provide a practical indication of the lexico-grammatical nature of meaning in the Firth-Halliday-Sinclair tradition.

One controversial aspect of collocation outside the scope of this chapter is the continued relevance of its role in idiomatic native-like speech, as discussed by Bolinger (1976) and Pawley and Syder (1983). In the Eastern European phraseological tradition collocational relations are identified with reference to a native speaker's judgement, and many corpora used in empirical approaches traditionally contain texts and spoken data produced by native speakers, and so the collocational tendencies identified normally reflect native speaker usage. Given that English is both a language with different standard versions around the world

(Kachru 1985) and a lingua franca in which most communication worldwide now involves one or more non-native speakers (Crystal 2003), it could be argued that the criterion of native-speaker acceptability may need to be re-assessed.

The collocational norms of the vocabulary of English as a lingua franca could eventually emerge over time through their use in specific contexts, and in the process it will be possible to identify empirically these new and continued tendencies of words to co-occur. Initial moves towards such identification have already been made, with the VOICE corpus (Seidlhofer 2001) and descriptions of collocational patterning in English as a lingua franca (Mauranen 2003; 2004), which suggest that non-native speaker use continues at times to approximate to native speaker use.

9.3 Studies of Extended Empirical Collocations

The progression beyond the word as a useful unit of meaning (c.f. Danielsson 2007; Gardner 2007) has led to a great deal of research on what might be collectively termed 'extended empirical collocations': multi-word phrases of varying lengths, degrees of fixedness and variability whose status as linguistic units is not yet determined. At the same time, more attention has been paid to the communicative conventions that characterize different 'contexts of situation', and linguistic features of registers and genres and the pragmatic features of communication within discourse communities have been described in more detail (Biber et al. 1998; Hyland 2000). Multi-word forms of various kinds have been seen as the means by which users conform to the communicative norms of a particular discourse community in order to bid for inclusion in that community. Current attempts to model language use are based on the interplay between the conventional and appropriate use of these multi-word forms and the individual language user's creativity in communicating with others in the context of a particular social situation.

Since computers process text as a progression of strings of characters with spaces between them, however, extended empirical collocations do not always respect traditional grammatical boundaries. Frequently occurring 'n-grams', computational linguistic parlance for strings of *n* words where *n* is greater than one, are identified irrespective of their meaning, use, or the word classes their constituent words might belong to. Below, I discuss work on some of these extended collocations, taking the academic research article as the context of situation.

An important study which described extended collocations in different discourse types was *Lexical Phrases and Language Teaching* (Nattinger and DeCarrico 1992). Nattinger and DeCarrico's construct, the 'lexical phrase', is a continuous or discontinuous, fixed or variable collocation which has a pragmatic discourse organizing function. Nattinger and DeCarrico presented a taxonomy of lexical phrases, based on their form and function. For example, they describe a type of lexical phrase called a 'phrasal constraint' which could take a form like *the ____er the ____er*, which would structure a phrase like *the more the merrier*. These shorter lexical phrases, according to Nattinger and DeCarrico's model, can be built up into extended collocations. For example turning a phrasal constraint into a 'sentence builder' requires the addition of noun groups or verb groups as in *the ____er X, the ____ Y,* which occurs in phrases like *the harder they come, the harder they fall.* Sentence building lexical phrases can be taken much further to offer paradigmatic choices of verbs with optional choices marked by brackets, to produce quite complex frames, as in Example 9.1:

> **Example 9.1** *this paper will compare/contrast/describe/demonstrate that X (first) (by analysing/comparing/demonstrating (that Y) (then by ____ing Z, and finally by ____ing A;*

The lexical phrase was conceived as a pedagogical unit, and Nattinger and DeCarrico specified discourse models, such as those underlying informal and business letters or academic essays, together with the lexical phrases which they intended learners to use when writing these texts. This meant, however, that the lexical phrase is of limited application across the English language as a whole, since for a particular collocation in a text to be classed as a lexical phrase, it must have the specified communicative function according to the discourse model for that text proposed by Nattinger and DeCarrico. In this case the model for academic writing was a rather simple sequence of opening, body, and closing, and the lexical phrases themselves were specified from somewhat vague data, for example, 'written discourse collected from a variety of textbooks for ESL, textbooks for academic courses, letters to the editor of various news publications, and personal correspondence' (Nattinger and DeCarrico 1992: xvi).

As lexical phrases were not supported by much empirical evidence, corpus-based work on a selection of lexical phrases was conducted by Oakey (2002) in a subset of the BNC. It was found that extended collocations with the same form as Nattinger and DeCarrico's lexical phrases were indeed used in academic writing, but these extended collocations performed more than one identifiable discourse function. It seemed that by proposing a form-function relationship for lexical phrases, Nattinger and DeCarrico had made their lexical phrase model too dependent on their own discourse model, and thus reduced the potential applicability of lexical phrases certainly to other genres such as research articles, and possibly to academic writing in general.

The work of Hyland (1996; 1998*b*) is concerned primarily with how writers use extended collocations to construct academic discourse and to indicate their stance towards the knowledge they are creating. He takes a corpus-based approach in order to illustrate the use of metadiscourse, a theoretical concept from the field of pragmatics which fits in with Hallidayan notions of evaluation, the creation of stance and the construction of discourse. Hyland (1998*a*) used a corpus of research articles from eight different academic disciplines to make statements about the use of language across different disciplines, but his study ultimately reinforces the existing theory of pragmatics rather than describing extended collocations in research articles, since Hyland's corpus searches were based on a list of 180 pre-existing items compiled from 'grammars, dictionaries and earlier studies' (Hyland 1998*a*: 355).

An extended empirical collocation commonly described in academic discourse (Hyland 2007) is the 'lexical bundle'. This construct originated in the corpus-based study by Biber et al. (1999) which produced the *Longman Grammar of Spoken and Written English*. Lexical bundles are frequently recurring fixed strings of three or more words which 'commonly go together in natural discourse' (ibid.: 990) and which Biber et al. claim are 'a basic linguistic construct with important functions for the construction of discourse' (2004: 398). The lexical bundle in theory is similar to one of Nattinger and DeCarrico's lexical phrases, as it is a collocation with a pragmatic discourse function, but it is also an empirical unit, since a fixed string needs to occur at least 40 times per million words in five or more texts in the corpus before it can be termed a lexical bundle. Examples of lexical bundles are *one of the, part of the, the use of, in contrast to the* and *on the other hand.*

When the definition of an extended empirical collocation is as strict as that for the lexical bundle, the composition of the corpus used to describe it becomes crucial. In making comparisons of the use of lexical bundles by users in different contexts of situation, such as spoken versus written academic registers (Biber and Barbieri 2007), or by student and expert writers of academic prose (Cortes 2004), it can be difficult to ensure that like is being compared with like. The next section outlines some of the issues in corpus construction which need to be considered when designing such comparative studies.

9.4 Corpora and Academic Discourse

While there are several sources of academic writing data available in existing 'off-the-shelf' corpora such as the Brown, LOB and BNC, the design principles underlying these corpora mean that they are not suitable for comparative studies. The language in these corpora was primarily balanced so that they were a representative sample of the language as a whole; they were not intended for comparison of similar amounts of language between their different subcategories. If a similar number of tokens in different categories is collected as a representative sample of a language, none of the individual categories can on their own be representative of that category in the language as a whole, simply because they were collected as part of a larger representative whole sample. The Brown corpus 'Learned' category of 160,000 words, for example, only consists of eighty 2000-word samples from academic texts which were collected as part of a larger sample representing American written English, and therefore cannot themselves be seen as being representative of all American learned writing. Similarly, comparisons of American learned writing with the 160,000 words of British learned writing in the 'Learned' category of the LOB corpus cannot be treated as comparisons of the two varieties of 'Learned' writing. This point is made repeatedly by Sinclair: 'a sample corpus will be discontinuous; its subdivisions will not stand as samples themselves' (Sinclair 1991: 24), and 'it is perfectly possible, and indeed very likely, that a corpus component can be adequate for representing its variety within a large normative corpus, but inadequate to represent its variety when freestanding' (Sinclair 2005: 3).

In the case of the written BNC, texts were originally grouped into a series of domains: Imaginative, Natural Science, Applied Science, Social Science, World Affairs, Commerce, Arts, Belief and Thought, Leisure and Unclassified. Samples in each domain were drawn from a variety of text media: books, periodicals, published and unpublished miscellaneous texts, texts which were written to be spoken and unclassified texts. Lee (2001) proposed a reclassification of the text samples into the following 'genres': Academic and Non-Academic (Humanities, Medical, Natural Science, Politics/Law/Education, Social Science, Technical/Engineering), Administrative, Advertising, Biography, Broadsheet News (Arts, Commerce, Editorial, Miscellaneous Reportage, Science, Social), Tabloid News, Scripted News, Commerce, Email, School and University Essays, Fiction (Drama, Poetry, Prose), Hansard Reports, Instructional, Personal and Professional Letters, Miscellaneous, Official Documents, Popular Lore and Religion.

While Lee's categories made it easier to see what sort of text a particular instance of language use came from, it also meant that the number of texts – and the number of tokens – in each new category was unequal, as seen in three subcorpora of academic writing shown in Figure 9.1.

For occurrences of linguistic features such as extended collocations to be compared between the above three subcorpora, results would either have to be normalized down to the level of the subcategory with the fewest tokens, in this case the approximately 500,000 tokens of Technical and Engineering writing, or normalized up to the level of the subcategory with the most tokens, namely the 2,500,000 or so tokens of Social Science writing. The former method would involve dividing the results for Medicine roughly by three and those for Social Science roughly by five. The latter method would involve multiplying results for Technical and Engineering by five, and those for Medicine roughly by three. In this case the

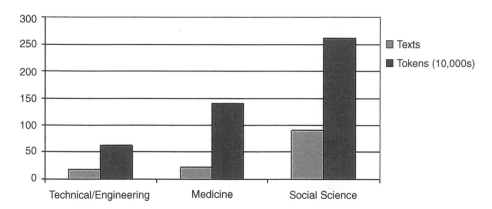

Figure 9.1 Comparison of three different academic writing subcorpora in the BNC.

results would be highly dubious, since it cannot be assumed that, for example, extended collocations which occur *n* times in 500,000 tokens of Technical and Engineering writing will occur *5n* times in 2,500,000 tokens.

Biber and Barbieri (2007) identify this problem in their comparative study of lexical bundles in subcorpora of academic discourse which are uneven in size; some contain more than a million tokens, while others are much smaller. The process of normalizing results in order to compensate for these imbalances risks creating phantom results. Lexical bundles are hard to identify in subcorpora which contain fewer than a million words, as the definition of a lexical bundle, as mentioned in the previous section, is an extended collocation which occurs at least 40 times per million words. But an extended collocation which occurs 21 times in 500,000 words will not necessarily occur 42 times in a million words and meet the lexical bundle definition criterion. Biber and Barbieri call for 'more comprehensive analyses based on much larger samples, with the sample design more evenly matched across registers' (ibid.: 268ff).

When data within the genre of academic writing from a single text type, such as the periodical, is isolated from the BNC using Lee's criteria, the resulting subcorpora are further imbalanced, as can be seen in Fig. 9.2.

The proportionally larger amount of words taken from two journals, *Gut* and the *Weekly Law Reports*, is particularly noticeable. It has been found that this

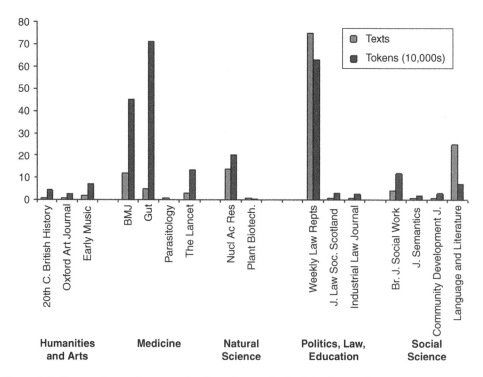

Figure 9.2 Comparison of texts and tokens for periodicals in the BNC.

imbalance causes normally infrequent words such as *gastric* (adj), *mucosa* (n) and *colitis* (n) to 'leap up into the top 8,000 frequent words of English' (Kilgarrif 2002: 1). The wide disparity between the numbers of tokens and texts between the different academic subjects in the BNC arises principally because it was not the intention of the BNC designers for it to be used for comparisons between genres (Aston 2001).

One other reason why existing corpora are not suitable for comparative descriptions of academic writing is related to the pragmatic role of extended collocations in the discourse. In many existing corpora whole texts were not included, as, in order to keep the sample size balanced in terms of tokens, text samples, rather than whole texts, were used. In a Sinclairian tradition, the inclusion of text fragments in a corpus means that the data is incomplete (Sinclair 1991: 23–4), implying that 'context of situation' by definition cannot be investigated because the situation, namely the text, is incomplete. If a text is to be studied as a communicative act, then all the language used to perform that act needs to be available for study. As a brief illustration of this difficulty, we can propose the existence of an extended empirical collocation which plays an important role in the introduction section of texts. If a corpus consisting of randomly selected text fragments is searched in order to test this hypothesis, the results will inevitably prove inconclusive, since the sampling construction method may or may not have included the introduction sections of the texts in the corpus.

From the above discussion it can be seen that by using existing corpora it is not possible to compare a similar number of tokens between academic areas; a truly comparative corpus would need to be constructed with freestanding subcorpora of similar dimensions, as pointed out by Biber and Barbieri. The remainder of this paper outlines a proposed method of addressing the above two problems so that occurrences of extended empirical collocations in different academic disciplines can be counted and compared.

9.5 Isolexical and Isotextual Versions of a Corpus

An isolexical (from 'same number of words') corpus of research articles was collected containing an equal number of tokens from each discipline to be compared. An isolexical corpus allows comparisons to be made with previous work on different types of extended collocations, for example, Moon (1998); Oakey (2002) and Cortes (2004), all of which talk about frequency in terms of occurrences per million. The isolexical corpus consists of eight independent subcorpora, four from Science disciplines and four from Social Science/Arts disciplines, and is similar in composition to Hyland's research article corpus (Hyland 1998*a*), apart from the substitution of Economics for Applied Linguistics. Each subcorpus contains approximately one million tokens each from five prestigious journals in that discipline, making it larger by an order of magnitude than previous corpora of research articles. The composition of the isolexical corpus can be seen in Fig. 9.3.

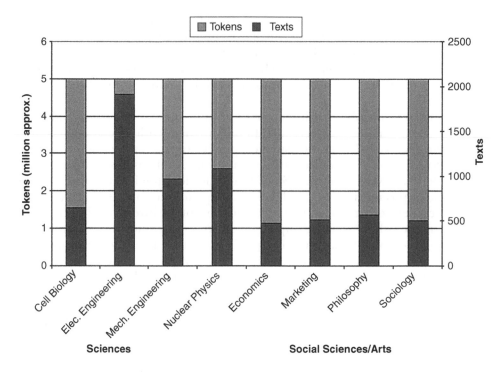

Figure 9.3 Texts and tokens in the isolexical version of the research article corpus.

It is noticeable from Fig. 9.3 that a far smaller number of texts is required in Social Science/Arts disciplines to obtain five million tokens than is required in Science disciplines. The subcorpora for each of the former disciplines contain around 500 texts each, whereas the subcorpora for the latter disciplines contain more than twice as many in the case of Mechanical Engineering and Nuclear Physics, and over three times as many in the case of Electrical Engineering. This variation between disciplines in the corpus is an obvious consequence of the fact that research articles in different academic disciplines vary greatly in length. For example, 750 texts are required to obtain a million Electrical Engineering tokens, but only 75 texts are needed to obtain a million Sociology tokens.

This imbalance of texts, however, means that a corpus of research article data with equal numbers of tokens in different disciplines is only balanced for the amount of language that it contains; it is not evenly balanced for the amount of meaning or communication that it contains. If there are different numbers of texts in the corpus, there are different numbers of communicative acts or situations in the corpus. This means that, despite the fact that the subcorpora are evenly balanced in terms of the number of tokens, consequently addressing the problem pointed out by Biber and Barbieri, they contain different numbers of introductions, conclusions, and so on which might bias any quantitative results in favour of the discipline with the largest number of texts.

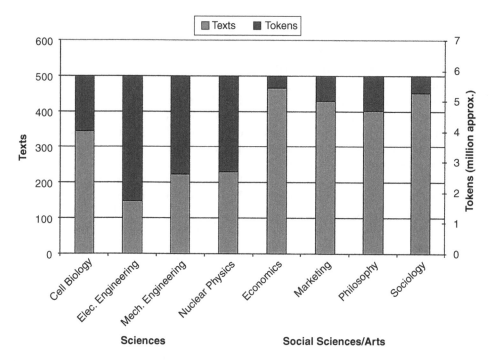

Figure 9.4 Texts and tokens in the isotextual version of the research article corpus.

For studies of the function of extended collocations, i.e. their possible roles in the act of communication, this possible bias needs to be addressed. This can be done by creating another isotextual (from 'same number of texts') version of the corpus containing an equal number of texts. In this case, 500 texts (the 500 most recent) were chosen from each of the five journals in each discipline. The isotextual corpus is almost completely a subset of the isolexical corpus, with the exception of 27 texts from three Economics journals to bring the total number of texts for those journals up to 100. Figure 9.4 shows the composition of the isotextual version of the corpus.

It is noticeable again from Fig. 9.4 that the differences in text lengths mean that the subcorpora in the Science disciplines contain between a third to a half fewer tokens than in the subcorpora in Social Science/Arts disciplines.

9.6 Isolexical and Isotextual Frequencies of 3-word Strings

Once these two versions of this corpus are collected, two basic comparisons can be made: one between isolexical frequencies of linguistic forms across different disciplines, and the other between isotextual frequencies of linguistic forms across different disciplines. The final section of this chapter compares the most frequent 3-word strings in each discipline and again assesses the effect of controlling for number of tokens and number of texts. The term *3-word string* is used, since the discourse function of these forms is not being investigated here.

The contrast between isolexical and isotextual occurrences of frequent (occurring more than 100 times) 3-word strings can be seen in Fig. 9.5. Comparing isolexically, frequent 3-word strings in general tend to occur more often in Science disciplines than in Social Science/Arts disciplines. In a given number of tokens, research articles in Science disciplines consequently contain a larger number of frequent 3-word strings. The one exception to this is in the subcorpus of Philosophy, an Arts related subject, which has the joint second highest number of frequent 3-word strings in the corpus.

The comparison of the occurrence of 3-word strings between subcorpora in the isolexical version of the corpus reveals that variation is not totally dependent on text length or the number of texts in the subcorpus, as can be seen by comparing the light columns in Fig. 9.5 with the light areas of the columns in Fig. 9.3. Even though Electrical Engineering has the shortest texts, and its isolexical subcorpus consequently requires the collection of the largest number of texts to yield 5 million words, it does not have the highest number of frequent 3-word strings. The highest number of 3-word strings on an isolexical comparison is in fact in the Nuclear Physics subcorpus, which has half as many texts as in Electrical

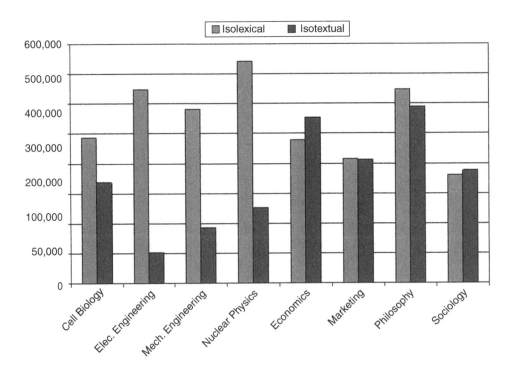

Figure 9.5 Distribution of 3-word strings occurring 100 times or more in each version of the research article corpus.

Engineering. Similarly in the Social Science/Arts subcorpora, all of which contain a similar number of texts, the Philosophy subcorpus contains appreciably more 3-word strings.

When an isotextual comparison is made, the tendency is reversed, and frequent 3-word strings occur considerably more in Social Science/Arts disciplines than in Science disciplines. Again, however, the number of 3-word strings is not totally dependent on the length of texts or the number of tokens in the subcorpus, as can be seen by comparing the dark columns in Fig. 9.5 with the light areas of the columns in Fig. 9.4. While Philosophy has the fewest number of tokens from 500 texts, it has the highest number of frequent 3-word strings.

When the form of the most frequent 3-word strings is compared in each discipline in the two versions it is apparent that the most frequent 3-word strings in the isolexical subcorpus for a particular discipline are also the most frequent 3-word strings in the isotextual subcorpus for that discipline. This is a rather surprising result, given the wide disparity between the numbers of texts in the isolexical version of the corpus, and between the number of tokens in the isotextual version of the corpus. The point of comparing isolexical and isotextual corpora is to eliminate any possible bias caused by under-representation of strings in disciplines with shorter texts or over-representation of strings in disciplines with longer texts, but the above result suggests that there is no such bias in the first place. It is plain that 3-word strings which are found frequently in a fixed number of tokens are also found frequently in a fixed number of texts. The large disparities in the frequencies of contexts of situation appear to have little effect on the rank orders of frequent 3-word strings.

The actual frequencies of the 3-word strings in the isolexical and isotextual versions in each discipline are shown in Tables 9.1–9.8, together with their rank order in each version of the corpus.

Table 9.1 Ten most frequent 3-word strings in the Cell Biology subcorpus.

3-word string	Isolexical frequency	Isolexical rank	Isotextual frequency	Isotextual rank	Rank difference
the presence of	3,176	1	2,564	1	0
in the presence	2,353	2	1,939	2	0
is required for	1,708	3	1,289	4	−1
the absence of	1,703	4	1,364	3	1
in the absence	1,576	5	1,274	5	0
the plasma membrane	1,359	6	1,134	6	0
as well as	1,279	7	1,018	7	0
at 37° c	1,217	8	998	8	0
in response to	1,194	9	959	9	0
at 4° c	1,106	10	891	10	0

Table 9.2 Ten most frequent 3-word strings in the Electrical Engineering subcorpus.

3-word string	Isolexical frequency	Isolexical rank	Isotextual frequency	Isotextual rank	Rank difference
shown in fig	5,574	1	1,954	1	0
due to the	2,812	2	1,048	2	0
as shown in	2,218	3	771	4	−1
a function of	2,043	4	788	3	1
in fig 1	1,971	5	554	9	−4
in fig 2	1,876	6	547	10	−4
as a function	1,844	7	706	5	2
in order to	1,827	8	646	6	2
the number of	1,699	9	637	7	2
is shown in	1,685	10	577	8	2

Table 9.3 Ten most frequent 3-word strings in the Mechanical Engineering subcorpus.

3-word string	Isolexical frequency	Isolexical rank	Isotextual frequency	Isotextual rank	Rank difference
shown in fig	3,862	1	2,001	1	0
in order to	2,273	2	1,209	2	0
as shown in	1,714	3	834	6	−3
the number of	1,684	4	946	3	1
due to the	1,648	5	901	4	1
based on the	1,609	6	875	5	1
the effect of	1,489	7	800	7	0
with respect to	1,486	8	738	8	0
the case of	1,254	9	617	9	0
in terms of	1,174	10	585	10	0

Table 9.4 Eleven most frequent 3-word strings in the Nuclear Physics subcorpus.

3-word string	Isolexical frequency	Isolexical rank	Isotextual frequency	Isotextual rank	Rank difference
in order to	2,270	1	1,223	1	0
a function of	2,234	2	1,021	6	−4
due to the	2,231	3	1,205	3	0
as a function	2,100	4	941	7	−3
in terms of	1,996	5	1,214	2	3
the case of	1,778	6	1,026	5	1
the number of	1,673	7	931	8	−1
is given by	1,571	8	1,047	4	4
shown in fig	1,515	9	764	12	−3
as well as	1,499	10	834	9	1
with respect to	1,337	13	792	10	3

Table 9.5 Eleven most frequent 3-word strings in the Economics subcorpus.

3-word string	Isolexical frequency	Isolexical rank	Isotextual frequency	Isotextual rank	Rank difference
the number of	1,910	1	2,147	1	0
the United States	1,416	2	1,484	2	0
there is a	1,334	3	1,355	4	1
the effect of	1,251	4	1,369	3	1
the fact that	1,218	5	1,315	5	0
with respect to	1,147	6	1,203	7	1
the set of	1,107	7	1,110	8	1
the value of	1,105	8	1,205	6	2
there is no	1,028	9	1,063	10	1
in which the	983	10	1,046	11	1
as well as	947	12	1,077	9	3

Table 9.6 Ten most frequent 3-word strings in the Marketing subcorpus.

3-word string	Isolexical frequency	Isolexical rank	Isotextual frequency	Isotextual rank	Rank difference
the number of	1,585	1	1,586	1	0
as well as	1,573	2	1,538	2	0
the effect of	1,441	3	1,481	3	0
the effects of	1,413	4	1,431	4	0
in terms of	1,399	5	1,339	7	2
the impact of	1,355	6	1,356	5	1
the use of	1,313	7	1,352	6	1
the role of	1,167	8	1,122	9	1
the basis of	1,093	9	1,127	8	1
on the basis	1,033	10	1,068	10	0

Table 9.7 Eleven most frequent 3-word strings in the Philosophy subcorpus.

3-word string	Isolexical frequency	Isolexical rank	Isotextual frequency	Isotextual rank	Rank difference
that it is	2,660	1	2,468	1	0
it is not	2,304	2	2,096	2	0
the fact that	2,245	3	2,060	3	0
there is a	2,211	4	2,006	6	2
there is no	2,205	5	2,051	4	1
that there is	2,121	6	2,032	5	1
in terms of	1,933	7	1,791	7	0
in order to	1,613	8	1,499	8	0
to say that	1,366	9	1,254	9	0
it is a	1,184	10	1,088	12	2
with respect to	1,155	12	1,165	10	2

It can be seen from the tables that, while the isolexical and isotextual rank order of some strings is slightly different, the largest difference is no more than 5 places. The mean difference in rank order is no more than 2.4 places, as shown in Table 9.9. The rank order of 3-word strings between the isolexical and isotextual versions of the corpus is most similar in the disciplines of Cell Biology and Sociology, both of which have a mean difference of less than one place.

This is a potentially intriguing finding for the study of fixed collocational patterns, as it suggests that the relationship between collocation and meaning is not a straightforward one. As discussed above, the principal reason for constructing an isotextual version of a corpus is to hold the 'meaning' variable constant when

Table 9.8 Eleven most frequent 3-word strings in the Sociology subcorpus.

3-word string	Isolexical frequency	Isolexical rank	Isotextual frequency	Isotextual rank	Rank difference
in terms of	1,757	1	1,784	1	0
as well as	1,717	2	1,766	2	0
the United States	1,227	3	1,475	3	0
in order to	1,149	4	1,123	7	3
one of the	1,144	5	1,124	6	1
a number of	989	6	1,011	8	2
the role of	945	7	952	10	3
the number of	918	8	1,129	4	4
the effects of	910	9	1,125	5	4
the fact that	901	10	878	14	4
in the united	801	14	965	9	5

Table 9.9 Mean difference in isolexical and isotextual rank of frequent 3-word strings in the research article corpus.

Discipline	Mean rank difference
Cell Biology	0.2
Electrical Engineering	1.8
Mechanical Engineering	0.6
Nuclear Physics	2.1
Economics	1
Marketing	0.6
Philosophy	0.7
Sociology	2.4

comparing fixed collocational patterns across disciplines. Comparing a similar quantity of texts allows a similar quantity of communicative situations to be compared, and thus, if meaning is defined as context of situation, this allows a similar quantity of meanings to be compared. However, the finding in this study, i.e. that the most frequent fixed collocational patterns between the isolexical and isotextual versions of the corpus are largely similar, suggests that these patterns would occur frequently regardless of the number of communicative situations in the sample.

The above findings may therefore suggest size criteria to guide designers of other comparative corpora, when studying fixed collocational patterns, to reduce the possibility of introducing bias into their results through an imbalance between tokens or texts between disciplines. If an isolexical corpus is being constructed, then its subcorpora should contain at least 500 texts; if an isotextual corpus is being constructed then each subcorpus should contain five million words. If either of these criteria are followed, then there will be less risk of bias being introduced.

9.7 Conclusion

This chapter has surveyed how approaches to collocation have developed since the introduction of corpus data and computer software to investigation of the phenomenon. It is clear that the definition of collocation has become more fluid as the field has grown and applications have become more diverse. The study of collocation in the Firthian tradition was initially concerned with the effect on the meaning of an individual word brought about by its use with another word in a particular text, or within a particular span around the word in a text. Some studies have taken this to further levels of abstraction as previous work has revealed the limitations of the usefulness of the word as a unit of meaning.

Another line of enquiry has been to look at extended collocations and describe their use in and between different contexts of situation, such as registers or genres. This chapter has discussed some of the corpus construction issues in this latter approach to collocation, and has presented some preliminary results relating to 3-word strings. Particularly striking has been the finding that frequent 3-word strings are frequent whether identified isolexically or isotextually. Corpus linguistics has bought this study of collocation up to the point where the prevalence of the most frequent 3-word strings has been quantified, but the implications of the present results will need to be assessed in future work by examining how each of these forms is used in the discourse in each text.

10

Corpus Linguistics and Language Variation

Michael P. Oakes

The creation of balanced corpora representing national varieties of English throughout the world has enabled statistical comparisons of word frequencies in each of these corpora. This chapter examines some of the statistical techniques that have been used in order to carry out such comparisons. Starting with the chi-squared test, I examine studies carried out on the Brown family of corpora, and note how use of dispersion measures (Juilland et al. 1970) and the Bonferroni correction (Altman 1991) can improve such comparisons. I then examine studies of style, genre and register variation, which have used multivariate techniques such as factor analysis and hierarchical clustering. Automatic genre differentiation by a Support Vector Machine (SVM) will be described, not with the objective of making new linguistic discoveries, but because automatic genre identification is useful in itself – in this case as a component in genre-sensitive search engines. Finally, the chapter concludes with a discussion of the difficulties of isolating single factors in corpora for comparison.

10.1 Introduction

Hofland and Johansson (1982: 39) state that quantitative studies of linguistic variation 'shed new light on the utilization of words in different varieties of English, and can, in addition, serve as a starting point for stylistic and grammatical studies as well as for cultural observations'. Biber (1988: 3) writes that many linguists are interested in differences between speech and writing, which can be considered as poles of one dimension of linguistic variation. However, certain types of stylistic research are not amenable to computer analysis, either because they involve a good deal of expert intuition (such as the identification of Semitisms in the Greek New Testament), or because they consider linguistic features which are found only rarely, such as the hapax legomena (words which appear only once) in a text, although these words tell us much about the writer's background and experience. Computer analyses of linguistic variation thus tend to be restricted to comparisons of the use of frequently occurring, objectively countable linguistic features, which are focussed on in this chapter.

Variationist research questions often take the form of 'what are the differences in the ways that feature x is used in corpus y and corpus z?' It should be noted that such questions also implicitly address *similarities* (although researchers tend to find differences more interesting to report), and that multiple (rather than two) corpora can be compared (as discussed later in this chapter). Additionally, the examination of differences is usually frequency-based (e.g. how often does feature x occur in corpus y and is this significantly more or less than in corpus z), although frequencies can often be approached from more complex perspectives, for example, if feature x has three specific functions a, b and c, how are these functions proportionally represented in corpora y and z?

Clearly, in order to carry out comparisons, it is important to use corpora that are matched in as many ways as possible to reduce the number of independent variables that could impact on variation. For example, if a researcher wanted to compare the spoken language of males with the language of females, then he/she would try to gather two corpora (male speech and female speech) that were of similar sizes, had similar numbers of speakers who were talking in similar contexts, in similar time periods and in similar regions of the world. Clearly, the more variables that are different between the two corpora being studied, the more difficult it becomes to say that any differences are the result of the factor we want to examine (such as sex). The Brown corpus family, discussed below, are a good example of corpora that have been carefully constructed using the same sampling model to carry out studies of diachronic and synchronic variation.

10.1.1 The Brown Corpus Family

Before examining the various statistical techniques which have been used to examine corpus variation, I will briefly review the well-known family of corpora based on the original Brown corpus, consisting of a million words of written American English texts that had been published in 1961 (Francis and Kučera 1964). The LOB (Lancaster-Oslo/Bergen) corpus is the British English equivalent of the Brown corpus, published in 1961. Hofland and Johansson (1982: 22) point out that 'One of the major advantages of the LOB and Brown corpora is that their composition enables a comparison of the characteristics of different types of texts'. The two corpora are 'balanced', in that the material in the two corpora were selected to match as much as possible. Both corpora consist of 500 text samples of about 2,000 words each, making about a million words in total. Table 10.1 shows the breakdown of text categories that are represented in both the LOB and the Brown corpora.

The corpora were assembled using identical sampling procedures. The whole population of texts were obtained from three published compendia, one consisting of samples from books, one taken from newspapers and periodicals and one consisting of government documents. Titles from these sources were chosen using a random number table, and articles obviously not written by British authors were excluded. Having chosen each title, the next task was to randomly select the page at which to start the 2,000 word extract. Non-random criteria were also used, such as excluding articles mainly consisting of dialogue, and weighting the sampling process so that articles from the national press were more likely to be chosen than articles from the local press (Hofland and Johansson 1982: 2).

Table 10.1 Text categories in the Brown family (data derived from Biber et al. 1998: 14).

Broad text category		Text category letter and description ('genre')	Number of texts	
			Brown Frown	LOB FLOB
	Press	**A** Press: Reportage	44	44
		B Press: Editorial	27	27
		C Press: Reviews	17	17
Informative		**D** Religion	17	17
		E Skills, Trades and Hobbies	36	38
		F Popular Lore	48	44
	General Prose	**G** Belles Lettres, Biographies, Essays	75	77
		H Miscellaneous: Government documents, industrial reports etc.	30	30
	Learned Writing	**J** Academic prose in various disciplines	80	80
		K General Fiction	29	29
		L Mystery and Detective Fiction	24	24
Imaginative	**Fiction**	**M** Science Fiction	6	6
		N Adventure and Western	29	29
		P Romance and Love story	29	29
		R Humour	9	9

10.1.2 Diachronic Corpora

Two other corpora, balanced with respect to LOB and Brown, are the FLOB (Freiberg-LOB) and Frown (Freiberg-Brown) corpora, designed to represent British English in 1991 and American English in 1992 respectively. Comparisons of these corpora are thus ideal for diachronic studies, enabling observation of changes in language over a thirty-year gap. More recently, further corpus building projects are underway: Leech and Smith (2005) have produced the Lancaster 1931 corpus of British English and are planning a 1901 version, while Baker (2008) has built the mid-2000s equivalent. Comparisons of these corpora will enable researchers to determine whether an observed linguistic change is speeding up, slowing down, remaining constant or reversing (although, it should be borne in mind that a gap of 30 or even 15 years may not give a full picture regarding linguistic change, but rather presents information as static 'snap-shots').

In contrast to the BNC Conversational Corpus (see Section 10.2.2), the Brown family corpora do not record any biographical or demographic information, since this is often not known. However, the Brown corpus family have all been annotated with a common grammatical tagset known as C8 (Leech and Smith 2005).

10.1.3 Sources of Linguistic Variation

As shown in Table 10.1, the Brown family corpora are subdivided into categories, which correspond loosely to 'genre', 'text type' or 'register'. Biber (1998: 208) uses the term 'genre' for classes of texts that are 'determined on the basis of external criteria relating to author's or speaker's purpose'. On the other hand, he uses 'text type' to refer to classes of text that are grouped on the basis of 'similarities in intrinsic linguistic form, irrespective of their genre classifications'. For example, particular texts from press reportage, biographies and academic prose might be very similar in having a *narrative* linguistic form, and thus would be grouped together as a single text type, even though they represent different genres. Register (Biber 1998: 135) refers to variation in language arising from the situations it is used in, and depends on such things as its purpose, topic, setting, interactiveness and the intended addressee. Registers may be highly specific, such as novels by Jane Austen, or the 'Methods' sections of academic papers describing biological research. A fourth source of variation recognized by Biber is 'dialect', which is defined by association with different speaker groups, based on region, social group or other demographic factors. Genre can swamp changes in language change 'proper' as observed in diachronic studies. To quote Hundt and Mair (1999: 222) differences in balanced corpora may 'reflect a change in stylistic preference rather than a change in grammatical rules'.

10.1.4 Feature Selection

For many text classification tasks, an essential early stage is to decide which linguistic features (called 'attributes' in machine learning applications) should be used to characterize the texts. Often, texts are characterized by the single word tokens they contain. Another possibility is to reduce all the words in a text to their lemmas, and record how many of each lemma is found in that text. If the texts are annotated with a state-of-the-art semantic tagger (e.g. Rayson et al. 2004a), then they can be characterized by the frequency with which each semantic tag is found. Even when selecting single word tokens as attributes, some decisions must be taken. For example, Hofland and Johansson (1982: 7) specified that a word token should consist of 'alphanumeric characters surrounded by white space, but may contain punctuation', thus allowing *2.33* and *5,000* to be counted as words. They also devised a capitalization principle, incidentally providing a basis for the different task of named-entity or proper noun recognition: 'words which are spelled with capitals in all their occurrences in the material are reproduced with capitals in the lists'. Some words were given interpretive codes, for example, AB (abbreviation), SF (neologism from science fiction), FO (foreign words and expressions), so another basis for comparison between two varieties of English could be the relative prevalence of these codes. For example, does British English make more use of abbreviations than American English?

One of the simplest and most widely used techniques for examining language variation in different corpora is the chi-squared test. The following section explains how the test is carried out and describes corpus variation studies which have used it. Additionally, I discuss limitations of the chi-squared test in order to demonstrate when its use is appropriate, and the advantage of using it in conjunction with a measure called Yule's Q.

10.2 The Chi-Squared Test

The chi-squared test is a widely used statistical test for the comparison of count data, such as word frequencies. One question which might be tackled by this test could be 'is the word *mother* more typical of female speech than male speech?' In the BNC Conversational Corpus, the word *mother* occurs 272 times in a corpus of 1,714,433 words of male speech, and 627 times in a 2,593,452 corpus of female speech (Rayson et al. 1977). The so-called 'observed' (directly counted) data is

(a) the word *mother* was spoken 627 times by females;
(b) *mother* was spoken 272 times by males;
(c) words other than *mother* were spoken 2,593,452 – 627 = 2,592,825 times by females, and;
(d) words other than *mother* were spoken on 1,714,433 – 272 = 1,714,161 occasions by males.

These values are set out in a 'contingency table', as shown in Table 10.2(a). However, do these numbers show that females really do say *mother* more than men? The first step in answering this question is to calculate the 'expected' values, which are the values for (a) to (d) we would have obtained if there was absolutely no difference in how often the two sexes say this word. The grand total, which is the total number of words in the combined corpora, is 1,714,433 + 2,593,452 = 4,307,885. Of this total, the word *mother* was spoken 272 + 627 = 899 times (the row total), and 1,714,433 words were spoken by men (the column total). So we might expect that of the 899 times that *mother* occurred, it would have been spoken by males 899 times the proportion of words in the combined corpus spoken by males, which is 899 × (1,714,433/4,307,885). Analogously, we work out the expected frequencies for the other three cells in the contingency table, using the formula

$$\text{Expected frequency} = \frac{\text{Row total} \times \text{Column total}}{\text{Grand total}}$$

The expected values are shown in Table 10.2(b). Now that we have corresponding tables of observed and expected values, we can derive a third table of contributions

Table 10.2 Calculation of chi-squared for the use of the word *mother* in male and female speech.

(a) Observed values

	Male speech	Female speech	Row total
mother	272	627	899
any other word	1,714,161	2,592,825	4,306,986
Column total	1,714,433	2,593,452	Grand Total = 4,307,885

(b) Expected values

	Male speech	Female speech
mother	357.8	541.2
any other word	1,714,074.9	2,592,910.6

(c) Contributions to the overall chi-squared value made by each cell

	Male speech	Female speech
mother	20.6	13.6
any other word	0.0	0.0

to the overall chi-squared value made by each cell. The value in each cell of this table (shown in Table 10.2(c)) is given by the formula:

$$\frac{(\textit{Observed value for that cell} - \textit{Expected value for that cell})^2}{\textit{Expected value for that cell}}$$

The four values in this table (one for each cell) are added together, to give an overall chi-squared value (34.2 in this example). We then obtain a quantity called the degrees of freedom, which depends on the size of the original contingency table, as follows:

Degrees of freedom = (number of rows − 1) × (number of columns − 1)

Thus for a 2 by 2 table, we have one degree of freedom. Using this data, we can look up what are called the 'critical values' for the chi-squared statistic in tables which can be found at the back of many statistics textbooks, such as Table A5 in Woods et al. (1986). If chi-square is > 3.84 with one degree of freedom, we can be 95 per cent confident that there really is a difference in the number of times males and females say mother; if chi-squared > 6.64 we can be 99 per cent confident; and if chi-squared is > 10.8 (as is the case in the *mother* example), we can be 99.9 per cent confident.

The chi-squared test can be extended for comparisons of more than two corpora. For example, Hofland and Johansson (1982: 19) simultaneously compared word frequencies in LOB and Brown, and two other corpora created by Carroll et al. (1971) and Jones and Sinclair (1974). Oakes and Farrow (2007) used the chi-squared test to compare the word frequencies in the variants of English used in Australia, Britain, India, New Zealand and the United States. Here the aim was to find words which occurred significantly more often in one variety of English than any of the others. The Australian corpus (ACE) had significantly more names of Australian people and places, and terms related to employment rights such as *unions, unemployed* and *superannuation*. As previously found by Leech and Fallon (1992) when comparing LOB and Brown, the British corpus (in this case FLOB) had many more aristocratic titles. The Kolhapur corpus of Indian English contained the terms *crores* for tens of millions, and *lakhs* for tens of thousands. There were also significantly more words related to the caste system, particularly *caste, castes* and *dalit*, and more terms coming from a wide variety of religions. The Wellington corpus of New Zealand English not surprisingly had many more names of New Zealand people and places, and also more sporting terms (*rugby* was sixteenth on the list of most typical New Zealand words) and words describing the natural world such as *bay, beach* and *cliff*. The Frown corpus had more terms reflecting concerns about diversity and equality: *black, gender, white, diversity* and *gay*. While many of these observations indicate cultural differences between these countries where English is widely spoken, linguistic differences were found as well. For example, the Kohlhapur corpus had more high frequency function words. Spelling differences between American English and the other types of English were regularly found, with *color* for example being highly typical of American English. Many concepts for transport were found to be typical of Frown, such as *pickup, railroad, highway* and *transportation*. These concepts exist in other English-speaking countries, but other terms are used for them.

When using the chi-squared test, a number of common errors should be avoided. First, some people feel that the test can only be used when comparing corpora of equal size. This is not so; it can be used for corpora of any relative size, as long as the rule-of-thumb is followed that expected values should all be five or more (for exact details of this, see Rayson et al. (2004*b*)). Second, some authors have disregarded data because some of the *observed* frequencies are less than five – but the criterion is that only words for which the *expected* values are less than five should be excluded from the analysis. Third, some authors have 'normalized' their data, so that instead of using raw frequency counts (the actual number of times each word was observed), they have expressed figures as ratios, for example, the occurrence of each word per thousand words of text. The problem with this is that different values of chi-squared would be obtained if the ratios were expressed as, say, words per million, so it is essential to use raw frequency counts rather than ratios, when carrying out chi-squared tests.

A potential problem regarding the value placed on results of the chi-squared tests relates to dispersion. For example, *thalidomide* occurs very frequently in the FLOB corpus, but only in a single article. Thus it would be dangerous to conclude that this word is somehow very typical of the British English of the 1990s. Therefore, a number of authors have pointed out that it is important to take into account some sort of criterion of 'dispersion' when carrying out comparisons of word frequencies across corpora, so conclusions are not based on words which appear often, but are clumped into a very small number of texts. The criterion of Kučera and Francis (1967) for the Brown corpus is that words should be distributed through at least five texts. Finally, if we are making multiple comparisons, such as simultaneously comparing the frequencies of many different words in two corpora, there will be an increased risk of Type I errors. These occur when a statistical test shows that a significant difference has been found in the frequency of a word in two corpora, even though this difference was simply due to chance variation. If we are looking for significance at the 5 per cent level, a type I error will occur in about one in twenty of the comparisons we make. This problem can be compensated for by using the Bonferroni correction (Oakes and Farrow 2007). In the past, people (e.g. Dunning 1993) have argued that related measures such as log-likelihood, also known as G^2, can be used with very low frequency data. There are indications that the log-likelihood test is becoming more popular among corpus linguists (see, e.g. King, this volume). However, the 'minimum of 5 for Expected values' rule should still be used when using this test (Moore 2004).

Lucy (2005: 51) writes that 'one of the properties of the chi-squared test is that variables showing only a weak relationship can show highly significant values of chi-squared'. This is because the chi-squared value reflects how confident we can be that there really is a relationship between two variables (such as a word and a genre). If we repeat a chi-squared experiment with a much larger data set, we would be more confident of our findings, and the resulting chi-squared values would be greater than before. However, the strength of the relationship between word and genre remains the same, irrespective of the size of the data set. The chi-squared test also does not show the direction of any relationship. For example, if the relationship between the word *grandma* and speaker gender produces a chi-squared value of 35.5, we can be confident that these two variables are indeed related, but is *grandma* indicative of male or female speech? For 2 × 2 contingency tables, Yule's Distinctiveness Coefficient (DC), also known as Yule's Q, is a useful measure of both strength and direction of relationship. This measure will be described further in Section 10.3. For 2 × n contingency tables, where either the number of rows or columns is more than 2, the strength of relationship can be found by Φ^2, where we divide the chi-squared value by the sample size. If both the number of rows and the number of columns are more than 2, we take the smaller of the number of rows and columns, and then subtract one. Φ^2 should be divided by this number to yield a measure called Cramer's V^2 (Lucy 2005: 48–51).

10.2.1 Comparisons Between British and American English

Hofland and Johansson (1982: 32) used the chi-squared technique to examine differences in the vocabulary used in American English and British English. They found, among other things, that British English prefers the –*t* form of the past

Table 10.3 Complete and absolute associations in LOB and Brown.

(a) A complete association		
	Brown	*LOB*
theatre	0	63
theater	95	30

(b) An absolute association		
	Brown	*LOB*
south-west	0	10
southwest	16	0

tense, as in *learnt* and *dreamt* as opposed to *learned* and *dreamed*. Here it is useful to note Lucy's (2005: 49) distinction of 'complete' and 'absolute' associations between variables. In the case of British and American English, these associations could be between the choice of alternative word forms and the choice of corpus. For example, the prevalence of the two forms *theatre* and *theatre* can be tabulated as in Table 10.3(a). The association is said to be complete because there is a 0 in one of the cells, in this case denoting that *theatre* never occurred in the sample of American English (although *theater* sometimes occurs in the LOB corpus of British English). In an absolute association there is a 0 in both the cells on one diagonal. Table 10.3(b) shows the absolute association between the choice of *south-west* and *southwest* and the type of corpus. The former is never used in Brown, and the latter is never used in LOB. Complete and absolute associations can only be identified in 2 by 2 tables.

Leech and Fallon (1992), who also used the chi-squared test, regarded that differences in the relative frequency with which words were used in the United States and Britain could be indicative of cultural differences between the two countries. An obvious example of this would be the prevalence of *baseball* in Brown, and the prevalence of *cricket* in LOB.

10.2.2 Social Differentiation in the Use of Vocabulary

Rayson et al. (1997) studied the demographically sampled and spoken English component of the British National Corpus. They used the chi-squared test to look for differences in word frequency with gender, age and socio-economic group. Some of their results are shown in Table 10.4. In each case, the 20 words with the highest chi-squared score are presented.

In general, males use more taboo words and number words, while women use more first person and third person feminine pronouns. In fact, Rayson, Leech and Hodges report that 'taboo vocabulary is highly characteristic along all three dimensions of gender, age and social group', that is, among male speakers below 35 years of age in the C2/D/E social range. Such findings suggest that it is

Table 10.4 Vocabulary used predominantly by certain social groups.

	A	B
Gender: Male (A) vs Female (B)	fucking, er, the, yeah, aye, right, hundred, fuck, is, of, two, three, a, four, ah, no, number, quid, one, mate	she, her, said, n't, I, and, to, cos, oh, christmas, thought, lovely, nice, mm, had, did, going, because, him, really
Age: Under 35 (A) vs Over 35 (B)	mum, fucking, my, mummy, like, wan 'na, goes, shit, dad, daddy, me, what, fuck, really, okay, cos, just, why	yes, well, mm, er, they, said, says, were, the, of, and, to, mean, he, but, perhaps, that, see, had
Socio-economic group: ABC1 (A) vs C2DE (B)[1]	yes, really, okay, are, actually, just, good, you, erm, right, school, think, need, your, basically, guy, sorry, hold, difficult, wicked, rice, class	he, says, said, fucking, ain't, yeah, its, them, aye, she, bloody, pound, I, hundred, well, n't, mummy, that, they, him, were, four, bloke, five, thousand

important to take into account the fact that variation may be the result of different factors acting in combination (e.g. the high prevalence of *lovely* in female speech is more due to the fact that it is older female speakers who use this word, rather than all females). Multivariate techniques are discussed in more detail in Section 10.3.

10.3 Genre Analysis

As described in Section 10.1, the LOB and Brown corpora were sampled according to text genre. The chi-squared test, as described in Section 10.2, can also be used to compare the vocabulary used in different genres. However, in this section, we will look at four other techniques for examining vocabulary differences in different genres, namely Yule's DC, hierarchical clustering, factor analysis and the SVM.

10.3.1 Yule's Distinctiveness Coefficient

Hofland and Johansson (1982, chapter 7) recorded the word frequencies in the following 'super-category' groups created by combining certain genres in the LOB corpus: A-C (newspaper text), D-H (informative prose), J (learned and scientific English), and K-R (fiction). The words for each super-category were ranked by their DC, which is a measure of the degree of over- or under-representation of a word in each category group. They give the example of the word *spokesman* which occurs 19 times (the 'absolute frequency') in one category, which we will call X. Taking into account the absolute frequency and total number of words in category

X, there is a relative frequency for *spokesman* of 107 words per million, using the formula:

> relative frequency = absolute frequency × 1 million/number of words in the category.

The word *spokesman* occurs 20 times in the million-word corpus as a whole (the corpus frequency). If the relative frequency is greater than the corpus frequency then the word is over-represented in that category, but if the relative frequency is less than the corpus frequency then the word is under-represented in that category. Since the relative frequency is 107 and the corpus frequency is only 20, *spokesman* is over-represented in category X by 87 words per million. The most over-represented words in category J and super-category K-R found by Hofland and Johansson are reproduced in Table 10.5. The words are listed in order of their DCs, highest first.

The 'distinctiveness coefficient' was originally developed by Yule (1944), and has since found acceptance outside linguistics. It appears, for example, in a book on forensic statistics (Lucy 2005: 48), where it is referred to as Yule's Q. It ties in with the ideas of complete and absolute associations described in Section 10.1, since in both cases Q is either −1 or 1. The form used by Hofland and Johansson is as follows:

$$DC = \frac{Freq_{LOB} - Freq_{BROWN}}{Freq_{LOB} + Freq_{BROWN}}$$

The DC always falls in the range −1 (for words exclusive to the Brown corpus) to +1 (for words exclusive to the LOB corpus). All other words have a DC somewhere in

Table 10.5 Most over-represented words in categories J vs K-R of the LOB corpus, listed in descending order of their DCs.

Grammatical category	J (science)	K-R (fiction)
Nouns	constants, axis, equations, oxides, equation, theorem	mister, sofa, wallet, cheek, living-room, café
Lexical verbs	measured, assuming, calculated, occurs, assigned, emphasized	kissed, heaved, leaned, glanced, smiled, hesitated
Adjectives	thermal, linear, radioactive, structural, finite	damned, asleep, sorry, gay, miserable, dear
Adverbs	theoretically, significantly, approximately, hence, relatively, respectively	impatiently, softly, hastily, nervously, upstairs, faintly

Table 10.6 Comparison between the parts of speech of the words with highest distinctiveness ratio for two genres.

Grammatical category	J (science)	K-R (fiction)
Nouns	58	23
Lexical verbs	1	31
Adjectives	12	2
Adverbs	0	4
Others	29	40
Total	**100**	**100**

between these two extremes. For example, the word *abandoned* is found 43 times in LOB and 25 times in Brown. Yule's DC is therefore $(43 - 25)/(43 + 25) = 18/68 = 0.26$. This positive value indicates that the word is over-represented in the LOB corpus, while a negative value would have shown that the word was under-represented in the LOB corpus (or over-represented in the Brown corpus).

Hofland and Johansson (1982: 32) made a comparison between the parts-of-speech of the 100 most over-represented words in both the J and K-R categories as determined by the distinctiveness ratio. In Table 10.6 there are more nouns and adjectives which are distinctive of J (learned and scientific articles) than for K-R (fiction), while there are more lexical verbs which are distinctive for fiction than for learned and scientific articles.

10.3.2 Hierarchical Clustering

The statistical techniques looked at so far are called univariate because a single variable is measured for each sampling unit. In the examples given in Sections 10.2 and 10.3.1, the single variable was frequency count, and the sampling units were single words or other countable linguistic feature. Sections 10.3.2 to 10.3.4 will examine multivariate approaches, where many different variables are all measured on the same sampling units. This section will focus on examples where a single genre (the sampling unit) is represented by a whole list of characteristic linguistic features, such as the frequency counts for each of 50 frequent words. The first multivariate technique examined will be a form of cluster analysis, which is a type of automatic categorisation – similar things (such as related genres) are grouped together, and dissimilar things are kept apart.

10.3.2.1 Correlation in word-frequency rankings
The starting point for many clustering algorithms, such as the one described in the following section, is the similarity matrix, which is a square table of numeric scores reflecting how much each of the items (such as texts) to be clustered have in common with each of the others. The production of such a matrix is described

by Hofland and Johansson (1982: 19). To study the relationships between four corpora (LOB, Brown, Carroll et al.[2] (1971) and Jones and Sinclair[3] (1974)), they calculated the Spearman rank correlations (see below) for the frequencies of the 89 most common words in the LOB corpus. Common single words can often be indicators of grammatical and stylistic differences between genres. For example *by* indicates use of the passive voice, *which* indicates the use of relative clauses, *the* indicates the use of nouns, and *an* the use of Latinate vocabulary (ibid.: 22). To illustrate their method of producing the similarity matrix for the four corpora, it is repeated here for just the ten most frequent words in the LOB corpus. These ten words and their ranks in each of the corpora (where the most frequent word would have a rank of 1) are listed in Table 10.7(a). This data is rewritten in Table 10.7(b),

Table 10.7 The ten most frequent words in the LOB corpus compared with the ranks of the corresponding words in three other corpora.

(a) Considering all words

	LOB	*Brown*	*Carroll et al. (1971)*	*Jones and Sinclair (1974)*
the	1	1	1	1
of	2	2	2	8
and	3	3	3	3
to	4	4	5	6
a	5	5	4	5
in	6	6	6	9
that	7	7	9	11
is	8	8	7	12
was	9	9	13	14
it	10	12	10	7

(b) Considering only the top ten words in the LOB corpus

	LOB	*Brown*	*Carroll et al. (1971)*	*Jones and Sinclair (1974)*
the	1	1	1	1
of	2	2	2	6
and	3	3	3	2
to	4	4	5	4
a	5	5	4	3
in	6	6	6	7
that	7	7	8	8
is	8	8	7	9
was	9	9	10	10
it	10	10	9	5

except that the words that were ranked tenth and eleventh in the Brown corpus are ignored, and only the ranks of each word among the top ten words in LOB are considered. Similarly, *was* is recorded in Table 10.7(a) as being the 13th most common word overall in the Carroll et al. corpus. Ignoring the words that were 11th and 12th most common in Carroll et al., since these words are not among the top ten in LOB, we record in Table 10.7(b) that of the words which appear in the top ten of LOB; *was* was the 10th most frequent in the Carroll et al. corpus.

A correlation coefficient measures the similarity between two corresponding sets of data. One such measure is the Spearman rank correlation coefficient (see, e.g. Woods et al. 1986: 170–1), which is given by the following formula:

$$r_s = 1 - \frac{6 \times \Sigma\ (R - S)^2}{n(n^2 - 1)}$$

When comparing the word frequency rankings for LOB and Jones and Sinclair, the top line of this formula can be calculated by taking the following steps. In Table 10.8 R is the rank of a word in LOB and S is the rank of the same word in Jones and Sinclair. In column 3 the difference in the ranks is recorded, and in column 4, the squares of the differences between the ranks is calculated. The summation symbol Σ in the bottom row means that the sums of the squares of the differences between the ranks must be added together, giving a total of 50. Finally, n is the number of words considered in the analysis, which is 10.

Spearman's rank correlation coefficient is then:

Table 10.8 Calculation of the top line of the Spearman formula (comparing LOB and Jones and Sinclair).

	R = Rank (LOB)	S = Rank (Jones and Sinclair)	$R - S$	$(R - S)^2$
the	1	1	0	0
of	2	6	−4	16
and	3	2	1	1
to	4	4	0	0
a	5	3	2	4
in	6	7	−1	1
that	7	8	−1	1
is	8	9	−1	1
was	9	10	−1	1
it	10	5	5	25
				Σ = **Total = 50**

$$1 = \frac{6 \times 50}{10 \times 99} = 0.697$$

A correlation coefficient is given as a number between −1 and +1. A coefficient of +1 means that two sets of scores have perfect positive correlation, whereas −1 indicates perfect negative correlation (as one score increases, the other decreases). Scores closer to zero indicate weaker correlation while a score of zero means that there is no correlation at all between the two sets of scores.

Once all of the corpora have been compared against each other in this way the similarity matrix in Table 10.9 can be obtained. The trivial observation that the word frequency ranking for a corpus is identical with itself does not need to be recorded, so the principal diagonal from top left to bottom right can be left empty. Note also that the matrix is symmetrical, so for example the similarity between Brown and Carroll is the same as that between Carroll and Brown. Since the rankings for LOB and Brown were identical, the Spearman correlation between them is +1. Hofland and Johansson also found that although Brown and Carroll contain American English, and the other two corpora contain British English, the most similar pair of corpora based on the word frequency rankings were LOB and Brown. It could be concluded that this is because these corpora were sampled to match each other with respect to the number of texts of each type they contain.

The similarity matrix of Table 10.9 can also be calculated using the Matlab statistical toolbox. The input data is that of Table 10.7(b), in a form where each corpus is allocated a row rather than a column:

```
Data = [ 1   2   3   4   5   6   7   8   9 10;
         1   2   3   4   5   6   7   8   9 10;
         1   2   3   5   4   6   8   7 10   9;
         1   6   2   4   3   7   8   9 10   5 ]
```

The command M = pdist(Data,'spearman') then produces a *difference* matrix called M, showing the differences between the corpora rather than their similarities. To transform this into a similarity matrix called N, we need the

Table 10.9 Similarity matrix for four corpora based on the word frequency rankings for ten common words.

	LOB	Brown	Carroll et al.	Jones and Sinclair
LOB	–	1.000	0.9636	0.6970
Brown	1.000	–	0.9636	0.6970
Carroll et al.	0.9636	0.9636	–	0.7576
Jones and Sinclair	0.6970	0.6970	0.7576	–

command N = 1 - M. When this matrix is printed out it consists of the six numbers in the top right-hand corner of Table 10.9. Since Table 10.9 is symmetrical, it is not necessary to reproduce the data for both corners. Thus Matlab gives the matrix in the following form:

N = [1.000 0.9636 0.6970 0.9636 0.6970 0.7576]

10.3.2.2 Production of a dendrogram

This section describes how clustering procedures are used in order to show relationships between groups of data (in this case the 15 different genres in LOB). Clustering is a technique which starts by considering all of the groups separately and calculating which two are the most similar. Then the two most similar groups are joined together to form a single cluster and the similarity calculation is carried out again, with the next two most similar groups being joined together, and so on, until there is only one 'super-cluster' left. The process can be visually represented as a dendogram – a type of tree diagram which shows the relationships between the groups.

Starting with the similarity matrix of genres produced by Hofland and Johansson (1982: 23), based on the rankings of the most common 89 words in LOB in each genre, these are rewritten in the linear format of matrix N as shown in the previous section. The matrix is then transformed into a distance matrix M with M = 1 – N. The Matlab statistical tool box can then be used to cluster the genres and produce the dendogram in Fig. 10.1. The letters along the bottom of Fig. 10.1 refer to the various genres in LOB, while the numbers down the side axis are difference scores – the lower the score here, the more similar the genres are. Therefore, the most similar pair of genres were K (fiction) and P (romance) which have a similarity of 0.97 or a difference of 1 – 0.97 = 0.03. The first step then, is to join these two genres into a single cluster. Henceforth, these two genres are considered as a singe entity.

The next most similar pair of nodes are L (mystery and detective fiction) and N adventure and western fiction), with a difference of 0.04, so these two are now fused to form a single entity. At the third stage, the two most similar entities are not individual nodes, but the clusters formed at the previous two stages. The distance between two clusters can be calculated in various ways. Here 'average linkage' was used, where the distance between two clusters is the average difference of all the members of one cluster and all the members of the other cluster. When using the 'single linkage method', the distance between two clusters is taken as the distance between the most similar member of one cluster to the most similar member of the other. The two clusters created so far are now joined together to form a larger cluster of four nodes. At each subsequent stage of the process the two most similar entities (clusters or individual nodes) are fused, until a single cluster remains. Matlab conducts the clustering process, described here in response to the command Z = linkage(M,'average'), where N is the name of the original difference matrix.

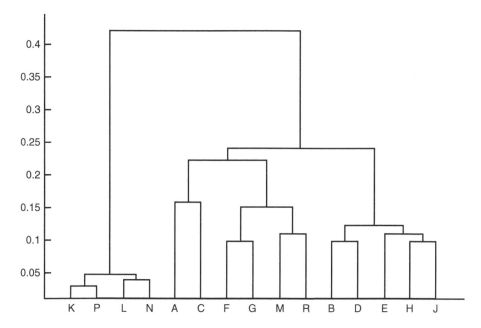

Figure 10.1 Dendrogram for the Genres in the LOB corpus.

The resulting dendogram can be plotted out on Matlab using the command `H = dendrogram(Z)`. The clusters are normally labelled numerically (in this case 1 to 15), but in order to allow the genres to be recognized according to the alphabetic labels in Table 10.1, it was necessary to input a couple of additional commands into Matlab in order to create the matrix `V = [A; B; C; D; E; F; G; H; J; K; L; M; N; P; R]`, and then `H = dendrogram(Z,'labels',V)`.

In Fig. 10.1, Genres K (General fiction), P (Romance and love story), L (Mystery and detective fiction) and N (Adventure and western fiction) form the most tightly bound cluster – not only were they closely related to each other, but they were quite distinct from all the other genres. It is not surprising that four types of fiction should be closely related to each other. If a criterion is set that all genres with less than 0.3 difference to each other belong in the same cluster, then there are just two clusters: the cluster containing K, L, N and P vs the rest. However, if a stricter criterion is set, that only genres with less than 0.2 difference should be considered as members of a common cluster, then the data set splits into four clusters. As before, the first of these is the cluster of K, L, N and P. After that, reading from left to right, a second cluster consists of two types of newspaper material: A (Press reportage) and C (Press reviews). It seems that these two genres are more intimately related to each other than they are to B (Press editorial), which appears in the fourth cluster (but remember that the second, third and fourth clusters are not so distantly removed from each other as they are from the first cluster). The third cluster suggests that M (Science fiction) and R (Humour) have much more in common with each other, along with F (Popular lore) and G (Belles lettres) than they do with the other types of fiction in the first cluster. Finally, the fourth cluster consists of B (Press editorial), D (Religion), E (Skills, trades and hobbies), H (Government documents), and J (Learned and scientific writings). Perhaps these five genres all aim at a common 'factual' writing style.

It should be noted again that the criteria for comparison in Fig. 10.1 were based on the rankings of the most common 89 words in each genre. It is possible that other types of criteria (e.g. standardized type-token ratio, overall proportion of nouns, mean word length) might produce different clustering patterns.

Although Hofland and Johansson used a visual representation of the similarity matrix, where dark coloured squares indicated very similar genres and lighter squares indicated less similar genres (ibid.: 24–5), their findings were similar to those shown in the dendrogram: the corpus was seen to have two major groups of texts (informative and imaginative prose), bridged by categories of what they called 'essayistic prose' – popular lore, belles lettres, science fiction and humour (ibid.: 27).

10.3.3 Factor Analysis

Biber (1988) writes that texts can be quantitatively characterized by any countable features such as single word frequency counts. Biber also used other countable features such as suasive verbs (*agree, arrange, ask, beg, command*, etc.), contractions, and the type-token ratio. In the technique of factor analysis however, text types are characterized not so much by individual markers, but by their regular co-occurrences within these text types. Groups of features which consistently co-occur in texts, using Biber's terminology, are said to define a 'linguistic dimension'. Such features are said to have positive loadings with respect to that dimension, but it is also possible for dimensions to be defined by features which are negatively correlated with them, that is, negative loadings. Biber's approach is to group the features first, and then to identify the linguistic dimensions, such as formal vs informal, or involved vs detached. The relative importance of factors is measured by values called eigenvalues. It is something of an art to empirically assess how many dimensions there really are in a set of texts, but one technique is to manually examine a graph of eigenvalues called a scree plot. A one-dimensonal example, showing a single linguistic dimension is given by Biber (1988: 17). At one pole is 'many pronouns and contractions', near which lie conversational texts, and almost as close, panel discussions. At the opposite pole, 'few pronouns and contractions', are scientific texts and fiction. Biber (1988: 63) gives the following methodological overview of factor analysis.

1. The use of computer corpora, such as LOB, which classify texts by a wide range of genres.
2. The use of computer programs to count the frequencies of linguistic features throughout the range of genres.

3. Use of factor analysis, to determine co-occurrence relations among the features.
4. Use of the linguist's intuition to interpret the linguistic dimensions discovered.

In a small experiment, the author wrote a Perl script to count the raw frequencies within each genre of the 50 most common words in the LOB corpus. These data were stored in a matrix called B, where the columns referred to genre and the rows referred to linguistic feature (word). Following Biber (1998: 94), these raw frequency data were standardized to a mean of 0 and a standard deviation of 1, using the Matlab command [S, meanp, stdp] = prestd(p), which creates a matrix of standardized data called S. The use of standardized data prevents those features that occur very frequently (such as the word *the*) from having an undue influence on the computed factor scores. The factor analysis itself uses a process called 'rotation', which simplifies the analysis by ensuring that each feature loads on as few factors as possible. Thus each factor becomes characterized only by its most representative features. One type of rotation called 'varimax' assumes the factors are uncorrelated, while another called 'promax' permits factors to overlap in features. Matlab uses varimax for the calculation of a matrix of factor loadings (called lambda) and promax for producing a convenient visual representation of the data called a biplot. The feature loadings in lambda should all be in the range −1 to +1. The factor analysis itself takes our matrix of standardized frequency counts S, with the command:

```
[lambda, psi, T, stats, F] = factoran(S, 2)
```

This will give a solution with two factors, and ignore all other factors with smaller eigenvalues than these. The number '2' can be replaced with higher numbers if desired, in order to enable the extraction of more factors. The value 2 was simply chosen here to produce the clearest biplot for illustration purposes, and the author did not attempt to calculate the optimal number of factors from a mathematical point of view. As stated above, lambda is a matrix of factor loadings. F is the matrix of scores for each of the features, indicating which words are associated with which factors.

Having performed the factor analysis, the next step is to produce a visual representation called a 'biplot' which shows the relationships between the factors, the text genres, and the individual linguistic features (in this case, frequent words). The biplot in Fig. 10.2 was produced using the following Matlab command:

```
biplot(lambda, 'scores', F, 'varlabels', V)
```

Here, 'scores' is a command used to plot the individual frequently occurring words on the biplot as dots. V is a one-dimensional matrix of genre labels created beforehand, using the command V = [A;B;C;D;E;F;G;H;J;K;L;M;N;P;R]. The term 'varlabels' is the command used to print these labels next to the appropriate text genre vectors. The scores are scaled by the biplot, so the word

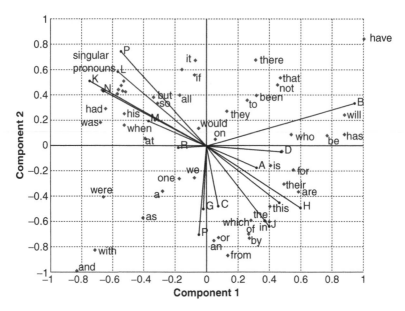

Figure 10.2 Biplot for a factor analysis.

points all fit inside the unit square. In Fig. 10.2, the word points have been labelled manually. As was the case for the dendrogram shown in Fig. 10.1, it can be seen that the four types of fiction K (General), L (Mystery and detective), N (Adventure and Western) and P (Romance and love story) are closely related to each other, scoring highly on factor 2 but loaded highly and negatively on factor 1. The genres M (Science fiction) and R (Humour) are again closely related. Like the other fictional texts, they are loaded positively on factor 2 and negatively on factor 1, but with much smaller loadings. B (Press: Editorial) is unique in that it is the only genre to be positively loaded on both factors, but as with the dendrogram, its closest neighbour is D (religion). The genres F (Popular lore), G (Belles lettres) and C (Press: Reviews) are again closely related, this time all independent of factor 1 and negatively loaded on factor 2. The genres D (Religion), E (Skills, trades and hobbies), H (Misc) and J (Science) were also close neighbours in both analyses, here negatively loaded on factor 2 but positively loaded on factor 1. Only genre A (Press: Reportage) is somewhat differently located with respect to its neighbours compared with the dendrogram. Table 10.10 shows the words most closely associated (positively and negatively) with factors 1 and 2.

The most striking features of Table 10.10 are:

(a) the word *have* had the most positive score with respect to both factors,
(b) the word *and* had the most negative score with respect to both factors, and
(c) the singular personal pronouns (*I, you, he, she, his, him, her*) were clustered very closely together.

Table 10.10 Scores for factors 1 and 2.

		Factor 1				Factor 2	
Positive loadings		Negative loadings		Positive loadings		Negative loadings	
word	score	word	score	word	score	word	score
have	1.00	and	−0.83	have	0.83	and	−0.99
will	0.88	with	−0.72	it	0.68	from	−0.87
has	0.88	was	−0.68	no	0.60	with	−0.83
be	0.77	were	−0.65	if	0.56	an	−0.75
are	0.58	had	−0.64	that	0.53	by	−0.74
who	0.54	you	−0.57	she	0.50	or	−0.73
their	0.48	him	−0.56	her	0.48	of	−0.70
that	0.47	I	−0.54	not	0.45	in	−0.61
not	0.45	she	−0.53	him	0.44	the	−0.60
this	0.40	when	−0.53	I	0.43	which	−0.59
in	0.40	he	−0.52	he	0.34	as	−0.58
		his	−0.52			this	−0.48
		as	−0.40			were	−0.41

In Fig. 10.2 the six points between the lines for genres K (General fiction) and L (Mystery and detective fiction) correspond to *she, her, him, he, I* and *you*. This shows that singular personal pronouns are very characteristic of fictional texts.

10.3.4 Linguistic Facets and SVMs

Santini (2006) developed an alternative approach to the automatic classification of web texts based on genre. Some web genres are 'extant', in that they have long existed in other media, such as the printed word. Examples of these are found in the BBC Web Genre Collection, namely editorials, do-it-yourself, mini-guides, short biographies and features articles. 'Variant' genres, on the other hand, have only arisen since the advent of the world-wide web, such as those found in the 7-Web-Genre collection: blogs, e-shops, frequently-asked-questions, listings (such as site maps or indexes), personal home pages and search pages (which include dynamic content, especially some form of search engine). The 7-Web-Genre collection also contains an extant genre: that of online newspaper front pages. It is anticipated that new web genres will emerge in the not too distant future. Web pages often belong to more than one genre, while others do not fit into any genre at all. Thus Santini's automatic genre identifier allows zero, one or more than one genre to be assigned to a given input text. As was the case with Biber's factor analysis, the first stage in genre analysis involves counting automatically extractable genre-revealing features. These include the identification of such features as function words and punctuation marks, which require no pre-processing by the computer. Other, more linguistically sophisticated features require the use of a tagger and a parser, such as part-of-speech trigrams. The third group of genre-identifying features are called 'facets', sets of features sharing a common textual interpretation, such as 'first person facet', which include all first person pronouns. Other facets consist of genre-specific referential vocabulary, such as the set '£, *basket, buy, cart, catalogue, checkouts, cost . . .*', all of which suggest the 'e-shop' genre, and facets based on the presence of HTML tags in the text. For example, the 'functionality facet' includes tags such as '<button>' and '<form>' which indicate the presence of buttons and forms in an interactive web page.

Having identified a range of countable features for describing texts, the next step is to choose a classifier capable of discriminating between sets of features in a text to predict the most likely genre or genres. The selected classifier is an SVM (Support Vector Machine), which is a form of supervised learner. This means that the classifier has to be presented with an adequate number of training examples, consisting both of the numbers of each feature found in a test, and the genre or genres a knowledgeable human has assigned to them. Once the classifier is able to discriminate between sets of features belonging to different genres, a new phase begins, called the test phase. Now the feature sets of previously unseen texts are presented to the classifier, and the classifier alone assigns genres to them. This approach contrasts with hierarchical clustering and factor analysis, which are unsupervised learning approaches. In unsupervised learning, at no stage is any human annotator required to classify any examples. The classifier is able to learn everything it needs to know from the unannotated texts presented to it. The objective of this work was not to make new linguistic discoveries, although questions such as 'what constitutes an e-shop genre?' will have been partially answered by the qualitative analysis required in compiling the linguistic facets. The main finding was that automatic genre analysis has practical uses, in this case helping to realise the goal of genre-sensitive search engines, which will answer queries such as 'Find me an academic article about X'.

10.5 Computational Stylometry

Up to now, differences between types of text have been considered, with each text type having been produced by many different authors or speakers. In this section, I briefly discuss how some of the techniques encountered in this chapter have been used to examine the writing styles of individual authors (see also Mahlberg, this volume).

The chi-squared test has been used by Forsyth (1999) to compare the poetry writing styles of the younger and the elder Yeats. His choice of linguistic feature was the 'substring', any sequence of up to eight characters, including spaces and punctuation, which appeared in a set of Yeats' poems. Since there are so many of

Table 10.11 Top six discriminators for the younger and older Yeats.

Rank	Substring	Chi-squared	YY-count	OY-count
1	what	35.1	30	100
2	can	34.3	21	82
3	s, an	25.4	63	19
4	whi	25.4	67	21
5	with	22.3	139	74
6	?	21.9	30	83

these, a random selection was taken. Having determined which substrings were most typical of the younger and the elder Yeats, Forsyth was able to estimate the dates of other Yeats' poems by how many 'older' and 'younger' features they contained, using a 'Youthful Yeatsian Index' measure similar to Yule's DC. The substrings most characteristic of the younger and of the older Yeats are shown in Table 10.11. Although these substrings were randomly selected, they do reveal some higher level linguistic constructs. Both *what* and *?* indicate that the poems of the older Yeats contain more questions.

Hierarchical clustering techniques were effectively used by Holmes (1992) in a comparison of Mormon scripture, Joseph Smith's personal writings and sections of the Old Testament. The main finding was that although these three sources could easily be distinguished from one another, the various prophets who had supposedly written the Mormon books over a period of many centuries could not be distinguished from each other. Holmes et al. (2001) used Principal Components Analysis, a technique closely related to factor analysis, to determine the provenance of a collection of letters, purportedly by an American War General, George Pickett, and published in a book called *The Heart of a Soldier*. They compared these letters with the autobiography of LaSalle Pickett, George's widow, George Pickett's personal pre- and post-war letters, George Pickett's war reports, genuine handwritten letters by George Pickett (the Inman Papers), and Walter Harrison's book *Pickett's Men*. Each set of texts was internally consistent, forming close clusters on the chart. However, the texts from *The Heart of a Soldier* also lay very close to LaSalle Pickett's autobiography, suggesting that she may have been the true author of the letters supposedly written by her husband. Finally, Popescu and Dinu (2007) used an SVM to discriminate between the possible authors of the disputed 'Federalist Papers'. These papers, written in 1787–1788 to encourage the American people to accept the new constitution, and published in various newspapers under the pseudonym 'Publius', were either written by Alexander Hamilton or James Madison. They are an ideal test bed for trying out new techniques in computational stylometry, because although the writing styles of these two writers were very similar, there are only two of them to choose between. The SVM indicated that Madison was the more likely author in all 12 cases, a finding which is in accordance with previous computer analyses and most historians.

10.6 Discussion

This chapter has examined various statistical methods for distinguishing between different text types, arising through such factors as demographic variation in writers or speakers, genre differences, topic differences or individual writing styles. I wish to end by discussing some of the potential issues that need to be taken into account when using these statistical techniques to examine variation in corpora.

As mentioned previously, the main difficulty with these approaches is the fact that each of these sources of linguistic variation can obscure any of the others. One way that authors have tried to compensate for this is by using texts that are as similar as possible. For example, in their study of the frequencies of syntactic structures used by different authors, Baayen, van Halteren and Tweedie (1996) used only science fiction texts, so the individual stylistic differences they were looking for did not get swamped by genre differences.

When carrying out comparisons, however, it is often difficult to build corpora that only differ on a single factor. For example, although little has been said here about cultural corpora, the main deviation from matching the LOB and Brown corpora text-for-text as closely as possible was due to cultural factors. So more extracts from westerns are found in category N (Adventure and western fiction) of the Brown corpus, since more westerns are written in the United States (Hofland and Johansson 1982: 3). Another issue arises regarding whether a diachronic corpus be exactly balanced text-for-text, or whether the diachronic corpus should take into account actual cultural differences. In using the same sampling model for the Brown family of corpora, the corpus builders chose the first option. However, it could be argued that perhaps the sampling model should have been changed over time in order to reflect changing patterns of text production and reception. For example, the 1960s could be seen as the heyday of science fiction, with more people writing and buying science fiction than in later decades. Perhaps the composition of a diachronic corpus should take this into account, although this would strongly impact on the amount and type of variation within the corpus.

In addition, it needs to be borne in mind that individual authors do not have a homogenous writing style, even when writing in a single genre. For example, DeForest and Johnson (2001) were able to show linguistic variation within a single author, by finding the proportion of Latinate vocabulary used by various characters in Jane Austen's novels. They found that a high proportion of Latinate vocabulary was indicative of, among other things, education, maleness and euphemism. A corpus with a small number of authors may result in variation that is due to individual writing styles. However, the more authors we include in a corpus (with the aim of averaging out individual differences) the more likely it is to introduce yet more factors that have to be balanced for. So if we build two corpora (say from culture a and culture b or from time period a and time period b) each containing equal-sized samples of writing from say, 500 authors, we might also need to take into account their age, gender, social class, education level and the like, otherwise imbalances in any of those factors could impact on any variation found.

Anecdotally, differences in subject matter are said to mask other types of linguistic variation. However, the linguistic features most suitable for differentiating texts according to subject matter are mid-frequency terms, while other types of linguistic features have proved effective at telling apart genres (such as the high frequency words used in this chapter, and Santini's linguistic facets), chronology (Forsyth's substrings) and individual authors (function words said to be outside the author's conscious control). All this suggests that the problem of different types of linguistic variation masking each other can be alleviated by finding linguistic features which are particularly good at identifying one source of linguistic variation, without being indicative of others. Such a proposal suggests a way forward for a more robust form of studies of corpus variation.

Notes

1 ABC1 and C2DE refer to the British government's classification of socio-economic status. Group A (3% of the population) represents professional people, senior managers or top level civil servants. Group B (20%), are middle-management executives, owners of small businesses or principle officers in local government. Group C1 (28%) are people in junior managerial positions and everyone else in non-manual positions. Group C2 (21%) are skilled manual workers. Group D (18%) are semi-skilled and unskilled manual workers. Group E (10%) are people on state benefit, the unemployed or casual workers. See *Occupation Groupings: A Job Dictionary* (2006), The Market Research Society.

2 The corpus reported in Carroll et al. (1971) consists of 5 million words of written American English used in schools over a range of subject areas and grades of writing.

3 The Edinburgh-Birmingham corpus used by Jones and Sinclair (1974) consists of collections of transcribed British speech from the 1960s.

11

Integrating Learner Corpus Analysis into a Probabilistic Model of Second Language Acquisition

Yukio Tono

This chapter considers recent research directions that have taken place in the field of learner corpora. I explore how multifactorial analytical techniques that use log-linear analyses can help to identify the extent to which different individual factors (and combinations of factors) influence the output of learners. Additionally, I show how probability-based theories such as the Bayesian approach can be used to explain the second language acquisition process. Using examples, I show how Bayesian probability theory enables statements to be made based on the partial knowledge available (e.g. patterns in corpus data) regarding as yet unobserved L2 competence. Finally, I outline the basic features of the Data Oriented Parsing model (another probabilistic model) and discuss the possibilities of analysing learner language within this framework.

11.1 Introduction

A learner corpus is a collection of texts, normally essays, produced by people who are learning a second or foreign language. Learner corpora have grown into one of the major types of specialized corpora in corpus linguistics. As James (1992: 190) notes 'The really authentic texts for foreign language learning are not those produced by native speakers for native speakers, but those produced by learners themselves.'

Learner corpora are therefore compiled with several different purposes in mind. First, they are used for providing information on learners' common errors for producing reference materials such as dictionaries or grammars (see, e.g. Gillard and Gadsby 1998). Two commercial learner corpora, the Longman Learners' Corpus (LLC) and the Cambridge Learner Corpus (CLC) have been used for these purposes. Second, learner corpora can be used for describing the characteristics of interlanguage produced by second language (L2) learners. The International Corpus of Learner English (ICLE) (Granger 1998) is a project which aimed to identify those features (overuse/underuse phenomena as well as errors) which are common to learners with different first language (L1) backgrounds and those which are unique to each L1. As well as comparing native speakers of different L1s, learner analysis can also carry out comparisons of learners at different levels of proficiency, see for example, research carried out on the NICT JLE (National Institute of Information and Communications Technology Japanese Learner of English) Corpus (Izumi et al. 2003) or the JEFLL (Japanese EFL Learner) Corpus (Tono 2007). Third, learner corpora can be used to provide classroom language teachers with an opportunity to monitor their students' performance in the framework of Action Research. Action Research is a reflective process of progressive problem solving led mainly by the teacher herself in a specific classroom context. Action Research usually takes place in a collaborative context with data-driven analysis (Johns 1997) or research designed to enable predictions about personal (e.g. teacher or student) and organizational (e.g. school or education board) change. For this kind of analysis, the use of small sets of learner corpora sampled in a specific learning context has become increasingly popular. For more information on types and features of learner corpora, see Pravec (2002).

This chapter will argue that research using learner corpora has come to a turning point methodologically and theoretically. Methodologically, it is necessary to integrate multiple variables concerning learners and learning environments into the analysis of learner corpora. Theoretically, learner corpus researchers need to consider how much contribution they could make to second language acquisition (SLA) theory construction as they investigate the patterns of use in L2 in terms of frequencies and distributions of learner errors and over/underuse phenomena. With this aim in mind, I will first discuss the complex nature of learner corpus research and the importance of multifactorial research design. Then I will introduce how probabilistic analysis can contribute to the formulation of linguistic and acquisition theories and discuss the possibility of theoretical reformulation of problems in SLA in light of probability theories. Finally, I will propose a framework of SLA theory using the concept of the Bayesian network as an underlying theoretical assumption and the Data Oriented Parsing (DOP) model as an attempt to integrate learner corpus findings into a probabilistic model of SLA.

11.2 Recent Challenges for Learner Corpus Research

As more and more learner corpora become available and the findings based on the analysis of such corpora are published, it is becoming clear that there are discrepancies between the approaches taken by learner corpus researchers and mainstream SLA researchers. While researchers working on learner corpora tend to look at overall patterns of language use (and misuse) across proficiency (e.g. native speaker vs non-native speaker; different ability levels of learners) and describe similarities and differences between the groups, SLA researchers have a tendency to set specific hypotheses to test against the data in order to identify causal relationships between variables. SLA researchers usually have specific theoretical frameworks on which their hypothesis is built upon while learner corpus researchers tend not to have such a theory a priori and often pursue data-driven, theory-generating approaches. The corpus-based approach to SLA has emerged among corpus linguists and not SLA specialists, which makes learner corpus research look rather weak in terms of theoretical perspectives. However, learner corpus researchers have argued that it is worth accumulating facts about SLA processes first before moving onto theory construction.

The problem is how can this be achieved? There are groups of researchers who set specific hypotheses within a certain framework of SLA theories and use learner corpora where appropriate to test these hypotheses. Such people do not always have sufficient knowledge about corpus design criteria and may lack technical skills in extracting necessary linguistic observations from the corpus. Other groups of people working in SLA research construct their own corpus data which suit their needs and methodological assumptions. It is often the case, however, that their corpora are limited in size from a standard corpus linguistic point of view and therefore generalization beyond the corpus under examination is difficult. Most of the studies so far exhibit such methodological shortcomings.

It is also difficult to relate corpus findings to actual educational settings. Corpus building/analysis projects such as ICLE largely ignore the educational contexts in each country and they assume that the findings could be applicable for advanced learners of English in general. This is reasonable as long as the performance of advanced learners is relatively stable and less vulnerable to a specific learning environment in each country. In the case of younger or less advanced learners, however, observed data are heavily dependent upon the nature of input and inter-actions in the classroom. For example, the order of acquisition could be a reflec-tion of the order of instructions given to learners. It would be ideal to relate corpus findings to specific input sources such as textbooks used in the class or classroom observation data (cf. the SCoRE Project in Singapore; Hong 2005). Therefore, one future direction will be to integrate educational and contextual as well as linguistic variables into corpus analysis, together with specific SLA hypotheses in mind. In dealing with multiple variables, a careful statistical treatment should be made to ensure internal and external validity. In the following section, I will illustrate such an approach in further detail.

11.3 Multifactorial Analyses and Beyond

Tono (2002) investigated the acquisition of verb subcategorization patterns by Japanese-speaking learners of English. This issue is related to the acquisition of argument structure and has been discussed with reference to both L1 and L2 acquisition (Pinker 1989; Juffs 2000). Tono compiled a corpus of free composi-tions written by beginning to intermediate level learners of English in Japan, called the JEFLL (Japanese EFL Learner) Corpus. The JEFLL Corpus consists of English compositions written by approximately 10,000 students, ranging from the first year of junior high school to the third year of senior high school (Year 7 to 12), totalling a little less than 700,000 tokens. Composition tasks were strictly controlled: all compositions were written in the classroom without the help of a dictionary. Additionally, a twenty-minute time limit was imposed. Students chose one of six topics (based on three narrative and three argumentative composition questions).

What makes Tono's (2002) design multifactorial? The primary goal of his research is to identify relative difficulties in acquiring different verbs in terms of the use of their subcategorization frame (SF) patterns.[1] A simple picture of the design would be illustrated as follows:

(1) Independent variable: proficiency level (defined for the purpose of the study as 'years of schooling')
     Dependent variable: use of verb SF patterns

However, a more wide-reaching analysis would take into account (a) whether only one verb or multiple verbs are being examined, (b) types of verb SF, and (c) distinctions between use and misuse. Thus, (1) should be rewritten as (2):

(2) Independent variables: a. proficiency level
                                b. types of verbs
                                c. types of SF patterns
     Dependent variable: frequencies of use vs misuse of SF patterns

Tono's study also took into account L1 influence, L2 inherent factors and input from the classroom. L1 influence was defined as the similarities in SF patterns between the English verbs under study and their translation equivalents in Japanese. For L2 inherent factors, Levin's (1993) verb semantic categories were used to classify the verbs in the study. The influence of classroom input was defined as the amount of exposure to specific verbs and their SF patterns in the textbooks, measured by their frequencies in the English textbook corpus. Thus, the overall relations among multiple variables are shown in (3):

(3) Independent variables:

     - Learner factor: (a) Proficiency level   (Factor 1)
     - L1 factors: (b) Degree of similarity/difference in SF patterns
                              between L1 Japanese and L2 English   (Factor 2)
                         (c) Frequencies of SF patterns in English   (Factor 3)
                         (d) Frequencies of SF patterns in Japanese   (Factor 4)
     - Input factor: (e) Frequencies of SF patterns in the textbooks
                                                                              (Factor 5)
     Dependent variable: Frequencies of use vs misuse of SF patterns
                                                                              (Factor 6)

Since many of the factors described in (3) are categorical or nominal data, we need to deal with multi-way frequency tables. For this, Tono employed log-linear analysis. The term 'log-linear' derives from the fact that one can, through logarithmic transformations, restate the problem of analysing multi-way frequency tables in terms that are very similar to ANOVA. Specifically, one may think of a multi-way frequency table as reflecting various main effects and interaction effects that add together in a linear fashion to bring about the observed table of frequencies.

Table 11.1 The results of log-linear analysis for the verb
get (from Tono 2002).

Verb	The final model by log-linear analysis
get	643, 543, 532, 432, 61, 1

Log-linear analysis can also be used for evaluating the relative importance of
each independent variable against the dependent variable. By taking a model
fitting approach with backward deletion using the saturated model, we could
reduce the number of independent variables to the most parsimonious sets of
variables. Table 11.1 shows the results of log-linear analysis performed on the use
of the verb *get*. Each number in the table consists of the factors which interact with
each other. For example, 643 signifies that there is a significant interaction between
factors 6, 4 and 3.

The table shows that the verb *get* can be best explained by a model consisting
of the three-way interaction effects of Factors 6-4-3, 5-4-3, 5-3-2 and 4-3-2 and
the two-way interaction effects of Factors 6 and 1, with the main effect being
Factor 1. This shows that there is a significant effect of school year (Factor 1) and
interaction effects between school year and use/misuse (Factors 6 and 1). Factor 6
is also related to frequencies of subcategorization frame (SF) patterns of the
Japanese-equivalent verb *eru* (Factor 4) and degrees of matching in SF patterns
between English and Japanese equivalents (Factor 2). This kind of analysis makes
it possible to identify which factors play a significant role in explaining the complex interactions of multiple variables. The results show the following interesting
findings. See Tono (2002) for further details:

(4) a. There is a significant relationship between school years and frequencies of
       use of SF patterns in major verbs.
    b. Frequencies in SF patterns have a strong correlation with frequencies
       in English textbooks, which means students use more verbs with various
       SF patterns as they are exposed to more variations in the textbooks.
    c. Despite the findings in (b), there is no significant correlation between
       frequencies of 'correct' use of SF patterns and frequencies in textbooks.
       The amount of exposure does not ensure correct use of the forms.
    d. The factors affecting the use/misuse of the SF patterns are mainly cross-
       linguistic factors, such as degrees of similarities in SF patterns between the
       target language and the mother tongue, or frequencies of SF patterns
       in the first language (Japanese).

Following Tono (2002), other studies have emphasized the value of multi-factorial
corpus analysis as a methodological innovation (see, e.g. Gries 2003). Second language acquisition is a multi-faceted phenomenon, composed of complex factors
related to learner's cognitive and affective variables, environmental variables

(types of formal instruction, school settings, curriculums, educational policies of the country), as well as linguistic (L2) or cross-linguistic (L1 vs L2) factors. Therefore it is sensible to adopt an integrative approach which takes multiple variables into account when tackling specific problems in SLA using corpus-based methodologies. Also since the primary information from learner corpora is based on frequencies and distributions of language features in interlanguage, it would be important to consider how the findings can fit into existing SLA theory. Below I argue that corpus-based approaches can help to shed light on theoretical perspectives in SLA. The following section outlines a new framework in learner corpus research, bridging the gap between purely descriptive studies using learner corpora and theoretical perspectives in SLA.

11.4 Motivating Probabilities

In recent years, a strong consensus has emerged that human cognition is based on probabilistic processing (cf. Bod et al. 2003). The probabilistic approach is promising in modelling brain functioning and its ability to accurately model phenomena 'from psychophysics and neurophysiology' (ibid.: 2). Bod et al. also claim that the language faculty itself displays probabilistic properties. I argue that this probabilistic view also holds for various phenomena in L2 acquisition and could have a significant impact on theory construction in SLA. I will briefly outline the nature of this evidence below.

11.4.1 Variation

Zuraw (2003) provides evidence that language change can result from probabilistic inference on the part of listeners, and that probabilistic reasoning could explain the maintenance of lexical regularities over (historic) time. Individual variations in SLA can also be explained by probabilistic factors such as how often learners are exposed to certain linguistic phenomena in particular educational settings. Variations in input characteristics could be determined by such probabilistic factors as frequencies and order of presentation of language items in a particular syllabus or materials such as textbooks or course modules.

11.4.2 Frequency

One striking clue to the importance of probabilities in language comes from the wealth of frequency effects that pervade language representation, processing and language change (Bod et al. 2003: 3). This is true for SLA. Frequent words are recognized faster than infrequent words (Jurafsky 1996). Frequent words in input are also more likely to be used by learners than infrequent words (Tono 2002). Frequency affects language processes, so it must be represented somewhere. More and more scholars have come to believe that probabilistic information is stored in human brains to assist automatic processing of various kinds.

11.4.3 Gradience

Many phenomena in language may appear categorical at first glance, but upon closer inspection show clear signs of gradience. Manning (2003) shows that even verb subcategorization patterns should better be treated in terms of gradients, as there are numerous unclear cases which lie between clear arguments and clear adjuncts (ibid.: 302). Rather than maintaining a categorical argument/adjunct distinction and having to make in/out decisions about such cases, we might instead represent subcategorization information as a probability distribution over argument frames, with different verbal dependents expected to occur with a verb with a certain probability (ibid.: 303). This type of analysis is readily applicable to cases in L2 acquisition. A strong claim can be made regarding the gradient nature of language in terms of a probability distribution over linguistic phenomena based on comparisons between native speaker's corpora and learner corpora.

11.4.4 Acquisition

Bod et al. (2003: 6) claim that 'adding probabilities to linguistics makes the acquisition easier, not harder'. Generalizations based on statistical inferences become increasingly robust as sample size increases. This holds for both positive and negative generalizations: as the range and quantity of data increase, statistical models are able to acquire negative evidence with increasing certainty. In formal L2 classroom settings, it is also very likely that learners will be exposed to negative evidence as well. Instructed knowledge of this type could serve to form a part of probabilistic information in a learner's mind besides actual exposure to primary data, which facilitates the processing of certain linguistic structures more readily than others.

11.4.5 What Does the Evidence Show?

The evidence above seems to indicate that a probabilistic approach will be very promising in theory-construction, not in only linguistics but also second language acquisition. It could be argued that corpus linguistics can provide a very strong empirical basis for this approach. By analysing various aspects of learner language quantitatively and at the same time integrating the results of the observations into the probabilistic model of learning, we could possibly produce a better picture of L2 learning and acquisition. In the next section, I will further explore this possibility and introduce one of the most promising statistical approaches, Bayesian statistics and network modelling as an underlying principle of language acquisition.

11.5 Integrating Probabilities into SLA Theory

One of the strengths of corpus linguistics is its data-driven nature: findings are supported by a large amount of attested language use data. This feature has been increasingly highlighted as electronic texts become increasingly available online. The dramatic increase in the size of available corpus data has also changed the way that people use statistics. Traditional mathematical statistics have been replaced by computational statistics, involving robust machine-learning algorithms and probabilistic inferencing on large-scale data. This shift towards more data-centred approaches should also be applied in the formulation of SLA theory by using learner corpora. By working on large amounts of learner data using probabilistic methods, it is possible to create a totally new type of learning model. In the following sections, I will introduce Bayesian network modelling as the basis of such probability theories and discuss how to view acquisition theory from Bayesian viewpoints.

11.5.1 Bayes' Theorem

Let me briefly describe Bayes' theorem and how it is useful for theory construction in SLA.[2] *Bayes' theorem* is a probability rule, currently widely used in the information sciences to cope with uncertainty from known facts or experience. It serves as a base theory for various problem solving algorithms as well as data mining methods. Bayes' theorem is a rule in probability theory that relates to conditional probabilities. *Conditional probability* is the probability of the occurrence of an event A, given the occurrence of some other event B. Conditional probability is written $P(A|B)$, and is read 'the probability of A, given B'. Bayes' theorem relates the conditional and marginal probabilities of stochastic events A and B and is formulated as in (5):

(5) $$P(A|B) = \frac{P(B|A)P(A)}{P(B)}$$

Each term in Bayes' theorem has a conventional name as in (6):

(6) a. $P(A)$ is the *prior probability* or marginal probability of A. It is 'prior' in the sense that it does not take into account any information about B.
  b. $P(A|B)$ is the conditional probability of A, given B. It is also called the *posterior probability* because it is derived from or depends upon the specified value of B.
  c. $P(B|A)$ is the conditional probability of B given A.
  d. $P(B)$ is the prior or marginal probability of B, and acts as a normalizing constant.

Bayes' theorem can also be interpreted in terms of *likelihood*, as in (7):

(7) $$P(A|B) \propto L(A|B)P(A)$$

Here $L(A|B)$ is the likelihood of A given fixed B. The rule is then an immediate consequence of the relationship $P(B \mid A) = L(A \mid B)$. In many contexts the likelihood function *L* can be multiplied by a constant factor, so that it is proportional to, but does not equal the conditional probability *P*. With this terminology, the theorem may be paraphrased as in (8):

(8)
$$posterior = \frac{likelihood \times prior}{normalizing}$$

In words, the posterior probability is proportional to the product of the prior probability and the likelihood.

An important application of Bayes' theorem is that it gives a rule regarding how to update or revise the strengths of evidence-based beliefs in light of new evidence *a posteriori*. This is a kind of probabilistic formulation of our daily activities. In a sense, we make a judgement about everything at every moment in our lives; things we are going to do next, things we are going to say, how we evaluate the things we see or hear and so on. Every human judgement, whether conscious or unconscious, is influenced by our prior probability of the events (i.e. past experiences or personal beliefs), adjusted by some likelihood of the events, given new data (i.e. likelihood), which yields *a posteriori* probability (i.e. new ideas or something learned). Therefore, Bayes' theorem can be viewed as a probabilistic model of human learning. The architecture of human cognitions will be modular and need specifications in their own right, but the overall learning algorithm can be explained in Bayesian terms.

There are a growing number of researchers in different disciplines of sciences who have adopted the Bayesian model as a theoretical basis. While Bayes' rule itself is quite simple and straightforward, it is very flexible in the sense that the same rule and the procedure can be adapted to varied sample sizes, from a very small to a huge set. Unlike *frequentist* probability, Bayesian probability deals with a subjective level of knowledge (sometimes called 'credence', i.e. degree of belief). This is intuitively more likely as a model of human learning, because we all have personal beliefs or value systems on which every decision is based. Some of these subjective levels of knowledge are formed via instructions in specific social and educational settings in a country. The levels of knowledge about what is appropriate in what situations are also partially taught and partially learned through experiences. In Bayesian terms, every time people are exposed to new situations, they learn from new data and revise their posterior probability including their belief system. I argue that exactly the same process is also applied to the acquisition and the use of second language.

11.5.2 Bayesian Theory in SLA

How could we realize Bayesian modelling in SLA? The overall picture is simple. Since Bayes' theorem itself is a formulation of 'learning from experience', in other words, obtaining posterior probability by revising prior probability in light of new attested data, we could give a model of language learning based on Bayes' rule in (7), as in (9):

(9)   (a revised system given the new data) ∝
          (likelihood) × (an old system of language)

What is promising is that corpus-based approaches will suggest a very interesting methodological possibility in providing input for these empty arguments in the model in (9). For example, if we compile a corpus of learners at different proficiency levels, we could formulate the model in such a way that probability scores for given linguistic items obtained at a certain proficiency level (Stage x, for instance) serve as the prior probability, while the scores obtained at the next level (Stage x + 1) will serve as the condition for posterior probability, as in (10).

(10)   (Language at Stage x+ 1) ∝ (Likelihood) × (Language at Stage x)

While the real picture would be much more complex than above, Bayesian reasoning can still provide the interesting possibility of describing a model of SLA from a probabilistic viewpoint. In order to illustrate this point, let us now come back to the example of verb SF pattern acquisition. Suppose we are interested in the occurrence of a particular SF pattern of a verb, we might try to represent subcategorization information as a probability distribution over argument frames, with different verbal dependents expected to occur with a verb with a certain probability. For instance, we might estimate the probability of SF patterns for a verb *get* as in (11):

(11) $P(NP_{[SUBJ]} \mid V= \textit{get})$ = 1.0

$P(NP_{[SUBJ]}\ NP_{[OBJ]} \mid V= \textit{get})$ = 0.377

$P(NP_{[SUBJ]}\ ADJ \mid V= \textit{get})$ = 0.104

$P(NP_{[SUBJ]}\ PP \mid V= \textit{get})$ = 0.079

$P(NP_{[SUBJ]}\ NP_{[OBJ]}\ PP \mid V= \textit{get})$ = 0.056

$P(NP_{[SUBJ]}\ NP_{[OBJ]}\ NP_{[OBJ]} \mid V= \textit{get})$ = 0.053

(Note: Probabilities are derived from the British National Corpus. Other constructions are omitted.)

So, for instance, the probability of choosing the SF pattern *get up* can be described by modelling the probability that a VP is headed by the verb *get*, and then the probability of certain arguments surrounding the verb (in this case, SUB + *get* + PART[up]), as in (12):

(12) $P(VP \rightarrow V[\textit{get}]\ PART[\textit{up}]) = P(VP[\textit{get}] \mid VP) \times$
          $P(VP[\textit{get}] \rightarrow V\ PART \mid VP[\textit{get}]) \times P(PART[\textit{up}] \mid PART, VP[\textit{get}]).$

The probabilities in (12) can be computed from corpora and the formal grammatical description can be given by yet another stochastic language model called a DOP model, described in Section 11.6.

If such probabilistic descriptions for the choice of verb SF patterns can be extracted from learner corpora, this information can then be integrated into a general probabilistic inference system. Suppose we wish to reason about the difficulty in acquiring verb SF patterns by Japanese learners of English. Let M be the misuse of a particular subcategorization frame pattern of the given verb, allowing 'yes' and 'no'. For explanatory purposes, let possible causes be J: the match in subcategorization pattern between English and L1 Japanese, with $P(J = yes) = 0.5$, and T: Textbook influence (whether the same subcategorization pattern occurs in the textbook as a source of input), with $P(T = yes) = 0.2$. We adopt the following hypothetical conditional probabilities for the correct use:

(13)
$$
\begin{aligned}
P(M = yes \mid J = no, T = no) &= 0.7 \\
P(M = yes \mid J = no, T = yes) &= 0.4 \\
P(M = yes \mid J = yes, T = no) &= 0.3 \\
P(M = yes \mid J = yes, T = yes) &= 0.1
\end{aligned}
$$

The left-hand diagram in Fig. 11.1 shows a directed graphical model of this system, with each variable labelled by its current probability of taking the value 'yes'.

Let me describe how to obtain probability scores in Fig. 11.1 in more detail. Suppose you observe the learner corpus data and found the correct use of the SF pattern *get up*, and you wish to find the conditional probabilities for J and T, given this correct use. By Bayes' theorem,

(14)
$$
P(J, T \mid M = yes) = \frac{P(M = yes \mid J, T)\, P(J, T)}{P(M = yes)}
$$

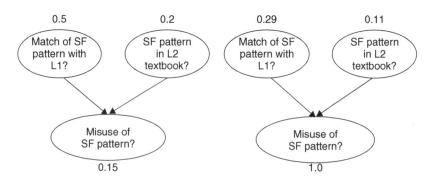

Figure 11.1 Directed graphical model representing two independent potential causes of the misuse of a verb SF pattern, with probabilities of a 'yes' response before and after observing the misuse.

The necessary calculations are laid out in Table 11.2. Note that, owing to the assumed independence, $P(J, T) = P(J)P(T)$. Also $P(M = \text{yes}, J, T) = P(M = \text{yes} | J, T)P(J, T)$, and when summed this provides $P(M = \text{yes}) = 0.45$.

By summing the relevant entries in the joint posterior distribution of J and T we thus obtain $P(J = \text{yes} | M = \text{yes}) = 0.27 + 0.02 = 0.29$ and $P(T = \text{yes} | M = \text{yes}) = 0.09 + 0.02 = 0.11$. These values are displayed in the right-hand diagram of Fig. 11.1. Note that the observed misuse has induced a strong dependency between the originally independent possible causes.

We now extend the system to include the possible misuse of another SF pattern of the given verb, denoted by M2, assuming that this verb pattern is not dealt with in the textbook and that

(15)
$$P(M2 = \text{yes} | T = \text{yes}) = 0.2$$
$$P(M2 = \text{yes} | T = \text{no}) = 0.8$$

so that $P(M2 = \text{yes}) = P(M2 = \text{yes} | T = \text{yes})P(T=\text{yes}) + P(M2 = \text{yes} | T = \text{no})P(T = \text{no}) = 0.2 \times 0.2 + 0.8 \times 0.8 = 0.68$. The extended graph is shown in Fig. 11.2.

Table 11.2 Calculations of probabilities for possible causes J and T.

J [P(J)]		no [0.5]		yes [0.5]	
T [P(T)]	no [0.8]	yes [0.2]	no [0.8]	yes [0.2]	
P(J,T)	0.4	0.1	0.4	0.1	1
P(M=yes|J,T)	0.7	0.4	0.3	0.1	
P(M=yes, J,T)	0.28	0.04	0.12	0.01	0.45
P(J,T|M=yes)	0.62	0.09	0.27	0.02	1

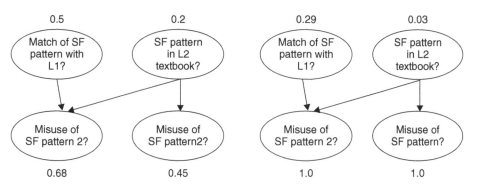

Figure 11.2 Introducing another misuse of an SF pattern into the system, before and after observing that neither of the patterns is correctly used.

Suppose we now find that the other SF pattern is incorrectly used (M2 = yes). Our previous posterior distribution P(J, T | M=yes) now becomes the prior distribution for an application of Bayes' theorem based on observing that the second SF pattern has failed.

The calculations are displayed in Table 11.3.

We obtain P(J = yes|M = yes, M2 = yes) = 0.299, P(T = yes|M = yes, M2 = yes) = 0.03. Thus, observing another misuse of SF patterns has decreased the chance of the influence of English textbooks on the use of verb SF patterns. This ability to withdraw a tentative conclusion on the basis of further information is extremely difficult to implement within a system based on logic, even with the addition of measures of uncertainty. In contrast, it is both computationally and conceptually straightforward within a fully probabilistic system built upon a conditional independence structure. Although the example shown above is rather limited in scope, it is possible that we can add more variables to the model and apply exactly the same procedure to obtain probabilistic inference from the observed data.

The above example has heuristically argued for the explanatory power of probabilistic models based on Bayesian reasoning. I have informally introduced the idea of representing qualitative relationships between variables by graphs and superimposing a joint probability model on the unknown qualities. When the graph is directed and does not contain any cycles,[3] the resulting system is often called a *Bayesian network*. Using the terms introduced earlier, we may think of this network and its numerical inputs as forming the knowledge base, while efficient methods of implementing Bayes' theorem form the inference engine used to draw conclusions on the basis of possibly fragmentary evidence.

The above example assumes that the random variables involved are discrete. However, the same formula holds in the case of continuous variables (or a mixture of discrete and continuous variables), as long as, when M is continuous (e.g. instead of yes/no, the accuracy rate of SP patterns in a certain learner group), we interpret P(M) as the probability density of M. See Pearl (1988) for more work related to this.

Table 11.3 Re-calculations of probabilities after observing another misuse of the SF pattern.

J [P(J)]	no [0.5]		yes [0.5]		
T [P(T)]	no [0.8]	yes [0.2]	no [0.8]	yes [0.2]	
P(J,T | M=yes)	0.62	0.09	0.27	0.02	1
P(M2=yes | J,T, M=yes)	0.8	0.2	0.8	0.2	
P(M2=yes, J,T | M=yes)	0.496	0.018	0.216	0.004	0.734
P(J,T | M=yes, M2=yes)	0.676	0.025	0.294	0.005	1

11.5.3 Advantages of the Bayesian SLA Model

So far we have seen how Bayesian networks can be adopted for describing phenomena in SLA. By using Bayesian reasoning, we could possibly define the whole framework of SLA as one realization of an expert system. An expert system consists of two parts, summed up in the equation:

(16)   Expert System = Knowledge Base + Inference Engine.

The *knowledge base* contains the domain specific knowledge of a problem. It is a set of linguistic descriptions of a language. For this, I assume a DOP model, which will be described in detail in the following section. The *inference engine* consists of one or more algorithms for processing the encoded knowledge of the knowledge base together with any further specific information at hand for a given application. It is similar to what cognitive scientists call 'declarative vs procedural' knowledge.

   As the knowledge base is the core of an expert system, it is important to define it properly. To achieve this, probabilistic information obtained from a large amount of learner data will be useful. Linguistic features with probability scores will be stored in the knowledge base in each of the language domains such as phonology, morphology, syntax, semantics and lexicon. The probabilistic data of linguistic features from each stage of learners will be used to form the input for the Bayesian network described in the previous section. Additional information or variables will constantly change the posterior probability, which will subsequently be used as the prior distribution for the new input.

   This whole picture of obtaining new posterior probability is assumed to be similar to what is happening cognitively in the brain. The Bayesian network model of SLA will have a strong explanatory power for human cognition. The following section will describe how a probabilistic view should be dealt with precisely in a formal language theory and introduce the basic notion of a DOP model as a candidate for such a theory. This model will help to better integrate probabilistic information of a language into the acquisition model based on Bayesian reasoning.

11.6 Implementation: A DOP Model

As we integrate Bayesian network modelling into SLA theory construction, it is necessary to look for a framework for linguistic description. Some people (Manning 2003, for example) claim that probabilistic syntax can be formalized within existing formal grammatical theories. I argue that it would be desirable to look for a more data-driven approach as a theoretical framework. For this purpose, the DOP model proposed by Bod (1992, 1998) seems to be promising. Here I will outline the basic features of DOP and discuss the possibilities of analysing learner language within this framework.

11.6.1 Probabilistic Grammars

Before explaining DOP, let me briefly describe probabilistic grammars in general. Probabilistic grammars aim to describe the probabilistic nature of a large number of linguistic phenomena, such as phonological acceptability, morphological alternations, syntactic well-formedness, semantic interpretation, sentence disambiguation and sociolinguistic variation (Bod 2003: 18).

The most widely used probabilistic grammar is the *probabilistic context-free grammar* (PCFG). PCFG defines a grammar as a set of phrase structure rules implicit in the tree bank (phrase structure trees) with probabilistic information attached to each phrase structure rule. Let us consider the following two parsed sentences in (17). We will assume that they are from a very small corpus of phrase structure trees:

(17)   a. (S (NP John) (VP (V gave) (NP Mary) (NP flowers))).
            b. (S (NP Mike) (VP (V gave) (NP flowers) (PP (P to) (NP Mary)))).

Table 11.4 gives the rules together with their frequencies in the Treebank.

Table 11.4 allows us to derive the probability of randomly selecting the rule S → NP VP from among all the rules in the Treebank. For example, the rule S→ NP VP occurs twice in a sample space of 10 possible rules, so its probability is 2/10 = 1/5. We are usually more interested in the probability of a combination of rules (i.e. a derivation) that generates a particular sentence. For this, we compute the probability by dividing the number of occurrences of rules involved in the derivation of a certain sentence by the number of occurrences of all rules. Note that this probability is actually the conditional probability P(structure A | structure B), and thus

Table 11.4 The rules implicit in the sample Treebank and their probabilities.

Rule	Frequency	PCFG Probability
S → NP VP	2	2/2 = 1
VP → V NP NP	1	1/2 = 1/2
VP → V NP PP	1	1/2 = 1/2
PP → P NP	1	1/1 = 1
NP → *John*	1	1/6 = 1/6
NP → *Mike*	1	1/6 = 1/6
NP → *Mary*	2	2/6 = 1/3
NP → *flowers*	2	2/6 = 1/3
V → *gave*	2	2/2 = 1
P → *to*	1	1/1 = 1
Total	**14**	

the sum of the conditional probabilities of all rules given a certain non-terminal to be rewritten is 1. The third column of Table 11.4 shows the PCFG probabilities of the rules derived from the Treebank.

Let us now consider the probability of the derivation for *John gave Mary flowers*. This can be computed as the product of the probabilities in Table 11.4, that is, 1 (S → NP VP) × 1/6 (NP → *John*) × 1/2(VP → NP NP) × 1(VP → *gave*) × 1/3 (NP → *Mary*) × 1/3(NP → *flowers*) = 1/108. Likewise, we can compute the probability of *John gave flowers to Mary*: 1 × 1/6 × 1/2 × 1 × 1/3 × 1 × 1/3 = 1/108.

What is important in these probabilistic formalisms is that the probability of a whole (i.e. a tree) can be computed from the combined probabilities of its parts. The problem of PCFG is its derivational independence from previous rules, since in PCFG, rules are independent from each other. For example, if we consider a larger Treebank, it surely contains various derivational types of prepositions: P → *to*; P → *for*; P → *in*, and so forth. The probability of observing the preposition *to*, however, is not equal to the probability of observing *to* given that we have first observed the verb *give*. But this dependency between *give* and *to* is not captured by a PCFG.

Several other formalisms, such as *head-lexicalized probabilistic grammar* (Collins 1996; Charniak 1997) and *probabilistic lexicalized tree-adjoining grammar* (Resnik 1992), have tried to capture this dependency and the DOP model (Bod 1992, 1998) is one of such models. A DOP model captures the previously mentioned problem dependency between different constituent nodes by a subtree that has the two relevant words as its only lexical items. Moreover, a DOP model can capture arbitrary fixed phrases and idiom chunks, such as *to take advantage of* (Bod 2003: 26).

11.6.2 A DOP Model

There is no space to elaborate on a DOP model in detail here, but let me provide a simple example of how a DOP model works. If we consider the example in (17a): *John gave Mary flowers*, we can derive from this treebank the following subtrees:

(18)   (S (NP John) (VP (V gave) (NP Mary) (NP flowers)))
       (S (NP) (VP (V gave) (NP Mary) (NP flowers)))
       (S (NP John) (VP (V) (NP Mary) (NP flowers)))
       (S (NP John) (VP (V gave) (NP) (NP flowers)))
       (S (NP John) (VP (V gave) (NP Mary) (NP)))
       (S (NP) (VP (V) (NP Mary) (NP flowers)))
       (S (NP) (VP (V gave) (NP) (NP flowers)))
       (S (NP) (VP (V gave) (NP Mary) (NP)))
       (S (NP John) (VP (V) (NP) (NP flowers)))
       (S (NP John) (VP (V) (NP Mary) (NP)))
       (S (NP John) (VP (V gave) (NP) (NP)))
       (S (NP) (VP (V) (NP) (NP flowers)))

```
(S (NP) (VP (V) (NP Mary) (NP)))
(S (NP) (VP (V gave) (NP) (NP)))
(S (NP John) (VP (V) (NP) (NP)))
(S (NP) (VP (V) (NP) (NP)))
(VP (V) (NP Mary) (NP flowers))
(VP (V gave) (NP) (NP flowers))
(VP (V gave) (NP Mary) (NP))
(VP (V) (NP) (NP flowers))
(VP (V) (NP Mary) (NP))
(VP (V gave) (NP) (NP))
(VP (V) (NP) (NP))
(V gave)
(NP John)
(NP Mary)
(NP flowers)
```

(Note: In actual DOP models in Bod (2003), all the subtrees are written in tree diagrams.)

These subtrees form the underlying grammar by which new sentences are generated. Subtrees are combined using a node substitution operation similar to the operation that combines context-free rules in a PCFG, indicated by the symbol 'o'. Given two subtrees T and U, the node substitution operation substitutes U on the leftmost nonterminal leaf node of T, written as T o U. For example, *John gave Mary flowers* can be generated by combining three subtrees from (18) as shown in Fig. 11.3.

The events involved in this derivation are listed in Table 11.5.

The probability of (1) in Table 11.5 is computed by dividing the number of occurrences of the subtree $[_S \text{NP} [_{VP} [_V \text{gave}] \text{NP NP}]]$ in (12) by the total number of occurrences of subtrees with root label S: 1/16. The probability of (2) is equal to 1/3, and the probabilities of (3) and (4) are also equal to 1/3 respectively.

The probability of the whole derivation is the joint probability of the four selections in Table 11.4. Since in DOP each subtree selection depends only on the root label and not on the previous selections, the probability of a derivation is the product of the probabilities of the subtrees, in this case $1/16 \times 1/3 \times 1/3 \times 1/3 = 1/432$.

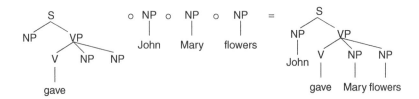

Figure 11.3 Generating *John gave Mary flowers* by combining subtrees from (18).

Table 11.5 The probability of a derivation is the joint probability of selecting its subtrees.

Event

---

(1) selecting the subtree [$_S$ NP [$_{VP}$ [$_V$ gave] NP NP]] from among the subtrees with root label S,

(2) selecting the subtree [$_{NP}$ John] from among the subtrees with root label NP,

(3) selecting the subtree [$_{NP}$ Mary] from among the subtrees with root label NP,

(4) selecting the subtree [$_{NP}$ flowers] from among the subtrees with root label NP.

The DOP model outlined here does not exhibit a one-to-one correspondence between derivation and tree, as with the PCFG. Instead, there may be several distinct derivations from the same tree. The probability that a certain tree occurs is the probability that any of its derivations occurs. Thus the probability of a tree is the sum of the probabilities of its derivations. Bod (2003) points out that this means that in DOP, evidence for a tree accumulates: the more derivations a tree has, the larger its probability tends to be (ibid.: 30). For further detail, see Bod (1992, 1998, 2003). He argues that language users store arbitrarily large sentence fragments in memory, and continuously and incrementally update its fragment memory given new input. Although language users cannot remember everything, they will initially store everything, as they process language input, and calculate the frequencies in order to accumulate the frequency information of subtrees. Thus, the DOP model fits very well with the Bayesian way of thinking described earlier. Another advantage is that the DOP model can effectively handle dependency problems that other models have. Since the model proposes that language users store sentence fragments in memory and that these fragments can range from two-word units to entire sentences, language users do not always have to generate or parse sentences from scratch using the rules of the grammar. Sometimes they can productively reuse previously heard sentences or sentence fragments. This will make language processing and language learning very easy, dealing with the problem of how to incorporate *idiom principles* (Sinclair 1991) or *lexicalized sentence stems* (Pawley and Syder 1983) into a stochastic model of language.

11.7 Integrative Perspectives of SLA as a Stochastic Language Model

I have shown that learner corpus research has come to a turning point, where a statistical linguistic analysis of learner language needs to be integrated into a formal theory of language acquisition. As an example, I have proposed a DOP model as a promising model of a probabilistic grammar. I have also argued that the entire SLA process can be explained by Bayesian reasoning.

Since this paper gave just a brief sketch of a new probabilistic model of SLA and how learner corpora play an important role there, it would be desirable to make a specific proposal as to how probabilistic data from learner corpora can form input for Bayesian network models. For this, not only a specific model of L2 acquisition of, for example, verb SF patterns, but also the general picture of L2 acquisition processes in the context of stochastic theories of human learning needs to be explored. Second language learners' use of a particular expression in a language depends on their intended meanings, various contextual as well as situational settings. All the choices made are affected by the prior probability of L2 learners' knowledge or belief. Once a certain string of a sentence is produced, then that string becomes a part of prior probability, leading to the prediction of what is going to be said next. This knowledge of a language is also influenced by many other factors, including learners' L1 knowledge, age, sex, cognitive maturity, L2 instructions, motivation and exposure to L2 input, among others. There are too many variables to consider, thus it would be extremely difficult to estimate the true value of L2 competence of a particular L2 learner. That is why we use Bayesian modelling in describing a complicated system of L2 acquisition. Instead of hoping to identify an exact state of abilities in L2, Bayesian methods enable statements to be made about the partial knowledge available (based on data) concerning 'state of nature' (unobservable or as yet unobserved) of L2 competence in a systematic way using probability as the yardstick.

The strength of Bayesian network modelling is that the same mathematical procedure can be applied to very small data or to larger, multilevel data. We can start from a very simple model in SLA and build up the model into a relatively complex one, without changing any statistical assumptions. The same Bayesian methods will always work on new data.

It is also important to place Bayesian networks in a wider context of so-called highly structured stochastic systems (HSSS). Many disciplines, such as genetics, image analysis, geography, marketing, predictions of El Niño effects among others, adopt this as a unifying system that can lead to valuable cross-fertilization of ideas. Within the artificial intelligence community, neural networks are natural candidates for interpretation as probabilistic graphical models, and are increasingly being analysed within a Bayesian statistical framework (see Neal 1996). In natural language processing, Hidden Markov models can likewise be considered as special cases of Bayesian networks (Smyth et al. 1997). By defining a model of SLA as a stochastic system, using probabilistic information from a large body of learner language production data at different levels of proficiency or developmental time frames, we could possibly describe and explain the SLA process from an innovative viewpoint.

11.8 Future Directions

In this chapter, I have argued that learner corpus research should be able to make a significant contribution to a probabilistic view of SLA theory based on Bayesian reasoning. This research is still at the preliminary stage of theory construction, and we need to further exploit the possibility of applying Bayesian networks for SLA modelling, but it would suffice to say that such an attempt will have a great potential and that learner corpora would play a significant role there. Further studies need to be done to provide specific procedures of building a stochastic model of SLA.

Notes

1 Verb subcategorization patterns are sometimes expressed in several different terms with slightly different connotations, such as verb patterns, verb complementation patterns, verb valency patterns or argument structures.
2 For a general introduction to Bayesian networks, see Cowell et al. (2007) and Sivia (2006).
3 Cycles in graph theory are loops starting from one node, forming arches among several nodes, and coming back to the same node again. This is not allowed in one-directional cause-effect relationships and is thus a necessary condition for a Bayesian network.

CHAPTER

12

English Language Teaching and Corpus Linguistics: Lessons from the American National Corpus

Randi Reppen

During the last ten years there has been increased interest in exploring how corpora can be used both to inform classroom instruction and as a source for class activities and materials development. This chapter explores some of the ways that corpus-based research can be incorporated into classroom instruction, and also describes the development of classroom activities using corpora for English language instruction.

The corpus used in the development of classroom activities described in this chapter is the American National Corpus (ANC). The ANC contains both spoken and written American English and covers a range of registers (e.g. casual conversation, speeches, fiction, academic prose, etc.) thus making it a rich resource for a range of teaching activities.

12.1 Introduction

With so many different types of texts now available electronically (many via internet access), the task of compiling a corpus could be seen as unnecessary (although see Lew, this volume for discussion of potential problems of using internet texts as a corpus). There is still considerable value in building carefully sampled, balanced corpora, as opposed to utilizing existing collections of texts in a more *ad hoc* way. However, as anyone who has compiled a corpus knows, there is always more to the task than expected. This chapter will offer a brief overview of some of the issues that are often encountered in corpus compilation. I focus on some of the major challenges in compiling a corpus that will be made publicly available, with particular insights from the on-going compilation of the American National Corpus (ANC). After addressing some of these challenges, I present ideas for using a corpus to enhance language teaching, again using examples from the ANC.

12.2 First Things First

As with any task or project it is important to know the goal. With corpus compilation the goal can range from representing a small specific slice of language use, for example the language of business meetings or office memos for a specific company. At the other end of the spectrum corpus compilers may have the goal of representing a more general variety, or varieties of language. An example of this type of project is the International Corpus of English (ICE), which is led by University College London. The ICE project has the goal of creating a number of equal sized corpora of different varieties of English as it is used around the world (e.g. Philippine English, Australian English).[1] The ICE project has involved researchers around the world collecting 10 million words from registers that are carefully specified in the design of the corpus (e.g. newspaper, conversation), thus allowing comparisons across a range of language varieties (see Greenbaum 1996). Because the types of language collected across the different varieties of English are carefully controlled, it is possible to compare language use across different varieties of English, such as comparing the English used in news stories from India, with news stories from the Philippines, Australia and Kenya.

Another ambitious example of representing a variety of language is the 100 million word British National Corpus (BNC). The corpus design of the BNC was carefully planned to represent a range of spoken and written situations of language use in the United Kingdom. Spoken language (including conversations among friends and formal speeches) comprises 10 per cent (roughly 10 million words) of the total corpus. The remainder of the corpus consists of written language, covering many different domains such as non-fiction, fiction, academic prose, personal letters and so on (see Aston and Burnard 1998). Initially only available to members of the EU, the BNC is now accessible online around the world and is a tremendous resource for language researchers and teachers.[2]

It could be argued that the BNC is rapidly becoming an historical corpus (the newest texts in it are from the early 1990s), and while other corpora of British English are also available (e.g. the Bank of English), they are not as easily accessible as the BNC. In terms of language teaching, many students across the world are taught using American English as a target model – and it could also be argued that American English is equally if not more influential than British English due to its role as a form of global media (see Ross 1995). Additionally, corpus studies on language variation and change, for example, Leech's (2002) study of modals and semi-modals or McEnery and Xiao's (2005) study of full and bare infinitives, have indicated that American English appears to be at the forefront of linguistic innovation. Such points suggest that there are strong justifications for building an equivalent contemporary American version of the BNC. Construction of such a corpus, the American National Corpus (ANC), is under way in an attempt to provide a similar resource for American English.[3]

The design of the ANC is modelled after the BNC, with a few notable differences (for a full description of the design of the ANC see Reppen and Ide 2004). For example, the material included in the ANC is from 1990 and onwards, whereas the material in the BNC was authored between 1960 and 1993. Another difference will be the inclusion of additional types of texts: the ANC includes categories for electronic communication such as blogs, chatrooms and webpages that reflect technological changes that have occurred since the compilation of the BNC. At the time of writing, the second release of the ANC consists of 20 million words of written and spoken American English.

Unlike the BNC, the ANC has not enjoyed the widespread support of publishers and funding agencies. Thus, some existing or previously collected spoken texts, such as texts from the Charlotte Narratives, some texts from the Michigan Corpus of Academic Spoken English (MICASE), and contributions from the Linguistic Data Consortium (e.g. Switchboard Corpus, Call Home Corpus) are included in the ANC. The ANC does not currently claim to represent the full range of American spoken English, a task that would be quite daunting, given the size of the United States and range of contexts of spoken language. However, it does provide access to the largest collection of spoken American English that is publicly available. It is hoped that at some point in the future, the ANC will provide a resource for researchers and language teachers that is similar in scope to that of the BNC. This chapter focuses on some of the ways that the current release of the ANC can be used as a resource for creating corpus-based language teaching activities.

12.3 Getting Ready for the Classroom

During the past ten years, the utility of using corpus findings to inform language teaching, and the actual use of corpora in language classrooms has been a topic of much interest and discussion (Gavioli and Aston 2001). Tim Johns was an early pioneer in bringing the corpus into the classroom, developing the concept of data driven language learning (DLL). In DDL, students are actively involved as 'language detectives' as they seek to discover patterns of language use that are revealed by concordance lines (Johns 1997). The notion of involving learners in language learning is one that has support from research in the area of second language acquisition (Schmidt 2001).

John Sinclair's 2004 edited volume, *How to Use Corpora in Language Teaching*, provides the reader with discussion that covers a range of uses of corpora in the classroom. The topics in this volume include using corpora of other languages, in this case, Pereira's use of a Portuguese corpus to inform language teaching and for classroom activities, such as disambiguating seemingly synonymous words. Mauranen's chapter describes the utility and challenges of using spoken corpora in the language classroom. Other chapters describe the use of corpora for teaching academic writing (Tankó), and Nesselhauf's use of learner corpora for writing. Römer's chapter compares textbooks and corpora to shed light on the possibilities that corpora might offer for materials development. All in all, Sinclair's edited volume provides a rich resource for readers interested in the range of uses of corpora for pedagogical purposes.

Research from corpus linguistics can provide a great deal of useful information to language teachers that can be used to inform course planning. For example, information from corpus linguistic research can provide insights as to what features of spoken language students will frequently hear outside the classroom, or what grammatical features students will encounter in the different types of texts that they will be reading or writing. The Longman Grammar of Spoken and Written English (Biber et al. 1999) carefully describes linguistic features of four registers of English (conversation, fiction, newspapers and academic prose) which are frequently encountered by both native English speakers and English language learners. This reference work can be a valuable resource for language teachers, including helping teachers as they decide how to arrange a syllabus, informing the selection of specific grammatical features to teach. Knowing the characteristics of the texts that students will encounter can be a useful factor to consider when making decisions about what to teach, and in what order.

Teachers can make use of the information from corpus linguistic research to help shape the features and structures of language that are presented in class to students. In addition to reference works, the many articles on English for specific purposes (ESP) or English for Academic purposes (EAP) that appear in professional journals can also provide a rich resource for teachers preparing students for a particular context of English use, such as writing business memos, the language of negotiation or writing biology articles.

12.4 On to the Classroom

This section provides two examples of activities that have been created using information derived from corpus analysis and also using a corpus as a source of teaching materials. In order to make use of a corpus or corpus findings for pedagogical purposes, the first task is to identify the structure or language features for instruction. For example, is there a particular grammatical structure that students need to practice? Is the goal to provide the teacher with information about the vocabulary load of reading texts that the students will be working with? Or, is the goal of the activity to raise student awareness of linguistic patterns in the texts that will be helpful to students as they produce these types of texts (e.g. the differences between informal conversation and an academic essay)?

The examples below describe classroom activities that have been developed using texts from the ANC. The first example will target a particular word and its different grammatical functions, while the second example will compare different types of texts in an effort to raise student awareness of register issues. The term *register* refers to the situational characteristics rather than linguistic characteristics of texts; these situational characteristics often have linguistic patterns associated with them (Biber 1988, 1995).

12.4.1 A Close Look at a Particular Word

One of the more challenging tasks confronting language learners is mastering words with multiple meanings or multiple functions. In English, many high frequency words often have multiple meanings. For example, the Longman Grammar of Spoken and Written English (Biber et al. 1999) identifies *get* as the second most frequent lexical verb when looking at a corpus that includes the registers of conversation, news, academic prose and fiction. These multiple meanings can present challenges for language learners as they fine-tune the contexts in which these different meanings occur.

In addition to one word having multiple meanings, it can also be the case that a word can also serve a number of different grammatical roles. That is, a particular word appearing in different contexts can be a noun, verb or even a preposition. In the example below, some of the different grammatical roles of the word *like* are explored. Using information from a corpus can help students see real world examples of the many uses of a particular word, in this case *like*. The activity below was created using the ANC. After the presentation of the activity, an explanation of how the activity was created is provided.

12.4.1.1 Example activity 1: The word like

Like is a word that can have many functions – this activity will focus on three of the grammatical roles that *like* can have. Read the examples below and then do the activity.

Like as a verb:
> I didn't **like** it.
> They don't **like** bed and breakfasts.
> She'll **like** that.
> How do you **like** that?
> They **like** their school.

Like as a preposition:
> It's not **like** Tom to be late.
> It was **like** being in the middle of a hurricane.
> It was **like** a traffic jam.
> It sounds **like** a nightmare.
> Why would they be treating me **like** this.
> You're going to look **like** a little old lady.

Like as a conjunction:
> It's almost **like** time doesn't exist.
> It was bouncing up and down **like** somebody had it on a yo-yo.
> It's **like** there's a bomb waiting to go off.
> They didn't look **like** they were doing it to be cool.
> I feel **like** I'm in the suburbs.

Read the sentences below and write the function of *like* in the space to the left of the sentence. The examples above should help you to decide which function of *like* is being used. Put the following abbreviations in the blanks below:

> V = verb; P = preposition; C = conjunction.

When you are finished, compare your answers with a classmate.

1. ___ I saw them walking down the street and it was **like** I was confused.
2. ___ Is it, is that **like** water on the knee? Is that what that is?
3. ___ It was a very nice letter, because it sounded **like** she went through very similar things that I did.
4. ___ I don't **like** the weather.
5. ___ He really looks **like** Ron.
6. ___ He seems to feel really **like** he's doing the right thing.
7. ___ It feels **like** maybe she made a compromise.
8. and 9. ___ ___ I don't really **like** going with Anne because she doesn't **like** to stay very long.
   (Answers: 1. C; 2. P; 3. C; 4. V; 5. P; 6. C; 7. C; 8. V; 9. V)

The concordancing program MonoConc was used to create the activity above. First, texts from the Call Home portion of the ANC were loaded into the program. Then concordances were created for the word *like*. These were then copied and pasted into a Word document where examples could be selected. The examples of the three different functions of *like* were designed to cover the types of examples that the students would encounter in the activity they were asked to do. Example sentences were selected based on the ability of the sentence to make sense in a stand alone context, and also based on the vocabulary load of the sentence. In this case, vocabulary load was determined by the teacher's knowledge of her students, and not by a more formal measure such as type token ratio.

It is possible to use this same format in order to develop a range of similar activities for other words with multiple meanings or functions. The uses of *like* presented above certainly do not encompass all of the possible functions of *like*.[4] The examples above, however, do provide a glimpse as to the different functions of *like*. The examples also highlight a use of *like* that is often not presented in traditional grammar textbooks, that is, the use of *like* as a conjunction with a copular verb, which as we see from the examples above is frequent in conversation.

12.4.2 Comparing Different Texts

In the example above, a word was selected as the focus of the activity. In addition to focusing on individual words, it is also possible to use the ANC to look at patterns found across different registers. As mentioned earlier, texts that are created for different purposes or under different conditions will have different linguistic features associated with them. For example, informal conversation is typically associated with a high number of personal pronouns, repetitions and many contractions, while at the opposite end of the spectrum, academic prose typically does not have a high use of those features, but is instead associated with a high use of nominalization and a much wider range of vocabulary use (i.e. high type/token ratio) (Biber 1988). The features that are associated with these different registers are in part a function of their production circumstances. Conversation is produced in real time and therefore is not carefully edited like academic prose. Conversation is often used for recounting personal information or sharing interactions with friends and family, thus resulting in the high use of personal pronouns. Due to time constraints of producing conversation, contractions are also used to lessen the processing burden for the listener. At the other end of the register spectrum, so to speak, academic prose is not produced under real time constraints in the same way that conversation is. In addition, academic prose is typically concerned with carefully packaging information and not usually delivering personal information. The focus is on the information and not the person, hence the use of the passive, and the minimal use of personal pronouns.

These patterns, of course, can vary from text to text, but in general they are typical of differences between informal conversation and academic prose. Being aware of some of the differences between spoken language and academic prose can help facilitate students' transition into more successful academic writing. Once students realize that academic prose is simply not spoken language written down, they will be on the path to greater success. The differences between speaking and writing can also be of use to students when preparing oral presentations. Although oral presentations do not have many features of informal conversation, and because oral presentations are prepared ahead of time, students often make the mistake of preparing an oral presentation with features associated with writing, therefore making the presentation difficult for the audience to process since the delivery mode is spoken. Looking at the characteristics of different types of texts that are created for different purposes and for different modes can be a valuable activity for students in academic English programmes.

The activity presented below outlines one way that corpora can be used in order to bring register awareness into the classroom. In this activity, students are asked to read through two short text examples and count four specific grammatical features: two that are typical of conversation (i.e. first person pronouns and contractions) and two that are typical of academic prose (i.e. nominalizations and passives). They must then enter the counts in the chart provided.

12.4.2.1 Example activity 2: Comparing texts
Read the two texts below. After reading the texts look at the chart listing four grammatical features. In each text identify the features listed in the chart. You might want to use a system for marking the features, such as circling the first person pronouns and underlining contractions.

Once you have marked the features compare your answers with a classmate. If you have any differences that cannot be resolved, ask your teacher. Once you have all the features marked, count them, and enter the numbers in the chart below the texts.

Text #1

On Bali, in November, 1946, Indonesian nationalist fighters, led by Ngurah Rai, found themselves trapped by Dutch forces close to Marga, north of Tabenan. Outnumbered and outgunned, Ngurah Rai and all 96 of his followers were killed in what is regarded as Bali's last puputan. Their sacrifice is commemorated by a monument and museum at the site, together with stones bearing the names of each of those who died on the island of Bali during the struggle for independence. Finally on 17 August 1950, five years to the day after independence was first declared, the fledgling Republic of Indonesia was recognized by the Netherlands. Sukarno, preeminent in the nationalist movement, emerged as the new nation's leader.

File: Berlitz Bali-history (116 words)

Text #2

KM: Do you think it will be strange to move up north when you've lived in Charlotte all your life? Do you think there'll be a very big culture shock?

TB: I don't know that it will be a very big culture shock, because I've grown up going to Boston all the time. So it's almost like a second home. It won't be too different, but the style of the city is a little different, so -

KM: Um-hmm. Why wouldn't you want to stay in Charlotte? Is there any particular reason?

TB: I need a change. I've lived here all of my life. So I need a change and Boston's the place I've always looked to live at, so -

File: Blanchardtracy (111 words)

	1st Person pronouns	*Contractions*	*Nominalizations*	*Passives*
Text 1				
Text 2				

Now that you have read the texts and completed the chart, what do you notice about the differences between these two texts? What does this tell you about differences between conversation and writing? Write down one tip that you will remember when you next write a paper for class.

(Answers)				
	1st Person pronouns	*Contractions*	*Nominalizations*	*Passives*
Text 1	6	10	0	0
Text 2	0	0	8	5

Corpora played multiple roles in the creation of this exercise – first, corpus based research (e.g. Biber 1988; Biber et al. 1999) was used to identify linguistic features that tend to be found in one register but not another. Second, such research also identifies linguistic features that are *frequently* found in a register as opposed to those that are relatively infrequent. Third, the two sample texts were taken from the ANC, which is easy to exploit as a source of teaching data, due to the fact that it contains a wide variety of registers. Finally, with a large and varied corpus like the ANC, subjects or concepts that are relevant for a particular class can be selected. For example, if a class consisted of L2 speakers of English who were living in Boston, the conversation above might be interesting to them. Because the ANC contains a range of texts, it is easy to 'hand-pick' examples for particular classes or students in this way.

A teacher can load a set of texts from one of the spoken registers in the corpus, and then carry out a concordance search for first person pronouns and contractions. By looking through concordance lines the teacher can quickly identify the texts that have high numbers of these features and then cut and paste such texts for the activity. Then the teacher can repeat that process to find a written text. The use of a corpus and a concordancing program therefore greatly simplifies the task of identifying texts with the features that are the focus of the activity. The discussion after the students have read the texts should result in a greater awareness of the differences between informal conversation and academic prose. One possible follow-up activity after doing the activity presented above could be to have students identify the features in the chart in an academic essay that they have written, and then have a class discussion about their texts and the features that they chose.

12.5 Wrapping Up

The activities presented in the previous section suggest just two ways to develop activities that use corpora and information from corpora in the language class-room. Although far from complete, the wide range of texts available in the ANC indicates that it is already a valuable resource for language teachers.

In addition to the ANC which is currently is available on CD, there are a number of other corpus resources that are available online. For example Mark Davies at Brigham Young University has a number of useful corpora with user-friendly inter-faces available at http://view.byu.edu. In addition, the University of Michigan has compiled a corpus of spoken academic language, MICASE (Michigan Corpus of Academic Spoken English). This corpus includes a variety of different contexts that are typical of American university spoken academic interactions ranging from advising sessions to class lectures. These are available on CD or via the web with an accessible search interface at http://legacyweb.lsa.umich.edu/eli/micase/index. htm. MICASE also provides audio files so that students can hear the language while reading transcripts.

Corpora and corpus linguistics provide yet another resource in the quiver of tools that are available for language teachers. As with any resource it needs to be applied appropriately. It is important not to let frequency be the only guide to selecting items for instruction. By knowing the learners' needs teachers can effec-tively use corpora to prepare learners for the wide range of situations and also for specialized situations of language use. In addition, as with other material that is brought into the classroom, teachers need to be aware of the appropriateness of the examples and the material in terms of vocabulary, grammar structures and cultural topics.

One of the principle goals of language instruction is to provide learners with the opportunity to interact with authentic materials that will enhance their learning and help them move along to language fluency. Corpus linguistics and the use of corpora in the classroom can help move learners towards this goal. Hopefully this chapter has provided some insights and ideas as to how corpora and information from corpus linguistics can be used to inform classroom teaching, and also how teachers might be able to use corpora to develop activities for their language learning classes.

Notes

1 At the time of writing, ICE corpora have been collected from Hong Kong, East Africa, Great Britain, India, New Zealand, the Philippines and Singapore. Other corpora from Australia, Canada, Fiji, Ireland, Jamaica, Kenya, Malaysia, Malta, Nigeria, South Africa, Sri Lanka, Tanzania and the United States are also planned. See http://www.ucl.ac.uk/english-usage/ice/ for more information.
2 See http://corpus.byu.edu/bnc/.
3 See http://www.americannationalcorpus.org/.
4 For example, *like* can also occur in spoken informal conversations as a colloquial discourse marker, e.g. *I was, like, confused about it.* The word can also take the form of a noun as in: *he'd never seen the like of it before.*

13

The Impact of Corpora on Dictionaries

Patrick Hanks

This chapter discusses how corpus-linguistic techniques have revolutionized dictionary creation since the 1980s. While arguing that corpora enable improved dictionaries, I address a number of issues which suggest that corpora should not be used unthinkingly, for example it is important for compilers to address questions such as whether a dictionary is intended primarily for decoding or encoding purposes, hence a corpus ought not to be used just to produce larger and larger new editions of dictionaries with more and more 'authentic' examples. Instead, corpus techniques should help dictionary creators to consider which words (or uses of words) should be left out of a dictionary (particularly if the dictionary is aimed at learners), and examples should be carefully and sparingly selected to illustrate normal usage. Additionally, I discuss the contribution of corpus approaches to lexicographic treatment of pragmatics, phraseology and grammar. The chapter ends with a brief look at research on the Pattern Dictionary, which is being compiled with evidence from the British National Corpus.

13.1 Early Corpora

Early electronic corpora, in particular, the Brown Corpus (Francis and Kučera 1964) and the LOB Corpus (Johansson et al. 1978) had little impact on lexicography, despite being consulted by some major dictionaries during the earliest days of corpus linguistics (in particular the *American Heritage Dictionary*, first edition, 1969; and the *Longman Dictionary of Contemporary English* (LDOCE), 1978). With the benefit of hindsight, the reason for this lack of impact was simple: these pioneering early corpora were not large enough to show significant facts about the behaviour of most individual words. They only contained one million words, so it was difficult to distinguish statistically significant co-occurrences of words from chance co-occurrences. The set of word forms in a language is not a fixed number, but we can estimate that something in the order of 250,000 types (unique words) are in regular use in English at any one time. Even allowing for Zipf's law (Zipf 1935) in relation to the distribution of words in a corpus – a phenomenon which can be crudely characterized as: 'most words occur very rarely; a few words occur very often', a corpus of only 1 million words has no chance of showing the user statistically significant collocations of any but a few very common individual items. In such a corpus, a few significant collocates for function words such as prepositions can be detected, but some perfectly ordinary words do not occur at all, and for those that do occur, their collocations with other words cannot be measured effectively. In small corpora, almost all of the co-occurrences appear to be random even if they are not. Similarly, for most mid-to-low frequency words, a corpus size of only a million words does not give reliable information about the extent to which a word has multiple meanings or belongs to multiple grammatical categories.

It was left to a few pioneers in corpus linguistics, notably Francis and Kučera, Sinclair, Leech, and Johansson and Hofland, to struggle on undaunted for almost 30 years in the face of misguided and sometimes virulent hostility from the dominant 'generative' school of linguistics, whose adherents arrogated to themselves the term 'mainstream' (though 'backwater' might now seem a more appropriate metaphor). The research method of these generative linguists characteristically relied almost entirely on the invention of data by introspection, followed by some explanation of whatever it was that had been invented. Though always suspect (being in danger of trampling unwittingly over some constraint of naturalness or idiomaticity), the invention of data may be regarded as unexceptionable when used to illustrate simple, normal structures of a language. However, the programme of generative linguistics was in many cases to discover a sharp dividing line between syntactically well-formed and syntactically ill-formed sentences. One of the important discoveries of corpus linguistics and corpus-driven lexicography has been that no such sharp dividing line exists. There is an infinitely large body of obviously well-formed sentences and an infinitely large body of ill-formed sentences in a language, but there is no sharp dividing line between them. Skilled language users often deliberately exploit the conventions of normal usage for rhetorical and other effects. For this reason, when a dictionary user (in particular, a foreign learner) asks, 'Can you say X in English?' the lexicographer is constrained to provide answers in terms that assume that the question really is, 'Is it normal to say X in English?' The boundary between possible and non-possible use of each word is always fuzzy; conventions are always open to exploitation.

In a prescient paper, published as early as 1966, John Sinclair argued that an essential task for understanding meaning in language would be the analysis of collocational relationships among words, which 'would yield to nothing less than a very large computer'.

13.2 Corpus-Driven Lexicography: From Cobuild to MEDAL

Things began to change with the first edition of Cobuild (1987). This was specifically designed as a tool to help foreign learners of English to write and speak natural, idiomatic English. In other words, it was designed as an encoding aid rather than a decoding aid. In 1983, after long struggles, both with issues such as rights and permissions and technical issues such as how to handle such a large corpus on the University of Birmingham's computer, a corpus of 7.3 million words was completed (tiny in today's terms, but more than seven times the size of any previous corpus), This was used as a basis for compiling the first draft of the dictionary.

The corpus yielded many new insights, large and small, but, with a corpus of only 7.3 million words, the lexicographers still allowed themselves to supplement its evidence by a combination of the evidence of their own intuitions and other dictionaries. By the time the final editing stage was reached (1986), the Birmingham Corpus had grown to 18 million words and lexicographers became rather more reluctant to trust their own intuitions in defiance of the absence of corpus evidence. In today's world, with corpora of hundreds of millions and even billions of words being available (see Culpeper, this volume), it is a foolhardy linguist or lexicographer who prefers his or her intuitions over very large samples of evidence, but that does not stop some people. Some generative linguists, cognitive linguists and construction grammarians (whatever their other merits) continue to blithely invent evidence purporting to demonstrate idiomatic uses of language where little or no empirical evidence exists. I recently received an email from an able and respected linguist (a non-native speaker) requesting advice on access to a corpus that would provide examples of constructions such as *I walked the letter to the post*, an example invented by Langacker which, not surprisingly, she had failed to corroborate in the British National Corpus (BNC). The possibility had apparently not occurred to her that Langacker's invented example is not idiomatic, and that her failure to find it in BNC might itself be an interesting piece of empirical data. Of course, lexicographers must be aware of the dangers of the failure-to-find fallacy (the fact that something is not found does not mean that it does not or cannot exist), but failure to find a phrase in a very large corpus suggests at the very least that it is not very idiomatic.

As an example of the new insights into word behaviour yielded by early work in corpus lexicography at Cobuild in the 1980s, consider the case of *–ly* adverbs. It was widely assumed by pre-corpus lexicographers that all (or almost all) *–ly* adverbs were adverbs of manner modifying the sense of a verb, an adjective, or another adverb and that the meaning of the adverb was always (or almost always) systematically derivable from the root adjective. There is some truth in this, of course: *walking slowly* is walking in a slow manner. But some *–ly* adverbs in English have special functions or constraints, which were not always well reported in pre-corpus dictionaries. For example, The *Oxford Advanced Learner's Dictionary* (OALD1-4), says nothing about the use of words like *broadly, sadly, unfortunately, luckily* and *hopefully* as sentence adverbs – linguistic devices that enable speakers and writers to express an opinion about the semantic content of what they are saying. Those pre-corpus dictionaries which did notice sentence adverbs did not succeed in noticing all of them systematically. They tended to be more concerned with questions about prescriptive rules, for example whether it is correct to say '*Hopefully, he will deliver his paper before the deadline.*' The problem here is that although '*sadly, he died*' can be paraphrased as '*It is sad that he died*', it is not the case that '*Hopefully, he will deliver*' can be paraphrased as '**It is hopeful that he will deliver*'. Corpus lexicographers now recognize that such concerns are based on a theory of language that assigns too great a role to lexical compositionality and too small a role to the idiosyncratic conventions that are associated with each word. The lexicon is indeed, in Bloomfield's phrase, a 'basic list of irregularities'.

However, whereas for Bloomfield (1933) and for Chomsky (1981) this was a reason for shying away from any attempt to show how words and meanings are related, for corpus lexicographers this is the central issue to be investigated. In the course of investigating such irregularities, new regularities are discovered. By the time of Crowther's corpus-based 5th edition, the OALD included a note at *hopefully* explaining adverbs which 'can modify the whole sentence'. For most (but not all) of them, an example (but not a definition) is given illustrating such use, for example at *sadly*: *Sadly, we have no more money.*

A glance at corpus evidence, even in quite a small corpus, shows the function of sentence adverbs, enabling a speaker to express their own attitude to the propositional content of what they are saying. It is a truism that '*Sadly, he died before completing the project*' does not mean that he died in a sad manner, but this was not always apparent to dictionary makers until they were confronted with overwhelming evidence.

Another example of what the early corpus evidence showed the Cobuild lexicographers is the fact that the supposed adverbs of manner – even those that really are adverbs of manner – do not always and regularly inherit the entire semantics of the root adjective. The adjective *lame*, for example, has two senses: 'unable to walk or run properly because of an injury to a leg' (applied to animate beings) and 'disappointingly feeble' (applied to excuses and other speech acts). The corresponding adverb, *lamely*, on the other hand, very rarely has the 'injured leg' sense. It is almost always used in the 'feeble excuse' sense. In an informal experiment, students at Birmingham University were asked to invent a short anecdote, ending with the sentence, 'She walked lamely out of the room'. The majority of them invented a story in which the person concerned felt that she had no adequate reply, rather than one in which she had injured her leg. This informal experiment needs to be repeated under better controlled experimental conditions, but it suggests that that even collocation with the verb *walk* is not always strong enough to activate the 'injured leg' sense of *lamely*. This is not a necessary condition for the idiomatic use of lamely – the BNC contains two or three examples (out of a total of 110) of the use of this adverb in the 'injured leg' sense (example 1) – but use with a speech-act verb (example 2) is overwhelmingly the norm. Example 1 is therefore possible but abnormal. Example 2 is normal.

1. The old dog ambled **lamely** towards them.
2. She hesitated, and then said **lamely**, 'That is all.'

It seems likely that the expected primary sense of this adverb is blocked by the existence of a lexicalization of 'walk lamely', namely *limp*. However this may be, the implications of this tiny example are far-reaching, as they suggest (among other things) that it is more important for lexicographers to research and describe the conventions associated with each lexical item individually than to accept unchallenged the assumptions inherited from theoretical linguists. It is on many thousands of such examples of conventional vs abnormal use of lexical items that the Theory of Norms and Exploitations (TNE; Hanks, forthcoming) is based.

Among many other innovations, Cobuild paid more attention than pre-corpus dictionaries to lexicographic issues such as the role of function words and the pragmatics of discourse organizers (*however, anyway*), which are discussed further in Section 13.6.

At Cobuild, the corpus was used by the lexicographers: (1) to structure the entries, placing the most important meaning of each word first; (2) to write accurate definitions reflecting actual usage; (3) as a source for example sentences and (4) to help decide what to leave out.

The first major impact of corpora on lexicography was therefore on a dictionary for foreign learners with a strong focus on use as an encoding tool. Subsequent newly compiled learners' dictionaries – the *Cambridge International Dictionary of English* (CIDE, first edition 1995), and the *Macmillan English Dictionary for Advanced Learners* (MEDAL, first edition 2002) were also corpus-based and used corpus-derived examples.

In due course complete recensions of the leading English dictionaries for foreign learners, OALD and LDOCE, were prepared on the basis of corpus evidence, though for marketing reasons the distinction between a dictionary as an encoding aid and as a decoding aid tended to be fudged by the publishers and hence by the lexicographers. So OALD (5th edition 1995, 6th edition 2000) is strong on collocates and verb patterns, but the examples are not as natural as either Cobuild or LDOCE, because many of them are deliberately concocted to illustrate underlying patterns of the kind that the editor of the first edition, A. S. Hornby, had described from the outset, rather than being selected without alteration from actual texts. See Section 13.5.

13.3 Coverage: Deciding What to Leave Out

Publishers, their marketeers and advisers (none of whom are lexicographers) often claim that one of the benefits of using corpus evidence is to enable a dictionary to give better coverage of the lexicon of a language. For example, Professor the Lord Quirk (the grammarian Randolph Quirk), wrote in the preface to the third edition of LDOCE (1995) – an edition which was heavily revised using the newly available evidence of the BNC:

> There are two core features of a dictionary in terms of which its degree of excellence and achievement must be measured: **coverage** and **definition**. . . . The advent of computerized corpora enables us to achieve a greatly enhanced coverage. . . . In consequence of new initiatives in coverage, the new LDOCE is about one fifth larger than its predecessors.

Other EFL dictionary publishers have written in similar terms. It is easy publicity to say that the corpus gives better coverage, providing an argument to justify investment in corpora which bean counters can easily understand. However, it is highly questionable whether one-fifth bigger necessarily means one-fifth better. Previous editions of LDOCE already had excellent vocabulary coverage for foreign learners.

The language does not change so fast that thousands of new entries need to be added to a learners' dictionary every few years. A few dozen, maybe, but not thousands. Many new terms are ephemeral and, if added, should be taken out again in the next edition. All too often they are not. The term *black-coated workers* (meaning 'office workers') is a case in point. It was already obsolescent in 1963, when it was added to OALD2, but it took the Oxford lexicographers 20 years to take it out again. So if LDOCE3 is one-fifth better than its predecessors (and in my opinion such a claim would not be unjustified, though hard to quantify), its added excellence is due at least in part to other factors such as sharper definitions and more natural examples, selected from the BNC.

Rather than offering more and more new words to be added, a more valuable benefit of corpus evidence for dictionary compilers – in particular compilers of smaller dictionaries and dictionaries for foreign learners – is that scarcity of corpus evidence can help to give a lexicographer the courage of his or her convictions in deciding what to leave out.

Dictionaries are and always have been full of rare and unusual words. This is especially true of dictionaries intended for decoding use (i.e. those compiled with native speakers in mind, where the lexicographer imagines a scenario in which readers want to find out the meaning of an unusual word more often than they seek information about the correct idiomatic use of more common words). Such dictionaries deliberately err on the side of including rare words because these are the very words that a reader is most likely to look up in the unlikely event of encountering one. However, for compilers of pedagogical dictionaries aimed at foreign learners, this presents an excruciating dilemma. On the one hand, the main purpose of a pedagogical dictionary is to help learners write and speak the language idiomatically. On the other hand, there is nothing more certain to destroy a user's confidence in a dictionary than the experience of looking up a word and not finding it. The problem is compounded when an EFL dictionary tries to meet the needs of learners for both encoding and decoding purposes.

To quote Jonathan Crowther (preface, 1995), the OALD:

> strives to satisfy the . . . basic needs of foreign students . . ., namely to develop their receptive and productive skills, the ability (as Tony Cowie wrote in his preface to the fourth edition) 'to compose as well as to understand'.

This is an ambitious goal, for there is a tremendous tension between the two objectives. Dictionaries such as the *Idiomatic and Syntactic English Dictionary* (ISED) and Cobuild1, which start out with the goal of restricting themselves to the encoding needs of advanced learners, are gradually seduced (mainly for marketing reasons) in successive editions into trying to serve as decoding tools as well, adding thousands and thousands of rare words and senses, which can only be there for decoding users and which clutter up the dictionary for those users who want to use it as an encoding tool.

This desire to meet two objectives is all the more seductive because there is no way of predicting all the many and various needs (both encoding and decoding) of advanced learners. It is a fair bet that no advanced learner will need to encode a term such as *black-eyed bean* and if one does, it is equally unlikely that he or she will consult MEDAL (where it is an entry) in order to do so. The entry can only be there for decoding users, and it is doubtful whether any of them will go to a learner's dictionary to find out about it.

One of the benefits of using corpus evidence is that it is possible to count the relative frequency of different words and expressions. The second edition of COBUILD introduced a system of diamonds to flag the relative frequency of different words in a corpus. Other EFL dictionaries (e.g. MEDAL, CALD) have followed suit. CALD (the *Cambridge Advanced Learner's Dictionary*) has a 'Frequency Information System' which 'gives students a clear guide to the most important words and meanings to learn':

E – Essential, about 4,900 terms
I – Improver, 3,300 terms
A – Advanced, 3,700 terms

In other words, about 12,000 terms are singled out, on the basis of corpus evidence, as what C.K. Ogden (1930) termed 'basic English' – a reasonable goal for an advanced learner. The blurb of CALD trumpets this feature: 'Frequency information showing you the most important words to learn'.

It must be admitted that dictionaries have not yet been very successful in calculating the relative frequency of meanings as opposed to words. CALD, for example, calculates comparative word frequency with great reliability, and this extends to certain fixed expressions such as phrasal verbs. But it does not do such a good job on the frequencies of different senses of a verb. So, for example, the use of *this* as an adverb, meaning 'as much as shown or to a particular degree' (e.g. *It was only about this high off the ground*) is flagged as E (for 'essential') along with the other uses of this very common word. However, in the BNC, the adverb use accounts for only about 0.16 per cent of all uses of *this*. It occurs 7.47 times per million words in the BNC, being similar in frequency to the words *symmetry, fittings, specifications, trinity* and *bilateral,* suggesting this use is not as essential (in terms of frequency at least) as the authors of CALD indicate.

A short case study of a borderline word will illustrate the encoding/decoding dilemma more clearly. The term *maulstick* is not in my active vocabulary: I had never encountered it and had no idea of its existence, still less about what it meant until, 20 years after first becoming a lexicographer, I stumbled across it in 1985 in the course of doing a lexicographical cross-check. It is in two EFL dictionaries of the 1970s: OALD3 (1974) and LDOCE1 (1978). I hope it is not excessively uncharitable to suppose that the LDOCE1 lexicographers did not dare to leave it out, because their main rival had it in. After all, what other evidence did they have? How could they know, with any confidence, that the word was so rare that it should be omitted? The worst mistake that a beginner in lexicography can make is to omit a term on the grounds, 'I don't know it'. You may not know it, and yet it may nevertheless be a common word or sense for other users of the language.

Lexicographers must make provision for the possibility of their own ignorance. So in it went. Or maybe the editors responsible for the 'maul-' section in these dictionaries were keen amateur oil painters, for, according to LDOCE1, it means 'a stick held by a painter to support the hand which holds the brush'.

By 1995, however, when corpus evidence was brought into play, this entry was deleted from both LDOCE and OALD, and other corpus-based learners' dictionaries have not included it.

That is not the end of the story, however, for there are other kinds of dictionaries besides learners' dictionaries. Even though there is scant corpus evidence for *maulstick* in the BNC (one occurrence), the word receives an entry in the *New Oxford Dictionary of English* (NODE 1998) and its successor, the *Oxford Dictionary of English* (ODE 2003), the only English dictionaries for native speakers that can justify a claim to be corpus-based. Although NODE made very full use of the evidence of the BNC, it did so mainly in order to improve the grammar, definitions and examples for everyday words. Improvements in vocabulary coverage of rarer terms owed more to other sources, in particular the Oxford Reading Programme (in which citation readers search texts for unusual terms and senses) and directed research in particular domains such as flora and fauna, and the vocabulary of sports and leisure activities, and of academic disciplines ranging from nuclear physics to art history. A balanced corpus of 100 million words is not nearly large enough to serve, unsupported, as a basis for an entry list for a native-speaker dictionary. Using corpus evidence to achieve coverage for such a dictionary is necessary, but not sufficient.

In the Oxford English Corpus of 1.5 billion words, there are two hits for *maulstick*. This tantalizing slither of evidence might have presented the lexicographical team with a dilemma – to include or not to include – if they had not already conducted directed research that tells them that it is an important term in art history – and, no doubt, would have substantially greater frequency in a dedicated corpus of art-history texts. Domain-specific corpora have much to contribute to future lexicography, but then questions will arise concerning the overlap between lexicography and terminology, the latter being a pitifully neglected subject in the English-speaking world, though strong in other languages.

In some aspects, dictionaries are being overtaken by other kinds of on-line resources. Anyone who really wants to know what a maulstick is might be well advised to go online (at the time of writing–May 2008, Google has 8,230 citations for the word), while at the relevant entry in Wikipedia, there are two nice pictures (at the time of writing) showing an artist using a maulstick. This is one of those entries where the best explanation is afforded by a visual representation of an example. The grammar, phraseology and definition of *maulstick* are of little linguistic interest.

13.4 Definitions

Does corpus evidence enable lexicographers to sharpen up definitions? It would be nice to be able to answer with an unequivocal 'yes', but the truth is more complex. The first editions of corpus-based dictionaries sometimes show the lexicographers seeming to struggle to find words to represent what they can see in the corpus, while partly or wholly rejecting definitions inherited from pre-corpus dictionaries. The lexicographers are trying to relate their definitions more closely to how the language is actually used. This calls for a great deal of effort and compression. The effort is sometimes (but not always) successful.

Consider, for example, the adjective *threadbare*. Here is a traditional pre-corpus definition (OALD2/3; 1963, 1974), buried in the entry for *thread*, for which a swung dash is substituted:

thread . . .

. . . **~bare**, *adj.* **1.** (of cloth) worn thin; shabby: *a ~bare coat.* **2.** (fig.) much used and therefore uninteresting or valueless; hackneyed: *~bare jokes (sermons, arguments).*

The apparatus and nesting seem a bit cumbersome to modern eyes, but this is a perfectly serviceable definition. Corpus lexicographers, however, want to get away from the Leibnizian brackets '(of cloth)', which are intended to make the definiens substitutable for the definiendum. They may also think that the corpus evidence does not chime well with 'uninteresting'.

Cobuild1 (1987) has:

threadbare, *adj.* **1 Threadbare** clothes, carpets, and other pieces of cloth are old and have been used so much that the cloth has become very thin: EG *O'Shea's suit was baggy and threadbare.*

2. Threadbare jokes, stories, excuses, etc. have been said so often that they are no longer funny, interesting, or believable.

Here, we can see the lexicographer struggling (and failing) to find a suitable superordinate word for 'jokes, stories, excuses, . . .' and eventually giving up, and, in defiance of the editor-in-chief's interdict, employing the forbidden escape word, 'etc.'. Something similar is happening in the second part of the explanation – the definiendum – with 'no longer funny, interesting, or believable.' It seems that what she wanted to say was something like, 'A threadbare joke is no longer funny; a threadbare story is no longer interesting; a threadbare excuse is no longer believable; . . . etc.'

Getting the right level of generalization in lexicography is extremely difficult. Struggling and failing to do so is one reason why many entries in corpus-based dictionaries tend to be rather wordy. Interestingly, it is often easier to find the right superordinate terms in definitions based on samples from very large corpora (billions of words) than in smaller corpora of only one or two hundred million words. The conventional norms of usage for a word tend to stand out in large samples, and these can sometimes suggest an appropriate superordinate. Nevertheless, this is an area in which serious lexicographical training is needed.

Cobuild2 (1995) tries again:

threadbare, *adj.* 1 **Threadbare** clothes, carpets, and other pieces of cloth look old, dull, and very thin, because they have been worn or used so much that the cloth has become very thin: *She sat cross-legged on a threadbare square of carpet.*

2. If you describe an activity, an idea, or an argument as **threadbare**, you mean that it is very weak, or inadequate, or old and no longer funny, interesting, or believable. . . . . *the government's threadbare domestic policies.*

This is hardly more successful. In fact, if anything, it is worse. The words 'dull' in sense 1 and 'activity' in sense 2 are very debatable, while in sense 2 the problem of getting the right level of generalization has not been addressed.

In MEDAL (2003), this is one of the entries which borrows Cobuild's full-sentence style, for two of its three definitions:

threadbare, *adj.* 1 threadbare clothing, carpet, or cloth is very thin and almost has holes in it because it has been worn or used a lot. 1 **a.** wearing or containing threadbare things: *the threadbare family apartment.* 2. a threadbare idea or excuse has been used a lot and is no longer effective.

Here at last the problem of the superordinate in sense 2 has been addressed, as indeed it has been in CALD ('a threadbare excuse, argument, or idea . . .'). But is it any better than Hornby's 1963 definition, quoted above? What the corpus dictionaries add – or try to add – is information about the semantic types of collocates: clothing and carpets, not just cloth, in sense 1, and an idea or excuse in sense 2. MEDAL also offers information about a sense extension (1a), typical of many adjectives.

In the first edition of the first corpus-driven dictionary (Cobuild), the definitions are undoubtedly verbose in places, not sharp. Reviewers of the first edition of Cobuild (1987) accused it, with some justice, of verbosity. However, some reviewers went on to associate this with the 'full-sentence' defining style. I think this criticism is mistaken. Let us look at another example. Definition 7 of *proportion* in Cobuild1 reads as follows:

If you say that something is big or small **in proportion to** something else, you mean that it is big or small when you compare it with the other thing or measure it against the other thing.

This is undeniably verbose. In the second edition, it was reduced to:

If something is small or large **in proportion to** something else, it is small or large when compared with that thing.

This is a full-sentence definition, but not especially verbose, nor is it significantly longer than the definitions of this difficult concept in other dictionaries.

MEDAL defines **proportion** (sense 2) as:

the correct, most useful, or most attractive relationship between two things,

and offers the phrase *in proportion to* with an example ('*his head is large in proportion to his small frame*') but no definition. An undefined example may be the best strategy for such a phrase.

One noticeable effect of corpus evidence is that corpus-based dictionaries – even dictionaries based on different corpora – are tending to converge in what they say about the meanings of words, compared with pre-corpus dictionaries, as described for example by Atkins and Levin (1991), who showed that there was simply no way of mapping the sense distinctions in one pre-corpus dictionary onto another. Such dictionaries were incommensurable. Now, it is clear that there are many different possible ways of carving up corpus data, but corpus-based dictionaries are, in many of their entries, commensurable. They may make more or less fine-grained sense distinctions, but the semantic space being described in two such dictionaries is very often recognizably similar. This is not because they copy from one another or because they are using the same corpus, but because the salient features of word meanings are generally the same across many different corpora. Minor details differ; old decaying senses are more fully represented in some dictionaries than in others, but the salient features of the architecture of a word's meaning are waiting there, to be discovered through painstaking corpus analysis. Corpus lexicography is very often a voyage towards the painful rediscovery of the obvious. After hours of painstaking corpus analysis and hunting for just the right generalizations to cover the bulk of the evidence, you know that you have got it right when your publisher says to you, 'That's obvious. Everyone in the whole world knows that.' To which the corpus lexicographer is minded to retort, 'If everyone in the whole world knows that, why didn't our pre-corpus dictionaries say so?'

A question that engages much lexicographical energy is, 'How many senses are there of this or that word?' To which the riposte is, 'How long is a piece of string?' that is there is no reliable way of deciding how many senses a word has: deciding this is, in each case, a matter of lexicographical art and judgement. Computational linguists often complain that sense distinctions in EFL and other dictionaries are too fine-grained, and this criticism is not totally ill-founded. Striving for a high level of generality obscures many contextually determined nuances. It is also difficult to get right.

Existing dictionary entries are all meaning-driven. A new kind of dictionary is proposed by Hanks and Pustejovsky (2005), which is pattern-driven. In other words, the lexicographers must first sort the corpus evidence for each word into patterns that are associated with it, and then attach a meaning to the pattern, not the word in isolation. An example of a pattern-dictionary entry is cited in Section 13.10.

13.5 Citing Examples

The selection or concoction of examples of usage to illustrate word senses or grammatical points is a vexed question, debated by two camps, with much misunderstanding on both sides. On one side, the editors of some corpus-based dictionaries have argued that only authentic examples – real sentences and phrases which have been uttered in earnest by real people for some real communicative purpose – are acceptable. Made-up examples are viewed as unreliable because they can trample unwittingly over selectional preferences and other unrecognized grammatical constraints and so mislead the user. On the other side, some pedagogical lexicographers argue that the purpose of an example in a dictionary is to illustrate some aspect of the linguistic competence that a dictionary user aims at, not merely to record a performance, and that therefore examples should be idealizations, based on corpus evidence perhaps, but shorter, neater and better focused than most real uttered sentences, which are full of digressions, loose ends and other imperfections. An obvious compromise would be to seek authentic sentences in the corpus that meet the criteria of the idealizers, but unfortunately suitable candidates are few and far between: for many words, they cannot be found at all.

The first edition of one otherwise excellent pre-corpus dictionary was marred by occasional bizarre invented examples, such as (s.v. *salvage*):

'We'll try to salvage your leg,' said the doctor to the trapped man.

There are several things wrong with this. In the first place, legs are not among the things that are normally salvaged (*ships, possessions,* and *pride* are among the more salient collocates in the direct object slot). Second, there are too many players: either 'the doctor' or 'the trapped man', in an authentic text, would probably have been mentioned before and would therefore be a pronoun here. The inventor of this example is trying to tell a whole story in a single sentence, which, of course, does not happen in real texts.

Determining the 'normal' uses of words turns out to be difficult – indeed, impossible without very large bodies of evidence and a theory of prototypical norms. Corpora occasionally throw up bizarre utterances that are implausible but nonetheless authentic:

Always vacuum your moose from the snout up, and brush your pheasant with freshly baked bread, torn not sliced.

> —Example cited by Judy Kegl (personal communication), from
> *The Massachusetts Journal of Taxidermy,* c. 1986, in an article cited
> in a corpus of Associated Press newswire texts.

This example is cited from memory, as I no longer have access to that early corpus. It deviates from normal usage in several ways – for example, the noun *moose* is not a canonical direct object of the verb *vacuum*. It would clearly not be a good example to put in a dictionary, but unfortunately, being human, lexicographers suffer from a temptation to use such examples because they are 'interesting' or because they illustrate some extreme boundary of possible usage. The purpose of a dictionary example is to illustrate normal usage, not the extreme boundaries of possibility.

Bizarre citations such as these have, indeed, been used as arguments to turn lexicographers and linguists alike away from corpus evidence. The obvious questions to ask are, 'What sort of thing do you normally vacuum in English – or is this verb normally intransitive?' The obvious way of answering is to look at the salient collocates in the direct object slot in a corpus (if there is one), either impressionistically or using a statistical tool such as the Sketch Engine (see Culpeper this volume). It is unlikely that *moose* will be found as a salient direct object of *vacuum* in any corpus. Although authentic empirical evidence is a necessary basis for linguistic analysis, it is not in itself sufficient. In other words, authenticity alone is not enough: evidence of conventionality is also needed.

The two sentences just discussed, one invented and the other authentic, are extreme cases on either side. Other badly chosen or badly invented examples are more quietly misleading. Because we cannot be sure that we know all the constraints that govern the idiomatic uses of a word – and because it is very clear that the 'anything goes' syntactic theories of the 1970s were simply wrong, though their legacy is still with us – it is safer to stick to authentic data, rather than making up examples, and to seek examples that are both typical and ordinary. Current dictionaries, both corpus-based and pre-corpus, contain many examples that are quietly misleading in one way or another.

An additional point may be made here about cognitive salience. The fact that, 20 years after hearing the 'vacuum your moose' example in conversation, I can still remember it suggests that it is somehow salient – cognitively salient, that is. I assume that I am a normal human being, at least in this respect, and that others too will find it memorable. It is memorable because it is unusual. But unusual examples do not belong in dictionaries. I remember few if any of the tens of thousands of more mundane sentences to which I must have been exposed in 1987. A large part of everyday language – the frequently recurring patterns, which we might call 'socially salient' – is conventional and for that very reason unmemorable. This suggests that cognitive salience and social salience are independent (or possibly inverse) variables.

Corpus lexicographers need to resist the temptation to select (and even more so, to invent) bizarre examples, regardless of how interesting they may seem. They should instead choose examples in which all the words are used normally, conventionally, and naturally, without unnecessary digressions or distractions. This is difficult.

13.6 Pragmatics

Section 13.2 contained some examples of sentence adverbs, illustrating the impact of corpora on dictionaries in respect of pragmatics. Lexical pragmatics is a very broad field, with many different realizations, and it is one where corpus evidence has been particularly beneficial. Pre-corpus dictionaries had got into the habit of trying to word all explanations in terms of substitutable definitions, no matter how absurd the result might seem, but corpus-based dictionaries pay much more attention to the pragmatic functions of certain words and expressions. Conversational pragmatics includes terms such as *I see, you know, right* and *of course.* No lexicographer inspecting a concordance for *see, know, right* and *course* could fail to notice the pragmatic force of these expressions. Thus, Cobuild2 has an entry for *right* in its pragmatic functions (separate from the many truth-functional and other semantic meanings of this word), with 'discourse functions' as a part-of-speech label and the following explanations:

1. You use '**right**' to attract someone's attention or to indicate that you have dealt with one thing, so you can go on to another. *Right, I'll be back in a minute | Wonderful. Right, let's go on to our next caller.*
2. You can use '**right?**' to check whether what you have said is correct. *They have a small plane, right? | So if it's not there, the killer must have it, right?*
3. You can say '**right**' to show that you are listening to what someone is saying and that you accept or understand it. (SPOKEN) '*Your children may well come away speaking with a broad country accent*' - '*Right*' - '*because they're mixing with country children.*'
4. You can say '**right on**' to express your support or approval (INFORMAL, SPOKEN, OLD-FASHIONED) *He suggested that many of the ideas just would not work. But the tenor of his input was 'Right on! Please show us how to make them work.'*
5. If someone says '**right you are**' they are agreeing to do something in a very willing and happy way. (INFORMAL, SPOKEN) '*I want a word with you when you stop.*' - '*Right you are.*'

Cobuild's initiative in this respect has been followed by other EFL dictionaries, though not by the corpus-based editions of OALD, which seem to be rather reluctant to let go of the traditional notion that the purpose of dictionary definitions is to define (not to comment on pragmatics).

One more example of the impact of corpus evidence on the description of conversational pragmatics in dictionaries will have to suffice. At its entry for *really*, the corpus-based LDOCE3 (1994) includes a box containing a graph showing that this word is used about 400 times per million words in written English, but approximately 1,800 times per million (i.e. 4½ times more often) in spoken English. The box goes on to illustrate the many different pragmatic uses of this word in speech:

4 **really?** a) used to show that you are surprised by what someone has said: '*There are something like 87 McDonalds in Hong Kong.*' '*Really?*' b) used in conversation to show that you are listening to or interested in what the other person is saying. '*I think we might go to see the Grand Canyon in June.*' '*Really?*' c) *AmE* used

to express agreement: *'It's a pain having to get here so early.' 'Yeah, really!'* d) especially BrE used to express disapproval: *Really, Larry, you might have told me!*

5 not really used to say 'no' or 'not completely': Do you want to come along? – 'Not really.'

6 I don't really know used to say that you are not certain about something: *I don't really know what he's up to. I haven't heard from him for ages.*

7 really and truly used to emphasize a statement or opinion: *really and truly, I think you should tell him.*

Many other examples of the impact of corpus evidence on the accounting for other kinds of pragmatic information in dictionaries could be given, but lack of space forbids.

13.7 Phraseology

Another aspect of the impact of corpora on dictionaries lies in the area of phraseology. This ranges from highlighting important phrases in examples to providing explicit lists of frequent collocations. Highlighting is a technique favoured by ODE, as in the following example sentence (s.v. *jaw*):

*victory was snatched **from the jaws of** defeat*

and at *plot*, contrasting with the transitive use in 'plotting a bombing campaign', an intransitive example with a salient preposition:

*brother plots **against** brother.*

OALD6 contains some useful 'help notes', which address phraseology, among other things. For example, at the entry for *really*, sense 4 ('(usually *spoken*) used, often in negative sentences, to reduce the force of sth. you are saying'), there is a help note that reads as follows:

The position of **really** can change the meaning of the sentence. **I don't really know** means that you are not sure about something. **I really don't know** emphasizes that you do not know.

Many modern dictionaries of current English for learners show lexical selections involving salient collocates based on statistical analysis of corpus data. For example MEDAL at *comfort* adds a note:

Words frequently used with comfort
verbs: bring, derive, draw, find, offer, seek, take

CALD at *threat* has:

> *Words that go with threat*
> be/pose a threat; issue/make a threat; receive a threat; carry out a threat;
> a threat hangs over sb; a growing/major/real/serious threat; an idle/
> immediate/potential/renewed threat; a threat to sb/sth; the threat of sth

Information of this kind, which can be extremely useful for encoding purposes, is comparatively easy to select from a corpus, given a good statistical analyser, but would be impossible to dream up out of one's head without corpus evidence. Oxford University Press devotes an entire volume, a companion volume to OALD called the *Oxford Collocations Dictionary for Students of English* (2002), to providing such information for a wide range of common words. The aim is to help learners to enrich their vocabulary and to select idiomatically correct (not merely logically correct) phraseology.

On the other hand, lexicographers must be alert and pay attention to the facts when encoding phraseological information. Several learners' dictionaries include the expression *black economy* in a form that implies that it is always used with the definite article *the*. This would be a useful piece of encoding information for a foreign learner, if it were true. Unfortunately it is not. Out of 43 genuine hits for *black economy* in the BNC, 39 are in a noun phrase governed by the definite article, but 6 are not. This sort of evidence presents lexicographers with another familiar dilemma: whether to represent the rule or to represent the predominant norm.

13.8 Grammar

Corpus evidence has enabled lexicographers to give better, streamlined accounts of English grammar. A notable example is ODE, which, unlike other dictionaries aimed at native speakers, has broken away from traditional simplistic obsessions (in particular, the subcategorization of verbs into merely transitive and intransitive, with occasional mention of prepositional choices). ODE gives an empirically sounder account, based on corpus evidence, of the syntactic patterns associated with each word. For example, ODE recognizes that a verb can have up to three arguments or valencies, and it says what they are: with verbs of movement, adverbial arguments ['with adverbial of direction]'; with linking verbs, a subject complement or object complement (as in 'she dyed her hair black'); and so on.

Old habits of caution in lexicography die hard, however. For example, CALD's entry for the verb **amble** gives the grammar as [I, usually + adv or prep]. 'I' stands for intransitive. In this example, 'usually' is unnecessary. *Amble* is indeed a manner-of-motion verb, so one would expect the adverbial of direction to be optional, but in fact it is obligatory in normal, non-contrastive text. The LDOCE3 entry for this verb is preferable:

> **amble** *v.* [I always + adv/prep] to walk in a slow relaxed way: [+ **along/across etc**] *the old man came out and ambled over for a chat.*

The relevant word in the example sentence here is 'over'. In the front matter, LDOCE3 comments: 'You cannot simply say "he ambled" without adding something like "along" or "towards me".' One needs corpus evidence to be able to make assertions like this in entry after entry with confidence.

Learner's dictionaries have built much of their grammatical apparatus on the insights of pre-corpus lexicographers such as A. S. Hornby, whose verb patterns are justly famous. Hornby and his mentor, H. E. Palmer, perceived the order underlying the apparent chaos of verb use in English. However, it is not surprising that many of the details of Hornby's verb patterns had to be revised in the light of corpus evidence in the 5th and 6th editions of OALD, for Hornby was reliant for the details on his intuitions and his wide reading. He did not have a corpus.

In one recent learners' dictionary, MEDAL, however, the grammatical apparatus is minimal. For example, at *amble*, MEDAL does not mention the more-or-less obligatory adverbial of direction, represented in LDOCE3 as '+ adv/prep'. This is surely a deliberate policy, since the principals involved in creating MEDAL had worked in one capacity or another on other learners' dictionaries, which have more sophisticated grammar patterns. Presumably, it was decided as a matter of policy that MEDAL should focus on meanings and examples, not on grammatical abstractions. After all, many learners learn by analogy, not by rule, so the grammatical abstractions will mean little or nothing to many readers.

13.9 The Role of Corpus Evidence in Dictionaries for Native Speakers

The one-volume *New Oxford Dictionary of English* (NODE 1998; subsequently rechristened the *Oxford Dictionary of English, ODE* 2001) is, so far, the only dictionary aimed at native speakers to have made extensive use of corpus evidence to compile a brand-new account of contemporary English for use by native speakers. It made use of three kinds of evidence: the BNC as a template for both the macrostructure and the microstructure of the dictionary and its entries; the Oxford Reading Program for rare and unusual words and senses; and technical literature for information about terminology in special domains, ranging from science to sport and from law to linguistics. *ODE* contrasts with the *Oxford English Dictionary* (Murray 1878–1928; 3rd edition in progress), which is a dictionary compiled on historical principles, placing the oldest meaning of a word first.

To date, *ODE* is the only dictionary of English for native speakers to be corpus-based. The *New Oxford American Dictionary* is an Americanization of it, not an original compilation. In other languages, the situation is rather different – for example, major corpus-based dictionaries for native speakers of languages as diverse as Danish, Modern Greek, and Malay are in compilation or have been published.

The impact of corpus data on lexicography since 1987 (the date of publication of Cobuild, the first corpus-driven dictionary) has been overwhelming. At last lexicographers have sufficient evidence to make the generalizations that they need to make with reasonable confidence. We can now see that pre-corpus lexicography was little more than a series of stabs in the dark, often driven by historical rather than synchronic motives. In word after word, pre-corpus lexicographers (consulting their intuitions and a bundle of more or less unusual citations collected by worthy and earnest citation readers) failed to achieve the right level of generalization regarding the conventions of present-day word meaning in a language, as can be seen by attempts to map the old definitions onto the new evidence. Of all the many possible uses and meanings that a word might have, lexicographers now have better chances of selecting the ones that are actually used and of writing reasonably accurate descriptive definitions of commonly used words. This has resulted in a clutch of completely new corpus-based dictionaries (Cobuild, CIDE, MEDAL, ODE) as well as completely rewritten editions of old favourites (OALD, LDOCE). But in truth the process of responding to the challenges posed by corpus evidence has hardly begun. What is now called for is a radical reappraisal of lexicological theory in the light of corpus evidence, with close attention to syntagmatics (the way words are normally and actually used), as well as what they mean. This will, if undertaken seriously and objectively, lead to completely new kinds of lexical resources, in particular hierarchically structured multipurpose on-line ontologies and lexicons.

13.10 The Future: FrameNet and the Pattern Dictionary

It seems certain that lexicography in future will be corpus-based, or even corpus-driven. More attention will be paid to the typical phraseology associated with each meaning of each word. Links will be set up between corpus evidence and meanings. One project that is doing this is FrameNet (Baker et al. 2003), which groups words of similar meaning into semantic frames and identifies the frame elements that participate in each frame. For example, in the 'Damaging' frame, there is an *Agent* (the person or thing that causes the damage), a *Patient* (the person or thing that suffers the damage), and a *Cause* (the event that causes the damage). Lexical units identified so far (May 2008) as participants in the 'Damaging' frame include: *chip*.v, *damage*.v, *deface*.v, *dent*.v, *key*.v, *mar*.v, *nick*.v, *rend*.v, *rip*.v, *sabotage*.v, *score*.v, *scratch*.v, *tear*.v, *vandalise*.v, *vandalism*.n. The semantic frame offers additional information about frame elements and lexical units. Annotated corpus examples are given.

FrameNet concentrates on words with similar meaning. A rather different project is the *Pattern Dictionary* (Hanks, in progress), which concentrates on meaning differences and how they can be recognized in texts. The project design is described in Hanks and Pustejovsky (2005); it is currently being implemented as part of the Corpus Pattern Analysis[1] project at the Masaryk University in Brno. The *Pattern Dictionary* aims to account for all the normal uses of all normal verbs in English. This is to say, it is a semantically motivated account of each verb's syntagmatic preferences, providing links between contexts and meanings, that is, there are 'pointers' from each pattern to the uses in a corpus that support it. The *Pattern Dictionary* is not aimed at everyday readers or learners, but is intended as a fundamental resource or benchmark for linguists, lexicographers, coursebook writers, computational linguists and lexicological theorists, with many possible applications. For example, if the Semantic Web (Feigenbaum et al. 2007) gets beyond processing lists of names and addresses, tagged documents and other entities, and starts to process unstructured texts, it will, sooner or later, have to address the question of what words mean – and how do we know what they mean? *The Pattern Dictionary* provides explicit links between meaning and use. Thus, while FrameNet annotates *scratch* as one of several words participating in the 'Damaging' frame, the Pattern Dictionary distinguishes 14 patterns for the verb *scratch*, only 3 of which have anything to do with 'Damaging'. Several of the meanings of *scratch* participate in frames that have not yet been compiled in FrameNet. Conversely, many verbs that are lexical units in FrameNet do not yet have a *Pattern Dictionary* entry. The two projects are complementary. Some of the *Pattern Dictionary*'s distinctions are quite fine-grained, but they are of vital importance in answering the question 'Who did what to whom?' No distinction is made between semantic and pragmatic implicatures, for both are part of the conventional meaning of these patterns.

scratch

1. PATTERN: [[Human | Physical Object 1]] scratch [[Physical Object 2]]
   PRIMARY IMPLICATURE: [[Human | Physical Object 1]] marks and/or damages the surface of [[Physical Object 2]]
   SECONDARY IMPLICATURE: Typically, if subject is [[Human]], [[Human]] does this by dragging a fingernail or other pointed object across the surface of [[Physical Object 2]]
   EXAMPLES: *I remember my diamond ring scratching the table.* | *'I'm sorry sir, but I'm afraid I've scratched your car a bit!'*
   FREQUENCY: 19%

2. PATTERN: [[Human]] scratch [[Language | Picture]] {on [[Inanimate = Surface]]}
   PRIMARY IMPLICATURE: [[Human]] writes or marks [[Language | Picture]] on [[Inanimate = Surface]] using a sharp edge or other sharp or pointed object
   EXAMPLES: *A Turkish schoolboy who had scratched the word 'Marxism' on his desk.* | *Names of infant Mulverins had recently been scratched on the wall.*
   FREQUENCY: 9%

3. PATTERN: [[Human | Animal]] scratch [[Self | Body Part]]
   PRIMARY IMPLICATURE: [[Human | Animal]] repeatedly drags one or more of his or her fingernails rapidly across [[Body Part]]
   SECONDARY IMPLICATURE: typically, [[Human | Animal]] does this in order to relieve itching
   EXAMPLE: *Without claws it is impossible for any cat to scratch itself efficiently.*
   FREQUENCY: 16%

4. PATTERN: [[Human]] scratch {head}
   PRIMARY IMPLICATURE: [[Human]] rubs his or her {head} with his or her fingernail(s)
   SECONDARY IMPLICATURE: often a sign that [[Human]] is puzzled or bewildered
   EXAMPLES: *He peered down at me and scratched his head as he replaced his cap.* | *Having just struggled through a copy of the Maastricht Treaty I can only scratch my head that anyone would wish to sign it* [METAPHORICAL EXPLOITATION].
   FREQUENCY: 14%

5. PATTERN: [[Human 1 | Animal 1]] scratch [[Human 2 | Animal 2]]
   PRIMARY IMPLICATURE: [[Human 1 | Animal 1]] uses the fingernails or claws to inflict injury on [[Human 2 | Animal 2]]
   EXAMPLE: *Mary was starting to pull her sister's hair violently and scratch her face in anger.*
   FREQUENCY: 9%

6. PATTERN: [[Inanimate]] scratch [[Human | Animal]]
   PRIMARY IMPLICATURE: [[Inanimate]] accidentally inflicts a superficial wound on [[Human | Animal]]
   EXAMPLE: *A nice old Burmese woman brought us limes – her old arms scratched by the thorns.*
   FREQUENCY: 2%

7. PATTERN: [[Bird = Poultry]] scratch [NO OBJ] (around)
   PRIMARY IMPLICATURE: [[Bird = Poultry]] drags its claws over the surface of the ground in quick, repeated movements
   SECONDARY IMPLICATURE: typically, [[Bird = Poultry]] does this as part of searching for seeds or other food.
   EXAMPLE: *A typical garden would contain fruit and vegetables, a few chickens to scratch around.*
   FREQUENCY: 3 %

8. PATTERN: [[Human]] scratch [NO OBJ] {around | about} {for [[Entity = Benefit]]}
   PRIMARY IMPLICATURE [[Human]] tries to obtain [[Entity = Benefit]] in difficult circumstances
   COMMENT: Phrasal verb.
   EXAMPLE: *Worrying his head off, scratching about for the rent.*
   FREQUENCY: 4%

9. PATTERN: [[Human]] scratch {living}
   PRIMARY IMPLICATURE: [[Human]] earns a very poor {living}
   COMMENT: Idiom.

EXAMPLE: *destitute farmers trying to scratch a living from exhausted land.*
FREQUENCY: 6%

10. PATTERN: [[Human 1]] scratch {[[Human 2]]'s {back}}
    PRIMARY IMPLICATURE: [[Human 1]] helps [[Human 2]] in some way
    SECONDARY IMPLICATURE: usually as part of a reciprocal helping arrangement
    COMMENT: Idiom.
    EXAMPLE: *Here the guiding motto was: you scratch my back, and I'll scratch yours—a process to which Malinowski usually referred in more dignified language as 'reciprocity' or 'give and take'.*
    FREQUENCY: 1%

11. PATTERN: [[Human | Institution]] scratch {surface (of [[Abstract = Topic]])}
    PRIMARY IMPLICATURE: [[Human | Institution]] pays only very superficial attention to [[Abstract = Topic]]
    COMMENT: Idiom.
    EXAMPLE: *As a means of helping Africa's debt burden, . . . it barely scratches the surface of the problem.*
    FREQUENCY: 11%

12. PATTERN: [[Human 1]] scratch [[Entity]]
    PRIMARY IMPLICATURE: [[Human 1]] looks below the obvious superficial appearance of something . . .
    SECONDARY IMPLICATURE: . . . and finds that the reality is very different from the appearance.
    COMMENT: Imperative. Idiom.
    EXAMPLE: *Scratch any of us and you will find a small child.*
    FREQUENCY: 2%

13. PATTERN: [[Human | Physical Object 1 | Process]] scratch [[Physical Object 2 | Stuff]] {away | off}
    PRIMARY IMPLICATURE: [[Human | Physical Object 1 | Process]] removes [[Physical Object 2 | Stuff]] from a surface by scratching it
    COMMENT: Phrasal verb.
    EXAMPLE: *First he scratched away the plaster, then he tried to pull out the bricks.*
    FREQUENCY: 2%

14. PATTERN: [Human]] scratch [[Language | Picture]] {out}
    PRIMARY IMPLICATURE: [[Human]] deletes or removes [[Language | Picture]] from a document or picture
    COMMENT: Phrasal verb.
    EXAMPLE: *Some artists . . . use 'body colour' occasionally, especially solid white to give that additional accent such as highlights and sparkles of light on water which sometimes give the same results as scratching out.*
    FREQUENCY: 1%

13.11 Conclusion

It would be no exaggeration to say that corpus evidence has had, is having and will continue to have a revolutionizing effect on lexicography. It has enabled lexicographers to get a new sense of proportion about the relative importance of different words and different meanings of words. It has led to the development of entirely new approaches to the lexicographic description of pragmatics, function words, phraseology and grammar. It has led to a heated and potentially productive debate about the role of example sentences in dictionaries. But corpus lexicography is still in its infancy. Computer programs are already in development to improve the selection of typical collocates of each word and typical examples of use. In future, we may expect development of new kinds of lexicographical work, where the microstructure of each entry is *pattern-driven* rather than meaning-driven. In other words, instead of asking, 'How many meanings does this word have, and how shall I define them?' the lexicographer will start by asking, 'How is this word used, how can I group the uses into patterns, and what is the meaning of each pattern?'

Dictionaries Cited

CALD: Woodford, K. et al. (2005), *Cambridge Advanced Learner's Dictionary* (= 2nd edn of CIDE). Cambridge: Cambridge University Press.

CIDE1: Procter, P. et al. (1995), *Cambridge International Dictionary of English*. Cambridge: Cambridge University Press.

COBUILD1: Sinclair, J. M., Hanks, P. et al. (1987), *Collins Cobuild English Language Dictionary*. London and Glasgow: HarperCollins.

COBUILD2, 3: Sinclair, J. M., Fox, G., Francis, G. et al. (1995, 2nd edn; 2001, 3rd edn). *Collins Cobuild English Language Dictionary*. London and Glasgow: HarperCollins.

COD1: Fowler, H. W. and Fowler, F. G. (1911), *Concise Oxford Dictionary of Current English*. Oxford: Oxford University Press.

COD8: Allen, R. et al. (1990), *Concise Oxford Dictionary of Current English,* 8th edn. Oxford: Oxford University Press.

CPA: Hanks, P. (in progress), *Corpus Pattern Analysis: The Pattern Dictionary*. Brno: Faculty of Informatics, Masaryk University: http://nlp.fi.muni.cz/projects/cpa/.

ISED: Hornby, A. S. Gatenby, E. V. and Wakefield, H. (1942), *Idiomatic and Syntactic English Dictionary*. Tokyo: Kaitakusha. Reprinted in 1948 from photographic plates by Oxford University Press as *A Learner's Dictionary of Current English*. See OALD.

LDOCE1: Procter, P. et al. (1978), *Longman Dictionary of Contemporary English*. Harlow: Longman.

LDOCE3: Rundell, M. et al. (1995), *Longman Dictionary of Contemporary English,* 3rd edn. Harlow: Longman.

LDOCE4: Bullon, S. et al. (2003), *Longman Dictionary of Contemporary English,* 'new edition'. Harlow: Longman.

MEDAL: M. Rundell. (2002), *Macmillan English Dictionary for Advanced Learners.* Oxford: Macmillan.

NODE (ODE): Hanks, P., Pearsall, J. et al. (1998), *New Oxford Dictionary of English.* Oxford: Oxford University Press. (2nd edn, 2003 published as *Oxford Dictionary of English.*)

OALD2: Hornby, A. S. et al. (1962), *Oxford Advanced Learner's Dictionary of Current English,* 2nd edn. Oxford: Oxford University Press. (2nd edn of ISED).

OALD3: Hornby, A. S., Cowie, A. et al. (1974), *Oxford Advanced Learner's Dictionary of Current English,* 3rd edn. Oxford: Oxford University Press.

OALD4: Cowie, A. et al. (1974), *Oxford Advanced Learner's Dictionary of Current English,* 4th edn. Oxford: Oxford University Press.

OALD5: Crowther, J. et al. (1995), *Oxford Advanced Learner's Dictionary of Current English,* 5th edn. Oxford: Oxford University Press.

OALD6: Wehmeier, S. et al. (2000), *Oxford Advanced Learner's Dictionary of Current English,* 6th edn. Oxford: Oxford University Press.

Using Corpora in Translation Studies: The State of the Art

Richard Xiao and Ming Yue

Translation Studies (TS) is an area of research that has benefited greatly from and been advanced by corpus methodologies over the past decade. This chapter first clarifies some terminological confusion in using corpora in translation and contrastive studies, which is followed by a review of the state of the art of corpus-based Translation Studies. On the basis of this review we present a case study from a genetically distinct language pair, namely English-Chinese translation, that has been undertaken in order to bring fresh evidence with regards to research on so-called translation universals, which has so far been confined largely to English and closely related European languages.

14.1 Introduction: Paradigmatic Shifts in Translation Studies

Translation Studies (TS) can be defined as a scholarly discipline that is concerned with 'the complex of problems clustered round the phenomenon of translating and translations' (Holmes 1987: 9). According to the Holmes-Toury map (Munday 2001), Translation Studies can be *theoretical, descriptive* or *applied.*

One of the advantages of the corpus-based approach is that it can reveal the 'regularities of actual behaviour' (Toury 1995: 265). The establishment of corpus-based Translation Studies as a new paradigm was preceded by two paradigmatic shifts in theoretical Translation Studies. The first shift is from 'prescriptive' to 'descriptive' accounts of translation. Prescriptive translation studies were dominant before the mid-1950s, including for example, Alexander Tytler's (1747–1814) three principles of translation; Friedrich Schleiermacher's (1768–1834) foreignizing translation; Yan Fu's (1854–1921) *xin* (fidelity) – *da* (fluency) – *ya* (elegance); Nida's (1964: 166) *dynamic equivalence;* and Newmark's (1981) distinction between semantic versus communicative translation. The 1950s saw a paradigmatic shift in Translation Studies from prescriptive to descriptive perspectives, which is represented by Descriptive Translation Studies (DTS, see Section 14.3.2).

The second shift is from the micro (i.e. linguistic) to macro (i.e. socio-cultural) perspective. The period between the mid-1950s and the mid-1980s was what Fawcett (1997: foreword) calls the 'heroic age' of linguistically oriented translation studies, which focused on word, phrase and sentence levels. Since the mid-1980s socio-culturally oriented translation studies have become mainstream, integrating with literary and linguistic theories such as feminism, post-colonialism, and discourse and ideology. In the 1980s, the traditional illusion of an 'ideal' translation gradually gave way to a more realistic view that translating is a communicative act in a socio-cultural context and that translations are an integral part of the receiving culture (cf. Bassnett and Lefevere 1990; Bassnett-McGuire 1991).

It is clear even from this brief review that different approaches have been taken to Translation Studies, from the earlier workshop approach, the philosophical and linguistic approach, the functionalist approach, to DTS, the post-structuralist and post-modernist approaches, and the cultural studies approach. Nevertheless, there has been a gap between translation theory and practice, and practice is lagging far behind theory. On the one hand, the same translation phenomenon can be explained by many different competing theories. On the other hand, the majority of phenomena in translation cannot be explained by existing translation theories.

Under the influence of New Firthian scholars such as Halliday and Sinclair, target-system-oriented translation projects were carried out in Australia and the United Kingdom (Bell 1991; Baker 1992). Meanwhile, the descriptive methodology continued to gain supporters among comparative literature scholars and polysystem theorists (cf. Tymoczko 1998: 652). Toury (1995: 1) argues that 'no empirical science can make a claim for completeness and (relative) autonomy unless it has a proper descriptive branch'. Arguments like this have had a great impact on DTS, which has shifted the focus in translation research from the relationship between source and target texts to translations themselves.

With the rapid development of corpus linguistics in the mid-1980s, corpus linguists started to become interested in translated texts, initially focussing on literary texts such as novels. For example, Gellerstam (1986) studied translated English from Swedish, casting new light on what has been known as 'translationese'. Bell (1991: 39) proposed observing translator performance by analysing the translation product through 'finding features in the data of the product which suggest the existence of particular elements and systematic relations in the process'. His proposal sparked great interest in building and exploring corpora of translated texts, with the aim of analysing features of translational language for evidence of the relationship between translation as a product and translation as a process. Corpora are useful in this respect because they help to reveal 'relations between frequency and typicality, and instance and norm' (Stubbs 2001*a*: 151). According to Baker (1993: 243), '[t]he most important task that awaits the application of corpus techniques in translation studies [. . .] is the elucidation of the nature of translated text as a mediated communicative event'. As we will see in Section 14.3, corpora and corpus linguistic techniques are powerful tools for identifying the characteristic features of translational language (i.e. the so-called 'translation universals'), which provide evidence for the translation process *per se*, or in Baker's (1993: 243) words, to 'understand what translation is and how it works'.

Laviosa (1998*a*: 474) observes that 'the corpus-based approach is evolving, through theoretical elaboration and empirical realisation, into a coherent, composite and rich paradigm that addresses a variety of issues pertaining to theory, description, and the practice of translation'. In our view, three factors have collaboratively contributed to the convergence between corpus research and Translation Studies. They are (1) the hypothesis that translation universals can be tested by corpus data (see Section 14.3), (2) the rapid development of corpus linguistics, especially multilingual corpus research in the early 1990s, and finally (3) the increasing interest in DTS. The marriage between DTS and corpora is only natural, in that corpus linguistics, as a discipline stemming from the description of real linguistic performance, supplies DTS with a systematic method and trustworthy data. Tymoczko (1998: 652) predicated that 'Corpus Translation Studies is central to the way that Translation Studies as a discipline will remain vital and move forward'. This predication has been realized by an ever-growing number of corpus-based Translation Studies, for example, van Leuven-Zwart and Ton Naaijkens (1991), Kenny (2001), Laviosa (2002), Granger et al. (2003), Mauranen and Kujamäki (2004), Hansen et al. (2004), Olohan (2004), Anderman and Rogers (2007) and Kruger and Wallmach (forthcoming), which have led to a better understanding of the scope, significance, usefulness and appropriateness of corpora in studying the processes, products and functions of translation. Corpus-based Translation Studies has increasingly been seen not only as a legitimate part of contrastive language study but also as a crucial way of revealing inherent features of translational language which as a special variant, like any other variants of a natural language, deserves to be investigated in its own right (cf. Mauranen 2002: 165).

On the 'applied' front of Translation Studies are (1) translation teaching, which includes curriculum design, teaching and assessment methods; (2) translation aids, including for example, paper-based and online references and dictionaries, machine translation (MT) systems, computer-aided translation (CAT), translation memories (TM) and terminology banks; (3) translation criticism including translation evaluation and review; and (4) interfaces with other disciplines such as audio-visual translation, software localization and Web translation, and global advertising strategies.

In the remainder of this chapter, we will first discuss the state of the art of theoretical, descriptive and applied corpus-based Translation Studies, highlighting significant works and their contributions to the development of DTS and those investigating translation universals (TU) hypotheses. We will then present a case study that seeks to uncover some features of core lexical use in translated Chinese fiction.

14.2 Corpora Used in Translation Studies

Given that corpus-based Translation Studies is a relatively new paradigm, it is hardly surprising that there is some confusion surrounding the terminology in relation to the diversity of corpora used in Translation Studies. Therefore, before we review the state of the art in corpus-based Translation Studies, it is appropriate to clear up some terminological confusion.

14.2.1 Monolingual Versus Multilingual Corpora

As the names suggest, the distinction between monolingual and multilingual corpora is based on the number of languages covered in a corpus. A monolingual corpus literally involves texts of a single language, and is primarily designed for intralingual studies. For the purpose of Translation Studies, a monolingual corpus usually consists of two subcorpora which are created using comparable sampling techniques, with one composed of non-translated native texts and the other of translated texts in the same language (see Section 14.2.3). This kind of monolingual comparable corpus is particularly useful in the study of intrinsic features of translational language (see Section 14.3.3). With that said, as we will see shortly (Section 14.3.1), even a simple monolingual corpus of either source or target language alone is useful in applied Translation Studies.

A multilingual corpus, in contrast, involves texts of more than one language. As corpora that cover two languages are conventionally known as 'bilingual', multilingual corpora, in a narrow sense, must involve more than two languages, though 'multilingual' and 'bilingual' are often used interchangeably in the literature, and also in this chapter. A multilingual corpus can be a parallel corpus, or a comparable corpus (see below). Both types are useful in Translation Studies, while a multilingual comparable corpus is also particularly useful for cross-linguistic contrasts.

14.2.2 Parallel Versus Comparable Corpora

Terminological confusion around multilingual corpora often centres on these two terms. For some scholars (e.g. Aijmer and Altenberg 1996; Granger 1996: 38), corpora composed of source texts in one language and their translations in another language (or other languages) are 'translation corpora' while those comprising different components sampled from different native languages using comparable sampling techniques are called 'parallel corpora'.

For others (e.g. Baker 1993: 248, 1995, 1999; Barlow 1995, 2000: 110; McEnery and Wilson 1996: 57; Hunston 2002: 15; McEnery et al. 2006), corpora of the first type are labelled 'parallel' while those of the latter type are comparable corpora. As argued in McEnery and Xiao (2007: 19–20), while different criteria can be used to define different types of corpora, they must be used consistently and logically. For example, we can say that a corpus is monolingual, bilingual or multilingual if we take the number of languages involved as the criterion for definition. We can also say that a corpus is a translation or a non-translation corpus if the criterion of corpus content is used. But if we choose to define corpus types by the criterion of corpus form, we must use the terminology consistently. Then we can say that a corpus is parallel if the corpus contains source texts and translations in parallel, or that it is a comparable corpus if its components or subcorpora are comparable by applying the same sampling frame. It is illogical, however, to refer to corpora of the first type as translation corpora by the criterion of content while referring to corpora of the latter type as comparable corpora by the criterion of form.

In addition, a parallel corpus, in our terms, can be either unidirectional (e.g. from English into Chinese or from Chinese into English alone), or bidirectional (e.g. containing both English source texts with their Chinese translations as well as Chinese source texts with their English translations), or multidirectional (e.g. the same piece of text with its Chinese, English, French, Russian and Arabic versions). In this sense, texts that are produced simultaneously in different languages (e.g. UN regulations) also belong to the category of parallel corpora. A parallel corpus must be aligned at a certain level (for instance, at document, paragraph, sentence, or word level) in order to be useful in Translation Studies. The automatic alignment of parallel corpora is not a trivial task for some language pairs, though alignment is generally very reliable for many closely related European language pairs (cf. McEnery et al. 2006: 50–1).

14.2.3 Comparable Versus Comparative Corpora

Another complication in terminology involves a corpus which is composed of different variants of the same language. This is particularly relevant to Translation Studies because it is common practice in this research area to compare a corpus of translated texts – which we call a 'translational corpus' – and a corpus consisting of comparably sampled non-translated texts in the same language. They form a monolingual comparable corpus (cf. Section 14.2.1).

To us, a multilingual comparable corpus samples different native languages, with its comparability lying in the matching or comparable sampling techniques, similar balance (i.e. coverage of genres and domains) and representativeness, and similar sampling period. By our definition, corpora containing different varieties of the same language (e.g. the *International Corpus of English, ICE*) are not comparable corpora because all corpora, as a resource for linguistic research, have 'always been pre-eminently suited for comparative studies' (Aarts 1998: ix), either intralingually or interlingually. The Brown, LOB, Frown and FLOB corpora are also used typically for comparing language varieties synchronically and diachronically. Corpora like these can be labelled as 'comparative corpora'. They are not 'comparable corpora' as suggested in the literature (e.g. Hunston 2002: 15).

Having discussed the main points of terminological confusion in corpus-based Translation Studies, it is worth pointing out that the distinctions discussed here are purely for the sake of clarification. In reality, there are multilingual corpora which are a mixture of parallel and comparable corpora. For example, in spite of its name, the *English-Norwegian Parallel Corpus* (ENPC) can be considered as a combination of a parallel and comparable corpus.

14.2.4 General Versus Specialized Corpora

General and specialized corpora differ in terms of coverage, that is, the range of genres and domains they are supposed to represent. As general corpora such as the *British National Corpus* (BNC) 'typically serve as a basis for an overall description of a language or language variety' (McEnery et al. 2006: 15), they tend to proportionally cover as many genres and domains as practically possible to ensure maximum balance and representativeness. Specialized corpora, on the other hand, tend to be composed of texts from a specific domain (e.g. engineering, or business) or genre (e.g. news text or academic writing). While balanced general corpora are undoubtedly very useful in translation research, as in many other areas, specialized corpora are of exceptional value for Translation Studies. This is because specialized corpora are often rich in terminology; they have practical value to translators of technical text; and they can provide a basis for studying the authorship of original texts, translatorship or any other traces of the many 'pragmatic texts' (cf. Baker 1995: 225–6).

Both monolingual and multilingual corpora, including parallel and comparable corpora, can be of specialized or general corpus type, depending on their purposes. For example, for exploring how general linguistic features such as tense and aspect markers are translated, balanced corpora, which are supposed to be more representative of any given language in general, would be used; for extracting terminologies or neologies, specialized parallel and comparable corpora are clearly of better use. However, since it is relatively easier to find comparable text categories in different languages, it is more likely for multilingual comparable corpora to be designed as general balanced corpora in relation to parallel corpora.

14.3 Corpus-Based Translation Studies

Corpora of different kinds can be used for different purposes in Translation Studies. For example, parallel corpora are useful in exploring how an idea in one language is conveyed in another language, thus providing indirect evidence to the study of translation processes. Corpora of this kind are indispensable for building statistical or example-based machine translation (EBMT) systems, and for the development of bilingual lexicons and translation memories. Also, parallel concordancing is a useful tool for translators.

Comparable corpora are useful in improving the translator's understanding of the subject field and improving the quality of translation in terms of fluency, correct choice of term and idiomatic expressions in the chosen field. They can also be used to build terminology banks.

Translational corpora provide primary evidence in product-oriented Translation Studies (see Section 14.3.2.1), and in studies of translation universals (see Section 14.3.3). If corpora of this kind are encoded with sociolinguistic and cultural parameters, they can also be used to study the socio-cultural environment of translations (see Section 14.3.2.3).

Even monolingual corpora of source language and target language are of great value in Translation Studies because they can raise the translator's linguistic and cultural awareness in general and provide a useful and effective reference tool for translators and trainees. They can also be used in combination with a parallel corpus to form a so-called translation evaluation corpus that helps translator trainers or critics to evaluate translations more effectively and objectively.

This section explores the state of the art of corpus-based Translation Studies on the Holmes-Toury map, that is, applied TS, descriptive TS and theoretical TS.

14.3.1 Applied Translation Studies

On the applied TS front, three major contributions of corpora include corpus-assisted translating, corpus-aided translation teaching and training, and development of translation tools. An increasing number of studies have demonstrated the value of corpora, corpus linguistic techniques and tools in assisting translation production, translator training and translation evaluation. For example, Bernardini (1997) suggests that 'large corpora concordancing' (LCC) can help students to develop 'awareness', 'reflectiveness' and 'resourcefulness', which are said to be the skills that distinguish a translator from those unskilled amateurs. Bowker (1998: 631) observes that 'corpus-assisted translations are of a higher quality with respect to subject field understanding, correct term choice and idiomatic expressions'. Zanettin (1998) shows that corpora help trainee translators become aware of general patterns and preferred ways of expressing things in the target language, get better comprehension of source language texts and improve production skills; Aston (1999) demonstrates how the use of corpora can enable translators to produce more native-like interpretations and strategies in source and target texts respectively; according to Bowker (2001), an evaluation corpus, which is composed of a parallel corpus and comparable corpora of source and target languages, can help translator trainers to evaluate student translations and provide more objective feedback; Bernardini (2002*b*), Hansen and Teich (2002) and Tagnin (2002) show that the use of a multilingual concordancer in conjunction with parallel corpora can help students with 'a range of translation-related tasks, such as identifying more appropriate target language equivalents and collocations, identifying the norms, stylistic preferences and discourse structures associated with different text types, and uncovering important conceptual information' (Bowker and Barlow 2004: 74); Bernardini and Zanettin (2004: 60) suggest that corpora be used in order to 'provide a framework within which textual and linguistic features of translation can be evaluated'. Finally, Vintar (2007) reports efforts to build Slovene corpora for translator training and practice.

Corpora, and especially aligned parallel corpora, are essential for the development of translation technology such as machine translation (MT) systems, and computer-aided translation (CAT) tools. An MT system is designed to translate without or with minimal human intervention. MT systems have become more reliable since the methodological shift in the 1990s from rule-based to text-based algorithms which are enhanced by statistical models trained using corpus data. Parallel corpora can be said to play an essential role in developing example-based and statistical MT systems. Well-known MT systems include examples such as

Systran, Babelfish, World Lingo and Google Translation. MT systems like these are mainly used in translation of domain-specific and controlled language, automated 'gisting' of online contents, translation of corporate communications, and locating text or fragments requiring human translation. CAT tools are designed to assist in human translation. There are three major types of CAT tools. The most important type are translation memory and terminology management tools which can be used to create, manage and access translation memories (TMs) and termbases. They can also suggest translation candidates intelligently in the process of translation. A second type are localization tools, which are able to distinguish program codes or tags from the texts to be translated (e.g. menus, buttons, error messages etc.), or even better, turn program codes or tags into what a program or webpage really looks like. Another type of tool is used in audiovisual translation (e.g. subtitling, dubbing and voice-over). Major products of CAT tools include SDL Trados, Déjà Vu, Transit, and Wordfast for TM and terminology tools, Catalyst for software localization, Trados TagEditor for webpage translation, and WinCap for subtitling. CAT tools have brought translation into the industrial age, but they are useless unless translated units and terminologies have been stored in translation memories and termbases. This is where corpora come into the picture.

14.3.2 Descriptive Translation Studies

Descriptive Translation Studies (DTS) is characterized by its emphasis on the study of translation *per se*. It answers the question of 'why a translator translates in this way' instead of dealing with the problem of 'how to translate' (Holmes 1972/1988). The target-oriented and empirical nature of the corpus methodology is in perfect harmony with DTS. Baker (1993: 243) predicted that the availability of large corpora of both source and translated texts, together with the development of the corpus-based approach, would enable translation scholars to uncover the nature of translation as a mediated communicative event.

Corpus-based DTS has revealed its full vitality over the past decade, which will be reviewed in this section in terms of its three foci: translation as a product, translation as a process and the function of translation (Holmes 1972/1988).

14.3.2.1 Product-oriented DTS
Presently, corpus-based DTS has primarily been concerned with describing translation as a product, by comparing corpora of translated and non-translational native texts in the target language, especially translated and native English. The majority of product-oriented translation studies attempt to uncover evidence to support or reject the so-called translation universal hypotheses (see Section 14.3.3).

As far as the English language is concerned, a large part of product-oriented translation studies have been based on the Translational English Corpus (TEC), which was built by Mona Baker and colleagues at the University of Manchester. The TEC corpus, which was designed specifically for the purposes of studying translated texts, consists of contemporary written texts translated into English from a range of source languages. It is constantly expanded with fresh materials, reaching a total of 20 million words by the year 2001. The corpus comprises full texts from four genres (fiction, biography, newspaper articles and in-flight magazines) translated by native speakers of English. Metalinguistic data such as information about translators, source texts and publishing dates is annotated and stored in the header section of each text. A subcorpus of original English was specifically selected and is being modified from the BNC to match the TEC in terms of both composition and dates of publication.

Presently, the TEC is perhaps the only publicly available corpus of translational English. Most of the pioneering and prominent studies of translational English have been based on this corpus, which have so far focused on syntactic and lexical features of translated and original texts of English. They have provided evidence to support the hypotheses of translational universals, for example, simplification, explicitation, sanitization, and normalization (see Section 14.3.3). For example, Laviosa (1998*b*) studies the distinctive features of translational English in relation to native English (as represented by the BNC), finding that translational language has four core patterns of lexical use: a relatively lower proportion of lexical words over function words, a relatively higher proportion of high-frequency words over low-frequency words, a relatively greater repetition of the most frequent words, and a smaller vocabulary frequently used (see Section 14.4 for further discussion). This is regarded as the most significant work in support of the simplification hypothesis of translation universals (see Section 14.3.3.2). Olohan and Baker's (2000) comparison of concordances from the TEC and the BNC shows that the *that*-connective with reporting verbs *say* and *tell* is far more frequent in translational English, and conversely, that the *zero*-connective is more frequent in native English. These results provide strong evidence for syntactic explicitation in translated English (see Section 14.3.3.1), which, unlike 'the addition of explanatory information used to fill in knowledge gaps between source text and target text readers, is hypothesized to be a subliminal phenomenon inherent in the translation process' (Laviosa 2002: 68). Olohan (2004) investigates intensifiers such as *quite, rather, pretty* and *fairly* in translated versus native English fiction in an attempt to uncover the relation between collocation and moderation, finding that *pretty* and *rather*, and more marginally *quite*, are considerably less frequent in the TEC-fiction subcorpus, but when they are used, there is usually more variation in usage, and less repetition of common collocates, than in the BNC-fiction corpus.

A number of corpus-based studies have explored lexical patterning in translational language. For example, Kanter et al. (2006) identify new universals characterizing the mutual overlaps between native English and translated English on the basis of Zipf's Law (Zipf 1949). Øverås (1998) explores the relationship between collocation and explicitation in English and Norwegian novels, demonstrating how a collocational clash in the source text is translated using a conventional combination in the target language. Kenny (2001) studies the relationship between collocation and sanitization on the basis of an English-German parallel corpus and monolingual corpora of source languages. Baroni and Bernardini (2003) compare the bigrams (i.e. two-word clusters) in a monolingual comparable corpus of native Italian texts and translated articles from a geopolitics journal, concluding that:

> Translated language is repetitive, possibly more repetitive than original language. Yet the two differ in what they tend to repeat: translations show a tendency to repeat structural patterns and strongly topic-dependent sequences, whereas originals show a higher incidence of topic-independent sequences, i.e. the more usual lexicalized collocations in the language. (Baroni and Bernardini 2003: 379)

One interesting area of product-oriented translation research involves corpora composed of multiple translations of the same source text for comparing individual styles of translators. One such corpus is the *Hong Lou Meng* Parallel Corpus,[1] which is composed of the Chinese original and four English translations of the classic Chinese novel *Hong Lou Meng* 'A Dream of Red Chamber'.

14.3.2.2 Process-oriented DTS

Process-oriented DTS aims at revealing the thought processes that take place in the mind of the translator while she or he is translating. While it is difficult to study those processes on-line, one possible way for corpus-based DTS to proceed is to investigate the written transcripts of these recordings off-line, which is known as Think-Aloud Protocols (or TAPs, see Bernardini 2002c). However, the process cannot be totally detached from the product. Stubbs (2001a) draws parallels between corpus linguistics and geology, both assuming a relation between process and product. A geologist is interested in geological processes, which are not directly observable, but individual rocks and geographical formations such as destruction and construction are observable traces of geological processes. As such, as Stubbs (2001a: 154) agues, 'By and large, the processes are invisible, and must be inferred from the products.' The same can be said of translation: Translation as a product can provide indirect evidence of translation as a process. Hence, both types of studies can be approached on the basis of corpus data. Process-oriented studies are typically based on parallel corpora by comparing source and target texts while product-oriented studies are usually based on monolingual comparable corpora by comparing translated target language and native target language. For example, Utka (2004) is a process-oriented study based on the *English-Lithuanian Phases of Translation Corpus*. Quantitative and qualitative comparisons of successive draft versions of translation have allowed him not only to reject Toury's (1995) claim that it is impossible to use a corpus to study the translation process, but also to report cases of normalization, systematic replacement of terminology and influence by the original language.

Chen (2006) presents a corpus-based study of connectives, namely conjunctions and sentential adverbials, in a 'composite corpus' composed of English source texts and their two Chinese versions independently produced in Taiwan and mainland China, plus a comparable component of native Chinese texts as the reference corpus in the genre of popular science writing. This investigation integrates product- and process-oriented approaches in an attempt to verify the hypothesis of explicitation in translated Chinese. In the product-oriented part of his study, Chen compares translational and native Chinese texts to find out whether connectives are significantly more common in the first type of texts in terms of parameters such as frequency and type-token ratio, as well as statistically defined common connectives and the so-called translationally distinctive connectives (TDCs). He also examines whether syntactic patterning in the translated texts is different from native texts via a case study of the five TDCs that are most statistically significant. In the process-oriented part of the study, he compares translated Chinese texts with the English source texts, through a study of the same five TDCs, in an attempt to determine the extent to which connectives in translated Chinese texts are carried over from the English source texts, or in other words, the extent to which connectives are explicitated in translational Chinese. Both parts of his study support the hypothesis of explicitation as a translation universal in the process and product of English-Chinese translation of popular science writing.

14.3.2.3 Function-oriented DTS

Function-oriented DTS encompasses research which describes the function or impact that a translation or a collection of translations may have in the socio-cultural context of the target language, thus leading to the 'study of contexts rather than texts' (Holmes 1972/1988: 72). There are relatively few function-oriented studies that are corpus-based, possibly because the marriage between corpora and this type of research, just like corpus-based discourse analysis (e.g. Baker 2006), is still in the 'honeymoon' period.

One such study is Laviosa (2000), which is concerned with the lexicogrammatical analysis of five semantically related words (i.e. *Europe, European, European Union, Union* and *EU*) in the TEC corpus. These words are frequently used in translated newspaper articles and can be considered as what Stubbs (1996, 2001*b*) calls 'cultural keywords', or words that are important from a socio-cultural point of view, because they embody social values and transmit culture. In this case they reveal the image of Europe as portrayed in data from translated articles in *The Guardian* and *The European*. Given that the TEC is a growing multi-source-language corpus of translational English, Laviosa (2000) suggests that it is possible to carry out comparative analyses between *Europe* and other lemmas of cultural keywords such as *Britain* and *British, France* and *French*, and *Italy* and *Italian*, and so on, which may lead to the direction of corpus-based investigation into the ideological impact of translated texts.

Similarly, Baker (2000) examines, on the basis of the fictional component of the TEC corpus, three aspects of linguistic patterning in the works of two British literary translators, that is, average sentence length, type/token ratio, and indirect speech with the typical reporting verbs such as *say*. The results indicate that the two translators differ in terms of their choices of source texts and intended readership for the translated works. One translator is found to prefer works targeting a highly educated readership with an elaborate narrative which creates a world of intellectually sophisticated characters. In contrast, the other chooses to translate texts for an ordinary readership, which are less elaborate in narrative and concerned with emotions. These findings allow Baker (2000) to draw the conclusion that it is 'also possible to use the description emerging from a study of this type to elaborate the kind of text world that each translator has chosen to recreate in the target language' (cf. Kruger 2002: 96).

Kruger (2000) examines whether the Afrikaans 'stage translation' of *The Merchant of Venice* reveals more spoken language features signaling involvement and interaction between the characters than a 'page translation'. She used an analytical tool that would not only enable her to quantify linguistic features of involvement in four Shakespeare texts (the original and three translations), but also to provide a 'norm' of the occurrence of such features in authentic spoken English. This type of investigation allows her to validate her assumptions that different registers of translated drama have different functions and therefore they present information differently.

Masubelele (2004) examines the changes in orthography, phonology, morphology, syntax, lexis and register of Zulu brought about by translation works. She compares the 1959 and 1986 translations of the *Book of Matthew* into Zulu in a translational corpus in order to research the role played by Bible translation in the growth and development of written Zulu in the context of South Africa. She finds that Toury's (1980) concept of the initial norm (i.e. the socio-cultural constraints) 'seems to have guided the translators of these translations in their selection of the options at their disposal' (Masubelele 2004: 201). The study shows 'an inclination towards the target norms and culture' – while the translators of the 1959 version adopted source text norms and culture, the translators of the 1986 version adopted the norms of the target culture (Masubelele 2004: 201).

14.3.3 Theoretical Translation Studies

Theoretical Translation Studies aims 'to establish general principles by means of which these phenomena can be explained and predicted' (Holmes 1988: 71). It elaborates principles, theories and models to explain and predict what the process of translation is, given certain conditions such as a particular pair of languages or a particular pair of texts. Unsurprisingly it is closely related to, and is often reliant on the empirical findings produced by DTS.

One good battleground of using DTS findings to pursue a general theory of translation is the hypothesis of so-called translation universals (TUs) and its related sub-hypotheses, which are sometimes referred to as the inherent features of translational language, or 'translationese'. It is a well-recognized fact that translations cannot possibly avoid the effect of translationese (cf. Hartmann 1985; Baker 1993: 243–5; Teubert 1996: 247; Gellerstam 1996; Laviosa 1997: 315; McEnery and Wilson 2001: 71–2; McEnery and Xiao 2002, 2007). The concept of TUs is first proposed by Baker (1993), who suggests that all translations are likely to show certain linguistic characteristics simply by virtue of being translations, which are caused in and by the process of translation. The effect of the source language on the translations is strong enough to make the translated language perceptibly different from the target native language. Consequently translational language is at best an unrepresentative special variant of the target language (McEnery and Xiao 2007). The distinctive features of translational language can be identified by comparing translations with comparable native texts, thus throwing new light on the translation process and helping to uncover translation norms, or what Frawley (1984) calls the 'third code' of translation.

Over the past decade, TUs have been an important area of research as well as a target of debate in DTS. Some scholars (e.g. Tymoczko 1998) argue that the very idea of making universal claims about translation is inconceivable, while others (e.g. Toury 2004) advocate that the chief value of general laws of translation lies in their explanatory power; still others (e.g. Chesterman 2004) accept universals as one possible route to high-level generalizations. Chesterman (2004) further differentiates between two types of TUs: one relates to the process from the source to the target text (what he calls 'S-universals'), while the other ('T-universals') compares translations to other target-language texts. Mauranen (2007), in her comprehensive review of TUs, suggests that the discussions of TUs follow the general discussion on 'universals' in language typology.

Recent corpus-based works have proposed a number of TUs, the best known of which include explicitation, simplification, normalization, sanitization and levelling out (or convergence). Other TUs that have been investigated include under-representation, interference and untypical collocations (see Mauranen 2007). While individual studies have sometimes investigated more than one of these features, they are discussed in the following sections separately for the purpose of this presentation.

14.3.3.1 Explicitation

The explicitation hypothesis is formulated by Blum-Kulka (1986) on the basis of evidence from individual sample texts showing that translators tend to make explicit optional cohesive markers in the target text even though they are absent in the source text. It relates to the tendency in translations to 'spell things out rather than leave them implicit' (Baker 1996: 180). Explicitation can be realized syntactically or lexically, for instance, via more frequent use of conjunctions in translated texts than in non-translated texts (see Section 14.4.2.3 for further discussion), and additions providing extra information essential for a target culture reader, and thus resulting in longer text than the non-translated text. Another result of explicitation is increased cohesion in translated text (Øverås 1998). Pym (2005) provides an excellent account of explicitation, locating its origin, discussing its different types, elaborating a model of explicitation within a risk-management framework, and offering a range of explanations of the phenomenon.

In the light of the distinction made above between S- and T-universals (Chesterman 2004), explicitation would seem to fall most naturally into the S-type. Recently, however, explicitation has also been studied as a T-universal. In his corpus-based study of structures involving NP modification (equivalent of the structure noun + prepositional phrase in English) in English and Hungarian, Váradi (2007) suggests that genuine cases of explicitation must be distinguished from constructions that require expansion in order to meet the requirements of grammar. While explicitation is found at various linguistic levels ranging from lexis to syntax and textual organization, 'there is variation even in these results, which could be explained in terms of the level of language studied, or the genre of the texts' (Mauranen 2007: 39). The question of whether explicitation is a translation universal is yet to be conclusively answered, according to existing evidence which has largely come from translational English and related European languages (see Section 14.4 for further discussion).

14.3.3.2 Simplification

Explicitation is related to simplification: 'the tendency to simplify the language used in translation' (Baker 1996: 181–2), which means that translational language is supposed to be simpler than native language, lexically, syntactically and/or stylistically (cf. Blum-Kulka and Levenston 1983; Laviosa-Braithwaite 1997). As noted in Section 14.3.2.1, product-oriented studies such as Laviosa (1998*b*) and Olohan and Baker (2000) have provided evidence for lexical and syntactic simplification in translational English. Translated texts have also been found to be simplified stylistically. For example, Malmkjaer (1997) notes that in translations, punctuation usually becomes stronger; for example commas are often replaced with semicolons or full stops while semicolons are replaced with full stops. As a result, long and complex sentences in the source text tend to be broken up into shorter and less complex clauses in translations, thereby reducing structural complexity for easier reading. Nevertheless, as we will see in Section 14.4.2.1, this observation is likely to be language specific.

The simplification hypothesis, however, is controversial. It has been contested by subsequent studies of collocations (Mauranen 2000), lexical use (Jantunen 2001), and syntax (Jantunen 2004). Just as Laviosa-Braithwaite (1996: 534) cautions, evidence produced in early studies that support the simplification hypothesis is patchy and not always coherent. Such studies are based on different datasets and are carried out to address different research questions, and thus cannot be compared.

14.3.3.3 Normalization

Normalization, which is also called 'conventionalization' in the literature (e.g. Mauranen 2007), refers to the 'tendency to exaggerate features of the target language and to conform to its typical patterns' (Baker 1996: 183). As a result, translational language appears to be 'more normal' than the target language. Typical manifestations of normalization include overuse of clichés or typical grammatical structures of the target language, adapting punctuation to the typical usage of the target language, and the treatment of the different dialects used by certain characters in dialogues in the source texts.

Kenny (1998, 1999, 2000, 2001) presents a series of studies of how unusual and marked compounds and collocations in German literary texts are translated into

English, in an attempt to assess whether they are normalized by means of more conventional use. Her research suggests that certain translators may be more inclined to normalize than others, and that normalization may apply in particular to lexis in the source text. Nevalainen (2005; in Mauranen 2007: 41) suggests that translated texts show greater proportions of recurrent lexical bundles or word clusters.

Like simplification, normalization is also a debatable hypothesis. According to Toury (1995: 208), it is a 'well-documented fact that in translations, linguistic forms and structures often occur which are rarely, or perhaps even never encountered in utterances originally composed in the target language'. Tirkkonen-Condit's (2002: 216) experiment, which asked subjects to distinguish translations from non-translated texts, also shows that 'translations are not readily distinguishable from original writing on account of their linguistic features.'

14.3.3.4 Other translational universals

Kenny (1998) analyses semantic prosody in translated texts in an attempt to find evidence of sanitization (i.e. reduced connotational meaning). She concludes that translated texts are 'somewhat "sanitized" versions of the original' (Kenny 1998: 515). Another translational universal that has been proposed is the so-called feature of 'leveling out', that is, 'the tendency of translated text to gravitate towards the centre of a continuum' (Baker 1996: 184). This is what Laviosa (2002: 72) calls 'convergence', that is, the 'relatively higher level of homogeneity of translated texts with regard to their own scores on given measures of universal features' that are discussed above.

'Under representation', which is also known as the 'unique items hypothesis', is concerned with the unique items in translation (Mauranen 2007: 41–2). For example, Tirkkonen-Condit (2005) compared frequency and uses of the clitic particle *kin* in translated and original Finnish in five genres (fiction, children's fiction, popular fiction, academic prose and popular science), finding that the average frequency of *kin* in original Finnish is 6.1 instances per 1,000 words, whereas its normalized frequency in translated Finnish is 4.6 instances per 1,000 words. Tirkkonen-Condit interprets this phenomenon as a case of under-representation in translated Finnish. Aijmer's (2007) study of the use of the English discourse marker *oh* and its translation in Swedish shows that there is no single lexical equivalent of *oh* in Swedish translation, because direct translation with the standard Swedish equivalent *åh* would result in an unnatural sounding structure in this language.

14.4 Core Lexical Features of Translated Novels in Chinese

As can be seen in the discussion above, while we have followed the literature in using the conventional term 'translation universal', the term is highly debatable in Translation Studies. Since the translational universals that have been proposed so far are identified on the basis of translational English – mostly translated from closely related European languages, there is a possibility that such linguistic features are not 'universal' but rather specific to English and/or genetically related languages that have been investigated. For example, Cheong's (2006) study of English-Korean translation contradicts even the least controversial explicitation hypothesis.

As noted, research on the features of translated texts has so far been confined largely to translational English translated from closely related European languages (e.g. Mauranen and Kujamäki 2004). Clearly, if the features of translational language that have been reported are to be generalized as translation 'universals', the language pairs involved must not be restricted to English and closely related languages. Therefore, evidence from 'genetically' distinct language pairs such as English and Chinese is undoubtedly more convincing.

We noted in Section 14.3.2.2 that the explicitation hypothesis is supported by Chen's (2006) study of connectives in English-Chinese translations of popular science books. Nevertheless, as Biber (1995: 278) observes, language may vary across genres even more markedly than across languages. Xiao (2008) also demonstrates that the genre of scientific writing is the least diversified of all genres across various varieties of English. The implication is that the similarity reported in Chen (2006) might be a result of similar genre instead of language pair. Ideally, what is required to verify the English-based translation universals is a detailed account of the features of translational Chinese based on balanced comparable corpora of native Chinese and translated Chinese. This is what we are aiming at on our project *A corpus-based quantitative study of translational Chinese in English-Chinese translation*, which compares the *Lancaster Corpus of Mandarin Chinese* (LCMC, see McEnery and Xiao 2004) and its translational match in Chinese – the newly built *ZJU Corpus of Translational Chinese* (ZCTC, see Xiao, He and Yue 2008).

In this section, we will present a case study of Laviosa's (1998*b*) core features of lexical use in translational language (see Section 14.3.2.1) on the basis of a parallel analysis of the fiction categories in the LCMC corpus and a corpus of translated Chinese fiction.

14.4.1 The Corpora

The corpus data used in this case study are the five categories of fiction (i.e. general fiction, mystery and detective stories, science fiction, adventure stories and romantic fiction) in the LCMC corpus (LCMC-Fiction hereafter) for native Chinese, amounting to approximately 200,000 running words in 117 text samples taken from novels and stories published in China around 1991.[2] The *Contemporary Chinese Translated Fiction Corpus* (CCTFC hereafter) is composed of over one million words in 56 novels published over the past three decades, with most of them translated and published in the 1980s and 1990s. These novels are mostly translated from English while other source languages are also represented including, for example, Russian, French, Spanish, Czech, German and Japanese.

Table 14.1 Corpus sizes.

Type	CCTFC	LCMC-fiction
Running word tokens	1,096,666	195,437
Unique word types	37,897	20,065

Both corpora are annotated with part-of-speech information using the same tagger and marked up in XML.

Table 14.1 shows the sizes of the two datasets.[3] Please note that the different sizes of our corpora of native and translated fiction will not affect our results significantly because, as we will discuss shortly, WordSmith (version 4.0 in this study) has taken account of this difference when computing type-token ratios. When frequencies are compared, they are either normalized to a common base or converted into proportional data.

14.4.2 Results and Discussions

This section presents and discusses the results of data analysis. We will first discuss the parameters used in Laviosa (1998*b*) in an attempt to find out whether the core patterns of lexical use that Laviosa observes in translational English also apply in translated Chinese fiction. We will also compare the frequency and use of connectives in translated and native Chinese.

14.4.2.1 Lexical density and mean sentence length

There are two common measures of lexical density. Stubbs (1986: 33; 1996: 172) defines lexical density as the ratio between the number of lexical words (i.e. content words) and the total number of words. This approach is taken in Laviosa (1998*b*). As our corpora are part-of-speech (POS) tagged, frequencies of different POS categories are readily available.[4]

The other approach commonly used in corpus linguistics is the type-token ratio (TTR), that is, the ratio between the number of types (i.e. unique words) and the number of tokens (i.e. running words). However, since the TTR is seriously affected by text length, it is reliable only when texts of equal or similar length are compared. To remedy this issue, Scott (2004) proposes a different strategy, namely, using a standardized type-token ratio (STTR), which is computed every *n* (the default setting is 1,000 in WordSmith) words as the Wordlist application of the WordSmith Tools goes through each text file in a corpus. The STTR is the average type-token ratio based on consecutive 1,000-word chunks of text (Scott 2004: 130).[5] It appears that lexical density defined by Stubbs (1986, 1996) measures informational load whereas the STTR is a measure of lexical variability, as reflected by the different ways they are computed.

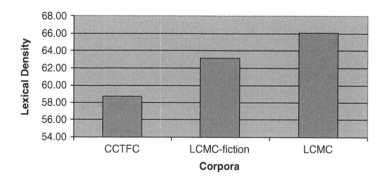

Figure 14.1 Lexical density in translated and native Chinese.

Let us first look at the Stubbs-style lexical density in native and translated Chinese fiction. As can be seen in Fig. 14.1, the lexical density in translated Chinese fiction (58.69 per cent) is considerably lower than that in native Chinese fiction (63.19 per cent). The difference is statistically significant ($t = -4.23$, $p < 0.001$). In relation to translated Chinese, LCMC-fiction's lexical density score is closer to the LCMC corpus as a whole, in spite of the fact that the LCMC covers genres with greater lexical density such as news. It is also of interest to note that while translated Chinese fiction and native Chinese fiction display a significant difference in their mean lexical density, the two groups of texts *per se* are very homogeneous, as indicated by their standard deviation scores, 2.22 for CCTFC and 2.98 for LCMC-fiction, which are not statistically significant ($F = 1.1$, $p = 0.298$ for Levene's test for equality of variances). These findings are in line with Laviosa's (1998*b*) observations of lexical density in translational English.

However, if lexical density is measured by the STTR, the difference between translated (mean = 47.59, standard deviation = 3.42) and native (mean = 48.42, standard deviation = 1.43) Chinese fiction is not statistically significant ($t = 0.531$, $p = 0.598$), though there is less variance in native Chinese fiction, as reflected by its smaller standard deviation score. This means that translated Chinese fiction displays a comparable level of lexical variability to native Chinese fiction.

In terms of lexical versus function words, native Chinese fiction registers a significantly greater ratio of lexical over function words than translated Chinese fiction (1.73 vs 1.43, $t = -2.9$, $p = 0.042$). The texts in the translated Chinese fiction corpus are also significantly more homogeneous than those in the native Chinese fiction corpus (standard deviation scores are 0.13 and 0.23 respectively, a significant difference: $F = 4.29$, $p = 0.043$). This result confirms Laviosa's (1998*b*: 8) initial hypothesis that translational language has a relatively lower proportion of lexical words over function words.

Figure 14.2 shows the mean sentence length in translated and native Chinese fiction. As can be seen, translated Chinese fiction has a mean sentence length of 22 words whereas it is 16 words in native Chinese fiction. This difference is

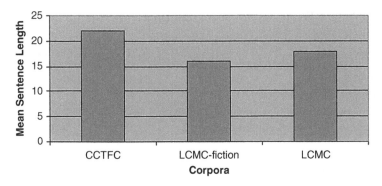

Figure 14.2 Mean sentence length in translated and native Chinese.

statistically significant ($t = 2.37$, $p = 0.021$). Native Chinese fiction is also slightly more homogeneous (standard deviation = 2.05) than translated Chinese fiction (standard deviation = 5.38), though the difference is not significant ($F = 2.19$, $p = 0.144$ for Levene's test for equality of variances). It is also clear in the figure that the mean sentence length in native Chinese fiction is very similar to that in the whole LCMC corpus (16 vs 18). It appears, then, that our data support Laviosa's (1998*b*: 5) observation that translated language has a significantly greater mean sentence length than non-translated language. On the other hand, this finding goes against Malmkjaer's (1997) expectation that stronger punctuation tends to result in shorter sentences in translated text (cf. Section 14.3.3.2). As this case study is based on translated Chinese fiction, our finding is tentative. We will wait to see what our balanced corpus of translated Chinese will tell us.

14.4.2.2 Frequency profiles

Laviosa (1998*b*) defines 'list head' or 'high frequency words' as every item which individually accounts for at least 0.10 per cent of the total tokens in a corpus. In Laviosa's study, 108 items were high frequency words, most of which were function words. In this case study, we also define high frequency words as those with a minimum proportion of 0.10 per cent. But the numbers of items included can vary depending on the corpus being examined. Table 14.2 shows the frequency profiles of translated and native Chinese fiction. As can be seen, while the numbers of high frequency words are very similar in the two corpora (118 and 112 respectively), high frequency words in translated Chinese fiction account for a considerably greater proportion of tokens in the corpus (47.9 per cent in comparison to 41.1 per cent for native Chinese fiction). The ratio of high over low frequency words is also greater in translated Chinese fiction (0.92) than in native Chinese fiction (0.70). Laviosa (1998*b*) hypothesizes on the basis of the results of lemmatization that there is less variety in the words that are most frequently used. As Chinese is a non-inflectional language, lemmatization is irrelevant; and as noted earlier, the

Table 14.2 Frequency profiles of translated and native Chinese fiction.

Type	CCTFC	LCMC-fiction
Number of items	118	116
Cumulative proportion	47.9%	41.1%
Repetition rate of high frequency words	4,447.02	692.09
Ratio of high/low frequency words	0.92	0.70

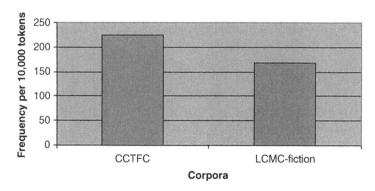

Figure 14.3 Normalized frequencies of connectives in translated and native Chinese fiction.

standardized type-token ratios as a measure of lexical variability are very similar in translated and native Chinese fiction. Nevertheless, it can be seen in Table 14.2 that high frequency words display a much greater repetition rate than comparable native Chinese fiction (4,447.02 and 692.09 respectively).

The above discussion suggests the core lexical features proposed by Laviosa (1998*b*) for translational English are essentially also applicable in translated Chinese fiction.

14.4.2.3 Connectives as a device for explicitation

Chen (2006) finds that in his Chinese corpus of popular science books translated from English, connectives are significantly more common than in a comparable corpus of original Chinese scientific writing; some connectives are also found to be translationally distinctive, that is, significantly more common in translated texts. Chen (2006) concludes that connectives are a device for explicitation in English-Chinese translations of popular science books. In the remainder of this section, we will compare corpora of translated and native Chinese fiction in terms of their frequency and use of connectives in an attempt to find out whether Chen's conclusion also applies in literary translation.

Table 14.3 Frequent connectives in translated Chinese fiction.

Connective	Gloss	Proportion
和	and	0.438
而	but	0.206
但	but	0.147
但是	but	0.087
如果	if	0.072
可是	but	0.068
而且	and	0.067
并	and	0.057
不过	but	0.054
然后	then	0.051

Figure 14.3 shows the normalized frequencies of connectives in translated and native Chinese fiction. As the two corpora are of different sizes, the raw frequencies of connectives are normalized to a common base of 10,000 tokens for easier comparison. As can be seen, connectives are by far more frequent in translated fiction (224.4 and 167.5 instances per 10,000 tokens respectively). The difference in frequencies is highly significant (log likelihood score 312.54 for 1 d.f., $p < 0.00001$).

Appendix A lists all frequently used connectives that account for at least 0.001 per cent of total words in the two corpora. It is clear that a substantially greater variety of frequent connectives are used in translated Chinese fiction. A total of 112 frequent items are found in translated fiction whereas only 64 are found in the original fiction. Of these, 63 items overlap in the two lists. One item on the list for original fiction (跟着 'then', the last item in the Appendix table) does not appear in the list for translated fiction, whereas 49 items listed for translated fiction do not appear in the original fiction list. The connectives listed for translated fiction also account for substantially greater proportions of the whole corpus. There is only one connective that takes up more than 0.05 per cent of the corpus of original fiction (i.e. 和 'and', 0.058 per cent). In contrast, there are ten connectives that account for more than 0.05 per cent of the corpus of translated fiction (see Table 14.3). While 和 ('and') is the most frequent item in both corpora, it is over seven times as frequent in translated fiction as in original fiction (0.432 per cent vs 0.058 per cent for translated and native fiction respectively). This result appears to suggest Chen's (2006) observations of explicitation via connectives in English-Chinese translations of popular science books also hold in literary translation, though a more conclusive investigation can only be based on balanced corpora.

14.5 Conclusions

The present chapter has explored how corpora have helped to advance Translation Studies as a scholarly discipline. On the basis of a clarification of the terminology in using corpora in translation and contrastive research, we reviewed the state of the art of corpus-based Translation Studies. A case study was also presented that was undertaken to bring fresh evidence from a genetically distinct language pair, namely English-Chinese translation, into the research of the so-called translation universals, which has so far been confined largely to English and closely related European languages. It is our hope that more empirical evidence for or against translational universals will be produced from our balanced monolingual comparable corpora of translated and native Chinese when our project is completed.

Acknowledgements

We are grateful to the China National Foundation of Social Sciences for supporting our project *A corpus-based quantitative study of translational Chinese in English-Chinese translation* (Grant Reference 07BYY011).

Notes

1 The corpus is searchable at http://score.crpp.nie.edu.sg/hlm/index.htm.
2 More details about the LCMC corpus and its availability can be found at http://www.lancs.ac.uk/fass/projects/corpus/LCMC/.
3 The statistics reported by WordSmith include actual words in the corpora excluding punctuations and symbols. All numeral tokens are collapsed and represented by the symbol # in the wordlist.
4 In this study, we follow Xiao et al. (2008) in treating adjectives (including non-predicate and descriptive adjectives), adverbs, idioms and formulaic expressions, nouns and verbs as lexical words. Function words include the following POS categories: auxiliaries, classifiers, conjunctions, directional locality words, interjections, morphemes, numerals and quantifiers, onomatopoeias, particles, prefixes, pronouns, prepositions, space words, suffixes, and time words. Unclassified words and symbols and punctuations are excluded in computing ratios of high and low frequency words.
5 If a text chunk is shorter than the set n (e.g. 1,000) words, the standardized type-token ratio of the text chunk is taken as 0.

Appendix A

Commonly used connectives in translated and native Chinese fiction.

No	Conn.	Gloss	% CCTFC	% LCMC-fiction
1	和	and	0.438	0.058
2	而	but	0.206	0.028
3	但	but	0.147	0.025
4	但是	but	0.087	0.006
5	如果	if	0.072	0.007
6	可是	but	0.068	0.011
7	而且	and	0.067	0.005
8	并	and	0.057	0.010
9	不过	but	0.054	0.006
10	然后	then	0.051	0.008
11	所以	so	0.047	0.006
12	因为	because	0.047	0.003
13	于是	then	0.046	0.007
14	或	or	0.040	0.004
15	接着	then	0.037	0.003
16	那么	(if . . .) then	0.037	0.002
17	或者	or	0.034	0.003
18	虽然	although	0.034	0.005
19	因此	so	0.032	0.003
20	然而	however	0.027	0.004
21	并且	and	0.025	0.002
22	只有	only if	0.023	0.005
23	尽管	although	0.022	0.002
24	只要	if	0.021	0.004
25	既	and	0.019	0.003
26	以及	and	0.019	0.002
27	而是	but	0.016	0.003
28	还是	or	0.016	0.006
29	即使	even if	0.016	0.002
30	同时	meanwhile	0.015	0.002
31	不管	regardless	0.013	0.002
32	既然	now that	0.013	0.002
33	要是	if	0.011	0.001
34	由于	because	0.011	0.001
35	就	then	0.010	0.001
36	又	and	0.010	0.002
37	也	even (if)	0.009	0.001
38	与	and	0.009	0.005
39	不仅	not only	0.008	0.001
40	无论	no matter how	0.008	0.001

(*Continued*)

No	Conn.	Gloss	% CCTFC	% LCMC-fiction
41	或是	or	0.007	
42	倘若	if	0.007	0.001
43	此外	besides	0.006	
44	假如	if	0.006	0.001
45	另外	besides	0.006	0.001
46	甚至	even	0.006	0.001
47	虽	although	0.006	0.003
48	除非	unless	0.005	0.001
49	否则	otherwise	0.005	0.002
50	及	and	0.005	0.001
51	哪怕	even if	0.005	
52	虽说	although	0.005	0.001
53	要么	or	0.005	
54	总之	in a word	0.005	0.001
55	不但	not only	0.004	0.001
56	不论	no matter how	0.004	0.001
57	不然	otherwise	0.004	
58	还	even, still	0.004	0.001
59	不是	either (or)	0.003	
60	才	not until	0.003	0.001
61	何况	let alone	0.003	0.001
62	即便	even if	0.003	
63	且	and	0.003	
64	若	if	0.003	0.001
65	因而	therefore	0.003	
66	只是	except that	0.003	0.002
67	不论是	no matter how	0.002	
68	从而	thus	0.002	
69	固然	admittedly	0.002	
70	假若	if	0.002	
71	可	but	0.002	
72	况且	moreover	0.002	
73	另一方面	on the other hand	0.002	
74	那末	then	0.002	0.002
75	却	but	0.002	0.001
76	无论是	now matter how	0.002	
77	一方面	on the one hand	0.002	0.001
78	以至	so that	0.002	
79	以致	so that	0.002	

80	与其	rather than	0.002	
81	则	then	0.002	
82	之所以	the reason for	0.002	
83	非但	not only	0.001	
84	果然	if really	0.001	0.001
85	换句话说	in other words	0.001	
86	及其	and	0.001	
87	继而	then	0.001	
88	假使	if	0.001	
89	紧接着	shortly after	0.001	
90	就是	even if	0.001	
91	就是说	that is to say	0.001	
92	可见	hence	0.001	0.001
93	其次	(first…)then	0.001	
94	恰恰相反	on the contrary	0.001	
95	然	but	0.001	
96	如	if	0.001	
97	若是	if	0.001	0.001
98	是因为	because	0.001	
99	首先	first	0.001	
100	虽则	although	0.001	
101	同	and	0.001	
102	要不	or	0.001	
103	要不然	or	0.001	
104	一旦	once	0.001	
105	一来	on the one hand	0.001	
106	以	so that	0.001	
107	以免	lest	0.001	
108	以至于	so that	0.001	
109	因	because	0.001	
110	与此同时	meanwhile	0.001	
111	总而言之	in a word	0.001	
112	纵然	even if	0.001	
113	跟着	then		0.001

CHAPTER

15

Corpus Linguistics and the Languages of South Asia: Some Current Research Directions

Andrew Hardie

The application of corpus-based methods to the languages of South Asia (India, Pakistan, Bangladesh, Sri Lanka and Nepal) is in its infancy, in comparison to the state of the field in other areas of the world. This is in part due to the technical difficulties surrounding computational manipulation of the very wide variety of non-Roman writing systems in use in South Asia. However, the advent, and increasing use, of Unicode has negated these difficulties to a large extent.

As a survey of work to date in the field demonstrates, corpus-based work on South Asian languages has so far primarily been focussed on corpus construction, and on the demands of computational linguistics, with some few exceptions. However, the exploitation of corpora to address linguistic questions, exemplified here by a corpus-based analysis of vocabulary differentiation in Hindi and Urdu, is increasingly common.

It has often been reported that, while Hindi and Urdu are mostly identical in terms of their phonology and their grammar, they differ strongly in terms of their lexis (cf. Bhatia and Koul 2000; Masica 1991). In this short exploratory study, the differentiation between Hindi and Urdu is characterized quantitatively, by means of an analysis based on frequency lists from a diverse set of five corpora created by the EMILLE project (Baker et al. 2004): Hindi news text, general Hindi written discourse, general Urdu written discourse, Hindi-Urdu speech transcribed as Hindi, and Hindi-Urdu speech transcribed as Urdu. The relative prominence of vocabulary items identifiable as Hindi or Urdu is traced across the different text types under study.

Methodological issues in the comparison of corpus texts written in the same language (phonologically and grammatically speaking) but two different alphabets are also addressed.

15.1 Introduction

This chapter addresses the application of corpus linguistics methodologies to the languages of South Asia (i.e. languages of the Indo-Aryan and Dravidian families). In Section 15.2, the current state of the field of South Asian corpus linguistics will be described, and a range of recent work summarized, in a number of related areas: corpus construction, corpus annotation, computational linguistics and the application of corpora to linguistic analysis. Because of technical problems associated with the creation of corpora using South Asian writing systems, the amount of corpus-based work on these languages has been to date relatively small, especially compared with the very great amount of non-corpus-based linguistic scholarship that these languages have inspired. But as will be argued below, it must be anticipated that the amount of corpus-based work focusing on South Asian languages will increase. For this reason, in Section 15.3, a relatively brief linguistic investigation is undertaken, examining two closely-related Indo-Aryan languages (or *dialects*, or *varieties* – see Section 15.3.1), namely Hindi and Urdu. The aim of this fairly basic analysis is to demonstrate and exemplify the potential of corpus-based methods to address new questions – and old questions in new ways – in the rapidly developing field of South Asian linguistics.

15.2 The State of the Art – Corpus Linguistics and South Asian Languages

At the time of writing, the field of corpus linguistics for South Asian languages may be said (speaking very generally) to be about ten to fifteen years behind English-language corpus linguistics. One explanation for this state of affairs relates to technical problems, associated especially with the alphabets used to write South Asian languages, that have inhibited the creation and use of corpora in these languages. However, as the first part of this section will explain, these problems have now largely been overcome. We may anticipate, then, that the field of South Asian corpus linguistics will now rapidly expand. Therefore, the remainder of this section very briefly surveys some current and recent work in a number of different areas of this field. The general picture that emerges is that while corpus construction and corpus annotation, and to a lesser degree corpus-based lexicography, are becoming well-established practices in South Asian corpus linguistics, other forms of corpus-based analysis are in their very earliest phases.

15.2.1 Corpus Construction

There have, until recently, been relatively few corpora of South Asian languages, and relatively little activity involving those corpora that do exist. As noted above, it is arguable that this has largely been due to the technical problems of storing and rendering text in the writing systems of South Asia. Unlike other major world regions where a non-Latin writing system is used (such as China, Japan, the Arabic-speaking world or Eastern Europe), South Asia does not use a single writing system but a wide array of scripts, some specific to one language, others (e.g. Devanagari, Indo-Perso-Arabic[1]) used by multiple languages. This diversity of *scripts* is clearly a consequence of the diversity of *languages* in South Asia (Nakanishi 1980: 48–56 provides an overview of scripts while Masica 1991 and Steever 1997 give a linguistic overview; for a demographic profile of the multilingual situation in the largest South Asian nation, India, see Mallikarjun 2004).

The high diversity of writing systems, and the consequent longstanding lack of effective standardization for computational handling of these scripts, was a major factor inhibiting the growth of corpus linguistics for South Asian languages. One piece of evidence for the central role of the script encoding and rendering problems in delaying the growth of South Asian corpus linguistics is the fact that the first corpus of Indian *English*, the Kolhapur Corpus (Shastri et al. 1986), was successfully constructed and distributed years before corpora of Indo-Aryan and Dravidian languages became available. Clearly, then, the obstacles to the establishment of corpus linguistics in South Asia are more likely to have been technical – the abovementioned encoding issues – than of any other kind. This section will briefly overview the encoding issues that previously hampered corpus construction, before describing corpora that *have* been constructed.

15.2.1.1 Technical issues for South Asian language corpora

A quintessential feature of modern corpora is that they must consist of machine-readable text (McEnery and Wilson 1996: 17; Biber et al. 1998: 4). Text is stored in computer memory as a sequence of numbers. The *encoding* of a machine-readable text is the set of correspondences between the characters (or *graphemes*) in a writing system and the numbers that represent them. The *rendering* of a machine-readable text is the set of procedures whereby a particular character in memory is made visible on screen or in print by the computer in the shape of some glyph. A single character may be realized by a range of glyphs – for example, the character <b>[2] may be realized as b or b or **b** or b – depending on the font being used, but the underlying number stored in memory is the same in each case. For the Latin alphabet, character encoding has long been standardized, in the form of the ASCII[3] character set, in which, for instance, the character <b> is encoded as 0x62 and the character <B> is encoded as 0x42.[4] Likewise, rendering for the Latin alphabet is straightforward: a single glyph for each character must be retrieved from memory and rendered in the appropriate position.

For the scripts used to write Indo-Aryan (e.g. Nepali, Punjabi, Hindi, Bengali) and Dravidian (e.g. Tamil, Kannada, Telugu) languages, rendering is much more difficult, since characters frequently merge with adjacent characters or have contextually conditioned variations in shape or positioning. Therefore, to render text in one of these alphabets, the computer cannot simply display a single given glyph for each conceptually distinct character. Rather, the relationship between characters or 'letters of the alphabet' and glyphs is highly complex, with one-to-one, one-to-many, many-to-one, and many-to-many mappings observable in one or more scripts of South Asia, as exemplified below for Devanagari (for an overview of the complexities see Hardie 2007*a*):

न स	Devanagari consonants <na> (left) and <sa> (right)
न्स	Devanagari consonant cluster <nsa>
र क	Devanagari consonants <ra> (left) and <ka> (right)
र्क	Devanagari consonant cluster <rka>
क्र	Devanagari consonant cluster <kra>

क ष	Devanagari consonants <ka> (left) and <sha> (right)
क्ष	Devanagari consonant cluster <ksha> (a unique form, often perceived as a separate letter)
क ि	Devanagari consonant <ka> and vowel diacritic <i>
कि	Devanagari consonant-plus-vowel combination <ki> (note that the diacritic *precedes* the consonant graphically, even though it *follows* the consonant orthographically)

The ISCII[5] standard sought to create a standard for character encoding for all those writing systems in use in India that descend from the Brahmi script. Thus ISCII covers, among others, the Devanagari, Gujarati, Bengali, Tamil and Malayalam scripts. This is accomplished by the establishment of a character set containing (1) the basic Latin letters, digits, punctuation and so on, as in ASCII, together with (2) a generalized collection of characters, each one of which relates to one 'letter of the alphabet' across the family of scripts. So, for instance, the code point for the letter <ka> could refer to the letter <ka> in Devanagari, or in Bengali, or in Gujarati and so on. The ISCII character encoding itself does not contain any information as to which writing system is being encoded at any particular point; this must be indicated separately. This is the standard's first disadvantage. While the same generalized set of code points in the ISCII character set can thus serve for all the different Brahmi-derived writing systems, the issue of visualizing the characters in context (according to complex rules that differ considerably from script to script) is left to the display software, so without a very powerful rendering engine (and, in some cases, a specialized hardware extension) the electronic text cannot be made legible on screen for a human being.

While ISCII was an important advance, and had the advantage of encoding both a South Asian script and the Latin alphabet within a single eight-bit[6] character set, its two disadvantages – the ambiguity of ISCII-encoded documents, and the need for powerful rendering software – mitigated against its use in environments such as the World Wide Web. Most web browsers could not (and cannot) render ISCII at all. Therefore, during the explosive growth of the Web in the mid-to-late 1990s, South Asian languages were encoded on the web and in other contexts (e.g. word processing software) using a hugely diverse range of incompatible, bespoke encodings. A typical news organization publishing in Hindi, for instance, would use a single eight-bit font for all text on its website.[7] That font would represent a collection of around 200 glyphs and glyph fragments. The visual forms of each Hindi word would be assembled by juxtaposing the appropriate glyphs and glyph fragments together. Thus, no complex rendering would be required. However, the cost was that the link between the character encoding and the underlying conceptual sequence of the orthography was broken. For instance, the character <ka> might be encoded by one of three, four or even more code points depending on the context in which it appeared. Similarly, the character <i>, which in the ISCII system is rendered *before* the consonant *after* which it occurs, must in one of these font-based encoding systems actually be encoded in the position in the character stream where it is rendered, that is, before the consonant.

These font-based encodings, created without reference to any standard, were incompatible not only with ISCII but also, nearly always, with one another. Hindi text from one website, displayed in the font from another website, would usually produce gibberish. Thus, while a mature *de jure* standard (ISCII) existed, the *de facto* situation was completely unstandardized. Furthermore, in the absence of a widely used standard, many publishers did not move away from hot-metal printing at a time when publishing in languages with well-standardized character encodings was becoming fully electronic. This situation was a major impediment to corpus construction. All very large corpora depend on pre-existing electronic text. It is simply infeasible for tens or hundreds of millions of words of data to be typed afresh in a corpus construction project. While some substantial South Asian language corpora (discussed below) were indeed created in ISCII encoding by re-typing printed text, the limitations on the size of these corpora meant that many key applications (such as corpus-based lexicography) were out of reach. Much electronic text was available via the web, but it was of no use because of the wide range of incompatible encodings.

The solution to this situation came in the form of the Unicode Standard,[8] which established a character encoding covering all the writing systems currently in use in the world. Unicode's encoding of the Brahmi-descended South Asian scripts was based on that of ISCII. However, because Unicode is not limited to the 256 code points of the eight-bit character space,[9] it was possible for each and every script to be given its own uniquely identifying set of code points, removing the ambiguity of ISCII documents. More importantly, while Unicode like ISCII requires a powerful rendering engine to manage the contextual variations in character shapes for South Asian alphabets, the fact that Unicode is a *general* standard, that has been generally implemented, means that sufficiently powerful rendering software is very widely available within a large range of non-purpose-specific tools. Unicode is supported by operating systems such as Microsoft Windows and Linux; it is an integral part of modern Web and text-markup standards such as XML; and it is built into newer programming languages such as Java. So someone creating a text in Hindi today and publishing it on the web can use Unicode and be very confident that their reader, even if equipped with no more than a basic web-browser, will be able to see the text rendered appropriately.

Simultaneously, and in consequence, Unicode has become the text encoding of choice for corpus construction projects (as McEnery and Xiao 2005 argue persuasively). Very many of the most widely used corpus and text analysis tools now support Unicode.[10] The widespread adoption and implementation of Unicode has had a very positive effect on corpus building for South Asian languages in particular. Text in these languages is becoming available that has been created in Unicode as its original form.[11] Moreover, now that a single encoding has emerged as a stable standard, the task of creating mappings between the various non-standard South Asian script encodings and Unicode becomes worthwhile (see Hardie 2007a for a description of a methodology for converting the type of eight-bit font encodings described above to Unicode).

15.2.1.2 Contemporary South Asian language corpora

While Unicode has largely solved the problems of encoding that inhibited the development of South Asian language corpora, there are still relatively few corpora in these languages, and fewer still that are widely available. However, many corpus-creation projects are now in progress.

The first large corpora to be developed for South Asian languages were created by a consortium of institutions in India in the TDIL initiative.[12] This data is now maintained and distributed by the Central Institute of Indian Languages (CIIL) and is generally referred to as the CIIL Corpus/Corpora.[13] These corpora were created as ISCII text, as noted above, sampled from a very wide range of written text genres. The cross-linguistic coverage is very wide: fourteen separate major languages of India are covered by the CIIL Corpora (Assamese, Bengali, Gujarati, Hindi, Kannada, Kashmiri, Maithili, Malayalam, Marathi, Oriya, Punjabi, Tamil, Telugu and Urdu). Each language's corpus contains between 2 and 4 million words. This does not however represent an absolute end point for these data collections. Work is in hand to expand the size of the original corpora by an order of magnitude, develop corpora for more languages (including minority languages) and collect new types of corpus data such as spoken data, child language data and historical data. A dedicated body has been set up to distribute the resulting corpora, the *Linguistic Data Consortium for Indian Languages* (LDC-IL),[14] hosted by the CIIL.

An initiative which, by contrast, focused on one single language was the work on Bengali corpus building undertaken at the Indian Statistical Institute, Kolkata (see Dash and Chaudhuri 2000; Dash 2000). The outcome of this work initiative is a written corpus, composed of texts from a variety of genres, which has been used by Dash (2000) as the basis for a quantitative study of pronouns – in particular, their patterns of inflection – in Bengali; and by Dash (2004) to develop a quantitative profile of the incidence of different letters in Bengali text, and their combinatorial properties.

Beyond India, a major initiative was the EMILLE Project,[15] undertaken by the universities of Lancaster and Sheffield (see Baker et al. 2004; Hardie et al. 2006). In collaboration with the CIIL, the EMILLE project created Unicode versions of the ISCII-encoded CIIL corpora. Larger amounts of data (but drawn from a much smaller range of sources and genres) were collected from the web. The data were not drawn solely from sources in India, Pakistan and Bangladesh – many text producers in the South Asian diaspora worldwide, including the United Kingdom, America and Canada contributed data. Data in Sinhala was gathered as well, to create the first ever corpus in that language (some 7 million words). A UK-based parallel corpus, consisting of English-language government leaflets and their translations into Hindi, Urdu, Gujarati, Punjabi and Bengali – all languages of significant minorities within the UK – was also collected. Most notably, 500,000 words of spoken data were collected for each of the same five languages, being sampled from the language of British South Asian communities rather than from South Asia itself. The EMILLE Corpora, including the Unicode version of the CIIL

Corpora, are available through ELDA.[16] Work was also undertaken within EMILLE to create a version of the text processing architecture, GATE,[17] with support for Unicode – which was therefore capable of processing the data collected (see Cunningham et al. 2002).

A more recent international project, *Nelralec*,[18] has turned to the development of resources for the Nepali language. The resulting *Nepali National Corpus* (Yadava et al. 2008) is constructed according to an innovative 'core and penumbra' model: that is, it combines a small, carefully designed core selection of texts with a larger penumbra collected without any strict sampling criteria. The two parts thus combine the advantages of size and representativeness. To facilitate foreseen cross-linguistic comparison using the corpus, the 'Core Sample' part has been designed as a match for the FLOB and Frown corpora (Hundt et al. 1998, 1999). Like them, it is a million words in extent. Much of it was re-keyboarded for the corpus. The penumbra, by contrast, was opportunistically collected from sources of text already in electronic format, without especial regard for balance and representativeness. While this 'General Collection' data is much less tidy in terms of its construction than the Core Sample, it has the advantage of size: it contains 13 million words of text. A quarter of a million words of spoken text, and four million words of data parallel with English, have also been collected.

The Centre for Research in Urdu Language Processing (CRULP) in Pakistan has also engaged in corpus-building activities, described by Hussain (2008) and Ijaz and Hussain (2007). This has led to the creation of an 18 million word corpus of Urdu news text, drawn principally from the Jang news website.[19] Within this dataset, the corpus is divided roughly evenly across a number of 'domains' such as sport, finance, and so on, although the news domain is represented more heavily than the other domains. For copyright reasons this corpus has not yet been publicly distributed.

New projects are established at a very substantial pace, and it is almost inevitable that some significant corpus-creation initiatives have been omitted from this, necessarily abbreviated account. Many very recent initiatives address yet further new languages from South Asia's vast linguistic diversity. For instance, despite the central position of Sanskrit in the history of the Indo-Aryan languages, no major corpus-building projected has to date included this classical language within its purview. Recently, however, steps have been taken towards making substantial amounts of Sanskrit literature, originally assembled for the purpose of new print editions in the 'Clay Sanskrit library', available as a searchable corpus.[20]

15.2.2 Corpus Annotation

Many of the corpus construction projects mentioned above have worked on, or are working on, part-of-speech (POS) tagging as a complement to the corpus text. This may be because POS tagging enhances the 'searchability' of a corpus, by grouping words into (hopefully) natural categories and by disambiguating (some) homonyms, as well as providing a basis for many further analyses such as parsing and (some types of) semantic tagging. So, for instance, tagging of Urdu (Hardie

2004, 2005) and Nepali (Yadava et al. 2008, Hardie et al. forthcoming) was under-taken in the context of the construction of the EMILLE corpora and the Nepali National Corpus, respectively.

Other than this, most work on annotation has been focused on POS tagging and parsing in particular. In many cases, the goal of the tagging is to support the requirements of computational linguistic techniques rather than linguistic analysis *per se*; a good example of this is the Urdu POS tagger developed by Sajjad (2007). For Hindi in particular, there has been much work done that addresses POS tagging and parsing simultaneously. For example, Bharati and Mannem (2007) describe a set of systems developed for the POS tagging and shallow parsing (syntactic chunk annotation) of Hindi, Bengali and Telugu. One notable feature of this work on grammatical annotation is the very high degree of variation in the size, form and structure of the tagsets used (compare, e.g. the POS tagsets pro-posed for Urdu and/or Hindi by Hardie 2003; Bharati 2006; and Sajjad 2007). This is, of course, true of some non-South Asian languages as well, but perhaps not to such a great extent, relative to the length of time that work on tagging has been under way. It remains to be seen whether future advances will bring stand-ardization or further increases in diversity of annotation schemes.

Moving away from strictly grammatical annotation, other common forms of textual annotation that have been applied to several languages include semantic tagging, tagging pragmatics features and the annotation of various discourse relationships. The annotation of discourse anaphora has been applied by Sinha (2007), in a study discussed further in Section 15.2.4. But semantic tagging (see for instance Wilson and Thomas 1997; Löfberg et al. 2003 on Finnish; Rayson et al. 2004*a* on English) has not as of yet been applied to the existing South Asian lan-guage corpora (though a comparable development has been the creation of Word-Net computational semantic resources for these languages: see Section 15.2.3). Nor has there yet been any application of pragmatic or stylistic tagging. It is to be anticipated that as POS tagging and parsing become better-established for these languages, more attention will be directed to these and other types of corpus annotation. Given the deep and rich range of South Asian literature which is now (or is becoming) available in electronic format, such as the Sanskrit literature mentioned above, the prospects for stylistic analysis in particular are extremely exciting.

15.2.3 Developments in South Asian Language Computational Linguistics

Computational linguistics[21] and corpus linguistics are distinct fields which overlap in some areas (e.g. the implementation and exploitation of automated corpus annotation). Therefore, although computational linguistics is not the central con-cern of the present survey, some relevant work in this field will be discussed here.

The majority of work within computational linguistics for South Asian languages has addressed one of three concerns. The first is the implementation of certain types of automatic corpus annotation, especially POS tagging and parsing; this has already been discussed above. The second is related forms of computational analysis that are not so directly linked to the task of corpus annotation. For instance, techniques have been developed for the automatic morphological analysis of words in Bengali (Dasgupta and Ng 2006) and Hindi-Urdu (Bögel et al. 2007). A detailed computational analysis of Urdu, based in the theory of Lexical Functional Grammar, has been developed by Butt and King (2002, 2007). Likewise, in the field of semantics rather than grammar, a Hindi WordNet[22] has been created (Narayan et al. 2002; Bhattacharyya et al. 2006) and work-in-progress on WordNets in other South Asian languages has been reported. There has also been work in the field of machine translation (see Rao 2001 for an overview).

The third major concern of computational linguistics in the languages of South Asia has been software localization, which is the process of modifying internally used software to create new versions whose interface is in some national or regional language (as opposed to an international *lingua franca* such as English), thus making the software in question accessible for speakers of more languages. Many of the challenges in this field are the same as those involved in corpus construction and utilization (e.g. issues associated with script encoding and rendering: see for instance Hussain 2004). Software localization is an important adjunct to corpus linguistics in these languages; for example, the corpus construction and corpus-based lexicography undertaken within the *Nelralec* project (see Section 15.2.1.2) was supported by a concurrent effort to produce localized versions of Linux and other not specifically linguistic software, without which the exploitation of the Nepali National Corpus would have been much less effective. However, an extensive discussion of this field is beyond the scope of this survey; the interested reader is referred to Singh (2004), Sasikumar and Hegde (2004), and Hall (2004) for overviews of the relevant issues. One single illustrative example may be cited of the kinds of practical issues which arise in this area of computational linguistics: Naseem and Hussain's (2007) exploration of spellchecking for Urdu.

15.2.4 South Asian Language Corpora in Linguistic Analysis

Compared to work in corpus construction, corpus annotation and computational linguistics, there has been relatively little specifically linguistic research into South Asian languages using corpus-based methodologies. However, some such studies have been undertaken on a range of languages including Hindi, Bengali and Nepali.

In Sinha's (2007) study of the discourse-anaphoric properties of Hindi demonstratives, a scheme for tagging demonstrative anaphor based on that used by Botley (2000) for English is developed. The features of the anaphora that are tagged include the recoverability and syntactic category of the antecedent, the syntactic function of the demonstrative and the direction of reference. Based on a manual application of this annotation scheme to 100,000 words of Hindi news text, a quantitative analysis of the frequency of different features and combinations of features is undertaken, in which in particular a high frequency of proximal demonstratives with clausal antecedents is observed (while distal demonstratives prefer nominal antecedents).

An approach to grammatical categories based on collocation has been applied to postpositions in Nepali (Hardie 2007*b*, 2008). The data used was a subset of the Nepali National Corpus. An analysis of the collocates of the most frequent postpositions, including especially those marking accusative-dative, ergative-instrumental and genitive cases, demonstrates two recurring patterns – one of collocates that are *semantically coherent* with the postposition, and one where the postposition functions as a *subcategorizer* for the collocate – which vary in prominence across the different postpositions. In a cross-linguistic comparison with English (Hardie 2007*b*), a generally similar pair of patterns was observable in both languages. In a similar way to Dash's (2004) corpus-based analysis of Bengali pronouns, mentioned above, this research is based on using quantitative data to extend and elaborate on what is already known about an oft-studied feature of the grammar of Nepali.

There has also been substantial work exploiting corpora in the field of lexicography. A very large corpus has long been an indispensible tool for lexicographers of English. With the advent of more and larger South Asian language corpora, corpus-based techniques are swiftly becoming equally critical for the creation of dictionaries in these languages. The recently released *Samakalin Nepali Sabdakos* ("Contemporary Nepali Dictionary"),[23] based on the Nepali National Corpus, exemplifies this trend. Similar corpus-based lexicography is currently being undertaken for Hindi and other languages. For Urdu, there has also been work on corpus-based lexicon development, in the form of the 50,000-type lexicon described by Ijaz and Hussain (2007) – although this research had the end goal of a lexicon for use in computational applications such as text-to-speech synthesis and speech recognition rather than a dictionary for human use. For this latter enterprise, one problem is that even the largest widely available South Asian language corpora, such as the 14 million word Nepali National Corpus, or the 20 million word EMILLE-CIIL written Tamil corpus, are still not large enough for fully corpus-based lexicography. This is because any word that an everyday-usage dictionary would ideally include may still occur only a very few times, or perhaps not at all, in a corpus of this size. It may be predicted, then, that the demands of lexicography will continue to drive the construction of larger and more balanced and representative corpora in the languages of South Asia – as has been the case for other languages, including, of course, English.

When a study of vocabulary, for the purpose of lexicography or any other reason, is undertaken using a relatively small corpus, then for the conclusions to be reliable it is necessary to concentrate the analysis on the most frequent items in the corpus. This principle will be adhered to in the short investigation of Hindi and Urdu vocabulary across a set of five corpora in the following section, which attempts to demonstrate just one of the avenues of research that the application of corpus linguistics to the languages of South Asia opens up.

15.3 A Corpus-Based Comparative Analysis of Hindi and Urdu Vocabulary

In this section, a short corpus-based investigation will be sketched out to show the kinds of avenues of analysis that are open to the South Asian language researcher using corpus data. The topic is a basic one – the vocabulary of Hindi-Urdu – and the discussion necessarily brief. However, even this relatively superficial study serves to exemplify the possibilities and potential of the corpus-based approach in these languages, and the kinds of questions that may now be asked and answered. In Section 15.3.1, the background on Hindi and Urdu that underlies this investigation's research questions will briefly be outlined. The data to be investigated, and the methods used to prepare it, will be addressed in Section 15.3.2; results will be presented in 15.3.3.

15.3.1 Hindi and Urdu

The linguistic and socio-political relationship between Hindi and Urdu is, perhaps, unique.[24] On *some* linguistic grounds – but not all – they are effectively the same language. On socio-political grounds, however, many or most speakers consider them to be separate languages based on the cultural identity association of Hindi with Hindus (and, thus, modern India) and of Urdu with Muslims (and, thus, modern Pakistan) – although, according to the Ethnologue (Gordon 2005), there are many more native speakers of Urdu in India than in Pakistan.

Hindi and Urdu derive from the New Indo-Aryan dialect spoken around Delhi in the twelfth and thirteenth centuries, a period of contact between the Indo-Aryan speakers and invaders from the West, especially Persia. As Kachru explains:

> Under court patronage and various other social pressures, two distinct styles, with two different scripts, developed in the course of the succeeding centuries. The one written in the Perso-Arabic script and looking to the West (i.e., Iran and the Arabic-speaking countries) for literary conventions and specialized vocabulary became known as Urdu. The one written in Devanagari script and adopting literary conventions and vocabulary mainly from Sanskritic sources came to be known as Hindi. (Kachru 2006: 2)

Due to this common origin, Hindi and Urdu share their syntax, morphology, phonology and core vocabulary in all but the smallest details. An example of a difference reported by Schmidt (1999: 109) is that in Hindi, the auxiliary verb within the verbal structure known as the *conjunctive participle* may be omitted in certain circumstances, whereas this is not possible in Urdu. However, all in all, the colloquial spoken forms of Hindi and Urdu are almost entirely mutually comprehensible. As modern linguistics has traditionally privileged the spoken form of language as primary, and concerned itself with structural aspects of language such as grammar and phonology rather than with literary, specialized lexis, it is perhaps not surprising that 'Hindi-Urdu' is often described as a single language in much of the literature (e.g. Kachru 1990). Some authors therefore describe Hindi and Urdu as dialects of a single language (as reported by Bhatia and Koul 2000: ix–x). Masica goes so far as to suggest that by one definition of a dialect, Urdu and Hindi 'are different *literary styles* based on the *same* linguistically defined subdialect' (Masica 1991: 27), although as Kachru (2006: 5) points out there are some dialectal differences *within* both Hindi and Urdu.

However, other linguistic criteria serve to separate Hindi and Urdu. First, due to their use of different scripts they do not (indeed, *cannot*) share a written standard, and in the written form mutual comprehensibility is obviously zero. Furthermore, in the spoken form mutual comprehensibility may be substantially less than 100 per cent due to the use of loanwords from different sources (Persian or Arabic in Urdu, Sanskrit in Hindi) in the lexis of more formal and specialized registers – for example the language of science, technology, literature, religion, philosophy and law.

The points outlined in the foregoing summary are generally agreed upon by most or all commentators on the relationship between Hindi and Urdu. What has not to date been investigated – what until the advent of suitable corpora *could not* be investigated – is how this linguistic situation is reflected in the frequency profile of vocabulary in use across a corpus of texts. The second part of this study is a necessarily cursory attempt to make some initial observations towards such an analysis.

In particular, the following issues will be addressed. How homogenous are the quantitative patterns of vocabulary usage in the data? If they are not homogenous, can we associate this with the Hindi-Urdu distinction? Are there quantitative or qualitative differences in the vocabulary of the five datasets (described below) that can be associated with the Hindi-Urdu distinction or with the text-type distinctions between the corpora? If there are, is the effect of text-type – that is, the variation in composition of the corpora – on these quantitative patterns more or less extensive than the effect of the Hindi-Urdu distinction? Finally, how quantitatively dominant are loanwords from Sanskrit (Hindi) or Persian and Arabic (Urdu)? Are the two languages mirror images in this respect?

15.3.2 Data and Method

The data for this analysis was drawn from the EMILLE and CIIL corpora, as described in Section 15.2.1.2. The version of the CIIL data utilized was that created by the EMILLE project to match the format of the EMILLE corpus files. This meant that all the datasets were in the same format – Unicode, as opposed to the ISCII of the original CIIL Corpus – and used the same system of mark-up, namely TEI/XCES-compatible XML.[25] This meant that all the data could be processed in the same way – although, as will be explained below, full compatibility of all the data could not be achieved.

The data fell into five distinct sections, each of which will be treated here as an independent corpus. Three of the datasets were in Hindi, and two in Urdu.

The first Hindi dataset was the CIIL corpus of written Hindi (originally gathered by the Indian Institute of Technology). The second was the written Hindi corpus collected for the EMILLE corpus. The distinction between the two is that the EMILLE dataset consists solely of 'webnews', that is, news text harvested from World Wide Web sites in Hindi, in the period 2000–2003. However, the CIIL Hindi corpus is drawn largely from published books from a very wide range of genres. In terms of text-type, then, the two written Hindi datasets are strongly distinct from one another.

The written Urdu dataset (originally gathered by Aligarh Muslim University) was also derived from the CIIL Corpus. It is a collection of texts from across a similar spread of written genres as the Hindi data. There is, for Urdu, no corresponding 'webnews' data. This is because, at the time these datasets were collected, no data source on the web could be found that published Urdu news text in an encoding that could be easily converted to Unicode (see Baker et al. 2004: 511–14 for an overview of some of the difficulties).

The remaining two datasets are the EMILLE Hindi and Urdu spoken corpora. These largely originate from a single, overlapping source. Because demographic sampling of natural, informal spoken dialogues from South Asian communities in the United Kingdom, which was the EMILLE project's original goal, proved infeasible (Baker et al. 2004: 515–17), the spoken corpora were instead constructed from transcriptions of BBC radio broadcasts in the languages being sampled. However, the main BBC radio station aimed at the UK South Asian diaspora community, the *BBC Asian Network*, did not distinguish between Hindi and Urdu. Rather, the programmes were labelled as Hindi-Urdu. The broadcaster's labels were the only criteria used to classify speech as Hindi or Urdu (in the light of the literature cited in the preceding section, there did not seem to be any safe way to do so on any linguistic basis). Thus, programmes from the BBC Asian Network were deemed to be equally valid as Hindi and as Urdu and the greater part of both spoken corpora consist of transcriptions of these programmes. However, both the Hindi and Urdu spoken corpora also contain a small amount of data from sources labelled explicitly as Hindi or as Urdu. The Hindi corpus contains a small amount of naturally collected speech, in the form of a monologue rather than a dialogue. The Urdu corpus contains some transcriptions from the *Jaltrang* programme on *BBC Radio Lancashire*, which unlike the other BBC programmes *were* explicitly labelled as Urdu rather than as Hindi-Urdu.

Therefore, to a very large extent, the Hindi and Urdu spoken corpora are effectively identical, the only difference being that one was transcribed into Devanagari script and the other was transcribed into Indo-Perso-Arabic script. While the transcribers had access to a 'foreign' tag for coding words not in the language of the main transcription, there are no instances of the vocabulary of the 'other' side of the divide being marked as 'foreign' (i.e. Arabic-derived words tagged as 'foreign' in text transcribed as Hindi, or Sanskrit-derived words tagged as 'foreign' in text transcribed as Urdu). This suggests that the vocabulary in use was perceived by the transcribers as neutral between Hindi and Urdu; it remains to be seen whether an analysis of the corpora confirms this.

Table 15.1 Datasets for study of Hindi and Urdu vocabulary.

Dataset	Abbreviation	Tokens
Hindi – CIIL written corpus	h-ciil	1,932,000
Hindi – EMILLE webnews corpus	h-webnews	9,919,000
Hindi – EMILLE spoken corpus	h-spok	542,000
Urdu – CIIL written corpus	u-ciil	2,341,000
Urdu – EMILLE spoken corpus	u-spok	455,000

These five corpora are of very different sizes, and their text-type composition was determined by the contingencies of the projects for which they were created. They were not designed to be directly comparable, and that makes the comparison which will be made here of their vocabulary, based largely on frequency, potentially problematic. However, the rather uneven composition of the various datasets actually allows some useful comparisons to be made. For instance, it is to be expected that there will be minimal or no differences between the Hindi and Urdu spoken data, if the method is reliable. Likewise, comparing differences between the Hindi-CIIL data and the Hindi-webnews data in the one hand, and between the Hindi-CIIL and the Urdu-CIIL data on the other, may allow some judgement to be made about whether the contrast between written Hindi and written Urdu is greater or less than text-type variation within Hindi. The sizes of the different datasets (together with the abbreviations that will be used to refer to the different datasets hereafter) are given in Table 15.1.

The Xaira[26] software was used to analyse the data. Frequency lists for each entire corpus were created (for ease of manipulation, only the 1,000 most frequent words were retained and the remainder discarded) and automatically transliterated to the Latin alphabet for ease of comparison, using one-to-one character replacement so that no information from the original script would be lost. Even so, there were still major typographic differences between the Urdu and Hindi texts (and even, in some minor details of the encoding, between the different Urdu data sources). This is because Indo-Perso-Arabic is a less explicit script than Devanagari; due to the script's roots in the phonology of Arabic, short vowels are typically omitted and some letters perform double duty as long vowels and consonants. So a direct transliteration does not actually result in the usual Latin-alphabet transcription of the word (which is typically close to, if not identical with, a transliteration of the more phonetically explicit Devanagari). These typographic variations are exemplified in Table 15.2.

In addition, there were some tokenization differences between Devanagari and Indo-Perso-Arabic: in Devanagari, case-marking postpositions and the future tense auxiliary are written as suffixes to the nouns and verbs they modify (e.g. *usake*, 'of it'), whereas in Indo-Perso-Arabic they are typically written as suffixes (e.g. the equivalent *ās ke*).

Table 15.2 Examples of words that are different in automatically transliterated Urdu and Hindi text.

Normal Latin transcription of word	Direct transliteration from Devanagari	Direct transliteration from Indo-Perso-Arabic
nahīṁ 'not'	nahīṁ	nhyṁ
bahut 'very'	bahuta[27]	bht
haiṁ 'are'	haiṁ	hyṁ
ek 'one'	eka	āyk
aur 'and'	aura	āvr
śukriyā 'thanks'	śukriyā	śkryh
koī 'someone'	koī	kv'yy

There was also spelling variation, in both Urdu and Hindi, of some very common words. For instance, there are *multiple* variant spellings of the Muslim greeting *assalāmu 'alaikum*, a loan-phrase from Arabic meaning 'peace be upon you', whose original Arabic spelling, put through the direct transliteration system used in Table 15.2 for Urdu, would produce *ālslām 'lykm*. The Urdu spellings that can be observed in the corpus, transliterated, include *slām* and *āslām* for the first word, and *'lykm*, *v'lykm* and *vā'lykm* for the second word.[28] It appears that the spelling variation seen here is reflected in Urdu dictionaries as well – Haq (1937 [2001]: 841) has *ālslām 'lykm* (i.e. the Arabic spelling) whereas the dictionary of the Oriental Book Society (p. 63) has *āslām v'lykm*. The Hindi spellings, although they cannot be compared to the Arabic for obvious reasons, are also multiple: they include *salāma* and *assalāma* for the first word, and *vālekuma* and *vālaiyakuma* for the second – note that the Hindi spelling given by McGregor's (1993: 994) dictionary is *salāma alaikuma*. The observed variants were all among the thousand most frequent types in the Hindi and Urdu spoken corpora – that is, they were not individual typographic errors, but persistent patterns of spelling variation. If spelling variation can affect such a common and easily spotted phrase, it may easily be anticipated that it may also impact on the shape and contents of the frequency list in less easily noticed ways.

For clarity, the results presented in the following section standardize all spellings to the usual Latin transcription. This has been done manually. In any extension of this study, it might prove useful to utilize an automated intra-language transliteration system to handle the gap between Devanagari to Indo-Perso-Arabic (or vice versa), such as the systems described by Malik (2006a, 2006b). However, this would still leave the inherent spelling variation to be dealt with.

The frequency lists were edited to remove punctuation marks. The frequencies of punctuation marks could not be meaningful in this study, since (a) the systems of punctuation in Devanagari and Indo-Perso-Arabic differ, (b) there appear to also have been different punctuation conventions in the two written Hindi datasets, and (c) any punctuation in the spoken texts would in any case be no more than an impressionistic indication of speech divisions by the (non-linguist) typist who happened to transcribe that text.

To make meaningful comparisons between such different-sized databases, it is necessary to normalize frequencies. In this study, frequencies *per million words* are used, based on Xaira's token counts for the corpora (since Xaira counts punctuation marks as tokens, the frequencies of the punctuation marks that were scrubbed from the lists were subtracted from the corpus sizes before frequency per million was calculated). However, there is some potential for noise in this frequency data, since all three written corpora were mapped into Unicode from other original encodings, and this process can leave a residue of 'junk' in a text if its original encoding was not entirely regular. For instance, the *h-ciil* corpus contains at least some tokens which consist solely of vowel diacritics and which are therefore not legal words in the Devanagari script. It is difficult to determine how great an impact such noise may have on the total number of tokens, and thus on the normalized frequency of different types – *and* on significance statistics such as log-likelihood, which are calculated using the total corpus sizes. For this reason, additional statistics (e.g. frequency relative to the most frequent type) will be used as a double-check, where appropriate, in the discussion that follows.

The spelling variation noted above may also impact on the statistics: where a word is spelt in two different ways, then unless the different variants are known and counted together, its frequency will appear to be lower than it actually is. It is impossible to be certain of identifying and cleaning up all of this type of noise in the data; however, this will be done wherever possible.

15.3.3 Results and Analysis

15.3.3.1 Homogeneity of the frequency profiles of the different datasets

The twenty most frequent words in each corpus, together with their raw frequencies and normalized frequencies per million words, are shown in Table 15.3.

The highest frequency per million for each corpus, as shown in Table 15.3, varies noticeably. This may be due to the issues of spelling variation and other noise, discussed above.

The different columns of Table 15.3 contain, by and large, the same words – though not in the same order. Table 15.4 shows the amount of overlap between the top twenty most frequent words of each pair of corpora. This is in each case equal to 15 ± 2. In terms of the patterning of the differences – such as they are – there may be a text-type effect (see the difference between h-ciil and h-webnews, and the similarity between h-spok and u-spok) but there is no clear effect of a Hindi versus Urdu distinction.

The two Urdu corpora are linked by a single factor: the high frequency of *is/us* 'him/her/this/that'. However, this is a trivial feature, as it is an artefact of the writing systems: *is* and *us* (proximal and distal demonstratives respectively) are homographs in Indo-Perso-Arabic but not in Devanagari. In the h-spok corpus, for instance, the sum of the frequencies of *is* and *us*, the 22nd and 75th most frequent

Table 15.3 Twenty most frequent words in the five datasets (see Table 15.7 for translations).

h-ciil			h-webnews			h-spok			u-ciil			u-spok		
Word	Freq	Per mill	Word	Freq	Per mill	Word	Freq	Per mill	Word	Freq	Per mill	Word	Freq	Per mill
ke	59,732	30,917	ke	469,800	47,364	hai	27,046	49,900	ke	86,015	36,743	hai	15,330	33,692
hai	52,693	27,274	meṁ	302,394	30,486	ke	20,235	37,334	kī	68,712	29,352	ke	13,426	29,508
meṁ	48,981	25,352	kī	261,233	26,337	aur	10,683	19,710	meṁ	66,466	28,392	āp	11,261	24,749
kī	39,888	20,646	hai	240,619	24,258	kī	9,755	17,998	hai	64,228	27,436	haiṁ	10,462	22,993
se	30,209	15,636	ko	194,912	19,650	se	8,403	15,504	aur	61,857	26,423	meṁ	9,694	21,305
aur	29,243	15,136	se	166,592	16,795	haiṁ	7,704	14,214	se	47,512	20,296	aur	9,604	21,108
kā	28,112	14,551	ne	161,031	16,235	to	6,109	11,271	is/us	45,013	19,228	ki	8,179	17,976
ko	24,555	12,710	ki	151,060	15,229	ye	6,081	11,220	kā	40,247	17,192	se	7,562	16,620
haiṁ	19,343	10,012	kā	140,100	14,124	jo	6,077	11,212	ko	30,901	13,200	kā	6,430	14,132
par	16,538	8,560	aur	115,263	11,620	meṁ	5,885	10,858	haiṁ	25,721	10,987	ye	5,875	12,912
bhī	15,840	8,199	par	109,038	10,993	me	5,747	10,603	ki	24,846	10,613	ko	5,298	11,644
nahīṁ	14,623	7,569	bhī	76,137	7,676	kā	5,460	10,074	par	21,753	9,292	to	5,077	11,158
ki	13,897	7,193	haiṁ	73,758	7,436	ki	5,284	9,749	ye	20,111	8,591	is/us	4,966	10,914
ek	13,076	6,768	is	69,460	7,003	ko	4,854	8,956	ek	19,392	8,284	ki	4,376	9,618
hī	12,662	6,554	nahīṁ	65,652	6,619	ek	4,713	8,696	ne	18,824	8,041	ne	4,279	9,404
ho	11,673	6,042	kahā	64,752	6,528	bahut	4,504	8,310	bhī	16,808	7,180	jo	4,175	9,176
thā	11,309	5,854	ek	59,983	6,047	bhī	4,125	7,611	in/un	16,788	7,171	bahut	4,154	9,130
to	10,990	5,688	lie	59,557	6,004	āp	4,067	7,504	kar	15,536	6,636	vo	3,207	7,048
ne	10,847	5,614	kar	54,341	5,478	vo	3,512	6,480	nahīṁ	14,411	6,156	bhī	3,137	6,895
yah	9,939	5,144	kiyā	51,458	5,188	kar	3,352	6,185	vo	14,394	6,149	jī	3,062	6,730

Table 15.4 Number of words overlapping among the twenty most frequent words: a comparison among all five corpora.

	h-ciil	h-webnews	h-spok	u-ciil	u-spok
h-ciil	–	15	13	15	13
h-webnews	15	–	13	17	13
h-spok	13	13	–	15	17
u-ciil	15	17	15	–	15
u-spok	13	13	17	15	–

words respectively, is 4,157 – which would make the *is/us* combination one of the twenty most frequent words in that corpus as well. A similar consideration applies to the *in/un* combination ('them/these/those'), a frequent form in u-ciil.

By contrast, a small number of real similarities link the two spoken corpora: *bahut* 'much/many/very' and *āp* 'you/oneself' are among the most frequent and *nahīṁ* 'not' is not. This is encouraging. However, although explanations for these patterns rooted in the difference between writing and speech as modes of language could easily be devised, care must be taken not to read too much into such a small number of similarities, as similar patterns can be observed linking corpora that do not form a natural set: for example *kar* 'do' is one of the twenty most frequent words in h-webnews, h-spok and u-ciil but not in h-ciil or u-spok.

In summary, then, it seems that the *content* of the top end of the frequency lists (if not their relative ranking) is rather homogenous across the five corpora. Is the same true of the *profile* of the frequency data, that is, the pattern of relative frequencies among the most frequent items? From an impressionistic examination of Table 15.3, it would seem that the frequencies per million fall off more drastically in, for instance, *h-webnews* than in either of the Urdu corpora. To examine this more rigorously, the frequencies of each of the top twenty words were recalculated as fractions of the frequency of the most frequent type (so, for instance, in *h-ciil* the recalculated relative frequency of *hai* was $27,274 \div 30,917 = 0.882$). These values were then plotted as Fig. 15.1.

An examination of this graph reveals that there is a degree of variation among the corpora in terms of how steep the 'fall-off' is after the most frequent type in the corpus. For h-ciil, u-ciil and u-spok, there is a much less rapid 'fall-off' in frequency than there is in h-spok. (h-webnews is somewhere between). This is perhaps a counter-intuitive finding, given that (as noted above) h-spok and u-spok are the two most similar corpora in terms of their provenance. Moreover, the group of three corpora with a similar profile (h-ciil, u-ciil and u-spok) includes Hindi and Urdu corpora, and spoken and written corpora. Clearly, this variant feature of the frequency profiles, if significant, does not map clearly onto the obvious external variables.

So while there *does* appear to be a lack of homogeneity in the frequency profile, it is not of a kind that can be traced back to the difference between Hindi and

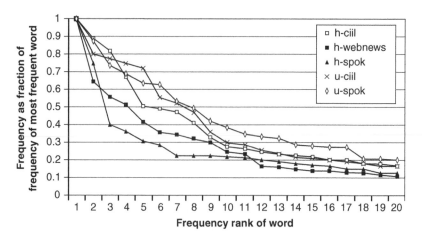

Figure 15.1 Relative frequencies of very frequent words in the Hindi and Urdu corpora.

Table 15.5 Number of words overlapping among the 100 most frequent words: a comparison of h-ciil to the other four corpora (shown in brackets for comparison: equivalent figures from Table 15.4 multiplied by 5).

	h-webnews	*h-spok*	*u-ciil*	*u-spok*
Number of types in top 100 overlapping with the h-ciil top 100	67 (75)	68 (65)	69 (75)	58 (65)

Urdu or to any demonstrable text-type effect – with the exception of a relatively few features which *may* possibly be characteristic of the spoken form of the language(s).

Is the picture radically different if we look at the 100 most frequent words, instead of just the 20 most frequent words? While the 'top twenty' is composed of function words, the 'top hundred' also includes content words – verbs and, especially, nouns. Thus, we would expect there to be rather more variation. Table 15.5 shows the amount of overlap among the corpora, considered in terms of types, at the level of the 'top hundred'. In Table 15.5, each of the other four corpora is compared to the h-ciil corpus, since Table 15.4 shows that this corpus has the least variable 'similarity' across the other four.

Table 15.5 clearly shows that considering the 100 most frequent types rather than the 20 most frequent, there is in three cases slightly less overlap. However the difference is not large. Surprisingly, in the comparison of h-ciil to u-spok – which

Table 15.6 Frequency profile statistics for the 100 most frequent types.

	h-ciil	*h-webnews*	*h-spok*	*u-ciil*	*u-spok*
Freq of 100th type [A]	1011	1077	1383	973	1211
Freq of 100th type [B]	0.033	0.023	0.026	0.027	0.036
% of corpus [C]	39	44	47	46	51

Note: A – Frequency of 100th most frequent type (per million words)

   B – Frequency of 100th most frequent type (as fraction of frequency of most frequent type)

   C – Total frequency of 100 most frequent types (as percentage of the total tokens in the corpus)

did not stand out particularly in the previous analysis – there is actually *more* overlap. In this light, it would seem that there is not significant vocabulary differentiation between Hindi and Urdu, or between the spoken and written forms, within the 100 most frequent types. The statistics presented in Table 15.6 assess the frequency profile of the 100 most frequent types in a variety of ways. The main finding, again, is that there is no clear differentiation, either by text type, or according to Hindi versus Urdu, of the various datasets. In fact, the percentage of the corpus accounted for by the 100 most frequent type, and the frequency of the hundredth type *are* highest for the two spoken corpora. This would fit with a prior expectation that spoken conversation would be less diverse in vocabulary than written discourse. However, there is no clear gap between the spoken and written corpora (h-spok is only 1 per cent higher on the former measure than u-ciil) and it would be unwise to build too much out of just this distinction – given that, if enough statistics are evaluated, *some* are bound to show a difference between speech and writing.

To summarize: on quantitative grounds the frequency profiles of datasets are heterogenous to a degree. But this heterogeneity does not appear to be linked to easy distinctions of variety (Hindi as opposed to Urdu) or text type (written versus spoken). What does a qualitative examination of the data – taking into account what these most frequent types actually *are* – reveal?

15.3.3.2 Shared and unique vocabulary across the datasets
Let us return first to the 20 most frequent words in each corpus, shown in Table 15.3. These most frequent words are all grammatical words and fall into a very few classes, as Table 15.7 illustrates.

Qualitatively there is little difference between these extremely frequent words in the five corpora. The same sets of words are found. There are certainly no differences that can be easily traced to the distinction between Hindi and Urdu. This is what we would expect, given the common observation that Hindi and Urdu are

Table 15.7 Classification of highly frequent types in the five corpora.

Category	Types	Translation
Postposition	kā, ke, kī	genitive (masc. sing., fem., masc. plrl./oblique)
	ko	accusative/dative, *to*
	ne	ergative
	meṁ	*in*
	par	*on, at*
	se	*from, by*
	lie	*for* (in the compound *ke lie*)
Personal pronouns	āp	*you/oneself*
Demonstrative pronouns	ye/vo,[29] is/us, in/un	*this/that/he/she/it/they*
	kahā	*what/which* (interrogative)
	jo	*who/which* (relative)
Emphatic particles[30]	hī	exclusive emphatic particle
	bhī	inclusive emphatic particle
	to	contrastive emphatic particle
Auxiliary verbs	hai, haiṁ, ho, thā	forms of *honā*, 'to be'
	kar, kiya	forms of *karnā*, 'to do'
Conjunctions	ki[31]	*that* (subordinator)
	aur	*and*
Other	nahīṁ	*not* (negative marker)
	bahut	*very*
	ek	*one*

grammatically near-identical (see Section 15.3.1). However, a small number of distinctions between the spoken corpora and the written corpora may be observed:

- *bahut* 'very' and *āp* 'you/oneself' are among the 'top twenty' in both spoken corpora, but none of the written corpora (with regard to *āp* in particular, compare the common finding for English that personal pronouns are significantly more common in spoken corpora than written corpora – see for instance Rayson et al. 2002: 302).
- *ke* is the most frequent word in all three written corpora. In both spoken corpora, however, the most frequent word is *hai* 'is', followed by *ke*. Again, we may compare the common finding that verbs are more common in speech and complex noun phrases (such as those that include nouns linked by adposition) are more common in writing in English (cf. Rayson et al. 2002: 301, 303).

Moving on to look more widely at the 100 most frequent words, a straightforward way to throw differences between the corpora into relief is to look at the words which are in the 'top hundred' for each corpus that are *not* in the 'top hundred' for any other corpus. For this analysis, all inflected forms of a single root were treated as 'the same word'; for instance, *cāhie* is (uniquely) highly frequent in h-ciil, and *cāhte* is (uniquely) highly frequent in u-spok, but as these are both inflections of *cāhnā* 'to want, to desire', neither was included in this step of the analysis. This process did cover over some points which might be worthy of study, for example the apparent fact that the u-spok corpus contains a large number of uniquely highly frequent verbs in the Hindi-Urdu polite imperative form. However, there is no space here to elaborate on this. The resulting list of words which are only highly frequent in one of the five corpora is given in Table 15.8.

The most notable feature of Table 15.8 is that it is the h-webnews corpus which has the most uniquely highly frequent types, and that they are, fairly obviously, topic-driven: they relate to the government and politics of India. The h-ciil corpus, from a more diverse range of source texts, does not have any such topic-specific vocabulary. The h-spok corpus has hardly any uniquely frequent words at all. On the Urdu side, u-spok's list contains a number of topic-driven vocabulary items from the field of music, presumably in reference to the music played by the radio shows that were sampled in the corpus, whereas u-ciil like h-ciil has a list containing non-topic-specific vocabulary.

Beyond this, there is a clear split between the Hindi and Urdu corpora, along the Sanskrit versus Persian and Arabic lines that we would expect (plus some English in all corpora except h-ciil and u-ciil). However, the terms are – except in h-webnews – neither especially technical nor especially clearly associated, semantically, with particular formal registers such as politics or religion. If frequency is taken as a proxy for saliency, then, the most prominent difference between written Hindi and Urdu corpora may not be so much in the vocabulary of the high registers as in the use of frequent, and semantically broad, words such as *adhik* and *prakār* on the one hand, and *ilm*, *ziṁdagī* and *muxtalif* on the other, as evident in h-ciil and u-ciil. Hindi and Urdu may not be direct 'mirror images' in this respect, as there is some slight evidence to suggest that the reliance on loanwords may be greater for Urdu than Hindi.

One further observation is that Arabic and Persian loanwords may be more important in Urdu than Sanskrit loanwords are in Hindi, on the basis that the list of uniquely highly frequent words for h-ciil is much shorter than that for u-ciil. This might be argued to be an effect of the h-webnews corpus being present in the comparison without there being an Urdu equivalent (since any Sanskrit-based words in that corpus's 'top hundred' that were shared with h-ciil's 'top hundred' would be eliminated from the analysis above). However, a manual survey of the 'top hundred' list for h-ciil and h-webnews suggests that this is not a major factor.

15.4 Conclusion

The very cursory study of Hindi and Urdu vocabulary in the preceding section – confined as it was to a rudimentary discussion of the 20 and 100 most frequent types in each corpus – may be said to suggest the following conclusions.

Table 15.8 Uniquely highly frequent types in the five corpora.

Corpus	Types in the top 100 that are not in the top 100 of other corpora	
h-ciil	adhik 'many, more' [S]	din 'day'
	kabhī 'sometimes, at one time'	prakār 'kind, sort, type, way' [S]
h-webnews	adhyakṣ 'person in charge, president' [S]	pradhānmaṁtrī 'prime minister'
	amerikā 'America' [E]	[S]
	anusār 'accordance, conformity' [S]	batāyā 'tell'
	anya 'other, different' [S]	bīc 'middle, average, between'
	kāṁgres 'Congress (political party)' [E]	baiṭhak 'sitting room, assembly
	jhārkhaṁd 'Jharkhand (Indian state)'	room'
	dillī 'Delhi'	bhājapā 'BJP (political party)'
	deś 'place, country, land' [S]	[abbreviation]
	pārṭī '(political) party' [E]	bhārat 'India' [S]
	pulis 'police' [E]	bhāratīya 'Indian' [S]
	pūrv 'forward, eastward, prior' [S]	maṁtrī 'minister' [S]
		rāṁcī 'Ranchi (a city)'
		rājya 'sovereignty, state' [S]
		sarkār 'master, government' [P]
		siṁha 'lion, hero (also a
		surname)' [S]
h-spok	cār 'four'	bāre (multiple homonym)
	tīn 'three'	matlab 'purpose, meaning' [A]
	bār (multiple homonym)	
u-ciil	ilm 'knowledge' [A]	dor 'distant' [P] *or* daur 'age,
	istemāl 'use, practice' [A]	time' [A]
	kam 'few, small' [P]	nazar 'look, sight' [A]
	jan 'person' or jin 'spirit'	pānī 'water'
	zabān 'tongue, language' [P]	pedā 'born, gain' [P]
	ziṁdagī 'life' [P]	muxtalif 'different, various' [A]
	zyādā 'many, more' [A]	vajah 'reason, basis, face' [A]
	taraf 'side, edge' [A]	sirf 'only' *or* sarf 'expense' [A]
	dūsre 'second'	hāsil 'product, gain' [A]
u-spok	āvāz 'sound, voice' [P]	film 'film' [E]
	janāb (an honorific) [A]	yahāṁ 'here'
	naγmā 'song, melody' [P]	sn (multiple homonym)
	nambar 'number' [E]	sāme'īn 'listeners' [A]
	nā 'no, not'	hāṁ 'yes; place'
	fon 'phone' [E]	

Note: Translations are simplified from those of Haq (1937 [2001]) and McGregor (1993). Where the word is indicated in these sources as a loanword, the language it is loaned from is indicated, as follows: [A] Arabic, [E] English, [P] Persian, [S] Sanskrit. One word in u-ciil, transliterated as *tvr*, could not be tracked down in these sources and has been omitted from consideration.

The quantitative analysis of the frequently used vocabulary suggests a degree of heterogeneity. However, what variation there is in the frequency profiles is insufficient to suggest any clear, hard-and-fast divisions among the corpora that might be linked to difference between Hindi and Urdu, or between spoken texts and written texts. In that respect, then, the corpora are all relatively similar, and it is not possible to say whether the spoken/written distinction or the Hindi/Urdu distinction has the greater effect.

In a qualitative analysis, the corpora are largely homogenous at both the 'top twenty' and the 'top hundred' level, although some slight differences between the spoken and written language can be identified (most notably *ke* being the most frequent word in writing and *hai* the most frequent word in speech). However, while all the 'top twenty' in each corpus are grammatical words – even where there are differences between the corpora – the 'top hundred' *does* contain non-grammatical words that are uniquely highly frequent in each corpus and an examination of these reveals both a text-type distinction and a Hindi versus Urdu distinction. The former is largely a reflection of topic homogeneity in the texts from which each corpus was sampled. The latter distinction is, of course, one of Sanskrit versus Persian or Arabic vocabulary, as was anticipated from the outset – but the analysis suggests that the most prominent difference between Hindi and Urdu may not be found in the specialist or technical vocabularies, but rather in some semantically very broad loanwords that are, presumably as a function of their non-specificity, highly frequent.

There is clearly much more work to be done here. With appropriate advances in automatic resolution of spelling variants, tokenization, and transliteration between Hindi and Urdu – all of which, it should be noted, present greater problems than the equivalent tasks for English – it may be possible to use computational techniques (e.g. a keywords analysis) to compare the datasets. Likewise, this will enable the use of more rigorous statistical tools (e.g. an analysis based on Zipf's Law), as opposed to the fairly impressionistic analysis of relative frequency that was employed here.

Since the differences among the corpora due to text-type were not always clearly distinguishable from those due to the Hindi-Urdu distinction, or to differences in the sampling underlying each corpus, another fruitful line of analysis may be a multidimensional analysis, after the fashion of Biber (1988) – but necessarily including vocabulary features as well as the grammatical features that Biber relied on. It might be hypothesized that the Hindi-Urdu distinction may be discernable as a dimension of variation in much the way that different aspects of text-type distinctions may be.

This type of study represents only the beginning of a corpus-based approach to the languages of South Asia. However, this investigation, like the work cited in Section 15.2.4, clearly indicates that innumerable new directions of research are now open to us by means of various corpus methodologies. With the problems of encoding and rendering discussed in Section 15.2.1.1 now largely a thing of the past, thanks to the wide establishment of the Unicode standard, the potential for creating new corpora in these languages is today very great. In particular, as corpus annotation (particularly grammatical annotation) develops, opportunities for cross-linguistic comparative analysis among South Asian languages will increase. The areal relationship of Indo-Aryan and Dravidian – contrasted with the genetic relationship of Indo-Aryan to the more westerly Indo-European languages – makes such comparisons, particularly if they bridge the two language families, an especially fascinating prospect.

In conclusion, then, the potential contribution from South Asian language corpora to linguists' understanding of the Indo-Aryan and Dravidian languages is evidently great; but perhaps as great, and ultimately more socially significant, is the associated practical potential of the field for enhancing the interests of the languages' speakers, in the form of such improvements to lexicography, language learning materials, language technologies and other resources that the corpus-based enterprise alone may afford.

Notes

1 The term *Indo-Perso-Arabic* is used here for the version of the Perso-Arabic alphabet used for Urdu and other Indo-Aryan languages such as Punjabi (distinguished from the form of that script used for Persian by possessing characters for retroflex consonants, for instance).

2 Graphemes (characters) are, as is customary, given in <angled brackets> parallel to the /slash brackets/ used to indicate phonemes.

3 American Standard Code for Information Interchange.

4 All character values in this discussion are hexadecimal numbers indicated by a leading *0x.*

5 *Indian Standard Code for Information Interchange.* A parallel PASCII standard (*Perso-Arabic Standard Code for Information Interchange*) covers Indo-Perso-Arabic.

6 Eight bits (binary digits) of memory can represent any number between 0 and 255 (0xff). A character set can be referred to as *eight-bit* if it uses only these numbers to encode characters. The number 8 is significant because the byte, the basic unit of computer memory, consists of eight bits.

7 This discussion actually represents a slight oversimplification of the situation. Some producers of online text in South Asian languages actually abandoned any attempt to encode their text at all, instead publishing text as JPEG images or PDF files, or requiring the use of a special plug-in piece of software (this last solution was common for the extremely difficult-to-render *nasta'liq* calligraphy style used in printed Indo-Perso-Arabic).

8 See http://www.unicode.org/.

9 Unicode is a sixteen-bit encoding (or, in some variants, a thirty-two-bit encoding), allowing many thousands more characters to be encoded than in an eight-bit character set.

10 These include GATE (see also below), WordSmith, Xaira, AntConc, and Nooj.

11 An example of a South Asian language site with large amounts of user-generated content created as Unicode text is the Hindi Wikipedia: see http://hi.wikipedia.org/.

12 *Technology Development for Indian Languages*, 1990–91.

13 See http://www.ciilcorpora.net/.

14 See http://www.ciilcorpora.net/ldcil.htm.

15 *Enabling Minority Language Engineering*, funded by the UK EPSRC, project reference GR/N19106. See http://www.emille.lancs.ac.uk/.

16 See http://www.elda.org/.

17 See http://gate.ac.uk/.

18 *Nepali Language Resources and Localization for Education and Communication*; funded by the EU Asia IT&C programme, reference number ASIE/2004/091-777. See http://www.bhashasanchar.org/.

19 See http://www.jang.net/urdu/.

20 See http://www.claysanskritlibrary.org/corpus.php.

21 For present purposes, the terms *computational linguistics* will be considered to include *language engineering* and *natural language processing*.

22 See http://www.cfilt.iitb.ac.in/wordnet/webhwn/. See Fellbaum (1998) and Miller and Fellbaum (2007) for background on WordNet, a major resource for computational semantic analysis.

23 See http://www.nepalisabdakos.com.

24 Possibly the most comparable situation is that of Punjabi. In Pakistan, Punjabi speakers use an Indo-Perso-Arabic script, *Shahmukhi* (and are mostly Muslim), whereas in India Punjabi speakers use a script related to Devanagari, *Gurmukhi* (and are mostly Sikh or Hindu). See also Malik (2006*a*).

25 See http://www.tei-c.org/, http://www.cs.vassar.edu/XCES/.

26 See http://www.oucs.ox.ac.uk/rts/xaira/; see also Xiao (2006).

27 In Devanagari, each consonant character implies a following <a> vowel, unless it is cancelled by a diacritic mark called *virama*. However, in writing a Hindi word that ends with a consonant, the final *virama* is very often not written even though no <a> is pronounced. This silent final inherent vowel is usually omitted in Latin transcriptions of Hindi, but an automated direct transliteration preserves it.

28 A <v> (representing original Arabic *wa*, 'and') does occur before *'alaikum* when the order of the two words is reversed in the usual response to the greeting. But in the spoken Urdu texts, a <v> is sometimes found in cases where *'alaikum* follows *assalāmu*, which is not a correct spelling but presumably reflects Hindi-Urdu pronunciation, as do the Devanagari spellings with initial <v> (there is no /v/ ~ /w/ distinction in Hindi-Urdu).

29 *yah*, the twentieth most frequent word in h-ciil, is another form of *ye* – the distinction is one of number (singular versus plural) but does not appear to be being made (or at least, not made as extensively) in the other Hindi corpora.

30 The characterizations of the emphatic particles given here are taken from Schmidt (1999: 210–15).

31 The word spelt *ki* in Hindi is often transcribed as *ke* in discussions of Urdu (see e.g. Schmidt 1999: 225); in this discussion, and in the tables above, the form is given as *ki* to avoid confusion with postposition *ke*.

16

The Web as Corpus Versus Traditional Corpora: Their Relative Utility for Linguists and Language Learners

Robert Lew

The Web, teeming as it is with language data, of all manner of varieties and languages, in vast quantity and freely available, is a fabulous linguists' playground.
Adam Kilgarriff and Gregory Grefenstette (2003: 333)

With the continued expansion of the World Wide Web and dramatic improvements in computational speed and software quality, the collective textual content of the Web is becoming a serious competitor to traditional language corpora, at least in some applications and for some categories of potential corpus users. The present chapter looks at the relative advantages and disadvantages of the textual Web as corpus, and examines its relative usefulness for different categories of users, both language professionals such as linguists, and less skilled users such as language learners. Also considered are the pros and cons of the various alternative mechanisms for accessing the textual resources of the World Wide Web: a desktop-based concordancing application, a dedicated concordancer running on a web-accessible server and a popular general-purpose search engine.

16.1 Introduction[1]

Electronic corpora of natural language have grown dynamically in the recent decades: in their number, volume, as well as in importance (Sinclair 1991; Biber et al. 1998; Walter and Harley 2002). The population of typical corpora users is no longer restricted to the inner circles of lexicographers, linguists and experts in Natural Language Processing (which includes speech and character recognition, machine translation, spellchecking and grammar checking). Increasingly, corpora are being embraced by representatives of the less esoteric and less technical language-related professions, such as translators and language teachers, but also by language learners themselves (Tribble 1991; Aston 1997*b*; Varantola 2003). It is a sign of the times that corpus samples have even made their way into learners' dictionaries (e.g. Sinclair 1995).

On the other hand, the World Wide Web, the hypertext, multimedia section of the internet,[2] generally assumed to have originated in 1994 (de Schryver 2002), is developing with such momentum that in some areas of applications it may encroach on the niches freshly filled by 'traditional' electronic text corpora. A number of authors have proposed to treat and use the textual content of the world's web pages as a corpus (Grefenstette 1999; Rundell 2000; de Schryver 2002; Smarr and Grow 2002; Kilgarriff and Grefenstette 2003; Resnik and Smith 2003; Fletcher 2004). As Kilgarriff and Grefenstette (2003: 333) rightly point out, '[l]anguage scientists and technologists are increasingly turning to the Web as a source of language data, because it is so big, because it is the only available source for the type of language in which they are interested, or simply because it is free and instantly available'.

In the present chapter, I will try to discuss the usefulness of the two types of resources (i.e. traditional text corpora and the WWW) for two broad categories of users (and uses). First, I want to evaluate their usefulness in the context of foreign language teaching, seen as a branch of applied linguistics, as a potential tool for solving ad hoc lexical queries. I will not address the (no doubt very interesting and important) issues of the role played by corpora in the creation of learning tools and aids, such as textbooks, grammar books, or dictionaries (e.g. Aston 1997*a*, 1997*b*; Partington 1998; Reppen this volume; Willis 2000); or the direct use of corpora for inductive data-driven learning (e.g. Johns 1991). The scope of my discussion will also be restricted to the English language and to the lexical dimension. The other category of user that I want to focus on here will be the professional linguist. Here, I would like to focus primarily on the use of such textual resources for the verification of language related hypotheses by those linguists of various specialisms who accept corpus linguistics as an empirical methodology to a greater or lesser degree. This type of fairly general linguistic application appears to be of most general interest to a broad range of linguists, as opposed to certain more specialized applications relevant to, for example, computational linguists. In what follows, I will try to trace where the expectations and needs of the linguist-researcher and language learner converge, and where they diverge.

Given the two types of corpus-like resources (traditional corpora and the WWW), and the two broad categories of their users outlined above, it seems that a further distinction would usefully be made, based on the mechanism of accessing the resources in question. This is so because the access mechanism used has a significant impact on the functional qualities of the resources, and thus their practical utility. I believe it is necessary to consider at least three different access mechanisms that the user (the practising linguist or the language learner, respectively) can employ to communicate with the textual database. These three mechanisms are: a dedicated concordance application running on the user's desktop computer; a server-based concordance application accessed through the hypertext protocol; and a publicly accessible general-purpose search engine.

In the present chapter, I will try to compare the usefulness of traditional corpora and the-World Wide Web-as-corpus with reference to the following criteria: size of the resources; linguistic representativeness; balancing and noisiness; functionality and access mechanism.

16.2 Size of Textual Resources

The resource that is most commonly identified as the first general electronic text corpus is the Brown University corpus (Kučera and Francis 1967), created in the early sixties. Usually referred to as the Brown corpus, this resource measures a million orthographic words (tokens). Twenty years later, a corpus created in Birmingham to assist in the well-known lexicographic COBUILD project (Sinclair 1987) was larger by a factor of ten. The next tenfold increase in corpus size is the 100 million words of the British National Corpus (BNC: Leech et al. 1994; Burnard 1995), also created with lexicographic applications foremost in the mind. The BNC has become a *de facto* standard of a national corpus, a model of sorts for other similar undertakings (cf. Fillmore et al. 1998). It is worth stressing at this point that the complete body of the BNC, and a subset of the Bank of English corpus (which has evolved out of the COBUILD corpus) are now searchable through the WWW.[3]

Today, the largest corpora have grown by yet another order of magnitude. The Bank of English, which has evolved out of the COBUILD corpus, has remained among the largest corpora of English, with the most recent available reports[4] placing the size at somewhat above 500 million words, although the corpus is to a large extent an opportunistic one. However, currently at least two other corpora are said to have exceeded 1 billion words of text: The Cambridge International Corpus[5] and the Oxford English Corpus.[6]

Turning to the size of the World Wide Web, the approximate size of the textual resources of the WWW can be extrapolated from the number and average length of documents indexed by search engines. Before it stopped publicizing the number of indexed pages in late August 2005 after the famous 'size war' with Yahoo,[7] the most popular search engine Google[8] claimed the number of pages in its indexes to be over 8 billion, by a very conservative estimate (excluding e.g., partially indexed pages). Applying to this number the estimation algorithm proposed by Lawrence and Giles (1999) puts a rough estimate of the total (indexed and unindexed) textual resources at five trillion (5,000,000,000,000) word tokens: that is about fifty thousand times the size of the BNC. Of course, such estimates will vary widely depending on the assumption of what type of content should be counted; and, such extrapolation is becoming more difficult and less dependable with the increasing reliance of the WWW on content generated on the fly from some type of underlying database (the so-called deep-web, cf. Bergman 2001). This last source of error is likely to lead to underestimation rather than otherwise, and there is no questioning the fact that the size of the WWW is greater by several orders of magnitude compared to traditional corpora.

The rate of growth of the English-language part of the internet can be appreciated by looking at the frequencies of specific phrases and comparing them against the BNC, as shown in Table 16.1. As the numbers indicate, the current size of indexed textual content of the English-language web exceeds by some four orders of magnitude the size of a large general corpus. One should not forget that, as indicated above, the number of pages reported by the search engine would typically be about one order of magnitude smaller than the number of pages that are

Table 16.1 Frequencies of occurrence of selected English noun phrases in the BNC, AltaVista[9] (1998, 2001) and AlltheWeb[10] (2003, 2004, 2006).

		WWW				
Phrase	*BNC*	*Autumn 1998*	*Autumn 2001*	*Spring 2003*	*2 Dec 2004*	*16 Oct 2006*
medical treatment	414	46,064	627,522	1,539,367	1,960,000	11,300,000
prostate cancer	39	40,772	518,393	1,478,366	2,420,000	15,300,000
deep breath	732	54,550	170,921	868,631	1,770,000	6,010,000
acrylic paint	30	7,208	43,181	151,525	225,000	1,350,000
perfect balance	38	9,735	35,494	355,538	498,000	2,370,000
electromagnetic radiation	39	17,297	69,286	258,186	272,000	1,580,000
powerful force	71	17,391	52,710	249,940	326,000	2,000,000
concrete pipe	10	3,360	21,477	43,267	63,700	648,000
upholstery fabric	6	3,157	8,019	82,633	111,000	981,000
vital organ	46	7,371	28,829	35,819	59,200	207,000

Note: The figures for the BNC and AltaVista refer to the number of individual tokens. AlltheWeb cites the number of pages, so there may be more than a single token of a given phrase on a single page. The 1998–2003 data are taken from Kilgarriff and Grefenstette (2003).

in fact available on the web, because a large proportion of the web content remains unindexed (Lawrence and Giles 1999).

Admittedly, 100 million is a very large number of words. However, the statistical nature of the distribution of lexical items in natural text is such that the large majority of tokens turn out to be forms of the most frequent lexemes, while the number of occurrence of tokens representing the less common words decreases exponentially (as described by Zipf's law, Zipf 1935; Guiraud 1959). Thus, while a corpus of 100-million-word tokens is large enough to adequately represent the systematic facts of syntax (though see some reservations later in the chapter), when it comes to lexical facts, a 100-million-word corpus gives a reasonably accurate picture for at most the 10 thousand most common lexemes. Less frequent items are represented by fewer than 50 occurrences each, which does not provide a strong enough basis for statistically stable generalizations (Kilgarriff 2003; Kilgarriff and Grefenstette 2003).

It is also telling that, as shown by Banko and Brill (2001), the effectiveness of resolving lexical ambiguity grows monotonically with corpus size up to at least one billion words. Now, language engineering applications are not our primary focus, but this empirical fact is suggestive of the wealth of linguistic information that is potentially usable in corpora of different sizes.

The issue of corpus size is also related to the epistemological problem of negative evidence: in principle, the fact that a given form is not present in a corpus cannot be used as deterministic proof that the form is a nonexistent one. This is true of a sample of any size, except when the sample consists of the whole population (but that is, arguably, impossible for the population of utterances or texts of a living language). However, in terms of statistical inference and fuzzy logic, the bigger the corpus, the stronger the basis for claiming the non-existence of a form from its absence in a corpus.

The size range of a language resource needs to be appreciably larger if it is to provide a useful coverage of lexical combinations: idioms, phrases and collocations. This is so because the textual frequency of the co-occurrence of two or more words is naturally smaller, and often very much smaller, than the occurrence frequency of each of the component elements separately (compare the low frequency figures in the BNC column of Table 16.1 for noun phrases which are, subjectively speaking, not at all uncommon).

While it is probably a relatively safe assumption that very infrequent lexical items are not the primary interest of a foreign language learner (but may be of interest to a linguist), the language learner will no doubt want to be able to learn about patterns of semantically motivated lexical co-occurrence (to avoid using the variously understood word *collocation*). This is all the more important for the fact that lexical co-occurrence information is difficult to find in a dictionary,[11] and indeed it is actually difficult to *represent* lexicographically in a satisfactory manner.[12] In the light of the above, it seems that the issue of corpus size would be quite important to both the linguist and the language learner. This quantitative aspect appears then to score a point in favour of the World Wide Web, when seen in opposition to traditional corpora.

16.3 Linguistic Representativeness and the Balancing of Corpora

The issue of corpus representativeness cannot be usefully taken up unless one specifies the population (in the statistical sense) which we would expect to be faithfully represented. But, as noted by Sambor, we are dealing here with 'trudność natury ściśle lingwistycznej – nie istnieje mianowicie żaden jednorodny makrotekst jako populacja generalna, wobec której badane teksty można byłoby traktować jako próby z niej wylosowane' [a purely linguistic problem – there exists no uniform macrotext or general population that our set of texts could be treated as a sample of – translation Robert Lew] (Sambor 1988: 54–5). So, if we accept the view that there is no agreed standard of comparison, there are serious problems with establishing the criteria for corpus representativeness, and thus the usefulness of the very notion becomes questionable, at least for a general corpus: perhaps specialized corpora or text genres might be more easily dealt with.

In turn, the notion of the balancing of corpora is usually taken to refer to the selection of texts that go into the corpus being done in such a way so as not to favour, or disfavour, any particular text type(s). One could say then that corpus balancing is a weaker criterion, and more easily met than corpus representativeness, although some authors actually use the two terms interchangeably (Fillmore et al. 1998; Smarr and Grow 2002). In practice, the text types most commonly overrepresented in language corpora are press archives and fiction, while the most severely underrepresented type is probably spontaneous speech. This, of course, is a consequence of the grading of difficulty in acquiring linguistic data of a given type.

The unbalanced quality of the language content of the World Wide Web is among the most often listed drawbacks of this resource when considered from the point of view of linguistic applications. Kilgarriff and Grefenstette appear to make light of the problem, maintaining that: '[t]he Web is not representative of anything else. But neither are other corpora, in any well-understood sense' (2003: 343). I do not think that it is fair to equate the World Wide Web with traditional corpora in this regard, as the very nature of the non-representativeness is different in the two cases. For example, it is obvious that an inordinately high proportion of web-based texts are about various aspects of the web itself, which constitutes an interesting kind of systematic reflexivity. Another important point to note is the clear dominance of a single text genre: the web page. Somewhat less obviously, the World Wide Web exhibits an overrepresentation of texts about high technology. While the above features of the web are in fact inherent qualities of the language of the internet, the reasons behind the lack of balance in traditional corpora are more incidental; they are largely within the control of their creators and can be subject to planning activity. For this reason, it seems that the two cases of textual imbalance need to be distinguished on theoretical grounds.

One new threat to the representativeness of the texts on the World Wide Web is the relatively recent practice of some web content creators flooding their pages with a high number of repeated keywords in a way that is unobtrusive to the human reader, such as through the use of a tiny background-coloured font. This practice is known under the term *web-spamming* (Gyongyi and Garcia-Molina 2005), and it is aimed at boosting the position of the offending pages on results displayed by search engines through artificially exaggerating the frequency of occurrence of words known to be frequently sought. Such manipulation can not only affect the positioning of the page in search results, but also lead to the misrepresentation of lexical frequency distribution figures. However, designers of search algorithms are defending themselves against the consequences of such deceitful practice by adding mechanisms capable of ignoring such artificially added material. Somewhat ironically, the newest and most insidious type of search-engine spam, the so-called *link farms* (an inevitable consequence of the recent increased reliance of search engines on the analysis of hyperlink patterns – see e.g. Drost and Scheffer 2005), presents less of a threat to the reliability of lexical frequency counts than the spamming of web page content proper.

Lack of balance must be seen as a serious problem for both our categories of users of corpus-like resources: the professional linguist and the foreign language learner. By this criterion, then, (balanced) traditional corpora should be seen as superior to the Web. However, when it comes to the sensitivity to corpus imbalance, linguists may be in a better position to compensate for the lack of balance, with their expert metalinguistic and linguistic knowledge, as well as the usual dose of scientific scepticism. On the other hand, one important argument for using corpora is the notorious unreliability of intuition for judging linguistic data, so there are limits to such compensation.

16.4 Noise

Texts that go into a traditional corpus are normally subjected to filtering and cleaning procedures. Moreover, not infrequently they will be texts of high editorial quality to start with. Things look very different when it comes to texts available on the World Wide Web, where the proportion of all kinds of errors and mistakes, including typos, is substantial. However, as soon as you compare the alternative forms, doubts should disappear: 'the Web is a dirty corpus, but expected usage is much more frequent than what might be considered noise' (Kilgarriff and Grefenstette 2003: 342).[13]

Just as for the dangers related to the lack of representativeness, the risk of misleading the users would be appreciably higher with language learners than with linguists, as the latter would be expected to have a higher degree of language awareness.

16.5 Functionality and Access Mechanism

Proposals to use universal search engines for accessing the textual resources of the Web, either directly or with various types of additional processing, have been made by a number of authors (Rundell 2000; Kilgarriff 2001; de Schryver 2002; Kehoe and Renouf 2002; Smarr and Grow 2002; Volk 2002; Resnik and Smith 2003; Schmied 2006). According to Kilgarriff and Grefenstette (2003: 344–45), for the working linguist, the most serious drawbacks of using search engines compared to dedicated corpora are as follows: restrictions on the number of hits returned, narrow textual context, awkward ordering of citations in the results lists, impossibility to specify linguistic criteria (such as part of speech) in search queries, and difficulty in searching for all word forms of a lexeme at the same time (i.e. lack of lemmatization or stemming). I will briefly discuss these problems below, taking into account the needs of the linguist and the foreign language learner.

A typical maximum number of citations returned by a search engine is of the order of a few thousand (Kilgarriff and Grefenstette 2003). It seems that a few thousand items should be more than satisfactory for the language learner. This amount of data should in most cases also satisfy the linguist, unless the goal is to generate mass data for further processing (especially as the limits on automatically run queries may be more stringent).

Narrowing the textual context (co-text) to (typically) a dozen or so words can indeed be awkwardly restrictive to both categories of users considered here. This is particularly true for issues related to phenomena surfacing at the suprasentential level, such as, for example, discourse-linking adverbs. Still, the interested user can in each case expand the context easily and arbitrarily, by clicking the relevant hypertext link.

When it comes to the ordering of results returned by search engines, most of the popular engines now tend to favour to some extent those pages where search keywords are found in structurally prominent positions, such as titles or document section headings. Preference is also given to those web pages which are the targets of hyperlinks from a large array of other sites. While this seems to be a sensible strategy for the typical users of search engines, likely to produce highly relevant hits at the top of the list of results, it is an undesirable feature for the linguist or language learner who are normally after examples of *typical use* of language.[14] In some search engines, there are mechanisms allowing the user to at least partially remedy the above problem. Unfortunately, they are poorly documented and largely unknown. In Google, for example, the prefix *allintext:* or *intext:* can at this time be used in the search query to eliminate the structural position bias, though this particular feature of query syntax is not documented anywhere on the Google help pages. In the current version of the MSN/Live Search engine one can control the weight of the page popularity parameter.[15]

The fact that it is impossible to specify linguistic criteria such as part of speech information (e.g. *hit* as a verb vs. *hit* as a noun) in web-based searches may be a serious limitation to both the linguist and the advanced language learner. One should not forget, though, that this disadvantage is shared by a substantial proportion of traditional corpora as well, as such an option is afforded only by corpora properly annotated for part of speech. A partial workaround for the lack of part-of-speech sensitivity might be to limit the query to a single inflectional form that is unique to a given syntactic category, but this is not always a viable option for a weakly inflected language such as English. Also, one must bear in mind the fact that a given inflectional variant of a lexeme may have specific lexicogrammatical patterns which will then be overrepresented from the point of view of the complete lexeme.

Searching for all word forms of a single lexeme is an option available only in morphologically analysed and annotated corpora. Kilgarriff and Grefenstette (2003: 345) note that search engines do not offer such an option. It is indeed true that lemmatization (or stemming[16]) has never been a mainstream functionality of search engines. The early search engines were rather basic, and although there was a period around the turn of the century when quite a few search engines did experiment with lemmatization or truncation, later they dropped the functionality, one by one. Presumably, lemmatization did not offer a satisfactory commercial return compared to its increased computational cost. At the time of Kilgarriff and Grefenstette's 2003 analysis, of the major search engines, MSN Search[17] offered lemmatization, but at the time of this writing (November 2006) it no longer does. Lemmatization and truncation (as well as proximity search) is currently offered by the Exalead[18] engine. Since recently, Google appears to be offering some degree of (what it calls) stemming.[19]

All these drawbacks of existing search engines have inspired work aiming to give linguists access to the enormous text resources of the World Wide Web through an interface that is similar to those familiar from concordancers used for corpus searching. Such work can be categorized into two types of projects.

The first option is to try and create a linguistic search engine from scratch, optimized to reflect the needs of linguists.[20] Within this rubric, one could name Adam Kilgarriff's (2003) Linguistic Search Engine, the Search Engine for Applied Linguists (Fletcher 2004) – both at present at the proposal stage, as well as the Linguist's Search Engine,[21] which has a functioning test version running on a relatively small material of 3.5 million sentences. This last resource allows the user to generate and store customized collections as texts, and supports grammatical parsing including a visualization module that draws structural marker trees. This is also the direction in which the WebCorp project (see below) is apparently heading.[22]

The second option is to provide a layer of pre- and post-processing (what some authors call *wrappers*), which redirect queries entered by the user to existing search engines (using either the hypertext protocol or the API interface), and then filter and present the results in appropriate format. Projects that work according to this principle may be further divided into those accessible through a web-page interface, and applications requiring installation on the users' computer. The first subset includes the following: WebCorp[23] (Kehoe and Renouf 2002; Morley et al. 2003; Fletcher 2004; Morley 2006; Renouf et al. 2006), WebCONC[24] and WebPhraseCount[25] (Schmied 2006), and Lexware Culler[26] (Dura 2006). The best-known application of the second subset is the KwicFinder[27] (Fletcher 2004).

It appears that at the present time most of the services of the second type above do not offer dramatic improvements over the basic search engine functionality, but they do have one significant disadvantage: inferior speed. Searches take much longer than is the case in search engines. This, incidentally, is also the disadvantage of large traditional corpora. In situations when the user needs to query the resource repeatedly at short intervals, the cumulative delay may become unacceptable and thus make such a resource unusable for practical purposes.

Paradoxically, in some cases involving heavily filtered searches, recall can fall way below that of a traditional corpus, as shown convincingly by Lüdeling et al. (2006).

Another aspect of the matter is that applications such as the KwicFinder cannot be utilized on public computers such as libraries, computer labs or internet cafes, since they require installation on the host machine.

On the other hand, dedicated linguistic search engines sound very promising, especially for the working linguist, although it is probably a little early to attempt a systematic evaluation for what is essentially still at the prototype or development stage.

16.6 Conclusion

Corpora, being electronic collections of authentic texts, are a valuable source of first-hand language data for the empirically minded linguist. For the foreign language learner they afford the possibility to verify in an instant, on-line fashion the many working micro-hypotheses regarding language usage against the material

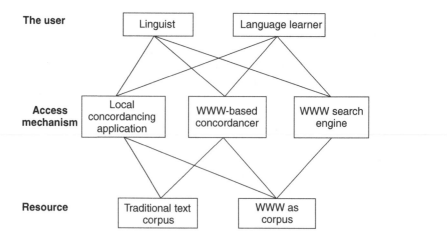

Figure 16.1 Configurations of access to the textual resources of traditional corpora and the World Wide Web by the working linguist and the language learner, divided into three layers.

representing authentic linguistic behaviour of native speakers of the target language. The World Wide Web can, in this context, be viewed as a unique, dynamic corpus.

The different access configurations to textual resources discussed in the present chapter are presented in Fig. 16.1. For ease of exposition, the figure ignores more detailed distinctions into further layers of structure within the search application and the search engine. These distinctions are rather important for the information technology expert, but from our perspective they would complicate the already rather complex relations.

Based on the above comparison of traditional electronic text corpora and the textual resources of the World Wide Web, it can be concluded that the WWW, despite its noisiness and poor balancing, can be an attractive and useful tool for on-line language reference. Its main virtues lie in the impressive size of the resource, and the speed with which it can be trawled using a general-access search engine. Such a configuration can be helpful in instantly resolving the language learner's immediate lexical problems, as well as serve the linguist in some types of situations. The more sophisticated needs of the working linguist may be better fulfilled by means of traditional corpora or the WWW enhanced with a specialized access interface. Plans to put online dedicated linguistic search engines appear to hold much promise in this regard. At the same time, we should keep in mind that the more sophisticated the tool, the greater its complexity and the skills required of the user. In view of the above trade-off relationship, it seems that for some groups of users, particularly language learners, maximally simplified tools will continue to hold the greatest attraction.

Notes

1 I am indebted to Przemysław Kaszubski and Włodzimierz Sobkowiak for their helpful comments on an earlier version of this chapter.
2 In its everyday sense, the internet is understood in the technically narrower sense of the World Wide Web.
3 http://sara.natcorp.ox.ac.uk/lookup.html, http://www.collins.co.uk/Corpus/CorpusSearch.aspx.
4 http://www.titania.bham.ac.uk/docs/about.htm.
5 http://www.cambridge.org/elt/corpus/what_can_corpus_do.htm.
6 http://www.askoxford.com/oec/mainpage/?view=uk.
7 http://www.yahoo.com/.
8 http://google.com.
9 http://www.altavista.com.
10 http://alltheweb.com; I specifically avoid using Google hit counts because of their now infamous instability, on which see e.g. http://aixtal.blogspot.com/2005/03/google-snapshot-of-update.html.
11 Things might be different for syntactically motivated co-occurrence (or colligation, in the terms of Sinclair 1991), where both smaller corpora and dictionaries appear to be mostly adequate.
12 Although attempts, more or less successful, have been made, notably the recent *Oxford Dictionary of Collocations* (Lea 2002).
13 The errors themselves may actually be of interest to linguists, EFL teachers and learners.
14 Of course, such structural bias might actually be an advantage for a researcher of the language of the web interested in, say, document titles.
15 Available from late 2004, initially as a test feature at http://beta.search.msn.com, now incorporated as a standard feature of http://search.live.com, the parameter may be set by dragging a graphic slider with the mouse under the Advanced, Results Ranking option, or directly by appending the popularity tag to the search expression, thus *{popl=0...100}*.
16 In the most common usage, the term *lemmatization* refers to the representation of all inflectional word forms of a lexeme by a citation form, or, in the context of search engines, another inflectional word form of this lexeme. In contrast, *truncation* refers to the use of a simple orthographic substring with a wildcard symbol representing any ending, without a true morphological analysis into lemmas. *Stemming* is often synonymous with *lemmatization*, though it is sometimes used in the same sense as *truncation*.
17 http://search.msn.com.
18 http://www.exalead.com/search.
19 Google's description of the feature at http://www.google.com/help/basics.html suggests some degree of derivational morphological analysis, so that including the word 'dietary' will also find 'diet'. This feature appears to be selectively active, for the less frequent keywords only.

20 It is worth noting at this junction that the prototype of chronologically the first
   search engine, Alta Vista, owes a lot to linguistic insight (Kilgarriff 2003).
21 http://lse.umiacs.umd.edu:8080, requires registration.
22 http://www.webcorp.org.uk/webcorp_linguistic_search_engine.html.
23 http://www.webcorp.org.uk.
24 http://www.niederlandistik.fu-berlin.de/cgi-bin/web-conc.cgi.
25 http://ell.phil.tu-chemnitz.de/cgi5/run.pl.
26 http://82.182.103.45/culler/.
27 http://www.kwicfinder.com.

CHAPTER

17

Building and Analysing Corpora of Computer-Mediated Communication

Brian King

This chapter addresses problems encountered during the construction and analysis of a synchronic corpus of computer-mediated discourse. The corpus was not primarily constructed for the examination of the linguistic idiosyncrasies of the online chatting medium; rather it is to be used for corpus-based sociolinguistic inquiry into the language use and identity construction of a particular social group (which in this case could be classed as 'vulnerable'). Therefore the corpus data needed considerable adaptation during compilation and analysis to prevent those idiosyncrasies from acting as noise in the data. Adaptations include responses to spam (in the form of 'adbots'), cyber-orthography, the ubiquity of names, overlapping conversations and challenges of annotation. Difficulties with gaining participant permissions and demographic information also required significant attention. Attempted solutions to these corpus construction and analysis challenges, which are closely bound to the fields of both cyber-research and corpus linguistics, are outlined.

17.1 Introduction

The usefulness of any given corpus, whether 'general-use' or 'project-based', 'raw' or 'annotated' (Beißwenger and Storrer 2007: 3), hinges upon sound corpus construction. As Lew (this volume) notes, the textual content of the Web is a serious competitor to traditional language corpora. Even if one does not use the whole Web as a corpus, it is still possible to 'harvest' a range of different text types from it. When contemplating the construction of a corpus for the purpose of investigating the language used during computer-mediated communication (CMC), the compiler could be forgiven for initially feeling somewhat smug about the task. The fact that the data is already digitized means that the time-consuming hurdle of electronic rendering can be sidestepped. In the case of the corpus analyst, however, the glow of relief soon fades because many hidden incompatibilities soon emerge between CMC data and corpus study. The purpose of this chapter is to explore solutions to the specific challenges that arise while compiling, annotating and analysing a corpus of 'synchronous' online communication (i.e. chat-room conversation) (see Beißwenger and Storrer 2007), using my own experience of building a 'chat-room corpus' where the majority of the participants were (or at least claimed to be) gay men. While all research involving human participants requires the researcher to address ethics, this particular case study also raises additional ethical concerns due to the potentially vulnerable nature of the participants (e.g. some men may not have disclosed their sexuality in 'real life', which raises issues about anonymity, confidentiality and obtaining consent).

This exploration will be structured as 'a walk through' the corpus project, from conception to analysis, revealing the attempted solutions to corpus-analytic problems encountered during that specific project, while also suggesting possible improvements. Creating a corpus involves countless subjective decisions, resulting in a need for step-by-step transparency about how the corpus used in a study has been constructed and analysed (Hunston 2002: 123). It is in this spirit that I shall proceed.

17.2 Corpus Construction

17.2.1 General Guidelines

Constructing a corpus requires attention to well-established (though continually evolving) guidelines for corpus size, representativeness, population sampling, and ethics of data collection. Numerous scholars have published useful information about these topics, including general advice (e.g. Biber et al. 1998; Kennedy 1998; McEnery and Wilson 2001; Meyer 2002; Baker 2006) as well as more specialized suggestions (e.g. Stenström et al. 2002; Dollinger 2006; Fritz 2006; Garcia et al. 2006; Lancashire 2006; Markus 2006). When constructing a corpus of synchronous CMC data one must strive to make the corpus as large as possible (in relation to the resources and time available) and gather the data in a way that attempts to include the full range of people, topics and whatever other variables might exist in the environment from which one is drawing the data. Similarly, all corpus compilers must be concerned with the ethics of data collection (see Section 17.4.1).

17.2.2 Digital Data: A Blessing Well-Disguised

Some of the general challenges that CMC data bring to corpus construction and analysis have been outlined by Beißwenger and Storrer (2007), who address the coding of hyperlinks and emoticons, the degree to which one might preserve the original screen layout, and the 'capturing of metadata' unique to online environments (e.g. delineating program functions versus user input). Claridge (2007) narrows focus for a specific look at the construction of corpora which consist exclusively of 'asynchronous' online communication (i.e. online message boards). Some problems identified by Beißwenger and Storrer are presented again by Claridge, but with suggested solutions for the purposes of corpus compilation and annotation. Specific issues Claridge raises for message-board data include quote-induced representativeness (the common tendency on message boards to quote sections of the posts of others and then respond to them), typos and misspellings, the need to encode graphic elements of some message boards (such as pictures and creative uses of punctuation), and the need to separate users' postings from language that repeats in the user interface (e.g. user signatures and prompts). The next section begins with relevant background to the study and then the article proceeds with a focus on solutions (both attempted and hypothetical) to problems which arose when compiling, preparing and analysing the corpus.

17.3 Background to the Project

17.3.1 Why a Queer[1] Chat-Room Corpus?

Starting with the conception of this corpus, its initial construction occurred as part of a project designed to examine *how* language is used to create social spaces in which queer sexual desires and/or sexual identities can be explored by individuals or communities.[2] The sociolinguistic investigation outlined in this paper could have proceeded without corpus analysis. However, it was decided that a combination of qualitative and quantitative analyses might enrich insights into 'the how' of language and queer spatiality by querying 'the who' plus 'the when' and 'the how often' on a larger scale than purely qualitative studies allow (cf. Baker 2005). By starting with a large body of data and commencing analysis with word lists and concordances created by the corpus software, the hope was that unexpected linguistic patterns might emerge. To put it another way, the hope was to minimize the effects of my own assumptions (as a white, western, middle-class, thirty-something gay man) concerning language use by queer participants. I say minimize rather than eliminate because intuition unavoidably still plays a role in corpus analysis (Hunston 2002: 22). Certainly looking at the data while wearing what I will call 'lavender-coloured glasses'[3] gives me the eyes (i.e. intuition) to see important patterns in the discourse of queer spaces (patterns that other eyes might miss). Of course it sometimes pays to remove those same spectacles in order to see patterns that might be hidden by those lenses, which is where the unbiased overview afforded by a corpus-driven analysis is especially helpful. A researcher (especially one with existing links to the population he or she is studying) may notice interesting features in the data, but a corpus analysis is more likely to highlight other aspects of the data, based on frequency and co-occurrence patterns, that might be overlooked by human eyes.

17.3.2 Peering over the Lavender-Coloured Glasses

Once the decision was made to complement qualitative discourse analysis with quantitative corpus analysis, corpus construction began. Between 27 October and 29 November 2005, data were gathered from the 'public' spaces of a number of queer chat-rooms. The resulting texts of the conversations were copied and pasted into word processing files and stored for future processing. By 29 November, there were about 300,000 words of data. In order to discover what words were present in the data a word list was created using Wordsmith 4. Baker (2006: 143–6) describes

Table 17.1 Examples of camp name conversions.

Participant	Turn	Original Nickname
A. Blueintown:	daveypoo is hot	(daveguy71)
B. Huntindan:	pervy only begins to cover it with soldierette	(soldierstud)
C. Dunstonnu:	GEEEEOOOORRRGGGIIIIIEEEE!!!!	(george44)
D. Homolulu23:	hola lolalarry	(ManLarry)

how one way of analysing corpus data involves semantically tagging all of the lexical items in the corpus in order to get an idea of which semantic categories are frequent or salient (when compared against a reference corpus). One issue that arises, however, is that traditional semantic taggers, for example, the USAS annotation scheme (Wilson and Thomas 1997) used by the tagger in WMatrix (Piao et al. 2005) would not be able to cope well with much of the language use in chat-rooms. Taggers normally require data that contain grammatically and orthographically 'correct' constructions, while chat-room data is often 'messy' or contains unusual (by written published standards) grammar or orthography (see Table 17.1 for examples). Therefore, rather than semantically tagging the corpus, I carried out an examination of an untagged word list, and grouped words that had similar semantic functions together by hand. I refer to these as 'key categories' (after Baker 2006: 143) although I have not carried out comparisons with reference corpora in order to obtain a measure of the statistical keyness of such categories.

By checking the concordance lines, and often by returning to the original source text, every incident of a word was checked in order to ensure that it was used in a way that was appropriate for the key category. For example, one such key category was 'Camp Names', which was subsequently selected for analysis (for details as to why it was selected, see King 2006, 2011). The composition of this key category is briefly outlined below.

As can be seen in Table 17.1, chat-room users alter the nicknames of other users. Out of concern for privacy, I've changed the participants' nicknames in Table 17.1, but effort was made to replace them with names similar to the original and convert them to Camp Names in a comparable manner. The term 'Camp Names' is inspired by historic studies of gay culture (see Chauncey 1994; Baker and Stanley 2003). Examples of camp names that Chauncey gives are *Toto* (named after the little dog in Wizard of Oz), *Maxine* (instead of Max) and *Blossom* (merely for its feminine ring). Similar but not identical to Chauncey's description, included in this category are name exclamations (see example C in Table 17.1). The use of 'catty femininity' by gay men (like 'screechy' greetings) challenges assumptions about how men talk (Harvey 2000: 253). Name diminutives have also been included in this category; that is suffixes added to names (connoting smallness, daintiness or babiness) and feminizations of names. For example, the hypothetical nickname *bigbear* might be changed to *bigbearette*, or perhaps *shane2231* might change to *shaniqua* (an oblique reference to pop divas) or to *shaneypoo*. There are diverse examples in the data, but tokens classified as Camp Names for this study are all transformations of online nicknames in one of the above ways.[4] In Section 17.6, I show how analysis of Camp Names was carried out. However, before this, I wish to return to corpus construction in order to look closely at how certain challenges with chat-room data are best dealt with while gathering and compiling the data.

17.4 Compiling the Queer Chat-Room Corpus (Problems and Solutions)

17.4.1 Eschewing the Online Research Paparazzi[5] (Corpus Ethics)

Ethical corpus construction is taken seriously by many researchers, and often considerable time is spent gaining permission to use print and spoken sources in a corpus (Kennedy 1998: 76). Obtaining informed consent online can be intensely difficult because of participant anonymity. This problem can be solved by gathering data from websites which enable communication with anonymous participants via e-mail. This was done for this corpus, and it offered an avenue for the ethical collection of corpus data. The remainder of this section explains the solutions which made the compiling of this corpus ethically (thus practically) possible. Without nuanced attention to ethics, chat-room corpora cannot be compiled, and the hope here is to provide other constructors of corpora with ideas that navigate the specific needs of participants in online chat-rooms.

Using e-mail addresses attached to online aliases, the chat-room participants were contacted. In order to facilitate this communication, a website group was set up with detailed information about what had been done already and what was to come. Figure 1 contains the original invitation e-mail that was sent to all those whose words could potentially end up in the corpus, informing them that I had saved files of their conversations, and asking for them to join the website group if they wished to be better informed.[6] All of the copied conversations were also posted on the website so that participants could scrutinize them and let me know if they wanted me to delete anything. Access to this website was strictly by invitation, so although those conversations had been taken out of their original context, they remained accessible only to those who might potentially have viewed them in the first place (namely those with registered nicknames). As Reid (1996) has stressed, it is doubtful whether the authors of CMC intend their words to be transferred to a different public domain, like print media or academic reports. Therefore, once participants had been informed, consent was needed to take those words and transfer them to a different public domain (the corpus and published analyses).

Participants were told their chat sessions had been saved in computer files. This sequence works contrary to the idea that participants in a corpus must be informed of 'recording' in advance (Baker et al. 2006: 68). Such prohibitions have been based on spoken data, and surreptitious recording of public spoken conversations is a practice that is considered unethical and which has become unacceptable in

---

You're invited!
Come join Queer Chatting Study.

Description: This group has been specially made in order to communicate with the men on XXX.com whose words I want to study.

[**Join now**]

_____ wrote you this personal note:

Hello, my name is _____, and I am a XXX.com user. I need your permission, please.

Back in October/November, I copied some public chat sessions from XXX.com and saved them on my computer. Some of your words appear in those files. I want to study those chat sessions and write a paper about them for my _____. Even though the data I gathered were from public chat-rooms, I still need your consent to study them.

Please join this private MSN Group, where you can learn more. This group is private, so only those invited can attend. It is for information and questions only.

All nicknames and places will be changed if I quote someone in the essay. If you really do not mind, you do not have to do anything. Joining the group merely gives you access to information about what I'm doing. There will be no monitoring of your chatting or further e-mails. I hope you will check it out.

Sincerely, _____ _____

» **Join the group* and you can:**

Post a message on the Message Board
Add some photos to the Photo Album

[**Join now**]

*Because this is a Private Group, you must **join the group** before access is allowed.

Figure 17.1 Invitation e-mail to chat-room participants.

language research (Cameron 2001). In online chat-rooms, though, saving public chat texts is a common practice (Kendall 2002: 60), so this procedure is often not viewed in the same way in cyber-research, perhaps because chat-room talk tends to blur the distinction between public and private. It could be argued that the difference is trivial because regardless of any perceived difference, researchers need to maintain certain standards of inquiry. However, on this point, a teleological view was taken because of the anonymous and spontaneous nature of online chat-rooms. The advantages of learning more about this form of language use were balanced against the questionability of surreptitious text copying, and it was decided (given the careful plan of action outlined in this section) that social harm would be mitigated. Once participants had been informed of the fact that their conversations had been saved, their consent had to be sought to continue to the next step (inclusion in the corpus).

Informed consent is not straightforward where queer corpus participants are concerned because of the increased need for measures to protect them from harm, considering prejudice in society against queer sexualities. Martin and Knox (2000) assert that 'gay and lesbian' (in this case, queer) participants should be allowed to give their consent anonymously if they so choose because written consent does not allow for added protection. They instead suggest 'implied consent' in the form of optional questionnaires, for example, in which consent is implied if participants send it in. If they choose not to send it, they have not consented. For this corpus, a modified version of implied consent was used. In the initial invitation to join the information website (see Fig. 17.1), it was stated that if they did not mind their words being used for study purposes, then they could signal their consent by remaining silent. In this way, they were permitted to remain anonymous yet give consent. Those who wanted to know more had the opportunity to join the website and get more actively involved. Finally, those who wanted to be excluded could contact me by e-mail, anonymously requesting that their online nickname and its accompanying text be deleted. There were no requests for exclusion received, while only 35 participants chose to come to the website and look at the data. Admittedly, it is possible that some participants might not have received the e-mail, but during the examination of participant profiles, it was noted that the vast majority viewed their accounts regularly. The idea that silence implies consent remains problematic, but these strategies manoeuvred along a difficult line between protection and consent, taking into consideration the specific needs of various participants.

17.4.2 Old Issues Encountered, New Solutions Required

Although sampling and representativeness are important during the construction of any corpus, there are some concerns which are specific to chat-room corpora. One such concern is the fact that one cannot be sure that participants are who, or where, they claim to be. This is also true of asynchronous CMC corpora (Claridge 2007: 94), but with chat-rooms it is possible to be selective about which chat-rooms to draw data from, in order to maximize the likelihood that the researcher can collect reliable demographic information. For example, in this case data were taken from chat-rooms named after cities in the United States and Australia because in such rooms (on this website) there is a basic assumption among those 'present' that the majority of people chatting there are in that city and hoping to meet face to face later (cf. Shaw 1997). In many cases they encounter offline acquaintances and friends there. There will be others who have logged in for a chat from afar, but other chat-rooms are provided for that kind of interaction, which are not 'anchored' to real-world locations. As there is always a concern then, that some users in CMC contexts will be classified incorrectly, it is essential for the researcher to acknowledge the level of potential for such incorrect classifications (although this should not mean that CMC research is infeasible).

As Meyer (2002: 49) points out, even with written or spoken corpora, data failing to match one's criteria inevitably creep in, but there is really no sure-fire way to balance features such as urban/rural, regional variation, sexual identity and race; rather the best one can do is deal with them as much as possible during corpus construction. For example, I tried not to collect a disproportionate amount of data from rooms which contained participants from large urban centres (even though such rooms tended to produce the most data). As Cameron and Kulick (2003: 85) have asserted, too often rural queer perspectives have been elided from language analyses in the past, so I attempted not to repeat this error. Another factor with online chat is that it can take place at any time of the day, and topics or moods could be affected by shifting social circumstances. For example on weekday afternoons, some participants are likely to be at work, while on Friday or Saturday nights, a 'party' atmosphere can develop. For this reason, the data were gathered seven days a week at various times (afternoon, evening and late at night) in order to avoid an overabundance of topics or styles that might dominate on certain days or at certain times of the day/night. Thus 'where' online chat-room participants are located and 'when' their chatting occurs can be somewhat controlled. However, the 'who' of chat-room participants is a more difficult question to address.

In most cases, when researchers are studying any type of online interaction, it is impossible to gather demographic data on the research participants. This problem is caused by the anonymity of much online interaction. One solution to this dilemma is to collect data from chat-rooms in which participants create personal public profiles for the purpose of conveying as much truthful information as possible about their corporeal selves, which was the solution employed in this project. From those profiles, I was able to construct Tables 17.2–17.4. Once again, this information is not verifiable, and some chat-room participants can be fluid about their self-descriptions (e.g. Laukkanen 2007). As outlined in the section on location above, though, it can be presumed that most were being reasonably forthright due to the desire to meet face to face (although some participants may change certain aspects of their identity – such as their age, in order to appear more widely attractive). As with all corpora, a certain level of uncertainty concerning the sources of the data must be accepted. I hope this section has demonstrated that by choosing carefully 'where' the data is drawn from and when, it is possible to get a representative corpus with sound sampling for sociolinguistic study.

Tables 17.2–17.4 show my efforts to create balanced corpora. While it was relatively easy to collect large amounts of data from both the American and Australian, and under 40 and over 40 demographics, Table 17.2 shows that most of the data were taken from white participants. However, this was reflective of what was actually happening in the chat-rooms I took data from, where the majority of the participants *were* white. Additionally, as Tables 17.3 and 17.4 show, while it was easier to balance the amount of participants from rural and urban concentrations in America, this proved to be more difficult in Australia, where most of the contributions I collected were from participants in urban areas. Clearly then, while balanced corpora allow for more accurate comparisons, corpus builders are also likely to be restricted by what is available to collect in the real world. Additionally, corpus

Table 17.2 Demographic information about chat-room participants (age, ethnicity, sexual identity). Where a field contains two sets of numbers (percentages and raw counts), the top set refers to the number of participants, and the bottom set refers to the number of turns taken in conversation.

		US over 40	*US under 40*	*AU over 40*	*AU under 40*
Number of participants		372	468	193	298
Turns	*Total turns*	18,045	16,234	11,363	15,192
	Mean turns	48	35	59	51
Age	*Median age*	48	30	47	31
Race	White	90% (336)	72% (337)	89% (172)	77% (228)
		89% (16133)	69% (11230)	88% (9956)	76% (11545)
	Unspecified	3% (10)	4% (19)	8% (15)	10% (31)
		5% (933)	5% (824)	6% (692)	14% (2172)
	Latino	1% (5)	4% (19)	–	–
		2% (319)	4% (700)		
	Asian	2% (7)	7% (32)	2% (4)	4% (13)
		2% (333)	10% (1557)	1% (81)	3% (453)
	Mixed	3% (12)	8% (37)	<1% (1)	7% (20)
		2% (309)	5% (851)	5% (530)	6% (923)
	Black	<1% (2)	4% (17)	–	–
		<1% (18)	6% (956)		
	All others	–	2% (7)	<1% (1)	2% (6)
			1% (116)	<1% (104)	<1% (99)
Sexual identity	Gay	81% (301)	77% (362)	71% (137)	63% (189)
		81% (14665)	77% (12420)	82% (9318)	68% (10318)
	Bisexual	7% (27)	3% (16)	10% (19)	5% (16)
		9% (1660)	3% (540)	4% (485)	4% (627)
	Unspecified	8% (30)	16% (73)	18% (34)	28% (84)
		8% (1450)	18% (2895)	13% (1521)	27% (4061)
	Queer	–	3% (12)	–	–
			2% (259)		
	All others	4% (14)	2% (7)	2% (3)	3% (9)
		2% (270)	<1% (120)	<1% (39)	<1% (186)

builders need to decide the extent to which their corpus accurately reflects the actual frequencies of types of people in a given population (in this case, gay chat-room users) or tries to balance every single variable so that every *possible* type of person is represented in the data equally (even if this does not reflect the reality of usage patterns). Along with availability of data, the sorts of research foci (e.g. what does the researcher want to compare) are likely to play a role in what is eventually collected. As my main comparison variables are location (Australia vs America)

Table 17.3 Demographic information about American chat-room
participants (location).[7]

Location		US over 40	US under 40
Specific area of the US	South	28% (103)	20% (93)
		52% (9461)	22% (3604)
	Midwest	28% (104)	20% (95)
		22% (3924)	18% (2972)
	West	17% (63)	25% (115)
		9% (1683)	26% (4289)
	New England	6% (22)	8% (38)
		4% (744)	6% (892)
	Middle Atlantic	11% (41)	9% (43)
		4% (792)	8% (1281)
	Southwest	6% (24)	8% (38)
		4% (672)	7% (1176)
	Hawaii	2% (8)	6% (29)
		3% (539)	9% (1532)
	Alaska	1% (4)	4% (17)
		<1% (113)	3% (432)
	Uncertain	1% (3)	<1% (3)
		<1% (117)	<1% (56)
Population concentration	Rural	52% (192)	47% (222)
		43% (7762)	41% (6684)
	Urban	48% (180)	53% (246)
		57% (10247)	59% (9550)

and age (over and under 40), these were the most important factors that I took
into account when collecting data (see also Oakes' discussion of taking multiple
variables into account, this volume).

17.4.3 Noisy Writing – What Counts as Valid Chat-Room Data?

Once confronted with the raw data, decisions had to be made about what to include
in the corpus. Although, ideally, keeping all contributions would seem like the
right thing to do, it soon became obvious that some contributions were problematic. For instance, a pattern was noticed in which people who contributed less
than five lines in one session were either adbots (automatic advertising programs
masquerading as participants) who always repeated the same line (which could
skew the data) or they were reticent participants, contributing nothing beyond
brief phatic communication (e.g. 'Hello, room'). After much deliberation, it was
decided that these contributions were not valuable enough to keep because even

Table 17.4 Demographic information about Australian chat-room participants (location).

Location		AU over 40	AU under 40
Specific area of Australia	New South Wales	36% (69)	25% (74)
		50% (5693)	24% (3609)
	Victoria	45% (87)	40% (118)
		31% (3540)	36% (5510)
	Queensland	17% (33)	32% (95)
		19% (2101)	38% (5834)
	South Australia	1% (2)	1% (5)
		<1% (17)	1% (95)
	All others	<1% (1)	2% (6)
		<1% (12)	1% (144)
Population concentration	Rural	17% (33)	11% (34)
		13% (1514)	9% (1324)
	Urban	83% (160)	89% (264)
		87% (9849)	91% (13868)

though they were part of the queer space under examination, the number of participants needed to be restricted because of limitations on my time and energy. Such brief contributors were relatively easy to remove with the use of Microsoft Word's 'find all' function to locate all instances of each nickname and then carrying out a word count on the resulting selected words. If the count was less than five, then the nicknames were shaded grey. After this process was finished, all shaded turns could be removed. Despite efforts to limit inclusion, there were still a large number of participants (1,321). Limiting the number of participants (while maintaining adequate corpus size) became a particularly important balancing effort. I wanted to avoid a punishing regime of work although, ethically, I felt motivated to communicate with the participants. With greater human resources, it would be advisable to keep all data in the corpus but tag suspected adbot and reticent-user turns in such a way that they can be ignored by analysis software if desired.

Another issue is the fact that some participants are 'casual senders' and some 'heavy senders' of text (Claridge 2007: 93); hence to simply count each participant equally can give a skewed perception of the demographic breakdown of a sample. For this reason, in this study the counts were based on the number of turns taken (see Tables 17.2–17.4). Turns were counted rather than words because turns could be easily tallied during the culling process described in the previous paragraph whereas to count the words of each participant would have been much more time consuming. With a team of researchers it would be more ideal to count the number of words. Counting turns as well as participants builds into the demographic summary the fact that one participant (e.g. a black, bisexual man in New York) might be a very heavy sender of text, meaning that his 'voice' or 'style' is present in the data to a disproportionate level. Counting him simply as one participant in the categories 'black' and 'bisexual' would fail to represent his contribution to the data accurately. So by counting the number of participants in each category as well as the number of turns they contributed to the corpus, a more accurate picture is presented concerning how much of the data in a corpus represents different categories of people, allowing one to adjust if necessary.

17.5 Annotating the Queer Chat-Room Corpus (Problems and Solutions)

The issue of noise in chat-room data certainly does not end once a corpus has been selectively compiled. In fact it is during annotation of a chat-room corpus that one truly begins to encounter the full variety of ways in which chat-room data can confound traditional corpus analysis. The primary roadblocks come in the form of cyber-orthography, randomly intertwined turn taking, and creative modes of expression which are unique to the chat-room medium. As Claridge (2007) reveals, some of these challenges also apply to asynchronous data like message boards, but corpus analysis of chat-room data has its own specific difficulties.

17.5.1 Cyber-orthography[8]

In many chat-room interactions accuracy is often sacrificed for speed. As participants type their contributions (sometimes frantically), hoping to keep up with fast-paced conversations, niceties like the backspace key, capitalization or punctuation can be ignored. Though accurate typing can confer a type of status among internet users, for the most part one is forgiven for a certain level of poor spelling and a reasonable number of typing errors. Hence there are many more typos than one would find even in asynchronous CMC because participants in message boards can edit their responses more carefully before posting them (more like an e-mail). Word truncations and misspellings can also be purposeful key-stroke-saving measures, and the ability to follow the conversation in spite of all these orthographic 'sins' can be an important aspect of in-group solidarity. Only newbies are confused by strings like 'wut r u up 2' (i.e. what are you up to). The problems that cyber-orthography creates for corpus analysis software are likely to be self-evident, but they are not wholly insurmountable problems, as will become more clear.

When dealing with vast amounts of data, the use of corpus tagging software can make a significant difference to the analyst's ability to handle the project. Common motivations for using automatic taggers include the desire to tag words according to their parts of speech or semantic categories. Without either automatic assistance or a large team of researchers, this level of annotation would be impossible in large corpora. Indeed even in the corpus for this study (a modest

300,000 words), without a tagger trained to handle chat-room data, manual gram-matical annotation would be a daunting task. Cyber-orthography sits in the way of automatic tagging of chat-room data because grammatical taggers such as CLAWS (Garside and Smith 1997), although trained to handle massive corpora of written discourse with impressive accuracy, are unable to handle cyber-orthography in a satisfactory manner (Ooi 2001: 95). Spelling variation is not a problem unique to CMC data. Corpus analysts who work with historical data have also put considera-ble resources into developing automatic tagging software that can successfully deal with Early-Modern English texts and their spelling variations (Archer et al. 2003; Rayson et al. 2005, 2007; Pilz et al. 2008). There is also effort being put into developing software that can better deal with CMC data (e.g. Ooi et al. 2006). These efforts to improve the efficiency of automatic taggers hold promise for the future, but for this study other strategies for dealing with spelling variation were required.

As this corpus was conceived as a basis for sociolinguistic-oriented discourse analysis, semantic and grammatical tagging (although potentially very useful) were not essential. By focussing on key categories (e.g. Camp Names – see Section 17.3.2) the task of carrying out a meaningful analysis became manageable because it was possible to use the 'find' and 'replace' functions from Microsoft Word in order to tag each token with its corresponding category name. This required a detailed reading of the word list, but each time suitable new words or spelling variations of existing category members were found, they were simply assigned to the broader key category. An example of this is that *chest* was sometimes spelt as *chst* – both versions received the same semantic tag in my categorization scheme. This was a tedious task, but manageable for one person considering the relatively small size of the corpus. The amount of work can also be minimized through the informed use of spreadsheet software to compile lists along with plenty of elec-tronic cutting, pasting and sorting. In this way, it became possible to at least draw frequency counts from chat-room data.

17.5.2 Turns for the Worse

Turn-taking in chat rooms is problematic for corpus analysis because conversa-tional turns are displayed in the order that the chat client (i.e. software of the chat-ting website) receives them. Compound this with the fact that one participant will often split one turn into many in order to keep up with the flow of conversation, and it soon becomes clear that concordance lines and collocational analysis are adversely affected. Table 17.5 shows an example from the chat-room corpus.

This example also raises the issue of separating turn markers (e.g. Joe_345:) from turn utterance, an issue that complicates word counts and collocations. As has been done with corpora of spoken data, this was dealt with by tagging all nick-names within turn prompts so that the software can easily be set to ignore them (e.g. <Joe_345>:). One must be careful to check the corpus for other creative uses of symbols such as '<' because their presence in the chat text (e.g. as an arrow <---) could cause problems with the software's analysis. Therefore, the colons (used by

Table 17.5 Extract from the chat-room.

1	Joe_345:	Hi everyone
2	Joe_345:	whats up this avo
3	Don_987:	hi Joe,
4	Joe_345:	in virtual lalaland?
5	Don_987:	my favourite chat buddy

this particular chat client to mark turns) were replaced with the symbol '|' because it was found to be absent in the corpus, whereas colons were often used in other contexts apart from marking turns. Names create further challenges because of 'addressivity' (a term taken from Werry 2004[1996]). Addressivity is a common conversation strategy in online chatting in which participants type the name of their addressee in order to get around the fact that it is not always clear who one is addressing due to intertwined turn display (see Section 17.5.2). As far as possible (despite variant spellings of nicknames by other participants as part of cyber-orthography as well as social forms of name manipulation), names within the chat text also need to be marked so that they can be ignored if necessary (e.g. 'Hi <Joe_345> what's up . . ..'). Failure to do so will result in word lists dominated by these names, which are more often noise than data. In the mark-up process, one should tag them as nicknames in preparation for those moments when it might be useful to include them in analysis.

The '|' symbol was set to be the boundary for all collocational analyses. Even though it would be ideal if one could treat lines 1 and 2 in Table 17.5 as one turn (with no collocational boundary after 'everyone'), while still treating lines 2 and 3 as separate turns (with a collocational boundary after 'avo') this is not possible unless one is willing to manually tag all turn markers (highly impractical). The solution suggested above is a workable compromise because for the most part turns are split into phrases and clauses (as in Table 17.5). Therefore one can still pull useful collocational data from the corpus despite losing some collocations to turn-splitting. This strategy also allowed the analyst to see the boundaries between speakers in concordance lines (marked by '|'), and of course if desired, the turn markers could be 'un-ignored' to facilitate reading of the text in its original context.

17.6 Analysing the Chat-Room Corpus (Problems and Solutions)

17.6.1 Sociolinguistic and Social Categories

As previously stated it was decided in this study to examine who was using various word categories, how frequently and in which situations. In order to do so the data needed to be manipulated in such a way that a key category such as Camp Names could be linked to the social categories of the person using that category during chat-room interaction. I adopted a system for conducting 'sociopragmatic annotation' (see Archer and Culpeper 2003; Archer 2005: 107–20), as it provides a useful model for preparing a corpus for sociolinguistic and pragmatic analysis. Under this system, a '<u> element' (inspired by the Text Encoding Initiative) is attached to every utterance, and it contains social information about the speaker (Archer 2005: 109). In this way, utterances can readily be linked to participants from various social categories. This system was applied to the chat-room corpus, making use of the demographic information summarized in Tables 17.2–17.4. The turn-marking nickname of each utterance was elaborated in the following way:

e.g. <u id='Joe_345' sexid='g' age='+' loc='au' race='w'>| *Hi everyone*</u>

This string identifies the participant whose turn was comprised of 'Hi everyone' as Joe_345, his sexual identity is gay ('g'), his age is over 40 ('+'), he is located in Australia ('au'), and his race is white ('w'). Using 'find and replace' on Microsoft Word, every instance of 'Joe_345:' in the corpus was replaced with the above string of information (remembering to include the colon so as to differentiate the turn-marking function of his name from the use of Joe_345 as a term of address by other participants). Then each paragraph mark (which must be typed as '^p' in the find field of Microsoft Word) was replaced with the string </u>^p. The result was that '</u>' was then placed at the end of every turn in the corpus. Because of the processing limits of automatic tagging software, sociopragmatic annotation remains a manually implemented, time-consuming approach, but at least one is left with text that allows the connection of social categories with the target language.

Once age and location had been chosen as categories for investigation, the sociopragmatic annotation allowed Camp Names to be counted by the software in relation to these two criteria. Within each file, the sequence of the chat-rooms was based upon country first, then region and finally date. Therefore data from the Atlanta Room were filed with data from the Mississippi Room (both being part of the USA South region), while Atlanta Room data from 5th November were filed before data from the same room on 12th November. Considering that the regions, dates and order of utterances were maintained, dispersion plots (charts that show whether terms are spread evenly throughout the corpus or gathered in particular places) could also be calculated using the entire corpus.

17.6.2 Investigating Context

In order to gain more insight into the contexts with which Camp Names are used in the various files, it was necessary to look closely at the concordance lines produced by Wordsmith. A coding scheme was created for the contexts in which Camp Names were used. This scheme was created as part of a process that Hunston (2002: 52) calls 'hypothesis testing', in which one views a small set of

Table 17.6 Camp names – context counts.

	US over 40	*US under 40*	*AU over 40*	*AU under 40*
Greetings and farewells	40%	45%	61%	61%
Addressivity	32%	38%	34%	32%
3rd Person reference	28%	17%	5%	7%

randomly selected lines in order to hypothesize about larger patterns and subsequently test those hypotheses. To clarify, Hunston reports that Sinclair (1999) advocates selecting 30 random concordance lines, observing the patterns in them, and then doing it again until no new patterns emerge. This was first done with the US+40 file because there were too many concordance lines to analyse them in their entirety. Following that process, there were three contexts as part of the coding scheme: Greetings and Farewells (e.g. 'STEVIIIIIIIIEEEEEE!!' or 'Hi, Steviepoops'), Addressivity (e.g. 'Steviepoops, I have a new DVD') and Third-Person References (e.g. 'John, Steviepoops doesn't need you tonight'). Once the encoding scheme had been created, based on a sample of the data, it was applied to all of the Camp Names in the whole corpus.

Table 17.6 displays the percentages of each context found in the four corpora after the source text was consulted to verify the context of each Camp Name sample. The various contexts (e.g. 'CAMPNAMES_G' – meaning Camp Name used in a 'greeting') were counted by Wordsmith Tools. Clear differences in this table include the larger number of Camp Names used by Australians in greetings and farewells (regardless of age) as well as the larger number of references to third parties in the United States over 40 corpus (indeed in the US corpora in general). It is difficult to speculate about what has caused these differences, but what is more striking is the basic similarity of the sub-corpora in terms of the contexts in which Camp Names are used. All three categories (greetings/farewells, addressivity and third-person reference) appear to various degrees in all the sub-corpora.

17.6.3 Investigating Frequency

One indicator of patterns of discourse is frequency of use. The frequencies of Camp Names in each file were then calculated by conducting counts of the tag 'CAMPNAME' using Wordsmith Tools software. To be able to demonstrate the patterns of frequency of Camp Names, it is necessary to investigate four null hypotheses in order to discover whether any differences in counts can be attributed to anything other than chance. The chi-square test is often used, but Dunning (1993) has proposed the log-likelihood calculation instead. He asserts that the chi-square test was developed to work with large datasets in which the data are very evenly distributed. The log-likelihood test, on the other hand, can be applied to 'very much smaller volumes of text . . . [and enable] comparisons to be made between the significance of the occurrences of both rare and common phenomena' (Dunning 1993: 62–3). Although it is difficult to say whether or not the data at hand would be classified as rare, his arguments are logical and other corpus linguists have adopted the log-likelihood test, particularly Baker (2005) and Meyer (2002). In this study the statistical significance of differences in the data counts was calculated using Paul Rayson's online *Log Likelihood Calculator* at the UCREL website. This calculator takes the size of each sub-corpus into consideration while calculating the probability (written as the value 'p') that any difference in word count is because of chance. Rayson (2008) provides a detailed explanation of how the log-likelihood test is conducted mathematically. For this study, the choice was made to trust the figures produced by the calculator.

Table 17.7 outlines the null hypotheses and summarizes whether they were accepted or rejected after statistical analysis. In Table 17.7, null hypothesis 1 must be rejected when US + 40 is compared to AU + 40 and null hypothesis 3 must be rejected when US + 40 is compared to US – 40. In both cases US + 40 contains a much higher relative frequency of Camp Names. To reject a null hypothesis means to reject the idea that differences in frequency are the result of mere chance, whereas to accept it is to admit that chance occurrence explains the frequency differences. Statistical analysis of Camp Names in the four sub-corpora clearly shows that they are used most frequently by the over-40 Americans, with no real difference in frequency between the other three cohorts. Table 17.8 shows the statistical data that were produced by comparing the frequencies of Camp Names according to locality. Chart A compares the number of Camp Names used by participants over 40 in the USA (US + 40) with those over 40 in Australia (AU + 40) and chart B compares the number of Camp Names used by participants under 40 in both

Table 17.7 Null hypotheses for camp names (locality and age).

	Null hypothesis	*Result*
1	Differences in the **frequency of Camp Names** between **AU over 40 and US over 40** are a result of chance.	Rejected
2	Differences in the **frequency of Camp Names** between **AU under 40 and US under 40** are a result of chance.	Accepted
3	Differences in the **frequency of Camp Names** between **US over 40 and US under 40** are a result of chance.	Rejected
4	Differences in the **frequency of Camp Names** between **AU over 40 and AU under 40** are a result of chance.	Accepted

Table 17.8 Camp names – log likelihood values by locality.

		AU over 40 <-> US over 40				AU under 40 <-> US under 40		
		Camp names	*Total words*				*Camp names*	*Total words*
A	AU + 40	44	50,711	B	AU – 40	46		74,447
	US + 40	166	84,750		US – 40	62		75,449
	Log Lklhd	26.57			Log Lklhd	2.17		
	p	< 0.001 US+40			p	INSIGNIFICANT		
	null hypothesis 1 is rejected				null hypothesis 2 is accepted			

Table 17.9 Camp names – log likelihood values by age.

		US over 40 <-> US under 40				AU over 40 <-> AU under 40		
		Camp names	*Total words*				*Camp names*	*Total words*
A	US + 40	166	84,750	B	AU + 40	44		50,711
	US – 40	62	75,449		AU – 40	46		74,447
	Log Lklhd	37.92			Log Lklhd	2.57		
	p	< 0.001 US+40			p	INSIGNIFICANT		
	null hypothesis 3 is rejected				null hypothesis 4 is accepted			

countries (AU – 40 and US – 40). First of all, chart A in Table 17.8 shows that the US + 40 sub-corpus contains more Camp Names than the AU + 40 sub-corpus, and the *probability* that this difference is a result of mere chance (p) is less than 0.001. This is a highly significant result (Oakes 1998), and the null hypothesis is rejected at better than the 1 per cent level (p < 0.01), meaning that an explanation for the difference (other than chance) exists. On the other hand, chart B shows that the null hypothesis is accepted in the case of the two under-40 sub-corpora because the log-likelihood value 2.17 is far too low. In other words, any difference in frequency is merely the result of chance in this case. In summary, the US + 40 group uses significantly more Camp Names than the AU + 40 group, which hints that maybe there is a difference based on locality. The under 40 participants complicate the picture, though, because the US – 40 group and the AU – 40 group are not significantly different in terms of Camp Names. Comparisons by age yield further insight.

To begin with, in Table 17.9, Chart A, we see that the US + 40 sub-corpus once again contains significantly more Camp Names – this time more than the US – 40 sub-corpus – and once again the null hypothesis is rejected at the 1 per cent level (p < 0.01), showing that mere chance does not explain this difference. The null hypothesis is accepted when the two Australian sub-corpora are compared, as can be seen in Chart B with a value of p that is insignificant. That means there is merely a chance difference in frequency based on age in the Australian data. Because the US + 40 sub-corpus has significantly more Camp Names than both the AU + 40 and US − 40 sub-corpora, and these two respectively show no difference with the AU − 40 sub-corpus, it becomes obvious that the US + 40 sub-corpus stands out as dominant in terms of frequency counts of Camp Names. Because of a shortage of space, this difference cannot be investigated more deeply. However, even such a restricted quantitative analysis enriches the qualitative investigation of the use of Camp Names by demonstrating that, in this corpus at least, they are being used in similar contexts, cross-generationally, in both Australia and the United States, with more frequent use by those over 40 in the United States. Further investigation, which takes advantage of other corpus analysis techniques and takes into account a qualitative analysis of data (or analysis beyond the corpus, e.g. interviews), would doubtless bring further insight.

17.7 Conclusion

Compiling, annotating and analysing a chat-room corpus brings its own unique challenges on top of those faced by all compilers of corpora. As I hope this chapter has demonstrated, in the case of corpus-based study at the project level with corpora of manageable size, these are not insurmountable challenges for the solo analyst. The Queer Chat-Room Corpus is an uncommon and valuable source of interaction between sexually marginalized people, which has been placed in a corpus with their permission. Since its original project-based conception, it has become increasingly clear that this corpus should be made available for the general use of other scholars. Because of the challenges that chat-room CMC data create for automatic tagging software, such availability is contingent upon pulling together a team for the daunting task of annotating it. Hopefully advances in the ability of tagging software to deal with spelling variations (on the scale present in chat-rooms) will soon be achieved; a worthy project considering that online data (and its challenges) are not likely to disappear anytime soon.[9]

Notes

1 Although the corpus I am building is mainly used for chat between men who (claim to) identify as gay (e.g. having same-sex desire), I use the term *queer* rather than *gay* as not all people who experience such desire identify as gay (some may identify as bisexual or refuse to label their sexual identity, for example). The term *queer*, then, is a wider term which focuses more on forms of sexual expression that are 'against the normal'. Sumara and Davis (1999: 192) have suggested that to be queer is to be cut off from '. . . the cultural rewards afforded those whose public performances of self are contained within that narrow band of behaviours considered proper to a heterosexual identity'.

2 So as to keep focussed on the issue of corpus linguistics, this chapter will give only directly relevant information about that project. Please refer to King (2011) for detailed information on qualitative aspects.

3 The metaphor 'lavender-coloured glasses' is an oblique reference to William Leap's use of the term 'lavender' in reference to gay and lesbian language use (Leap 1995, 2008).

4 Camp Names are used in these chat-rooms for various purposes, including gay identity performance, solidarity moves and as a form of resistance to cultural scripts which place recipients of male sexual interest in disempowered subject positions (see King, 2011 for more details).

5 This heading was inspired by Chen et al. (2004).

6 For further information on the details of the project website, please refer to King (2006).

7 States of the USA were divided into six categories according to a breakdown provided by the US Department of State (2008). The dividing line for urban vs rural was set at 300,000. The number 300,000 is admittedly subjective, being based on my own experience of cities, towns and rural areas. This is not to imply that people located in cities of 250,000 are living a 'rural' lifestyle; rather the primary goal was to separate 'big city' or metropolitan locations from non-metropolitan. The World Index website of Falling Rain Genomics (2008) was indispensable as a tool for quickly finding up-to-date population estimates of town and cities in both Australia and the United States.

8 Cyber-orthography is a term created by Al-sa'di and Hamdan (2005) during their corpus analysis of chat-room English.

9 See Gong (2005) for perspectives on the absence of CMC data from large, broadly used corpora.

Bibliography

Aarts, J. (1998), 'Introduction', in S. Johansson and S. Oksefjell (eds) *Corpora and Cross-Linguistic Research*. Amsterdam: Rodopi, pp. ix–xiv.

Adolphs, S. and Carter, R. (2002), 'Point of view and semantic prosodies in Virginia Woolf's *To the Lighthouse*', *Poetica* 58, 7–20.

Aijmer, K. (1997), 'I think – an English modal Particle', in T. Swan and O. J. Westvik (eds) *Modality in Germanic Languages: Historical and Comparative Perspectives*. Berlin: Mouton de Gruyter, pp. 1–47.

Aijmer, K. (2007), 'Translating discourse markers: a case of complex translation', in M. Rogers and G. Anderman (eds) *Incorporating Corpora. The Linguist and the Translator*. Clevedon: Multilingual Matters, pp. 95–116.

Aijmer, K., Altenberg, B. and Johansson, M. (eds) (1996), *Language in Contrast: Papers from a Symposium on Text-based Cross-linguistic Studies, Lund, March 1994*. Lund: Lund University Press.

Alder, J. (2005), *Constitutional and Administrative Law*. Basingstoke: Palgrave Macmillan.

Alexander, R. (2007), '"Mortgage repayments" is more than a phrase: The cultural content of Business English phraseology', in J. Engberg, M. Grove Ditlevsen, P. Kastberg and M. Stegu (eds) *New Directions in LSP Teaching*. Bern etc.: Peter Lang, pp. 207–29.

Al-sa'di, R. A. and Hamdan, J. M. (2005), '"Synchronous online chat" English: computer-mediated communication', *World Englishes* 24, 409–24.

Altman, D. G. (1991), *Practical Statistics for Medical Research*. London: Chapman and Hall.

Anderman, G. and Rogers, M. (eds) (2007), *Incorporating Corpora: The Linguist and the Translator*. Clevedon: Multilingual Matters.

Anthony, L. (2005), '*AntConc*: design and development of a freeware corpus analysis toolkit for the technical writing classroom', in *Proceedings of Professional Communication Conference*, pp. 729–37.

Anthony, L. (2006), 'Developing a Freeware, multiplatform corpus analysis toolkit for the technical writing classroom', *IEEE Transactions on Professional Communication* 49(3), 275–86.

Anthony, L. and Lashkia, G. V. (2003), 'Mover: a machine learning tool to assist in the reading and writing of technical papers', *IEEE Transactions on Professional Communication* 46(3), 185–93.

Archer, D. (2005), *Questions and Answers in the English Courtroom (1640–1760)*. Amsterdam: John Benjamins.

Archer, D. (2007), 'Computer-assisted literary stylistics: the state of the field', in M. Lambrou and P. Stockwell (eds) *Contemporary Stylistics*. London: Continuum, pp. 244–56.

Archer, D. and Culpeper, J. (2003), 'Sociopragmatic annotation: new directions and possibilities in historical corpus linguistics', in A. Wilson, P. Rayson and T. McEnery (eds) *Corpus Linguistics by the Lune: Studies in Honour of Geoffrey Leech*. Frankfurt: Peter Lang, pp. 37–58.

Archer, D., Culpeper J. and Rayson, P. (2006: online), 'Love – "a familiar or a devil"? An exploration of key domains in Shakespeare's comedies and tragedies'. Accessed April 2008 at http://www.methodsnetwork.ac.uk/redist/pdf/es1_08archer.pdf

Archer, D., McEnery, T., Rayson, P. and Hardie, A. (2003), 'Developing an automated semantic analysis system for Early Modern English', in *Proceedings of Corpus Linguistics 2003*. UCREL, Lancaster University, 22–31. Accessed on 23 April 2008 at http://www.comp.lancs.ac.uk/computing/users/paul/publications/cl2003_archer.pdf

Aston, G. (1997a), 'Enriching the learning environment: corpora in ELT', in A. Wichmann, S. Fligelstone, T. McEnery and G. Knowles (eds) *Teaching and Language Corpora*. London: Longman, pp. 51–64.

Aston, G. (1997b), 'Small and large corpora in language learning', in B. Lewandowska-Tomaszczyk and P. J. Melia (eds) *International Conference on Practical Applications in Language Corpora, Łódź, Poland, 11–14 April, 1997*. Łódź: Łódź University Press, pp. 51–62.

Aston, G. (1999), 'Corpus use and learning to translate', *Textus* 12, 289–314.

Aston, G. (2001), 'Text categories and corpus users: a response to David Lee', *Language Learning and Technology* 5(3), 73–6.

Aston, G. and Burnard, L. (1998), *The BNC Handbook: Exploring the British National Corpus with SARA*. Edinburgh: Edinburgh University Press.

Atkins, B. T. S. and Levin, B. (1991), 'Admitting impediments', in U. Zernik (ed.) *Lexical Acquisition: Using On-Line Resources to Build a Lexicon*. Hillsdale, NJ: Lawrence Erlbaum Associates, pp. 233–62.

Baayen, H. H., van Halteren, H. and Tweedie, F. (1996), 'Outside the cave of shadows: using syntactic annotation to enhance authorship attribution', *Literary and Linguistic Computing* 11, 121–32.

Baker, C. F., Fillmore, C. J. and Cronin, B. (2003), 'The structure of the FrameNet database', *International Journal of Lexicography* 16(3), 281–96.

Baker, M. (1992), *In Other Words*. London and New York: Routledge.

Baker, M. (1993), 'Corpus linguistics and translation studies: implications and applications', in M. Baker, G. Francis and E. Tognini-Bonelli (eds) *Text and Technology. In Honour of John Sinclair*. Amsterdam: John Benjamins, pp. 233–50.

Baker, M. (1995), 'Corpora in translation studies: an overview and some suggestions for future research', *Target* 7(2), 223–43.

Baker, M. (1996), 'Corpus-based translation studies: the challenges that lie ahead', in H. Somers (ed.) *Terminology, LSP and Translation: Studies in Language Engineering in Honour of Juan C. Sager*. Amsterdam: John Benjamins, pp. 175–86.

Baker, M. (1999), 'The role of corpora in investigating the linguistic behaviour of professional translators', *International Journal of Corpus Linguistics* 4, 281–98.

Baker, M. (2000), 'Towards a methodology for investigating the style of a literary translator', *Target* 12(2), 241–66.

Baker, P. (2005), *Public Discourses of Gay Men*. New York: Routledge.

Baker, P. (2006), *Using Corpora in Discourse Analysis*. London and New York: Continuum.

Baker, P. (2008), 'The 2000s corpus: issues regarding building a modern version of LOB using the internet, and some preliminary findings', Presentation at Corpus Research Group, Lancaster University, 16 June 2008.

Baker, P., Hardie, A. and McEnery, T. (2006), *A Glossary of Corpus Linguistics*. Edinburgh: Edinburgh University Press.

Baker, P., Hardie, A., McEnery, A., Xiao, R., Bontcheva, K., Cunningham, H., Gaizauskas, R., Hamza, O., Maynard, D., Tablan, V., Ursu, C., Jayaram, B. D. and Leisher, M. (2004), 'Corpus linguistics and South Asian Languages: corpus creation and tool development', *Literary and Linguistic Computing* 19(4), 509–24.

Baker, P. and McEnery, T. (2005), 'A corpus-based approach to discourses of refugees and asylum seekers in UN and newspaper texts', *Journal of Language and Politics* 4(2), 197–226.

Baker, P. and Stanley, J. (2003), *Hello Sailor!: The Hidden History of Gay Life at Sea*. London: Pearson.

Baldwin, T. and Villavicencio, A. (2002), 'Extracting the unextractable: a case study on verb-particles', *Proceedings of the 6th Conference on Natural Language Learning* (CoNLL-2002). Taipei, Taiwan, pp. 98–104.

Banko, M. and Brill, E. (2001), 'Scaling to very very large corpora for natural language disambiguation', Proceedings of the 39th Annual Meeting of the Association for Computational Linguistics and the 10th Conference of the European Chapter of the Association for Computational Linguistics, Toulouse.

Barcelona, A. (2000), 'On the plausibility of claiming a metonymic motivation for conceptual metaphor', in A. Barcelona (ed.) *Metaphor and Metonymy at the Crossroads: A Cognitive Perspective*. Berlin: Mouton de Gruyter, pp. 31–58.

Barlow, M. (1995), *A Guide to ParaConc*. Houston: Athelstan.

Barlow, M. (2000), 'Parallel texts and language teaching', in S. Botley, A. McEnery and A. Wilson (eds) *Multilingual Corpora in Teaching and Research*. Amsterdam: Rodopi, pp. 106–15.

Barlow, M. (2002), 'Software for corpus access and analysis', in J. McH. Sinclair (ed.) *How to Use Corpora in Language Teaching*. Amsterdam: John Benjamins, pp. 205–21.

Barnbrook, G. (1996), *Language and Computers: A Practical Introduction to the Computer Analysis of Language*. Edinburgh: Edinburgh University Press.

Baroni, M. and Bernardini, S. (2003), 'A preliminary analysis of collocational differences in monolingual comparable corpora', in D. Archer, P. Rayson, A. Wilson and A. McEnery (eds) *Proceedings of the Corpus Linguistics 2003 Conference*. Lancaster: UCREL, Lancaster University, pp. 82–91.

Bassnett-McGuire, S. (1991), *Translation Studies*, 2nd edn. London: Methuen.

Bassnett, S. and Lefevere, A. (1990), 'Introduction', in S. Bassnett and A. Lefevere (eds) *Translation, History and Culture*. London: Pinter.

Beißwenger, M. and Storrer, A. (2007), 'Corpora of computer-mediated communication', To appear as chapter 21 in A. Lüdeling and M. Kytö (eds) *Corpus Linguistics: An International Handbook*. Berlin: Mouton de Gruyter. Preprint accessed on 2 May 2008 at: http://www.michael-beisswenger.de/pub/hsk-corpora.pdf

Bell, R. (1991), *Translation and Translating: Theory and Practice*. London: Longman.

Berber Sardinha, T. (2007), 'A program for identifying metaphor candidates in corpora', Paper presented at the 4th Corpus Linguistics Conference, July 2007, University of Birmingham.

Berber Sardinha, T. (2008), 'Metaphor probabilities in corpora', in M. S. Zanotto, L. Cameron and M. C. Cavalcanti (eds) *Confronting Metaphor in Use: An Applied Linguistic Perspective.* Amsterdam: John Benjamins, pp. 127–48.

Bergman, M. K. (2001), 'The deep web: surfacing hidden value', *The Journal of Electronic Publishing* 7(1).

Bernardini, S. (1997), 'A "trainee" translator's perspective on corpora', Paper presented at the conference of *Corpus Use and Learning to Translate.* Bertinoro, November 1997.

Bernardini, S. (2002*a*), 'Corpora in the classroom', in J. McH. Sinclair (ed.) *How to Use Corpora in Language Teaching.* Amsterdam: John Benjamins, pp. 15–36.

Bernardini, S. (2002*b*), 'Educating translators for the challenges of the new millennium: The potential of parallel bi-directional corpora', in B. Maia, J. Haller and M. Ulrych (eds) *Training the Language Services Provider for the New Millennium.* Faculdade de Letras da Universidade do Porto, pp. 173–86.

Bernardini, S. (2002*c*), 'Think-aloud protocols in translation research: achievements, limits, future prospects', *Target* 13(2), 241–63.

Bernardini, S. and Zanettin, F. (2004), 'When is a universal not a universal? Some limits of current corpus-based methodologies for the investigation of translation universals', in A. Mauranen and P. Kuyamaki (eds) *Translation Universals: Do They Exist?* Amsterdam: John Benjamins, pp. 51–62.

Bharati, A. (2006), 'Part-of-speech tagger for Indian languages', available online at http://shiva.iiit.ac.in/SPSAL2007/iiit_tagset_guidelines.pdf

Bharati, A. and Mannem, P. R. (2007), 'Introduction to the Shallow Parsing Contest for South Asian Languages', in Proceedings of the workshop on Shallow Parsing for South Asian Languages (SPSAL-2007), available online at http://shiva.iiit.ac.in/SPSAL2007/proceedings.php

Bhatia, T. K. and Koul, A. (2000), *Colloquial Urdu.* London: Routledge.

Bhattacharyya, P., Chakrabarti, D. and Sarma, V. M. (2006), 'Complex predicates in Indian languages and wordnets', *Language Resources and Evaluation* 40(3–4), 331–55.

Biber, D. (1988), *Variation Across Speech and Writing.* Cambridge: Cambridge University Press.

Biber, D. (1995), *Dimensions of Register Variation: A Cross-linguistic Comparison.* Cambridge: Cambridge University Press.

Biber, D. and Barbieri, F. (2007), 'Lexical bundles in university spoken and written registers', *English for Specific Purposes* 26, 263–86.

Biber, D., Connor, U. and Upton, T. A. (2007), *Discourse on the Move. Using Corpus Analysis to Describe Discourse Structure.* Amsterdam/Philadelphia: John Benjamins.

Biber, D., Conrad, S. and Cortes, V. (2004), 'If you look at . . . lexical bundles in university teaching and textbooks', *Applied Linguistics* 25(3), 371–405.

Biber, D., Conrad, S. and Reppen, R. (1998), *Corpus Linguistics: Investigating Language Structure and Use.* Cambridge: Cambridge University Press.

Biber, D., Johansson, S., Leech, G., Conrad, S. and Finegan, E. (1999), *Longman Grammar of Spoken and Written English*. Harlow: Pearson Longman.

Blacker, T. (2007), 'A touch of class war', *The Independent*, 4 August 2007, 26–7.

Bloomfield, L. (1933), *Language*. Revised from the 1914 Edition. New York: Holt.

Blum-Kulka, S. (1986), 'Shifts of cohesion and coherence in Translation', in J. House and S. Blum-Kulka (eds) *Interlingual and Intercultural Communication: Discourse and Cognition in Translation and Second Language Acquisition Studies*. Tübingen: Gunter Narr, pp. 17–35.

Blum-Kulka, S. and Levenston, E. (1983), 'Universals of lexical simplification', in C. Faerch and G. Kasper (eds) *Strategies in Interlanguage Communication*. London: Longman, pp. 119–39.

Bod, R. (1992), 'Data-oriented parsing', in *Proceedings of COLING 1992*, Nantes, France, pp. 855–59.

Bod, R. (1998), *Beyond Grammar: An Experience-based Theory of Language*. Stanford, CA: CSLI Publications.

Bod, R. (2003), 'Introduction to elementary probability theory and formal stochastic language theory', in Bod, Hay and Jannedy (eds) *Probabilistic Linguistics*. Cambridge, MA: MIT Press, pp. 11–38.

Bod, R., Hay, J. and Jannedy, S. (2003), *Probabilistic Linguistics*. Cambridge, MA: MIT Press.

Boers, F. (1999), 'When a bodily source domain becomes prominent: the joy of counting metaphors in the socio-economic domain', in R. Gibbs and G. Steen (eds) *Metaphor in Cognitive Linguistics*. Amsterdam: John Benjamins, pp. 47–56.

Bögel, T., Butt, M, Hautli, A. and Sulger, S. (2007), 'Developing a finite-state morphological analyzer for Urdu and Hindi', in Proceedings of the Sixth International Workshop on Finite-State Methods and Natural Language Processing. Potsdam, September 2007. Available online at http://ling.uni-konstanz.de/pages/home/butt/boegeletal.pdf

Bok, L. (2004), *The Little Book of Chavs: The Branded Guide to Britain's New Elite*. Bath: Crombie Jardine Publishing.

Bolinger, D. (1976), 'Meaning and memory', *Forum Linguisticum* 1(1), 1–14.

Botley, S. P. (2000), 'Corpora and discourse anaphora: using corpus evidence to test theoretical claims', Unpublished Ph.D. thesis, Lancaster University.

Bowker, L. (1998), 'Using specialized native-language corpora as a translation resource: a pilot study', *Meta* 43(4), 631–51.

Bowker, L. (2001), 'Towards a methodology for a corpus-based approach to translation evaluation', *Meta* 46(2), 345–64.

Bowker, L. and Barlow, M. (2004), 'Bilingual concordancers and translation memories: a comparative evaluation', in *Proceedings of the Second International Workshop on Language Resources for Translation Work, Research and Training*, University of Geneva, 28 August 2004, pp. 70–83.

Brook, G. L. (1970), *The Language of Dickens*. London: Andre Deutsch.

Brown, P. and Levinson, S. C. (1987), *Politeness: Some Universals in Language Usage*. Cambridge: Cambridge University Press.

Burnard, L. (1995), *The BNC Reference Manual*. Oxford: Oxford University Computing Service.

Butt, M. and King, T. H. (2002), 'Urdu and the parallel grammar project', in *Proceedings of COLING 2002, Workshop on Asian Language Resources and International Standardization*, pp. 39–45.

Butt, M. and King, T. H. (2007), 'Urdu in a parallel grammar development environment', *Language Resources and Evaluation* 41(2), 191–207.

Cameron, D. (2001), *Working with Spoken Discourse*. London: Sage.

Cameron, D. (2004), 'Out of the bottle: The social life of metalanguage', in A. Jaworski, N. Coupland and D. Galasiński (eds) *Metalanguage: Social and Ideological Perspectives*. Berlin and New York: Mouton de Gruyter, pp. 311–21.

Cameron, D. and Kulick, D. (2003), *Language and Sexuality*. Cambridge: Cambridge University Press.

Cameron, L. (2003), *Metaphor in Educational Discourse*. London: Continuum.

Cameron, L., Cienki, A., Crisp, P., Deignan, A., Gibbs, R., Grady, J., Kovecses, Z., Low, G., Semino, E. and Steen, G. (2007), 'MIP: A method for identifying metaphorically used words in discourse', *Metaphor and Symbol* 22(1), 1–40.

Carroll, J. B., Davies, P. and Richman, B. (1971), *The American Heritage Word Frequency Book*. New York: American Heritage Publishing Co.

Carter, R. (2004), *Language and Creativity. The Art of Common Talk*. London: Routledge.

Chapelle, C. (2001), *Computer Applications in Second Language Acquisition: Foundations for Teaching, Testing, and Research*. Cambridge, UK: Cambridge University Press.

Charniak, E. (1997), 'Tree-bank grammars', in *Proceedings of the Thirteenth National Conference on Artificial Intelligence (AAAI '96)*, Menlo Park, CA, pp. 1031–36.

Charniak, E. (2001), 'Immediate-head parsing for language models', in *Meeting of the Association for Computational Linguistics*, pp. 116–23.

Charteris-Black, J. (2003), 'Speaking with forked tongue: a comparative study of metaphor and metonymy in English and Malay phraseology', *Metaphor and Symbol* 18(4), 289–310.

Charteris-Black, J. (2004), *Corpus Approaches to Critical Metaphor Analysis*. Basingstoke: Palgrave Macmillan.

Chauncey, G. (1994), *Gay New York: Gender, Urban Culture, and the Making of the Gay Male World, 1890–1940*. New York: Basic Books.

Chen, S. L. S., Hall, G. J. and Johns, M. D. (2004), 'Research paparazzi in cyberspace: the voices of the researched', in M. D. Johns, S. L. S. Chen and G. J. Hall (eds) *Online Social Research: Methods, Issues, and Ethics*. New York: Peter Lang, pp. 157–75.

Chen, W. (2006), 'Explication through the use of connectives in translated Chinese: a corpus-based study', Ph.D. thesis, University of Manchester.

Cheong, H. (2006), 'Target text contraction in English-into-Korean Translations: a contradiction of presumed translation universals?' *Meta* 51(2), 343–67.

Chesterman, A. (2004), 'Beyond the particular', in A. Mauranen and P. Kuyamaki (eds) *Translation Universals: Do they exist?* Amsterdam: John Benjamins, pp. 33–49.

Chinchor, N. and Robinson, P. (1998), 'MUC-7 named entity task definition', in Proceedings of Seventh Message Understanding Conference (MUC-7). http://www.itl.nist.gov/iaui/894.02/related_projects//muc/proceedings/muc_7_toc.html

Chomsky, N. (1962), Paper given at *Third Texas Conference on Problems of Linguistic Analysis in English*, 1958. Austin: University of Texas.

Chomsky, N. (1980), 'On binding', *Linguistic Inquiry* 11, 1–46.

Chomsky, N. (1981), *Lectures on Government and Binding* (1993 7th edn). Dordrecht: Foris Publications.

Claridge, C. (2007), 'Constructing a corpus from the web: message boards', in M. Hundt, N. Nesselhauf and C. Biewer (eds) *Corpus Linguistics and the Web*. Amsterdam: Rodopi, pp. 87–108.

COBUILD (1995). *COBUILD English Collocations on CD Rom*. London: Collins.

COBUILD (1996). *COBUILD Grammar Patterns 1: Verbs*. London: HarperCollins.

COBUILD (1996). *COBUILD Grammar Patterns 2: Nouns and Adjectives*. London: HarperCollins.

Collins, M. (1996), 'A new statistical parser based on bigram lexical dependencies', in *Proceedings of the 34th Annual Meeting of the Association for Computational Linguistics*. Santa Cruz, CA, pp. 184–91.

Conklin, K. and Schmitt, N. (2008), Formulaic sequences: are they processed more quickly than non-formulaic language by native and nonnative speakers? *Applied Linguistics*.

Cook, G. (1995), 'Theoretical issues: transcribing the untranscribable', in G. Leech, G. Myers and J. Thomas (eds) *Spoken English on Computer*. London: Longman, pp. 35–53.

Cortes, V. (2004), 'Lexical bundles in published and student writing in history and biology', *English for Specific Purposes* 23(4), 397–423.

Cotterill, J. (2001), 'Domestic discord, rocky relationships: semantic prosodies in representations of marital violence in the O. J. Simpson trial', *Discourse & Society* 12(3), 291–312.

Cowell, R. G., Dawid, A. P., Lauritzen, S. L. and Spiegelhalter, D. J. (2007), *Probabilistic Networks and Expert Systems*. New York: Springer.

Cowie, A. P. (1998), 'Phraseological dictionaries: some East-West comparisons', in A. P. Cowie (ed.) *Phraseology: Theory, Analysis, and Application*. Oxford: Clarendon Press, pp. 209–43.

Crystal, D. (2003), *English as a Global Language*, 2nd edn. Cambridge: Cambridge University Press.

Culpeper, J. (2002), 'Computers, language and characterisation: An analysis of six characters in Romeo and Juliet', in U. Melander-Marttala, C. Östman and M. Kytö (eds) *Conversation in Life and in Literature*. Uppsala: Universitetstryckeriet, pp. 11–30.

Culpeper, J. (2005), 'Impoliteness and entertainment in the television quiz show: The weakest link', *Journal of Politeness Research* 1, 35–72.

Culpeper, J. (2008), 'Reflections on impoliteness, relational work and power', in D. Bousfield and M. Locher (eds) *Impoliteness in Language*. Berlin: Mouton de Gruyter, pp. 17–44.

Culpeper, J., Bousfield, D. and Wichmann, A. (2003), 'Impoliteness revisited: with special reference to dynamic and prosodic aspects', *Journal of Pragmatics* 35, 1545–79.

Cunningham, H., Maynard, D., Bontcheva, K. and Tablan, V. (2002), 'GATE: A framework and graphical development environment for robust NLP tools and applications', in *Proceedings of the 40th Anniversary Meeting of the Association for Computational Linguistics (ACL'02)*.

Dahlmann, I. and Adolphs, S. (2007*a*), 'Pauses as an indicator of psycholinguistically valid multi-word expressions (MWEs)?' *Workshop on A Broader Perspective on Multi-word Expressions, 28 June 2007, ACL 2007.* Prague, pp. 49–56.

Dahlmann, I., Adolphs, S. and Rodden, T. (2007*b*), 'Multi-word units, fluency and pause annotation in spoken corpora', Paper presented at the 40th BAAL Annual Meeting, Edinburgh.

Danielsson, P. (2002), 'Simple Perl programming for corpus work', in J. McH. Sinclair (ed.) *How to Use Corpora in Language Teaching.* Amsterdam: John Benjamins, pp. 225–46.

Danielsson, P. (2007), 'What constitutes a unit of analysis in language?' *Linguistik Online* 31, 17–24.

Dasgupta, S. and Ng, V. (2006), 'Unsupervised morphological parsing of Bengali', *Language Resources and Evaluation* 40(3–4), 311–30.

Dash, N. S. (2000), 'Bangla pronouns: a corpus-based study', *Literary and Linguistic Computing* 15(4), 433–43.

Dash, N. S. (2004), 'Frequency and function of characters used in Bangla text corpus', *Literary and Linguistic Computing* 19(2), 145–59.

Dash, N. S. and Chaudhuri, B. B. (2000), 'The process of designing a multidisciplinary monolingual sample corpus', *International Journal of Corpus Linguistics* 5(2), 179–97.

de Beaugrande, R. (1997), 'The story of discourse analysis', in T. A. van Dijk (ed.) *Discourse as Structure and Process (Discourse Studies: A Multidisciplinary Introduction,* vol. 1). London, Thousand Oaks, CA, New Delhi: Sage, pp. 35–62.

DeForest, M. and Johnson, E. (2001), 'The density of Latinate words in the speeches of Jane Austen's characters', *Literary and Linguistic Computing* 16(4), 389–401.

Deignan, A. (1999*a*), 'Corpus-based research into metaphor', in L. Cameron and G. Low (eds) *Researching and Applying Metaphor.* Cambridge: Cambridge University Press, pp. 177–99.

Deignan, A. (1999*b*), 'Metaphorical polysemy and paradigmatic relations: a corpus study', *Word* 50, 319–38.

Deignan, A. (2005*a*), *Metaphor and Corpus Linguistics.* Amsterdam: John Benjamins.

Deignan, A. (2005*b*), 'A corpus linguistic perspective on the relationship between metaphor and metonymy', *Style* 39(1), 72–91.

Deignan, A. (2007), 'Image metaphors and connotation in everyday language', in F. Ruiz de Mendoza (ed.) *Annual Review of Cognitive Linguistics,* vol. 5. Amsterdam: John Benjamins, pp. 173–92.

Deignan, A. (2008), 'Corpus linguistic data and conceptual metaphor theory', in M. S. Zanotto, L. Cameron and M. C. Cavalcanti (eds) *Confronting Metaphor in Use: An Applied Linguistic Approach.* Amsterdam: John Benjamins, pp. 149–62.

Deignan, A. and Potter, L. (2004), 'A corpus study of metaphors and metonyms in English and Italian', *Journal of Pragmatics* 36, 1231–52.

Denyoyer, L. and Gallinari, P. (2005), *The Wikipedia XML Corpus.* SIGIR Forum.

de Schryver, G. -M. (2002), 'Web for/as corpus: a perspective for the African languages', *Nordic Journal of African Studies* 11(2), 266–82.

Diniz, L. (2005), 'Comparative Review: TEXTSTAT 2.5, *ANTCONC* 3.0, and COMPLEAT LEXICAL TUTOR 4.0', *Language Learning and Technology* 9(3), pp. 22–7.

Dollinger, S. (2006), 'Oh Canada! Towards the corpus of early Ontario English', in A. Renouf and A. Kehoe (eds) *The Changing Face of Corpus Linguistics*. Amsterdam: Rodopi, pp. 7–26.

Drost, I. and Scheffer, T. (2005), 'Thwarting the nigritude ultramarine: learning to identify link spam', *Machine Learning: Ecml 2005, Proceedings*, (Lecture Notes In Artificial Intelligence), pp. 96–107.

Dunning, T. (1993), 'Accurate methods for the statistics of surprise and coincidence', *Computational Linguistics* 19(1), 61–74.

Dura, E. (2006), 'Extracting current language use from the Web', *Poznań Studies in Contemporary Linguistics* 41, 73–85.

Eelen, G. (2001), *A Critique of Politeness Theories*. Manchester: St Jerome Publishing.

Ensslin, A. and Johnson, S. (2006), 'Language in the news: investigating representations of "Englishness" using WordSmith Tools', *Corpora* 1(2), 153–85.

Erman, B. and Warren, B. (2000), 'The idiom principle and the open choice principle', *Text* 20(1), 29–62.

Fairclough, N. (1992), *Discourse and Social Change*. Cambridge: Polity Press.

Fairclough, N. (1995), *Critical Discourse Analysis. The Critical Study of Language*. London: Longman.

Fairclough, N. (2000), *New Labour, New Language?* London: Routledge.

Fairclough, N. and Wodak, R. (1997), 'Critical discourse analysis', in T. A. van Dijk (ed.) *Discourse as Social Interaction (Discourse Studies: A Multidisciplinary Introduction*, vol. 2). London, Thousand Oaks, CA, New Delhi: Sage, pp. 258–84.

Falling Rain Genomics (2008), 'Global gazetteer version 2.1'. On *Falling Rain World Index Website*. Accessed on 21 May 2008 at: http://www.fallingrain.com/world/

Fawcett, P. (1997), *Translation and Language: Linguistic Theories Explained*. Manchester: St Jerome Publishing.

Feigenbaum, L., Herman, I., Hongsermeier, T., Neunmann, E. and Stephens, S. (2007), 'The semantic web in action', *Scientific American* 297(6), 90–7.

Fellbaum, C. (ed.) (1998), *WordNet: An Electronic Lexical Database*. Cambridge, MA: MIT Press.

Fillmore, C., Ide, N., Jurafsky, D. and Macleod, C. (1998), 'An American National Corpus: a proposal', in A. Rubio, N. Gallardo, R. Castro and A. Tejada (eds) *Proceedings of the First International Conference on Language Resources and Evaluation*. Granada.

Firth, J. R. (1935 [1957]), 'The technique of semantics', in J.R. Firth *Papers in Linguistics 1934–1951*. London: Oxford University Press, pp. 7–33.

Firth, J. R. (1957), 'A Synopsis of Linguistic Theory 1930-1955.' In J. R. Firth (ed.) *Studies in Linguistic Analysis*. Oxford: Basil Blackwell, pp. 1–32.

Fish, S. E. (1996), 'What is stylistics and why are they saying such terrible things about it?', in J. J. Weber (ed.) *The Stylistics Reader. From Roman Jakobson to the Present*. London: Arnold, pp. 94–116.

Fletcher, W. H. (2004), 'Facilitating the compilation and dissemination of ad-hoc web corpora', in G. Aston, S. Bernardini and D. Stewart (eds) *Corpora and Language Learners; (Studies in Corpus Linguistics 17)*. Amsterdam: John Benjamins, pp. 273–300.

Flowerdew, L. (2005), 'An integration of corpus-based and genre-based approaches to text analysis in EAP/ESP: countering criticisms against corpus-based methodologies', *English for Specific Purposes* 24(3), 321–32.

Flowerdew, L. (2008), *Corpus-based Analyses of the Problem–Solution Pattern. A Phraseological Approach*. Amsterdam/Philadelphia: John Benjamins.

Forsyth, R. S. (1999), 'Stylochronometry with substrings, or: a poet young and old', *Literary and Linguistic Computing* 14(4), 467–77.

Francis, W. N. (1965), 'A standard corpus of edited present-day American English', reprinted in G. Sampson and D. McCarthy (2006), *Corpus Linguistics*. London: Continuum, pp. 27–34.

Francis, W. N. and Kučera, H. (1964), *Manual of Information to Accompany a Standard Corpus of Present-Day English for Use with Digital Computers*. Providence: Brown University.

Frawley, W. (1984), 'Prolegomenon to a theory of translation', in W. Frawley (ed.) *Translation: Literary, Linguistic and Philosophical Perspectives*. London: Associated University Press, 159–75.

Fritz, C. (2006), 'Favoring Americanisms? <ou> vs. <o> before <l> and <r> in early English in Australia: a corpus-based approach', in A. Renouf and A. Kehoe (eds) *The Changing Face of Corpus Linguistics*. Amsterdam: Rodopi, pp. 27–44.

Garcia, A. M., Martin, J. C., Olalla, D. M. and González, G. M. (2006), 'The Old English Apollonius of Tyre in the light of the old English concordancer', in A. Renouf and A. Kehoe (eds) *The Changing Face of Corpus Linguistics*. Amsterdam: Rodopi, pp. 81–98.

Gardner, D. (2007), 'Validating the construct of word in applied corpus-based vocabulary research: a critical survey', *Applied Linguistics* 28(2), 241–65.

Garside, R. and Smith, N. (1997), 'A hybrid grammatical tagger: CLAWS4', in R. Garside, G. Leech and A. McEnery (eds) *Corpus Annotation: Linguistic Information from Computer Text Corpora*. London: Longman, pp. 102–21.

Gavins, J. (2007), *Text World Theory. An Introduction*. Edinburgh: Edinburgh University Press.

Gavioli, L. and Aston, G. (2001), 'Enriching reality: Language corpora in language pedagogy', *ELT Journal* 55(3), 238–46.

Gellerstam, M. (1986), 'Translationese in Swedish novels translated from English', in L. Wollin and H. Lindquist (eds) *Translation Studies in Scandinavia*. Lund: CWK Gleerup, pp. 88–95.

Gellerstam, M. (1996), 'Translations as a source for cross-linguistic studies', in K. Aijmer, B. Altenberg and M. Johansson (eds) *Language in Contrast: Papers from a Symposium on Text-based Cross-linguistic Studies, Lund, March 1994*. Lund: Lund University Press, pp. 53–62.

Gibbs, R. (1994), *The Poetics of Mind: Figurative Thought, Language and Understanding*. Cambridge: Cambridge University Press.

Gibbs, R. (1999), 'Taking metaphor out of our heads and putting it in the cultural world', in R. Gibbs and G. Steen (eds) *Metaphor in Cognitive Linguistics*. Amsterdam: John Benjamins, pp. 145–65.

Gibbs, R. (2006), *Embodiment and Cognitive Science*. Cambridge: Cambridge University Press.

Gillard, P. and Gadsby, A. (1998), 'Using a learners' corpus in compiling ELT dictionaries', in S. Grainger (ed.) *Learner English on Computer*. London: Longman, pp. 159–171.

Goatly, A. (1997), *The Language of Metaphors*. London: Routledge.

Gong, W. (2005), 'English in computer-mediated environments: a neglected dimension in large English corpus compilation', in S. Hunston (ed.) *Proceedings of Corpus linguistics conference series*. Birmingham, 14–17 July 2005. Accessed on 23 April 2008 at: http://www.corpus.bham.ac.uk/PCLC/Wengao.pdf

Goossens, L. (1995), 'Metaphtonymy: the interaction of metaphor and metonymy in expressions of linguistics action', in L. Goossens, P. Pauwels, B. Rudzka-Ostyn, A. Simon-Vanderbergen and J. Vanparys (eds) *By Word of Mouth: Metaphor, Metonymy and Linguistic Action in a Cognitive Perspective*. Amsterdam: John Benjamins, pp. 159–74.

Gordon, R. G. (ed.) (2005), *Ethnologue: Languages of the World*, 15th edn. Dallas, TX: SIL International. Available online at: http://www.ethnologue.com/

Gorji, M. (2007), *Rude Britannia*. London and New York: Berlin.

Grady, J. (1997), 'THEORIES ARE BUILDINGS revisited', *Cognitive Linguistics* 8(4), 267–90.

Granger, S. (1996), 'From CA to CIA and back: an integrated approach to computerized bilingual and learner corpora', in K. Aijmer, B. Altenberg and M. Johansson (eds) *Language in Contrast: Papers from a Symposium on Text-based Cross-linguistic Studies, Lund, March 1994*. Lund: Lund University Press, pp. 38–51.

Granger, S. (1998), *Learner English on Computer*. London: Addison-Wesley Longman.

Granger S., Lerot, J. and Petch-Tyson, S. (eds) (2003), *Corpus-based Approaches to Contrastive Linguistics and Translation Studies*. Amsterdam: Rodopi.

Greenbaum, S. (ed.) (1996), *Comparing English World-wide: The International Corpus of International English*. Oxford: Oxford University Press.

Grefenstette, G. (1999), 'The WWW as a resource for example-based MT tasks', Plenary talk at the ASLIB conference on Translating and the Computer. London: ASLIB.

Gries, S. (2003), *Multifactorial Analysis in Corpus Linguistics: A Study of Particle Placement*. London, New York: Continuum.

Guiraud, P. (1959), *Problemes et méthodes de la statistique linguistique*. Dordrecht: D. Reidel Publishing Company.

Gyongyi, Z. and Garcia-Molina, H. (2005), 'Spam: it's not just for inboxes anymore', *Computer* 38(10), 28–34.

Hall, P. A. V. (2004), 'Localising Nations, saving languages: moving from Unicode to Language Engineering', in Proceedings of the International Conference on Translating and the Computer 26. Available online at http://www.bhashasanchar.org/pdfs/localising_nationspaper_V2.pdf

Halliday, M. A. K. (1961), 'Categories of the theory of grammar', *Word* 17(3), 241–92.

Halliday, M. A. K. (1966), 'Lexis as a linguistic level', in C. E. Bazell, J. C. Catford, M. A. K. Halliday and R. H. Robins (eds) *In Memory of J. R. Firth*. London: Longman, pp. 148–162.

Halliday, M. A. K. (2004), *An Introduction to Functional Grammar*, 3rd edn. London: Arnold.

Hamilton, C., Adolphs, S. and Nerlich, B. (2007), 'The meanings of "risk": a view from corpus linguistics', *Discourse and Society* 18(2), 163–81.

Hanks, P. (forthcoming), *Lexical Analysis: Norms and Exploitations*. Cambridge, MA: MIT Press.

Hanks, P. and Pustejovsky, J. (2005), 'A pattern dictionary for Natural Language Processing', *Revue française de linguistique appliquée* 10(2).

Hansen, G., Malmkjaer, K. and Gile, D. (2004), *Claims, Changes and Challenges in Translation Studies*. Amsterdam: John Benjamins.

Hansen, S. and Teich, E. (2002), 'The creation and exploitation of a translation reference corpus', in E. Yuste-Rodrigo (ed.) *Proceedings of the Workshop on Language Resources in Translation Work and Research*. Paris: European Language Resources Association (ELRA), pp. 1–4.

Haq, A. (1937), *English-Urdu Urdu-English Combined Dictionary* [single-volume reprint, 2001]. New Delhi: Star.

Hardie, A. (2003), 'Developing a tagset for automated part-of-speech tagging in Urdu', in D. Archer, P. Rayson, A. Wilson and A. McEnery (eds) *Proceedings of the Corpus Linguistics 2003 Conference. UCREL Technical Papers Volume 16*. Department of Linguistics, Lancaster University.

Hardie, A. (2004), 'The computational analysis of morphosyntactic categories in Urdu', Unpublished Ph.D. thesis, University of Lancaster. Available online at http://eprints.lancs.ac.uk/106/

Hardie, A. (2005), 'Automated part-of-speech analysis of Urdu: conceptual and technical issues', in Y. Yadava, G. Bhattarai, R. R. Lohani, B. Prasain and K. Parajuli (eds) *Contemporary Issues in Nepalese Linguistics*. Kathmandu: Linguistic Society of Nepal, pp. 73–90.

Hardie, A. (2007a), 'From legacy encodings to Unicode: the graphical and logical principles in the scripts of South Asia', *Language Resources and Evaluation* 41(1), 1–25.

Hardie, A. (2007b), 'Collocational properties of adpositions in Nepali and English', in M. Davies, P. Rayson, S. Hunston and P. Danielsson (eds) *Proceedings of the Corpus Linguistics conference, CL 2007*. University of Birmingham, UK. Available online at http://www.corpus.bham.ac.uk/corplingproceedings07/

Hardie, A. (2008), 'A collocation-based approach to Nepali postpositions', *Corpus Linguistics and Linguistic Theory* 4(1), 19–61.

Hardie, A., Baker, P., McEnery, A. and Jayaram, B. D. (2006), 'Corpus-building for South Asian languages', in A. Saxene and L. Bori (eds) *Lesser-Known Languages in South Asia: Status and Policies, Case Studies and Applications of Information Technology*. Berlin: Mouton de Gruyter.

Hardie, A., Lohani, R. R., Regmi, B. N. and Yadava, Y. P. (forthcoming), 'A morphosyntactic categorisation scheme for the automated analysis of Nepali'.

Hardt-Mautner, G. (1995), 'Only connect: critical discourse analysis and corpus linguistics', UCREL Technical Paper 6, Lancaster: University of Lancaster. Available at http://www.comp.lancs.ac.uk/ucrel/tech_papers.html

Hartmann, R. (1985), 'Contrastive textology', *Language and Communication* 5, 107–10.

Harvey, K. (2000), 'Describing camp talk: language/pragmatics/politics', *Language and Literacy* 9, 240–60.

Hickey, T. (1993), 'Identifying formulas in first language acquisition', *Journal of Child Language* 20(1), 27–41.

Hockenmaier, J. (2006), 'Creating a CCGbank for a wide-coverage CCG lexicon for German', in *Proceedings of ACL 2006*. Sydney, Australia, pp. 335–442.

Hockenmaier, J. and Steedman, M. (2007), 'CCGbank: a corpus of CCG derivations and dependency structures extracted from the Penn Treebank', *Computational Linguistics* 33, 355–96.

Hockey, S. (2000), *Electronic Texts in the Humanities*. Oxford: Oxford University Press.

Hoey, M. (1991), *Patterns of Lexis in Text*. Oxford: Oxford University Press.

Hoey, M. (2004), 'The textual priming of lexis', in G. Aston, S. Bernardini and D. Stewart (eds) *Corpora and Language Learners*. Amsterdam and Philadelphia: John Benjamins, pp. 21–41.

Hoey, M. (2005), *Lexical Priming: A New Theory of Words and Language*. London: Routledge.

Hoey, M. (2007), 'Lexical priming and literary creativity', in M. Hoey, M. Mahlberg, M. Stubbs and W. Teubert, *Text, Discourse and Corpora. Theory and Analysis*. London: Continuum, pp. 7–29.

Hoffmann, S. and Evert, S. (2006), 'BNCweb (CQP-Edition) – The marriage of two corpus tools', in S. Braun, K. Kohn and J. Mukherjee (eds) *Corpus Technology and Language Pedagogy: New Resources, New Tools, New Methods*. Frankfurt: Peter Lang, pp. 177–95.

Hofland, K. and S. Johansson. (1982), *Word Frequencies in British and American English*. London: Longman.

Holmes, D. I. (1992), 'A stylometric analysis of Mormon scripture and related texts', *Journal of the Royal Statistical Society Series A* 155, 91–120.

Holmes, D. I., Gordon, L. J. and Wilson, C. (2001), 'A widow and her soldier: stylometry and the American Civil War', *Literary and Linguistic Computing* 16(4), 403–20.

Holmes, J. (1972 [1988]), 'The name and nature of Translation Studies', in J. Holmes (ed.) *Translated! Papers on Literary Translation and Translation Studies* (2nd edn 1988, 1st edn in 1972). Amsterdam: Rodopi, pp. 66–80.

Holmes, J. S. (1987), 'The name and nature of translation studies', in G. Toury (ed.) *Translation Across Cultures*. New Delhi: Bahri Publications, pp. 9–24.

Hong, H. (2005), 'SCoRE: a multimodal corpus database of education discourse in Singapore schools', in *Proceedings of the Corpus Linguistics Conference Series 1 (1)*. Birmingham, UK, July 14–17, 2005.

Hori, M. (2004), *Investigating Dickens' Style. A Collocational Analysis*. Basingstoke: Palgrave Macmillan.

Hornby, A. S. (1954), *A Guide to Patterns and Usage in English*. Oxford: Oxford University Press.

Howarth, P. A. (1996), *Phraseology in English Academic Writing*. Tübingen: Max Niemeyer.

Hundt, M. and Mair, C. (1999), 'Agile and uptight genres. The corpus-based approach to language change in progress', *International Journal of Corpus Linguistics* 4(2), 221–42.

Hundt, M., Sand, A. and Siemund, R. (1998), *Manual of Information to Accompany the Freiburg-LOB Corpus of British English ('FLOB')*. Englisches Seminar, Albert-Ludwigs-Universität Freiburg. Available online at http://khnt.hit.uib.no/icame/manuals/flob/index.htm

Hundt, M., Sand, A. and Skandera, P. (1999), *Manual of Information to Accompany The Freiburg-Brown Corpus of American English ('Frown')*. Englisches Seminar, Albert-Ludwigs-Universität Freiburg. Available online at http://khnt.hit.uib.no/icame/manuals/frown/index.htm

Hunston, S. (2002), *Corpora in Applied Linguistics*. Cambridge: Cambridge University Press.

Hunston, S. (2004), 'Counting the uncountable: problems of identifying evaluation in a text and in a corpus', in A. Partington, J. Morley and L. Haarman (eds) *Corpora and Discourse*. Bern: Peter Lang, pp. 157–88.

Hunston, S. and Francis, G. (2000), *Pattern Grammar: A Corpus Driven Approach to the Lexical Grammar of English*. Amsterdam: John Benjamins.

Hussain, S. (2004), 'Complexity of Asian writing systems: a case study of Nafees Nasta'leeq for Urdu', in *SCALLA 2004 Working Position Papers*. Available online at http://www.elda.fr/proj/scalla.html

Hussain, S. (2008), 'Resources for Urdu language processing', in *Proceedings of the Workshop on Asian Language Resources Network, IJCNLP'08, IIIT. Hyderabad, India*. Available online at http://www.crulp.org/Publication/papers/2008/Resources_for_Urdu_Language_Processing.pdf

Hyland, K. (1996), 'Nurturing hedges in the ESP curriculum', *System* 24(4), 477–90.

Hyland, K. (1998*a*), 'Boosting, hedging and the negotiation of academic knowledge', *Text* 18(3), 349–82.

Hyland, K. (1998*b*), 'Persuasion and context: the pragmatics of academic meta-discourse', *Journal of Pragmatics* 30, 437–55.

Hyland, K. (2000), *Disciplinary Discourses*. Harlow: Longman.

Hyland, K. (2007), 'As can be seen: lexical bundles and disciplinary variation', *English for Specific Purposes* 27(1), 4–21.

Ide, N. and Macleod, C. (2001), 'The American National Corpus: a standardized resource of American English', in Proceedings of Corpus Linguistics 2001, Lancaster, UK.

Ide, N. and Romary, L. (2007), 'Towards international standards for language resources', in L. Dybkjaer, H. Hemsen and W. Minker (eds) *Evaluation of Text and Speech Systems*. Springer, pp. 263–84.

Ide, N. and Suderman, K. (2004), 'The American National Corpus first release', in *Proceedings of LREC 2004*. Lisbon, Portugal, pp. 1681–4.

Ide, N. and Suderman, K. (2006), 'Integrating linguistic resources: the American National Corpus model', in Proceedings of the 6th International Conference on Language Resources and Evaluation, Genoa, Italy.

Ijaz, M. and Hussain, S. (2007), 'Corpus based Urdu lexicon development', in Proceedings of Conference on Language Technology (CLT07). University of Peshawar, Pakistan. Available online at http://www.crulp.org/Publication/papers/2007/corpus_based_urdu_lexicon_development.pdf

Izumi, E., Uchimoto, K. and Isahara, H. (eds) (2003), *Nihonjin 1200 Nin No Speaking Corpus*. [A spoken corpus of 1,200 Japanese learners of English]. Tokyo: ALC Press.

Jakobson, R. (1960), 'Closing statement: linguistics and poetics', in T. A. Sebeok (ed.) *Style and Language*. Cambridge, MA: MIT Press, pp. 350–77.

James, C. (1992), 'Awareness, consciousness and language contrast', in C. Mair and M. Markus (eds) *New Departures in Contrastive Linguistics*, pp. 183–97.

Jantunen, J. (2001), 'Synonymity and lexical simplification in translations: a corpus-based approach', *Across Languages and Cultures* 2(1), 97–112.

Jantunen, J. (2004), 'Untypical patterns in translations. Issues on corpus methodology and synonymity', in M. Rogers and G. Anderman (eds) *Incorporating Corpora. The Linguist and the Translator*. Clevedon: Multilingual Matters, pp. 101–26.

Jarvinen, T. (1994), 'Annotating 200 million words: the Bank of English project', in *Proceedings of COLING-94*, vol. 1, Kyoto, pp. 565–68.

Jaworski, A., Coupland, N. and Galasiński, D. (eds) (2004*a*), *Metalanguage: Social and Ideological Perspectives*. Berlin and New York: Mouton de Gruyter.

Jaworski, A, Coupland, N. and Galasiński, D. (eds) (2004*b*), 'Metalanguage: why now?', in A. Jaworski, N. Coupland and D. Galasiński (eds) *Metalanguage: Social and Ideological Perspectives*. Berlin and New York: Mouton de Gruyter, pp. 3–8.

Jiang, N. and T. M. Nekrasova (2007), 'The processing of formulaic sequences by second language speakers', *The Modern Language Journal*, 91(3), 433–45.

Johansson, S., Leech, G. and Goodluck, H. (1978), *Manual of Information to Accompany the Lancaster-Oslo/Bergen Corpus of British English, for Use with Digital Computers*. Oslo: Department of English, University of Oslo.

Johns, T. (1991), 'Should you be persuaded: two samples of data-driven learning materials', *English Language Research Journal* 4, 1–16.

Johns, T. (1997), 'Contexts: the background, development and trialling of a concordance-based CALL program', in A. Wichmann, S. Fligelstone, G. Knowles and A. McEnery (eds) *Teaching and Language Corpora*. London: Longman, pp. 100–15.

Johns, T. (2002), 'Data-driven learning: the perpetual challenge', in B. Kettermann and G. Marko (eds) *Teaching and Learning by Doing Corpus Linguistics*. Amsterdam: Rodopi, pp. 107–17.

Johnson, S., Culpeper, J. and Suhr, S. (2003), 'From "politically correct councillors" to "Blairite nonsense": discourses of political correctness in three British newspapers', *Discourse and Society* 14(1), 28–47.

Jones, S. and Sinclair, J. M. (1974), 'English Lexical Collocations', *Cahiers de Lexicologie*, 24, 15–61.

Juffs, A. (2000), 'An overview of the second language acquisition of links between verb semantics and morpho-syntax', in J. Archibald (ed.) *Second Language Acquisition and Linguistic Theory*. Oxford: Blackwell, pp. 187–227.

Juilland A. D., Brodin, D. and Davidovitch, C. (1970), *Frequency Dictionary of French Words*. The Hague: Mouton.

Jurafsky, D. (1996), 'A probabilistic model of lexical and syntactic access and disambiguation', *Cognitive Science* 20, 137–94.

Kachru, B. B. (1985), 'Standards, codification and sociolinguistic realism: the English language in the outer circle', in R. Quirk and H. G. Widdowson (eds) *English in the World: Teaching and Learning the Language and Literatures*. Cambridge: CUP.

Kachru, Y. (1990), 'Hindi-Urdu', in B. Comrie (ed.) *The Major Languages of South Asia, the Middle East and Africa*. London: Routledge, pp. 470–89.

Kachru, Y. (2006), *Hindi*. Amsterdam: John Benjamins.

Kanter, I., Kfir, F., Malkiel, B. and Shlesinger, M. (2006), 'Identifying universals of text translation', *Journal of Quantitative Linguistics* 13(1), 35–43.

Kärkkäinen, E. (2003), *Epistemic Stance in English Conversation. A Description of its Interactional Functions with a Focus on* I think. Amsterdam/Philadelphia: John Benjamins.

Kehoe, A. and Renouf, A. (2002), 'WebCorp: Applying the Web to linguistics and linguistics to the Web'. *WWW 2002 Conference*. Honolulu, HI.

Kendall, L. (2002), *Hanging Out in the Virtual Pub: Masculinities and Relationships Online*. Berkeley, CA: University of California Press.

Kennedy, G. (1998), *An Introduction to Corpus Linguistics*. London: Longman.

Kenny, D. (1998), 'Creatures of habit? What translators usually do with words', *Meta* 43(4), 515–23.

Kenny, D. (1999), 'The German-English parallel corpus of literary texts (GEPCOLT): a resource for translation scholars', *Teanga* 18, 25–42.

Kenny, D. (2000), 'Translators at play: exploitations of collocational norms in German-English translation', in B. Dodd (ed.) *Working with German Corpora*. Birmingham: University of Birmingham Press, pp. 143–60.

Kenny, D. (2001), *Lexis and Creativity in Translation. A Corpus-based Study*. Manchester: St Jerome Publishing.

Kettemann, B. and Marko, G. (2004), 'Can the L in TaLC stand for literature?', in G. Aston, S. Bernardini and D. Stewart (eds) *Corpora and Language Learners*. Amsterdam: John Benjamins, pp. 169–93.

Kilgarriff, A. (2001), 'Web as corpus', in P. Rayson, A. Wilson, T. McEnery, A. Hardie and S. Khoja (eds) *Proceedings of the Corpus Linguistics 2001 Conference, Lancaster University*, 29 March–2 April 2001. Lancaster: UCREL, pp. 342–44.

Kilgarriff, A. (2002), RE: [Corpora-List] ACL proceedings paper in the American National Corpus. Available online at: http://torvald.aksis.uib.no/corpora/2002-3/0239.html

Kilgarriff, A. (2003), 'Linguistic search engine', in K. Simov and P. Osenova (eds) *Proceedings of the Workshop on Shallow Processing of Large Corpora (SProLaC 2003)*, 27 March 2003, held in conjunction with the Corpus Linguistics 2003 conference, (University Centre for Computer Corpus Research on Language Technical Papers). Lancaster: UCREL, Computing Department, Lancaster University, pp. 53–8.

Kilgarriff, A. and Grefenstette, G. (2003), 'Introduction to the special issue on the web as corpus', *Computational Linguistics* 29(3), 333–48.

Kilgarriff, A. and Rundell, M. (2002), 'Lexical profiling software and its lexicographic applications – a case study', *Proceedings EURALEX*. Copenhagen, pp. 807–18.

Kilgarriff, A., Rychly, P., Smrz, P. and Tugwell, D. (2004), 'The Sketch Engine', *Proceedings EURALEX*. Lorient, France, pp. 105–16.

Kilgarriff, A. and Tugwell, D. (2001), 'WORD SKETCH: extraction and display of significant collocations for lexicography', *Proceedings of the ACL workshop on COLLOCATION: Computational Extraction, Analysis and Exploitation*. Toulouse, pp. 32–8.

Kincaid, J. R. (1971), *Dickens and the Rhetoric of Laughter*. London: Oxford University Press.

King, B. W. (2006), 'A corpus-based investigation into the discourses of men in online queer space'. Unpublished masters dissertation, Available from the University of Leicester library, Leicester, UK.

King, B. W. (2011), 'Language, sexuality and place: The view from cyberspace', *Gender and Language* 5, 1–30.

Knight, D., Bayoumi, S., Mills, S., Crabtree, A., Adolphs, S., Pridmore, T. and Carter, R. (2006), 'Beyond the text: construction and analysis of multi-modal linguistic corpora', Paper delivered at the 2nd Annual International e-Social Science Conference, June 2006, University of Manchester.

Koller, V. (2002), 'A Shotgun Wedding: co-occurrence of war and marriage metaphors in mergers and acquisitions discourse', *Metaphor and Symbol* 17(3), 179–203.

Koller, V. (2004), *Metaphor and Gender in Business Media Discourse. A Critical Cognitive Study*. Basingstoke: Palgrave Macmillan.

Koller, V. and Mautner, G. (2004), 'Computer applications in Critical Discourse Analysis', in Ann Hewings, Caroline Coffin and Kieran O'Halloran (eds) *Applying English Grammar*. London: Arnold, pp. 216–28.

Korte, B. (1997), *Body Language in Literature*. Toronto: University of Toronto Press.

Kovecses, Z. (2002), *Metaphor: A Practical Introduction*. Oxford: Oxford University Press.

Krek, S. and Kilgarriff, A. (2006), 'Slovene word sketches', Proceedings of the 5th Solvenian/First International Languages Technology Conference, Ljubljana, Slovenia.

Krishnamurthy, R. (1987), 'The process of compilation', in J. M. Sinclair (ed.) *Looking Up*. London: Collins ELT, pp. 62–86.

Krishnamurthy, R. (1996), 'Ethnic, racial and tribal: the language of racism?', in C. R. Caldas-Coulthard and M. Coulthard (eds) *Texts and Practices. Readings in Critical Discourse Analysis*. London and New York: Routledge, pp. 129–49.

Krishnamurthy, R. (2004), *English Collocation Studies, The OSTI Report by John M. Sinclair, Susan Jones and Robert Daley*. London: Continuum.

Kruger, A. (2000), 'Lexical cohesion and register variation in translation: *The Merchant of Venice* in Afrikaans', Ph.D. thesis, University of South Africa.

Kruger, A. (2002), 'Corpus-based translation research: its development and implications for general, literary and Bible translation', *Acta Theologica Supplementum* 2, 70–106.

Kruger, A. and Wallmach, K. (eds) (forthcoming), *Corpus-Based Translation Studies: Research and Applications*. Manchester: St Jerome Publishing.

Kučera, H. and Francis, W. N. (1967), *Computational Analysis of Present Day American English*. Providence, Rhode Island: Brown University Press.

Kurohashi, S. and Nagao, M. (1997), 'Kyoto University text corpus project', in *Proceedings of the ANLP*, Japan, pp. 115–18.

Labov, W. (1990), 'The intersection of sex and social class in the course of linguistic change', *Language Variation and Change* 2, 205–54.

Labov, W. (2001), *Principles of Linguistic Change. Volume 2: Social Factors*. Oxford, UK and Cambridge, USA: Blackwell.

Lakoff, G. (1993), 'The contemporary theory of metaphor', in A. Ortony (ed.) *Metaphor and Thought*, 2nd edn. Cambridge: Cambridge University Press, pp. 202–51.

Lakoff, G. (2003), 'Metaphor and war, again'. Available online at: http://www.alternet.org/story/15414

Lakoff, G. and Johnson, M. (1980), *Metaphors We Live By*. Chicago: University of Chicago Press.

Lancashire, I. (2006), 'Computing the lexicons of Early Modern English', in A. Renouf and A. Kehoe (eds) *The Changing Face of Corpus Linguistics*. Amsterdam: Rodopi, pp. 45–62.

Laukkanen, M. (2007), 'Young queers online: the limits and possibilities of non-heterosexual self-representation in online conversations', in K. O'Riordan and D. J. Phillips (eds) *Queer Online: Media Technology and Sexuality*. New York: Peter Lang, pp. 81–100.

Laviosa, S. (1997), 'How comparable can "comparable corpora" be?' *Target* 9(2), 289–319.

Laviosa, S. (1998*a*), 'The corpus-based approach: a new paradigm in translation studies', *Meta* 43(4), 474–79.

Laviosa, S. (1998*b*), 'Core patterns of lexical use in a comparable corpus of English narrative prose', *Meta* 43(4), 557–70.

Laviosa, S. (2000), 'TEC: a resource for studying what is "in" and "of" translational English', *Across Languages and Cultures* 1(2), 159–77.

Laviosa, S. (2002), *Corpus-based Translation Studies. Theory, Findings, Applications*. Amsterdam: Rodopi.

Laviosa-Braithwaite, S. (1996), 'The English Comparable Corpus (ECC): a resource and a methodology for the empirical study of translation', Ph.D. thesis, University of Manchester.

Laviosa-Braithwaite, S. (1997), 'Investigating simplification in an English comparable corpus of newspaper articles', in K. Klaudy and J. Kohn (eds) *Transferre necesse est. Proceedings of the Second International Conference on Current Trends in Studies of Translation and Interpreting*. Budapest: Scholastica, pp. 531–40.

Lawrence, S. and Giles, C. L. (1999), 'Accessibility of information on the Web', *Nature* 400, 107–9.

Lea, D. (ed.) (2002), *Oxford Collocations Dictionary for Students of English*. Oxford: Oxford University Press.

Leap, W. (ed.) (1995), *Beyond the Lavender Lexicon: Authenticity, Imagination, and Appropriation in Lesbian and Gay Languages*. Luxembourg. Gordon and Breach.

Leap, W. (2008), Welcome! On *Website of the 15th Annual Lavender Languages and Linguistics Conference*. Accessed on 2 May 2008 at: http://www.american.edu/cas/anthro/lavenderlanguages

Lee, D. (2001), 'Genres, registers, text types, domains, and styles: clarifying the concepts and navigating a path through the BNC jungle', *Language Learning and Technology* 5(3), 37–72.

Leech, G. (2002), 'Recent grammatical change in English: data, description, theory', in K. Aijmer and B. Altenberg (eds) *Proceedings of the 2002 ICAME Conference*, Gothenburg.

Leech, G. and Fallon, R. (1992), 'Computer corpora – what do they tell us about culture?' *ICAME Journal* 16, 29–50.

Leech, G., Garside, R. and Bryant, M. (1994), 'CLAWS4: the tagging of the British National Corpus', *Proceedings of the 15th International Conference on Computational Linguistics (COLING 94)*, Kyoto, pp. 622–8.

Leech, G. and Short, M. (1981), *Style in Fiction. A Linguistic Introduction to English Fictional Prose*. Harlow: Pearson Education.

Leech, G. and Smith, N. (2005), 'Extending the possibilities of corpus-based research on English in the 20th century: a prequel to LOB and FLOB', *ICAME Journal* 29, 83–98.

Levin, B. (1993), *English Verb Classes and Alternations: A Preliminary Investigation.* Chicago: University of Chicago Press.

Lin, D. (1998), 'Automatic retrieval and clustering of similar words', *COLING-ACL,* Montreal, pp. 768–74.

Löfberg, L., Archer, D., Piao, S. S., Rayson, P., McEnery, T., Varantola, K. and Juntunen, J-P. (2003), 'Porting an English semantic tagger to the Finnish language', in D. Archer, P. Rayson, A. Wilson and A. McEnery (eds) *Proceedings of the Corpus Linguistics 2003 Conference.* UCREL technical paper number 16. UCREL, Lancaster University, pp. 457–64.

Lonfils, C. and Vanparys, J. (2001), 'How to design user-friendly CALL interfaces', *Computer Assisted Language Learning* 14(5), 405–17.

Louw, B. (1993), 'Irony in the text or insincerity in the writer? – The diagnostic potential of semantic prosodies', in M. Baker, G. Francis and E. Tognini-Bonelli (eds) *Text and Technology: In Honour of John Sinclair.* Amsterdam and Philadelphia: John Benjamins, pp. 157–76.

Lucy, D. (2005), *Introductory Statistics for Forensic Scientists.* New York: John Wiley.

Lucy, J. A. (1993), 'Reflexive language and the human disciplines', in J. A. Lucy (ed.) *Reflexive Language: Reported Speech and Metapragmatics.* Cambridge: Cambridge University Press, pp. 9–32.

Lüdeling, A., Evert, S. and Baroni, M. (2006), 'Using web data for linguistic purposes', in M. Hundt, C. Biewer and N. Nesselhauf (eds) *Corpus Linguistics and the Web, (Language and Computers – Studies in Practical Linguistics 59).* Amsterdam: Rodopi, pp. 7–24.

MacKenzie, I. (2000), 'Improvisation, creativity, and formulaic language', *The Journal of Aesthetics and Art Criticism* 58(2), 173–79.

Macleod, C., Grishman, R. and Meyers, A. (1998), 'COMLEX Syntax', in *Computers and the Humanities* 31, 459–81.

Mahlberg, M. (2007a), 'A corpus stylistic perspective on Dickens' *Great Expectations*', in M. Lambrou and P. Stockwell (eds) *Contemporary Stylistics.* London: Continuum, pp. 19–31.

Mahlberg, M. (2007b), 'Clusters, key clusters and local textual functions in Dickens', *Corpora* 2(1), 1–31.

Mahlberg, M. (2007c), 'Corpus stylistics: bridging the gap between linguistic and literary studies', in M. Hoey, M. Mahlberg, M. Stubbs and W. Teubert, *Text, Discourse and Corpora. Theory and Analysis.* London: Continuum, 219–46.

Malik, A. (2006a), 'Punjabi Machine Transliteration', in *Proceedings of the 21st International Conference on Computational Linguistics and 44th Annual Meeting of the Association for Computational Linguistics,* July 2006, pp. 1137–44.

Malik, A. (2006b), 'Hindi Urdu machine transliteration system'. Unpublished MSc Thesis, University of Paris 7.

Malinowski, B. (1923), 'The problem of meaning in primitive languages', in C. K. Ogden and I. A. Richards (eds) *Meaning of Meaning: A Study of the Influence of Language upon Thought and of the Science of Symbolism.* London: Kegan Paul, Trench, Trubner and Company, pp. 451–510.

Mallikarjun, B. (2004), 'Indian multilingualism, language policy and the digital divide', in *SCALLA 2004 Working Position Papers.* Available online at http://www.elda.fr/proj/scalla.html

Malmkjær, K. (1997), 'Punctuation in Hans Christian Andersen's stories and their translations into English', in F. Poyatos (ed.) *Nonverbal Communication and Translation: New Perspectives and Challenges in Literature, Interpretation and the Media.* Amsterdam: John Benjamins, pp. 151–62.

Manning, C. D. (2003), 'Probabilistic syntax', in R. Bod, J. Hay and S. Jannedy (eds) *Probabilistic Linguistics.* Cambridge, MA: MIT Press, pp. 289–341.

Marantz, A. (1984), *On the Nature of Grammatical Relations.* Cambridge: MIT Press.

Marcus, M. P., Santorini, B. and Marcinkiewicz, M. A. (1994), 'Building a large annotated corpus of English: The Penn Treebank', *Computational Linguistics* 19(2), 313–30.

Markus, M. (2006), 'EFL dictionaries, grammars and language guides from 1700 to 1850: testing a new corpus on points of spokenness', in A. Renouf and A. Kehoe (eds) *The Changing Face of Corpus Linguistics.* Amsterdam: Rodopi, pp. 63–81.

Martin, J. I. and Knox, J. G. (2000), 'Methodological and ethical issues in research on lesbians and gay men', *Social Work Research* 24, 51–9.

Masica, C. P. (1991), *The Indo-Aryan Languages.* Cambridge: Cambridge University Press.

Mason, O. (1997), 'The weight of words: an investigation of lexical gravity', in *Proceedings of PALC'97.* Lodz, pp. 361–75.

Mason, Z. (2004), 'A computational, corpus-based conventional metaphor extractor', *Computational Linguistics* 30(1), 23–44.

Masubelele, R. (2004), 'A corpus-based appraisal of shifts in language use and translation policies in two Zulu translations of the Book of Matthew', *Language Matters* 35(1), 201–13.

Mauranen, A. (2000), 'Strange strings in translated language: a study on corpora', in M. Olohan (ed.) *Intercultural Faultlines. Research Models in Translation Studies 1: Textual and Cognitive Aspects.* Manchester: St Jerome Publishing, pp. 119–41.

Mauranen, A. (2002), 'Will "translationese" ruin a contrastive study?' *Languages in Contrast* 2(2), 161–86.

Mauranen, A. (2003), 'The corpus of English as lingua franca in academic settings', *TESOL Quarterly* 37(3), 513–27.

Mauranen, A. (2004), 'Formulaic sequences in Lingua Franca English', Paper presented at the 37th BAAL Conference, 10 September 2004, Kings College, London.

Mauranen, A. (2007), 'Universal tendencies in translation', in M. Rogers and G. Anderman (eds) *Incorporating Corpora. The Linguist and the Translator.* Clevedon: Multilingual Matters, pp. 32–48.

Mauranen, A. and Kujamäki, P. (2004), *Translation Universals: Do they exist?* Amsterdam: John Benjamins.

Mautner, G. (2005), 'Time to get wired: using web-based corpora in critical discourse analysis', *Discourse & Society* 16(6), 809–28.

Mautner, G. (2007), 'Mining large corpora for social information: the case of *elderly*', *Language in Society* 36(1), 51–72.

Mautner, G. (2008), 'Analysing newspapers, magazines and other print media', in R. Wodak and M. Krzyzanowski (eds) *Qualitative Discourse Analysis in the Social Sciences.* Basingstoke: Palgrave-Macmillan, pp. 30–53.

Mautner, G. (2009), 'Checks and balances: how corpus linguistics can contribute to CDA', in R. Wodak and M. Meyer (eds) *Methods of Critical Discourse Analysis*, 2nd edn. London: Sage, pp. 122–43.

McArthur, T. (1981), *Longman Lexicon of Contemporary English*. London: Longman.

McEnery, T. (2004), 'Europe's ignored languages', in G. Sampson and D. McCarthy (eds) *Corpus Linguistics: Readings in a Widening Discipline*. London: Continuum.

McEnery, A. and Wilson, A. (1996/2001), *Corpus Linguistics* (2nd edn in 2001). Edinburgh: Edinburgh University Press.

McEnery, A. and Xiao, R. (2002), 'Domains, text types, aspect marking and English-Chinese translation', *Languages in Contrast* 2(2), 211–29.

McEnery, A. and Xiao, R. (2004), 'The Lancaster Corpus of Mandarin Chinese: A corpus for monolingual and contrastive language study', in M. Lino, M. Xavier, F. Ferreire, R. Costa and R. Silva (eds) *Proceedings of the Fourth International Conference on Language Resources and Evaluation (LREC) 2004*, Lisbon, 24–30 May 2004, pp. 1175–78.

McEnery, A. and Xiao, R. (2007), 'Parallel and comparable corpora: what is happening?', in M. Rogers and G. Anderman (eds) *Incorporating Corpora. The Linguist and the Translator*. Clevedon: Multilingual Matters, pp. 18–31.

McEnery, A., Xiao, R. and Tono, Y. (2006), *Corpus-based Language Studies: An Advanced Resource Book*. London: Routledge.

McEnery, A. M. and Xiao, Z. (2005), *Help* or *Help To*: What do corpora have to say? *English Studies* Volume 86, 1/2.

McEnery, T. and Xiao, Z. (2004), 'Swearing in modern British English: the case of *fuck* in the BNC', *Language and Literature* 13(3), 235–68.

McEnery, T. and Xiao, Z. (2005), 'Character encoding in corpus construction', in M. Wynne (ed.) *Developing Linguistic Corpora: A Guide to Good Practice*. AHDS Literature, Languages and Linguistics, Oxford: Oxbow Books, pp. 47–58.

McGregor, R. S. (ed.) (1993), *Oxford Hindi-English Dictionary*. Oxford: Oxford University Press.

Meyer, C. F. (2002), *English Corpus Linguistics*. Cambridge, UK: Cambridge University Press.

Meyers, A., Fang, A. C., Ferro, L., Aübler, S. K., Jia-Lin, T., Palmer, M., Poesio, M., Dolbey, A., Schuler, K. K., Loper, E., Zinsmeister, H., Penn, G., Xue, N., Hinrichs, E., Wiebe, J., Pustejovsky, J., Farwell, D., Hajicova, E., Dorr, B., Hovy, E., Onyshkevych, B. A. and Levin, L. (2006), 'Annotation Compatibility Working Group Report', in ACL 2006 Workshop: Frontiers in Linguistically Annotated Corpora 2006: A Merged Workshop with 7th International Workshop on Linguistically Interpreted Corpora (LINC-2006) and Frontiers in Corpus Annotation III.

Meyers, A., Grishman, R. and Kosaka, M. (2002), 'Formal mechanisms for capturing regularizations', in Proceedings of LREC-2002, Las Palmas, Spain.

Meyers, A., Grishman, R., Kosaka, M. and Zhao, S. (2001a), 'Covering Treebanks with GLARF', in ACL/EACL Workshop on Sharing Tools and Resources for Research and Education.

Meyers, A., Grishman, R., Kosaka, M. and Zhao, S. (2001b), 'Parsing and GLARFing', in Proceedings of RANLP-2001, Tzigov Chark, Bulgaria.

Meyers, A., Ide, N., Denoyer, L. and Shinyama, Y. (2007), 'The shared corpora working group report', in *Proceedings of The Linguistic Annotation Workshop, ACL 2007*. Prague, Czech Republic, pp. 184–90.

Meyers, A., Reeves, R., Macleod, C., Szekely, R., Zielinska, V., Young, B. and Grishman, R. (2004), 'The NomBank project: an interim report', in *NAACL/HLT 2004 Workshop Frontiers in Corpus Annotation*, Boston, MA.

Miller, G. A. (1956), 'The magical number seven, plus or minus two: some limits on our capacity for processing information', *The Psychological Review* 63(2), 81–97.

Miller, G. A. and Fellbaum, C. (2007), 'WordNet then and now', *Language Resources and Evaluation* 41(2), 209–14.

Miltsakaki, E., Joshi, A., Prasad, R. and Webber, B. (2004), 'Annotating discourse connectives and their arguments', in A. Meyers (ed.) *NAACL/HLT 2004 Workshop: Frontiers in Corpus Annotation*. Boston, MA, 2–7 May. Association for Computational Linguistics, pp. 9–16.

Moon, R. (1987), 'The analysis of meaning', in J. Sinclair (ed.) *Looking Up: An Account of the COBUILD Project in Lexical Computing*. London: Collins, pp. 86–103.

Moon, R. (1998), *Fixed Expressions and Idioms in English*. Oxford: Clarendon Press.

Moon, R. (2007), 'Sinclair, lexicography and the COBUILD project: the application of theory', *International Journal of Corpus Linguistics* 12(2), 158–81.

Moore, R. C. (2004), 'On the Log-Likelihood ratios and the significance of rare events', *Proceedings of the 2004 Conference 'Empirical Methods in Natural Language Processing'*. Barcelona, Spain, pp. 333–40.

Morley, B. (2006), 'WebCorp: a tool for online linguistic information retrieval and analysis', in A. Renouf and A. Kehoe (eds) *The Changing Face of Corpus Linguistics*. Amsterdam: Rodopi, pp. 283–96.

Morley, B., Renouf, A. and Kehoe, A. (2003), 'Linguistic research with XML/RDF-aware WebCorp tool', *WWW 2003 Conference*. Budapest.

Munday, J. (2001), *Introducing Translation Studies: Theories and Applications*. London: Routledge.

Nakanishi, A. (1980), *Writing Systems of the World*. Rutland, VT: Charles E. Tuttle Company.

Narayan, D., Chakrabarti, D., Pande, P and Bhattacharyya, P. (2002), 'An experience in building the Indo WordNet – a WordNet for Hindi', in *First International Conference on Global WordNet*, Mysore, India, January 2002. Available online at http://www.cfilt.iitb.ac.in/wordnet/webhwn/papers/gwn-2002.ps

Naseem, T. and Hussain, S. (2007), 'A novel approach for ranking spelling error corrections for Urdu', *Language Resources and Evaluation* 41(2), 117–28.

Nattinger, J. R. and DeCarrico, J. S. (1992), *Lexical Phrases and Language Teaching*. Oxford: Oxford University Press.

Neal, R. (1996), *Bayesian Learning for Neural Networks*. New York: Springer Verlag.

Nelson, M. (2005), 'Semantic associations in Business English: a corpus-based analysis', *English for Specific Purposes* 25, 217–34.

Nevalainen, S. (2005), 'Köyhtyykö kieli käännettäessä? Mitätaajuuslistat kertovat suomennosten sanastosta', in A. Mauranen and J. Jantunen (eds) *Käännössuomeksi*. Tampere: Tampere University Press, pp. 141–62.

Newmark, P. (1981), *Approaches to Translation*. Oxford: Pergamon Press.

Nida, E. (1964), *Toward a Science of Translating*. Leiden: J. Brill.

Noguchi, J. (2004), 'A genre analysis and mini-corpora approach to support professional writing by nonnative English speakers', *English Corpus Studies* 11, 101–10.

Oakes, M. and Farrow, M. (2007), 'Use of the chi-squared test to examine vocabulary differences in English-language corpora representing seven different countries', *Literary and Linguistic Computing* 22(1), 85–100.

Oakes, M. P. (1998), *Statistics for Corpus Linguistics*. Edinburgh: Edinburgh University Press.

Oakey, D. J. (2002), 'Formulaic language in English academic writing: A corpus-based study of the formal and functional variation of a lexical phrase in different academic disciplines in English.' In R. Reppen, S. Fitzmaurice and D. Biber (eds) *Using Corpora to Explore Linguistic Variation*. Amsterdam: John Benjamins, pp. 111–30.

Ogden, C. K. (1930), *Basic English: A General Introduction with Rules and Grammar*. London: Paul Treber and Co.

O'Halloran, K. (2007*a*), 'Critical discourse analysis and the corpus-informed interpretation of metaphor at the register level', *Applied Linguistics* 28(1), 1–24.

O'Halloran, K. (2007*b*), 'The subconscious in James Joyce's "Eveline": a corpus stylistic analysis that chews on the "Fish hook"', *Language and Literature* 16(3), 227–44.

O'Halloran, K. (2007*c*), 'Corpus-assisted literary evaluation', *Corpora* 2(1), 33–63.

O'Halloran, K. and Coffin, C. (2004), 'Checking overinterpretation and underinterpretation. Help from corpora in critical linguistics', in A. Hewings, C. Coffin and K. O'Halloran (eds) *Applying English Grammar*. London: Arnold, pp. 275–97.

Olohan, M. (2004), *Introducing Corpora in Translation Studies*. London and New York: Routledge.

Olohan, M. and Baker, M. (2000), 'Reporting *that* in translated English: evidence for subconscious processes of explicitation?' *Across Languages and Cultures* 1(2), 141–58.

Ooi, V. B. Y. (2001), 'Aspects of computer-mediated communication for research in corpus linguistics', *Language and Computers* 36, 91–104.

Ooi, V. B. Y., Tan, P. K. W. and Chiang, A. K. L. (2006), 'Analysing weblogs in a speech community using the WMatrix approach', 27th Conference of the International Computer Archive of Modern and Medieval English (ICAME) (University of Helsinki, Finland). 24–28 May 2006.

Oriental Book Society (date unknown), *New Edition Popular Oxford Combined Dictionary*. Lahore: Oriental Book Society.

Orpin, D. (2005), 'Corpus linguistics and critical discourse analysis. Examining the ideology of sleaze', *International Journal of Corpus Linguistics* 10(1), 37–61.

Øverås, L. (1998), 'In search of the third code: an investigation of norms in literary translation', *Meta* 43(4), 557–70.

Palmer, M., Daniel G. and Kingsbury, P. (2005), 'The Proposition Bank: an annotated corpus of semantic roles', *Computational Linguistics* 31(1), 71–106.

Partington, A. (1998), *Patterns and Meaning: Using Corpora for English Language Research and Teaching*. Amsterdam: John Benjamins.

Partington, A. (2004a), 'Utterly content in each other's company. Semantic prosody and semantic preference', *International Journal of Corpus Linguistics* 9(1), 131–56.

Partington, A. (2004b), 'Corpora and discourse, a most congruous beast', in A. Partington, J. Morley and L. Haarman (eds) *Corpora and Discourse*. Bern: Peter Lang, pp. 11–20.

Pawley, A. (1986), 'Lexicalisation', in D. Tannen and J. E. Alatis (eds) *Language and Linguistics: The Interdependence of Theory, Data and Application*. Georgetown: Georgetown University Round Table on Languages and Linguistics 1985, pp. 98–120.

Pawley, A. and Syder, F. H. (1983), 'Two puzzles for linguistic theory: nativelike selection and nativelike fluency', in J. C. Richards and R. W. Schmidt (eds) *Language and Communication*. London: Longman, pp. 191–226.

Pawley, A. and Syder, F. H. (2000), 'The one-clause-at-a-time hypothesis', in H. Riggenbach (ed.) *Perspectives on Fluency*. Ann Arbor, MI: University of Michigan Press, pp. 163–99.

Pearl, J. (1988), *Probabilistic Inference in Intelligent Systems*. San Mateo, CA: Morgan Kaufmann.

Peters, A. M. (1983), *The Units of Language Acquisition*. Cambridge: Cambridge University Press.

Piao, S., Rayson, P., Archer, D. and McEnery, T. (2005), 'Comparing and combining a semantic tagger and a statistical tool for MWE extraction', *Computer Speech and Language* (Special issue on Multiword expressions) 19, 378–97.

Pilz, T., Ernst-Gerlach, A., Kempken, S., Rayson, P. and Archer, D. (2008), 'The identification of spelling variants in English and German historical texts: manual or automatic?', *Literary and Linguistic Computing* 23, 65–72.

Pinker, S. (1989), *Learnability and Cognition: The Acquisition of Argument Structure*. Cambridge, MA: MIT Press.

Piper, A. (2000a), 'Lifelong learning, human capital, and the soundbite', *Text* 20(1), 109–46.

Piper, A. (2000b), 'Some have credit cards and others have giro cheques: "Individuals" and "people" as lifelong learners in late modernity', *Discourse & Society* 11(4), 515–42.

Pollard, C. and Sag, I. A. (1994), *Head-Driven Phrase Structure Grammar*. Chicago and Stanford: University of Chicago Press and CSLI Publications.

Pollard, D., Parpworth, N. and Hughes, D. (2001), *Constitutional and Administrative Law. Text with Materials*, 3rd edn. London, Edinburgh and Dublin: Butterworths.

Popescu, M. and Dinu, L. (2007), 'Kernel methods and string kernels for authorship identification: the Federalist Papers', *Proceedings of Recent Advances in Natural Language Processing 2007*. Borovets, Bulgaria.

Postal, P. M. (1974), *On Raising*. Cambridge: MIT Press.

Postal, P. M. and Pullum, G. K. (1988), 'Expletive noun phrases in subcategorized positions', *Linguistic Inquiry* 19, 635–70.

Pravec, N. A. (2002), 'Survey of learner corpora', *ICAME Journal* 26, 81–114.

Project Gutenberg (2003–2006), accessed July 2006 at: http://www.gutenberg.org/

Pustejovsky, J., Ingria, B., Sauri, R., Castano, J., Littman, J., Gaizauskas, R., Setzer, A., Katz, G. and Mani, I. (2004), 'The specification language TimeML', in I. Mani, J. Pustejovsky and R. Gaizauskas (eds) *The Language of Time: A Reader*. Oxford: Oxford University Press.

Pustejovsky, J., Meyers, A., Palmer, M. and Poesio, M. (2005), 'Merging PropBank, NomBank, TimeBank, Penn Discourse Treebank and Coreference', in ACL 2005 Workshop: Frontiers in Corpus Annotation II: Pie in the Sky.

Pym, A. (2005), 'Explaining explicitation', in K. Károly and Á. Fóris (eds) *New Trends in Translation Studies*, Budapest: Akadémiai Kiadó, pp. 29–43.

Rao, D. (2001), 'Machine translation in India: a brief survey', in *Proceedings of SCALLA 2001*, available online at http://www.elda.org/en/proj/scalla/SCALLA2001.html

Ratnaparkhi, A. (1999), 'Learning to parse natural language with maximum entropy models', *Machine Learning* 34(1–3), 151–75.

Rayson, P. (2008), 'Log-likelihood calculator'. *UCREL web server*. Accessed on 22 June 2006 at: http://ucrel.lancs.ac.uk/llwizard.html

Rayson, P., Archer, D., Baron, A., Culpeper, J. and Smith, N. (2007), 'Tagging the bard: evaluating the accuracy of a modern POS tagger on Early Modern English corpora', in *Proceedings of Corpus Linguistics 2007*. University of Birmingham. Accessed on 23 April 2008 at: http://ucrel.lancs.ac.uk/people/paul/publications/RaysonEtAl_CL2007.pdf

Rayson, P., Archer, D., Piao, S. L. and McEnery, T. (2004*a*), 'The UCREL semantic analysis system', in proceedings of the workshop on 'Beyond Named Entity Recognition: Semantic labelling for NLP tasks' in association with the 4th International Conference on Language Resources and Evaluation (*LREC 2004*), 25 May 2004, Lisbon, Portugal, pp. 7–12. Available online at http://www.comp.lancs.ac.uk/computing/users/paul/publications/usas_lrec04ws.pdf

Rayson, P., Berridge, D. and Francis, B. (2004*b*), 'Extending the Cochran rule for the comparison of word frequencies between corpora.' *Le poids des mots: Actes des 7es journées internationals d'analyse statistique des données textuelles (JADT)*. Louvain-la-Neuve, Belgium, 10–12 Mar, pp. 926–36.

Rayson, P., Archer, D. and Smith, N. (2005), 'VARD versus WORD: a comparison of the UCREL variant detector and modern spellcheckers on English historical corpora', in *Proceedings of Corpus Linguistics 2005*. Birmingham University, 14–17 July 2005. Corpus Linguistics Conference Series on-line e-journal. Accessed on 23 April 2008 at: http://www.comp.lancs.ac.uk/computing/users/paul/publications/cl2005_vardword.pdf

Rayson, P., Leech, G. and Hodges, M. (1997), 'Social differentiation in the use of English vocabulary: some analyses of the conversational component of the British National Corpus', *International Journal of Corpus Linguistics* 2(1), 133–52.

Rayson, P., Wilson, A. and Leech, G. (2002), 'Grammatical word class variation within the British National Corpus sampler', in P. Peters, P. Collins and A. Smith (eds) *New Frontiers of Corpus Research: Papers from the Twenty First International Conference on English Language Research on Computerized Corpora, Sydney 2000*. Amsterdam: Rodopi, pp. 295–306.

Reid, E. (1996), 'Informed consent in the study of on-line communities: a reflection on the effects of computer-mediated social research', *The Information Society* 12, 169–74.

Renouf, A., Kehoe, A. and Banerjee, J. (2006), 'The WebCorp Search Engine: a holistic approach to web text search'. *Electronic Proceedings of CL2005*. Birmingham: University of Birmingham.

Reppen, R. and Ide, N. (2004), 'The American National Corpus: Overall goals and the First Release', *Journal of English Linguistics* 32(2), 105–13.

Resnik, P. (1992), 'Probabilistic tree-adjoining grammar as a framework for statistical natural language processing', *Proceedings of the 14th Conference on Computational Linguistics*, pp. 418–24.

Resnik, P. and Smith, N. A. (2003), 'The Web as a parallel corpus', *Computational Linguistics* 29(3), 349–80.

Ritchie, D. (2003), 'ARGUMENT IS WAR – Or is it a game of chess? Multiple meanings in the analysis of implicit metaphors', *Metaphor and Symbol* 18(2), 125–46.

Rosenbaum, P. S. (1967), *The Grammar of English Predicate Complement Constructions*. Cambridge: MIT Press.

Ross, N. J. (1995), 'Dubbing American in Italy', *English Today*, 11, 45–8.

Rundell, M. (2000), 'The biggest corpus of all', *Humanising Language Teaching* 2(3).

Sag, I., Baldwin, T., Bond, F., Copstake, A. and Flickinger, D. (2002), 'Multiword expressions: a pain in the neck for NLP', *Third International Conference on Intelligent Text Processing and Computational Linguistics (CICLing-2002)*. Mexico City, Mexico, pp. 1–15.

Sajjad, H. (2007), 'Statistical part of speech tagger for Urdu', Unpublished MSc thesis, National University of Computer and Emerging Sciences, Lahore, Pakistan. Available online at http://www.crulp.org/Publication/theses/2007/part_of_speech_tagger.pdf

Sambor, J. (1988), 'Lingwistyka kwantytatywna - stan badań i perspektywy rozwoju', *Biuletyn PTJ* 41, 47–67.

Santini, M. (2006), 'Automatic identification of genre in web pages', Ph.D. dissertation, University of Brighton.

Sasikumar, M. and Hegde, J. J. (2004), 'Software localisation: some issues and challenges', in *SCALLA 2004 Working Position Papers*. Available online at http://www.elda.fr/proj/scalla.html

Schimdt, R. (2001), 'Attention', in P. Robinson (ed.) *Cognition in Second Language Instruction*. Cambridge: Cambridge University Press, pp. 3–32.

Schmidt, R. L. (1999), *Urdu: An Essential Grammar*. London: Routledge.

Schmied, J. (2006), 'New ways of analysing ESL on the WWW with WebCorp and WebPhraseCount', in A. Renouf and A. Kehoe (eds) *The Changing Face of Corpus Linguistics*. Amsterdam: Rodopi, pp. 309–24.

Schmitt, N., (ed.) (2004), *Formulaic Sequences: Acquisition, Processing and Use*. Amsterdam, Philadelphia: John Benjamins.

Scott, M. (1999), *WordSmith Tools 3.0*. Oxford: Oxford University Press.

Scott, M. (2004), *WordSmith Tools 4.0*. Oxford: Oxford University Press.

Scott, M. (2008), *WordSmith Tools 5.0*. Oxford: Oxford University Press.

Scott, M. and Tribble, C. (2006), *Textual Patterns. Key Words and Corpus Analysis in Language Education*. Amsterdam: John Benjamins.

Seidlhofer, B. (2001), *Vienna-Oxford International Corpus of English*. Available online at: http://www.univie.ac.at/voice/

Semino, E. and Rayson, P. (2006), 'Corpus techniques for metaphor analysis: exploiting a semantic annotation tool'. Available online at http://creet.open.ac.uk/projects/metaphor-analysis/procedure.cfm

Semino, E. and Short, M. (2004), *Corpus Stylistics. Speech, Writing and Thought Presentation in a Corpus of English Writing*. London: Routledge.

Sharoff, S. (2006), 'Open-source corpora. Using the net to fish for linguistic data', *International Journal of Corpus Linguistics* 11(4), 435–62.

Shastri, S. V., Patilkulkarni, C. T. and Shastri, G. S. (1986), *Manual of Information to Accompany the Kolhapur Corpus of Indian English, for Use with Digital Computers*. Kolhapur: Department of English, Shivaji University. Available online at: http://khnt.hit.uib.no/icame/manuals/kolhapur/INDEX.HTM

Shaumyan, S. (1977), *Applicative Grammar as a Semantic Theory of Natural Language*. Chicago: Chicago University Press.

Shaw, D. F. (1997), 'Gay men and computer communication: a discourse of sex and identity in cyberspace', in S. G. Jones (ed.) *Virtual Culture: Identity and Communication in Cybersociety*. London: Sage, pp. 133–45.

Shinyama, Y. and Sekine, S. (2006), 'Preemptive information extraction using unrestricted relation discovery', in Proceedings of NAACL/HLT, New York, NY: Association for Computational Linguistics.

Sinclair, J. (1991), *Corpus, Concordance, Collocation*. Oxford: Oxford University Press.

Sinclair, J. (1999), 'A way with common words', in H. Hasselgard and S. Oksefjell (eds) *Out of Corpora: Studies in Honour of Stig Johansson*. Amsterdam: Rodopi, pp. 157–79.

Sinclair, J. (2003), *Reading Concordances. An Introduction*. London: Pearson Longman.

Sinclair, J. (2006), *Exploring a Corpus*. Special Lecture held on 19 August 2006 at Ritsumeikan University, Japan.

Sinclair, J. (2007), 'Introduction', in M. Hoey, M. Mahlberg, M. Stubbs and W. Teubert, (eds) *Text, Discourse and Corpora. Theory and Analysis*. London: Continuum, pp. 1–5.

Sinclair, J. (ed.) (1987), *Looking Up: An Account of the COBUILD Project in Lexical Computing*. London, Glasgow: Collins.

Sinclair, J. (ed.) (1995), *Collins COBUILD English Language Dictionary*, 2nd edn. London, Glasgow: Collins.

Sinclair, J. (ed.) (2004), *How to Use Corpora in Language Teaching*. Amsterdam: John Benjamins.

Sinclair, J. M. (1966), 'Beginning the study of lexis', in C. E. Bazell, J. C. Catford, M. A. K. Halliday and R. H. Robins (eds) *In Memory of J. R. Firth*. London: Longman, pp. 410–30.

Sinclair, J. M. (2005), 'Corpus and text – basic principles', in M. Wynne (ed.) *Developing Linguistic Corpora: A Guide to Good Practice*. Oxford: Oxbow Books, pp. 1–16.

Sinclair, J. M. (ed.) (2006), *Collins COBUILD Advanced Learner's English Dictionary 5th Edition*. Glasgow: HarperCollins.

Sinclair, J. McH. (2004), *Trust the Text: Language, Corpus and Discourse*. London: Routledge.

Singh, U. N. (2004), 'Language technology: a roadmap for South Asian languages', in *SCALLA 2004 Working Position Papers*. Available online at http://www.elda.fr/proj/scalla.html

Sinha, S. (2007), *Demonstrative Anaphors in Hindi Newspaper Reportage: A Corpus-based Study*. München: Lincom Europa.

Sivia, D. S. (2006), *Data Analysis: A Bayesian Tutorial.* New York: Oxford University Press.

Smarr, J. and Grow, T. (2002), 'GoogleLing: the Web as a linguistic corpus', Technical Report, Stanford University.

Smyth, P., Heckerman, D. and Jordan, M. I. (1997), 'Probabilistic independence networks for hidden Markov probability models', *Neural Computation* 9, 227–69.

Spencer-Oatey, H. (2000), 'Rapport management: a framework for analysis', in H. Spencer-Oatey (ed.) *Culturally Speaking: Managing Rapport Through Talk Across Cultures.* London and New York: Continuum, pp. 11–46.

Starcke, B. (2006), 'The phraseology of Jane Austen's Persuasion: phraseological units as carriers of meaning', *ICAME Journal* 30, 87–104.

Steever, S. (ed.) (1997), *The Dravidian Languages.* New York: Routledge.

Stefanowitsch, A. (2006), 'Corpus-based approaches to metaphor and metonymy', in A. Stefanowitsch and S. Th. Gries (eds) *Corpus-based Approaches to Metaphor and Metonymy.* Berlin: Mouton de Gruyter, pp. 1–16.

Stenström, A. -B., Andersen, G. and Hasund, I. K. (2002), *Trends in Teenage Talk: Corpus Compilation, Analysis and Findings.* Amsterdam: John Benjamins.

Stubbs, M. (1986), 'Lexical density: a computational technique and some findings', in M. Coulthard (ed.) *Talking about Text. Studies Presented to David Brazil on His Retirement.* Birmingham: English Language Research, University of Birmingham.

Stubbs, M. (1996), *Text and Corpus Analysis.* Oxford and Cambridge, MA: Blackwell.

Stubbs, M. (2001a), 'Text, corpora and problems of interpretation: a response to Widdowson', *Applied Linguistics* 22(2), 149–72.

Stubbs, M. (2001b), *Words and Phrases. Corpus Studies of Lexical Semantics.* Oxford and Malden, MA: Blackwell.

Stubbs, M. (2005), 'Conrad in the computer: examples of quantitative stylistics methods', *Language and Literature* 14(1), 5–24.

Stubbs, M. and Gerbig, A. (1993), 'Human and inhuman geography: on the computer-assisted analysis of long texts', in M. Hoey (ed.) *Data, Description, Discourse.* London: HarperCollins, pp. 64–85.

Sumara, D. and Davis, B. (1999), 'Interrupting heteronormativity: toward a queer curriculum theory', *Curriculum Inquiry* 29, 191–208.

Tagnin, S. (2002), 'Corpora and the innocent translator: How can they help him?', in M. Thelen and B. Lewandowska-Tomaszczyk (eds) *Translation and Meaning* (Issue 6), Maastricht: Hogeschool Zuyd, pp. 489–96.

Terkourafi, M. (2008), 'Toward a unified theory of politeness, impoliteness, and rudeness', in D. Bousfield and M. Locher (eds) *Impoliteness in Language.* Berlin: Mouton de Gruyter, pp. 45–74.

Teubert, W. (1996), 'Comparable or parallel corpora?' *International Journal of Lexicography* 9(3), 238–64.

Teubert, W. and Čermáková, A (2004), *Corpus Linguistics. A Short Introduction.* London and New York: Continuum.

Tirkkonen-Condit, S. (2002), 'Translationese – a myth or an empirical fact? A study into the linguistic identifiability of translated language', *Target* 14(2), 207–20.

Tirkkonen-Condit, S. (2005), 'Do unique items make themselves scarce in translated Finnish?', in K. Károly and Á. Fóris (eds) *New Trends in Translation Studies. In Honour of Kinga Klaudy*. Budapest: Akadémiai Kiadó, pp. 177–89.

Tognini-Bonelli, Elena (2001), *Corpus Linguistics at Work*. Amsterdam: John Benjamins.

Tono, Y. (2002), 'The role of learner corpora in second language acquisition and foreign language learning: the multiple comparison approach'. Unpublished Ph.D. thesis. Lancaster University.

Tono, Y. (2007), *Nihonjin Chukosei Ichiman-nin no Eigo Corpus*. (A Corpus of 10,000 Japanese secondary school students ˋof English: The JEFLL Corpus). Tokyo: Shogakukan.

Toolan, M. (1996), 'Stylistics and its discontents; or, getting off the Fish "hook"', in J. J. Weber (ed.) *The Stylistics Reader. From Roman Jakobson to the Present*. London: Arnold, pp. 117–35.

Toury, G. (1980), *In Search of a Theory of Translation*. Tel Aviv: Porter Institute for Poetics and Semiotics.

Toury, G. (1995), *Descriptive Translation Studies and Beyond*. Amsterdam: John Benjamins.

Toury, G. (2004), 'Probabilistic explanations in translation studies. Welcome as they are, would they qualify as universals?', in A. Mauranen and P. Kuyamaki (eds) *Translation Universals: Do They Exist?* Amsterdam: John Benjamins, pp. 15–32.

Tribble, C. (1991), 'Concordancing and an EAP writing program', *CAELL Journal* 1(2), 10–15.

Tribble, C. and Jones, G. (1997), *Concordances in the Classroom*. Houston: Athelstan. webcorp. 1999–2008. Research and Development Unit for English Studies. Accessed February 2008 online at: http://www.webcorp.org.uk/

Truss, L. (2005), *Talk to the Hand*. London: Profile Books.

Tymoczko, M. (1998), 'Computerized corpora and the future of translation studies', *Meta* 43(4), 652–60.

The Unicode Consortium (2006), *Unicode Standard, Version 5.0*. Boston: Addison-Wesley Professional.

US Department of State (2008), 'Travel and geography: the regions of the United States'. On US Diplomatic Mission to Germany Website. Accessed on 21 May 2008 at: http://usa.usembassy.de/travel-regions.htm

Utka, A. (2004), 'English-Lithuanian phases of translation corpus: compilation and analysis', *International Journal of Corpus Linguistics* 9(2), 195–224.

Van Lancker, D. and Canter, G. J. (1981), 'Idiomatic versus literal interpretations of ditropically ambiguous sentences', *Journal of Speech and Hearing Research* 46(1), 64–9.

Van Lancker, D., Canter, G. J. and Terbeek, D. (1981), 'Disambiguation of ditropic sentences acoustic and phonetic cues', *Journal of Speech and Hearing Research* 24(3), 330–5.

van Leuven-Zwart, K. and Ton Naaijkens, A. (1991), *Translation Studies: The State of the Art*. Amsterdam: Rodopi.

Váradi, T. (2007), 'NP modification structures in parallel corpora', in M. Rogers and G. Anderman (eds) *Incorporating Corpora. The Linguist and the Translator*. Clevedon: Multilingual Matters, pp. 168–86.

Varantola, K. (2003), 'Translators and disposable corpora', in F. Zanettin, S. Bernardini and D. Stewart (eds) *Corpora in Translator Education.* Manchester: St Jerome, pp. 55–70.

Verhagen, M., Stubbs, A. and Pustejovsky. J. (2007), 'Combining independent syntactic and semantic annotation schemes', in *Proceedings of The Linguistic Annotation Workshop, ACL 2007.* Prague, Czech Republic, pp. 109–12.

Vintar, Š. (2007), 'Corpora in translator training and practice: a Slovene perspective', in M. Rogers and G. Anderman (eds) *Incorporating Corpora. The Linguist and the Translator.* Clevedon: Multilingual Matters, pp. 153–67.

Volk, M. (2002), 'Using the web as a corpus for linguistic research', in R. Pajusalu and T. Hennoste (eds) *Tähendusepüüdja. Catcher of the Meaning. A festschrift for Professor Haldur Õim.* Tartu: University of Tartu, pp. 3–13.

Wall, L. (2000), *Programming Perl.* CA: O'Reilly.

Wallace, M. and Spanner, C. (2004), *Chav! A User's Guide to Britain's New Ruling Class.* New York: Bantam Books.

Walter, E. and Harley, A. (2002), 'The role of corpus and collocation tools in practical lexicography', in A. Braasch and C. Povlsen (eds) *Proceedings of the Tenth EURALEX International Congress, EURALEX 2002, Copenhagen, Denmark, August 12–17, 2002, Vol.2.* Copenhagen: Center for Sprogteknologi, Copenhagen University, pp. 851–57.

Watts, R. J. (2003), *Politeness.* Cambridge: Cambridge University Press.

Weinert, R. (1995), 'The role of formulaic language in second language acquisition: a review', *Applied Linguistics* 16(2), 180–205.

Werry, C. C. (2004[1996]), 'Linguistic and interactional features of Internet relay chat', in G. Sampson and D. McCarthy (eds) *Corpus Linguistics: Readings in a Widening Discipline.* London: Continuum, pp. 340–52.

Widdowson, H. G. (2004), *Text, Context, Pretext. Critical Issue in Critical Discourse Analysis.* Oxford: Blackwell.

Wiechmann, D. and Fuhs, S. (2006), 'Concordancing Software', *Corpus Linguistics and Linguistic Theory* 2(1), 109–30.

Williams, R. (1976), *Keywords: A Vocabulary of Culture and Society.* New York: Oxford University Press.

Willis, D. (2000), *The Lexical Syllabus.* London: Collins.

Wilson, A. and Thomas, J. A. (1997), 'Semantic annotation', in R. Garside, G. Leech and T. McEnery (eds) *Corpus Annotation: Linguistic Information from Computer Text Corpora.* Longman, London, pp. 53–65.

Wilson, A. and Thomas, J. (1997), 'Semantic annotation', in R. Garside, G. Leech and A. McEnery (eds) *Corpus Annotation: Linguistic Information from Computer Texts.* London: Longman, pp. 55–65.

Wilson, T. and Wiebe, J. (2005), 'Annotating attributions and private states', in ACL 2005 Workshop: Frontiers in Corpus Annotation II: Pie in the Sky.

Wodak, R. and Meyer, M. (eds) (2001), *Methods of Critical Discourse Analysis.* London, Thousand Oaks, CA, New Delhi: Sage.

Woods, A., Fletcher, P. and Hughes, A. (1986), *Statistics in Language Studies.* Cambridge University Press.

Wray, A. (1999), 'Formulaic language in learners and native speakers', *Language Teaching* 32, 213–31.

Wray, A. (2000), Formulaic sequences in second language teaching: principle and practice. *Applied Linguistics* 21(4), 463–89.

Wray, A. (2002), *Formulaic Language and the Lexicon*. Cambridge: Cambridge University Press.

Wray, A. and Perkins, M. R. (2000), 'The functions of formulaic language: an integrated model'. *Language and Communication* 20(1), 1–28.

Wynne, M. (2006), 'Stylistics: corpus approaches', in K. Brown et al. (eds) *The Encyclopedia of Language and Linguistics*. Oxford: Elsevier, pp. 223–6.

Xia, F. and Palmer, M. (2001), 'Converting dependency structures to phrase structures', in *Proceedings of the First International Conference on Human Language Technology Research*. San Diego, USA, pp. 1–5.

Xiao, R. (2008), 'Using an enhanced MDA model in study of world Englishes'. Paper presented at the Fourth Inter-Varietal Applied Corpus Studies (IVACS) Conference. University of Limerick, 13–14 June 2008.

Xiao, R. and McEnery, T. (2006), 'Collocation, semantic prosody, and near synonymy: a cross-linguistic perspective', *Applied Linguistics* 27(1), 102–29.

Xiao, R., He, L. and Yue, M. (2008), 'In pursuit of the third code: Using the ZJU Corpus of Translational Chinese in Translation Studies', paper presented at the International Symposium on Using Corpora in Contrastive and Translation Studies (UCCTS2008), 25–27 September 2008, Zhejiang University, Hangzhou.

Xiao, R., Rayson, P. and McEnery, A. (2008), *A Frequency of Mandarin Chinese: Core Vocabulary for Learners*. London and New York: Routledge.

Xiao, Z. (2006), 'Review of Xaira: an XML Aware Indexing and Retrieval Architecture', *Corpora* 1(1), 99–103.

Yadava, Y. P., Hardie, A., Lohani R. R., Regmi B. N., Gurung, S., Gurung, A., McEnery, T., Allwood, J. and Hall, P. (2008), 'Construction and annotation of a corpus of contemporary Nepali', *Corpora* 3(2).

Yule, G. U. (1944), *The Statistical Study of Literary Vocabulary*. Cambridge: Cambridge University Press.

Zanettin, F. (1998), 'Bilingual comparable corpora and the training of translators', *Meta* 43(4), 616–30.

Zhao, S., Meyers, A. and Grishman, R. (2004), 'Discriminative slot detection using kernel methods', in Proceedings of the 20th International Conference on Computational Linguistics (COLING-04), Geneva.

Zipf, G. K. (1935), *Psycho-Biology of Languages*. Boston: Houghton Mifflin.

Zipf, G. K. (1949), *Human Behaviour and the Principle of Least Effort*. Cambridge MA: Addison-Wesley

Zuraw, K. (2003), 'Probability in language change', in R. Bod, J. Hay and S. Jannedy (eds) *Probabilistic Linguistics*. Cambridge, MA: MIT Press, pp. 139–76.

Index

Type 1 error 166
type/token ratio 247, 253

Unicode 7, 95, 100–2, 266, 268, 273–4, 277
unique items hypothesis 251
Unstructured Information Management
 Architecture 113
Urdu 272–88

vocabulary 273–4, 283
VOICE corpus 144

web as corpus 289–300
WebCONC 297
WebCorp 297
WebPhraseCount 297
web spamming 294
Wordbanks 34, 41, 42

WordNet 18, 270
Word Sketch 74–5, 79
WordSmith Tools 7, 38, 89, 92, 102,
 253, 316
world Englishes 68–9, 77
World Wide Web 68, 88, 265, 289–300, 301
wrappers 297
writing systems 264–5

Xaira 275, 277
XML 135, 253, 266, 273

Yule's Q, also Yule's Distinctiveness
 Coefficient 163, 166, 168–70

Zipf's Law 214, 245, 285, 292
ZJU Corpus of Translational Chinese 252
Zulu 248

Lightning Source UK Ltd.
Milton Keynes UK
UKOW06f0520261114

242199UK00008B/153/P